DESCRIBING GREECE

The *Periegesis Hellados* (*Description of Greece*) by Pausanias is the most important example of non-fictional travel literature in ancient Greek. With this work Professor Hutton provides the first book-length literary study of the *Periegesis Hellados* in nearly a hundred years. He examines Pausanias' arrangement and expression of his material and evaluates his authorial choices in light of the contemporary literary currents of the day and the cultural milieu of the Roman Empire in the time of Hadrian and the Antonines. The descriptions offered in the *Periegesis Hellados* are also examined in the context of the archaeological evidence available for the places Pausanias visited. This study reveals Pausanias to be a surprisingly sophisticated literary craftsman and a unique witness to Greek identity at a time when that identity was never more conflicted.

WILLIAM HUTTON is Assistant Professor of Classical Studies at the College of William & Mary in Virginia.

GREEK CULTURE IN THE ROMAN WORLD

Editors
SUSAN E. ALCOCK, University of Michigan
JAS ELSNER, Corpus Christi College, Oxford
SIMON GOLDHILL, University of Cambridge

The Greek culture of the Roman Empire offers a rich field of study. Extraordinary insights can be gained into processes of multicultural contact and exchange, political and ideological conflict, and the creativity of a changing, polyglot empire. During this period, many fundamental elements of Western society were being set in place: from the rise of Christianity, to an influential system of education, to long-lived artistic canons. This series is the first to focus on the response of Greek culture to its Roman imperial setting as a significant phenomenon in its own right. To this end, it will publish original and innovative research in the art, archaeology, epigraphy, history, philosophy, religion, and literature of the empire, with an emphasis on Greek material.

Titles in series:

Athletics and Literature in the Roman Empire
Jason König

Describing Greece: Landscape and Literature in the Periegesis *of Pausanias*
William Hutton

Reading the Self in the Ancient Greek Novel
Tim Whitmarsh

Image, Place and Power in the Roman Empire: Visual Replication and Urban Elites
Jennifer Trimble

The Making of Roman India
Grant Parker

DESCRIBING GREECE

Landscape and Literature in the Periegesis *of Pausanias*

BY

WILLIAM HUTTON

CAMBRIDGE
UNIVERSITY PRESS

CAMBRIDGE UNIVERSITY PRESS
Cambridge, New York, Melbourne, Madrid, Cape Town, Singapore, São Paulo

Cambridge University Press
The Edinburgh Building, Cambridge CB2 2RU, UK

Published in the United States of America by Cambridge University Press, New York

www.cambridge.org
Information on this title: www.cambridge.org/9780521847209

© Cambridge University Press 2005

First published 2005

Printed in the United Kingdom at the University Press, Cambridge

A catalogue record for this book is available from the British Library

ISBN-10 0 521 84720 6 hardback
ISBN-13 978 0 521 84720 9 hardback

for Martha

Contents

Figures

Tables

Preface

When I was a graduate student I was once invited, along with a number of other students, to dine with a famous classicist who was visiting the campus. The dinner conversation eventually came around to dissertation topics, and I admitted that I was thinking about working on Pausanias. This elicited a scornful *hmmph!* from our eminent guest. "Well, I realize he's not Herodotos or Thucydides . . ." I stammered diffidently, and the visitor replied, "*Hmmph!* He's not even Aelius Aristeides!"

This experience, of course, only confirmed me in my path, and the present volume is the ultimate result. In the years since that conversation, work on Aelius Aristeides has continued to languish while the study of Pausanias has blossomed, a development that neither I nor my distinguished dinner companion had any means of foreseeing at the time. This was before Karim Arafat's monograph on Pausanias appeared; before Jaś Elsner began publishing his groundbreaking articles on Pausanias as traveler, observer, and pilgrim; before the work of such scholars as Susan Alcock began shedding new light on the little-known period of Greek civilization to which Pausanias belonged; before the teams of Italian and French scholars producing the new series of commentaries on Pausanias had progressed very far in their work; even before the efforts of Christian Habicht and Paul Veyne on Pausanias had come to be fully appreciated. It is these scholars, and many others I haven't named, whom I wish to thank first for laying the foundation upon which this book rests, along with the many archaeologists who continue the painstaking and indispensable work of uncovering the realities of the Greece that Pausanias saw. Thanks to them, Pausanias is currently, with the possible exception of Plutarch and the authors of the New Testament, the most talked-about and written-about Greek author of the Roman period. I can only hope that in these circumstances my own work can make some small contribution to what my pioneering predecessors have already accomplished.

I first learned to love Pausanias as a student at the American School of Classical Studies in Athens, under the tutelage of John Camp, who was then Mellon Professor at the school. On two occasions, John invited me to accompany him and Alison Adams on research expeditions in Greece with Kendrick Pritchett, a man whose topographical and historical knowledge no ten scholars, such as they are now, could hope to equal. I fully expect that those trips will prove to be the most inspiring experiences of my entire academic life. None of my work on Pausanias would have been possible without the excellent facilities of the American School, both in Athens and in Corinth, where I was hospitably received at Hill House by Charles Williams and Nancy Bookidis, who were always generous with their knowledge and advice. Subsequently, other Corinthian archaeologists, including Guy Sanders, Benjamin Millis, and David Romano, have shared their time and their expertise in helping me understand the complexities of the site. In my years at the school I have benefitted from the companionship and counsel of many scholars and fellow-students. Among them, I particularly wish to thank Aileen Ajootian and Jennifer Tobin. Many librarians have provided invaluable assistance to my studies, including Camilla McKay and Phyllis Graham at the American School, and Ellen Ross and Erica Bainbridge at the Center for Hellenic Studies in Washington. I would also like to thank Michael Krumme of the German Archaeological Institute in Athens for his help with the illustrations and for trudging all the way up to Souidias Street in the middle of the Athens summer to bring them to me.

This work has a distant genetic relationship with the dissertation I wrote for the University of Texas. For that dissertation I had the benefit of the most erudite, helpful, and encouraging committee one could hope for, including Michael Gagarin, Peter Green, Jack Kroll, Cynthia Shelmerdine, and the late Charles Edwards. My thanks to them, and particularly to my dissertation director, Paula Perlman, without whom neither the dissertation nor this descendant of it would have ever seen the light. In addition, many other people have read parts of my work on Pausanias and have saved me from many errors and omissions. These include Christian Habicht, Jaś Elsner, Martha Jones, Gregory Hutton, and the members of the Down Under Writing Group: Natalie Alexander, David Christiansen, Janet Davis, and Martha Rose.

Pauline Hire was the first to suggest Cambridge University Press as a venue for publication of this work, and I have never regretted that advice. Michael Sharp, Pauline's successor at the Press, and Sinead Moloney have been models of efficiency and encouragement in shepherding me through the process. I would also like to thank the series editors for their speedy agreement to include my work in their series, and the anonymous reader for the Press, particularly for not being too careful about maintaining his or her anonymity in the course of his or her detailed and constructive comments.

The research and writing of this work was supported by two fellowships from the American School in Athens, by a University Fellowship from the University of Texas, and by two summer research grants from the College of William and Mary. I wish to express my gratitude to all of my extraordinarily collegial and accommodating colleagues in the Department of Classical Studies at William and Mary, and particularly to my old friends from Athens Linda Reilly, Barbette Spaeth, and John Oakley. To John Oakley I owe a particular debt of thanks; without his gentle but persistent encouragement I would probably still be dithering over footnotes.

I have incurred many personal debts in the course of writing this book, including to those who provided me with accommodation as well as friendship in the course of my research: Greg, Joann, Rollie and Kirk Willis, Mary Malone, Greg, Andrew and Vera Kochanowsky Hutton, and Seth Carpenter and Mi Hillefors. I also thank Georgia Irby-Massie and Keith Massie for services far beyond the call of friendship. My parents, Sybil and Robert Hutton have never been anything but encouraging in their son's unusual choice of careers, and they, along with my brothers Wilson and Greg, provided me with a love of learning and of language and a passion for looking at things differently. I have also been fortunate to have extremely supportive parents-in-law in William and Catherine Jones. Finally, my wife, Martha Taylor Jones, has been my constant supporter and companion in my life, my travels, and in the long and agonizing journey of book-writing. That only begins to express what I owe to her.

In what follows, abbreviations of ancient authors and texts follow the standards of Liddell–Scott and the *Oxford Classical Dictionary* (3rd edition). The titles of classical-studies journals are abbreviated as in *L'Année philologique*. Quotations of the Greek text of Pausanias follow the Teubner edition by F. Spiro, unless otherwise noted. Translations from Greek, Latin, German, French, and Italian are my own unless otherwise noted. On the subject of the transliteration of Greek names, my attitude is similar to that expressed by Jeffrey Hurwit in his book *The Athenian Acropolis* (Cambridge, 1999): "My transliteration of ancient Greek is admittedly inconsistent (using 'c' in 'Acropolis' but 'k' in 'Perikles', for instance): I have my reasons but they do not matter much."

CHAPTER I

Introduction

On the Mouseion hill in Athens, south-west of the acropolis, stand the conspicuous remains of a richly sculptured marble edifice. The Philopappus Monument, as the structure is called, was erected as a tomb for Gaius Julius Antiochus Epiphanes Philopappus, suffect consul of Rome, archon of Athens, friend to philosophers, and scion of the royal house of the Euphrates-valley kingdom of Commagene.[1] How did this Eastern prince come to hold the chief magistracies of two foreign cities? Why was such a monumental tomb erected for him in Greece, so far from his homeland? These are the sorts of questions that frequently arise when one contemplates the century in which Philopappus died, the second century CE. This was a time when members of a well-educated cosmopolitan elite associated freely with one another across ethnic boundaries. It was a period in which Greece, long subject to Rome, economically impotent, strategically irrelevant, a depopulated, dilapidated shadow of its classical self, still enjoyed a potent reputation for cultural preeminence from one end of the Roman Empire to the other.

Over the course of several years in the middle of the second century, a man named Pausanias traveled among the cities and shrines of mainland Greece. He took careful note of what he saw and prevailed on the inhabitants for information about local artifacts, traditions, and cult practices. Either before or after his visits, he researched the sites, learned what previous writers had recorded about their myths and histories, and added this information to the storehouse of knowledge and associations that his classical education had already made part of his basic mental make-up. Eventually, he compiled what he had seen and learned in a ten-scroll work that has come down to us under the title *Periegesis Hellados* ("Description of Greece"), a work that perfunctorily[2] describes Philopappus' grand tomb as "a monument built for a Syrian man" (1.25.8), but lavishes considerably more

<hr />

[1] On the monument, see Kleiner 1983.   [2] See, however, Steinhart 2003.

I

Figure 1.1. The Philopappus Monument in Athens.

respect and attention on monuments of greater antiquity. The *Periegesis* is a record of one native Greek speaker's view of his ancestral land at a period in history when what it meant to be Greek was more enigmatic than ever.

Only recently has Pausanias' significance as a witness to this era begun to be appreciated. For much of the twentieth century, the main emphasis in scholarship was on the utilitarian value of his text as a source of archaeological information. When one considers how valuable a source the *Periegesis* is, it is easy to understand why. As an eyewitness to the state of Greece in the second century, Pausanias gives us a priceless picture of a world forever lost to us: the Parthenon, with its walls and columns standing; races still being run at Olympia; gold and silver offerings still festooning the temple of Apollo at Delphi. Modern archaeologists use Pausanias as a guidebook for where to dig, and for identifying what they uncover. Likewise, historians, art historians, and students of Greek society mine his account for information preserved by no other ancient author. A good portion of our image of what ancient Greece was like is derived from Pausanias' descriptions. The oddly shaped building adjacent to the Parthenon in Athens, for instance, is called the "Erechtheion" because (and only because) Pausanias seems to refer to it by that name (1.26.5). The tallest standing remains in the site of ancient Corinth, the columns of an archaic temple, are commonly ascribed to a "temple of Apollo" because (and only because) Pausanias locates a temple of Apollo in that vicinity (2.3.6). Heinrich Schliemann used Pausanias' text as a treasure map for his excavation of Mycenae, and the great tholos tombs found there are still named after the mythical heroes Atreus, Aegisthus, and Clytemnestra, whom Pausanias reports as being buried outside the citadel walls (2.16.6–7). The *Periegesis* is one of the more useful texts that survive from antiquity. Open nearly any modern book on Greek history, literature, culture, or art and you will find citations of Pausanias.

As one might expect in the case of a text of such practical value, modern scholarship that deals with the *Periegesis* has tended to focus not on Pausanias himself but on the things he mentions, offering explanations of the myths he relates, verifications or debunkings of his historical accounts, and detailed correlations of his descriptions with the latest archaeological finds.[3] Within the last two decades, however, the focus of scholarship on Pausanias has begun to change significantly. Inspired by a volume of lectures by Christian Habicht,[4] by a thought-provoking monograph by Paul Veyne,[5] and by a general upswing of interest in Greek culture and literature

---

[3] Numerous archaeological/historical commentaries on Pausanias have been written and continue to be written, beginning with the deluxe edition of Xylander and Sylburg 1583, and continuing in the modern age with those of Hitzig and Blümner 1896–1910, Frazer 1898, Meyer 1954 (with abridged translation), Papachatzes 1974–1981; and the current ongoing efforts of teams of scholars writing in Italian (Musti et al. 1982–) and French (Casevitz et al. 1992). There have also been important commentaries on individual sections: Trendelenberg 1914 (Olympia), and Roux 1958 (Corinthia), for example.

[4] Habicht 1998.   [5] Veyne 1988, especially Chapter 8: "Pausanias Entrapped" (95–102).

in the Roman era,[6] a number of new studies have appeared that recognize Pausanias himself as a subject worthy of interest. So far, this new output includes five books, three collections of essays, and a rising tide of separate articles.[7] Welcome as these newer studies are, however, they frequently suffer from a certain narrowness of perspective. Like previous scholars whose focus was squarely on the factual data that Pausanias preserves, Pausanias' new followers tend to concentrate on isolated passages or on individual recurring features of the *Periegesis*, such as his references to Roman emperors or his efforts at writing history.[8] What is missing is a comprehensive view of the *Periegesis* and of the context that helps to give these separate elements their full meaning. The result is something like the proverbial blind men pawing the elephant: we have eloquent and insightful analyses of the separate parts but the animal as a whole remains something of a mystery.

Part of the explanation for this tendency can be found in the history of scholarship on Pausanias, a topic that will be addressed more fully toward the end of this chapter. In brief, an attitude has developed over the course of the past century or so that binds Pausanias' value as a source to what is perceived to be his lack of sophistication as an author. To preview a phrase that I will be using later, he is often regarded as a "dependable dullard," an author whose ability to report straightforward facts is uncontaminated by intellectual pretensions and artistic flights of fancy. Few of Pausanias' most recent students would acquiesce in the description of him as a "dependable dullard," yet the momentum of this characterization has been difficult to overcome, and has caused the potential value of a comprehensive literary analysis of the text to be overlooked. As a result of this attitude, the literary study of the *Periegesis* has languished. Aside from a brief monograph on metrical clausulae[9] and one on some of Pausanias' stylistic idiosyncrasies,[10] there has been no book-length study on the literary features of the *Periegesis*,

---

[6] Confining ourselves to book-length studies in the past decade or so, and still being far from exhaustive: Cartledge and Spawforth 1989; Engels 1990; Alcock 1993; Anderson 1993 and 1994; Quass 1993; Fein 1994; Flinterman 1995; Gleason 1995; Swain 1996; Schmitz 1997; Whitmarsh 2001.

[7] Monographs: Bultrighini 1990a; Bearzot 1992; Arafat 1996; Pritchett 1998 and 1999. Collections of essays: Bingen, ed. 1996; Alcock, Cherry, and Elsner, eds. 2001; Knoepfler and Piérart, eds. 2001; also a significant proportion of the essays in Pirenne-Delforge, ed. 1998 are on Pausanias. Substantial sections of monographs: Elsner 1995: 125–155; Swain 1996: 330–356; Hartog 2001: 140–150. Separate journal articles (post 1990, and hardly a complete list): Arafat 1992, 1995, 2000; Auberger 1992, 1994, 2000; Bearzot 1988; Birge 1994; Bommelaer 1999; Calame 1990; Eide 1992; Meadows 1995; Ekroth 1999; Elsner 1992, 1994, etc.; Tzifopoulos 1993; Jacquemin 1991a, 1991b, 1996 and 2000; Kreilinger 1997; Lacroix 1992; Lafond 1994; Schneider 1997; Steinhart 2002a and 2002b, 2003.

[8] Emperors: Arafat 1996; Jacquemin 1996. History: Bearzot 1992; Meadows 1995; Bingen, ed. 1996.

[9] Szelest 1953.   [10] Strid 1976.

its language and style, the literary affinities of the text, and the literary aims of the author since Carl Robert published *Pausanias als Schriftsteller* in 1909. Since Robert's time, archaeological and topographical studies have brought us much more knowledge about the sites and monuments Pausanias was describing, and have allowed us a clearer view of the ways in which Pausanias transforms his experience of landscape into prose. For this reason alone, reconsideration of the *Periegesis* from a literary perspective is long overdue.

A fundamental hypothesis of this book is that the *Periegesis* is not the naïve outpouring of a simple and ingenuous spirit or the mechanical and sequential recording of a traveler's impressions; it is instead the work of an author who was striving consciously for literary effect and was shaping his text, consciously or unconsciously, in response to a literary tradition and a contemporary intellectual milieu. Each separate section, paragraph, and sentence in Pausanias' work has the function not only of providing information for the reader, but also of contributing to the maintenance of a complex literary architecture. The text as we have it is the result of choices that the author made in order to express his understanding of the physical and cultural landscapes of Greece. In the course of this book, I will be examining those choices and the effect they had in determining the shape that the work eventually took. Reasonable scholars may differ on the issue of whether Pausanias succeeded in achieving his literary ambitions, so my intention here is not to recover Pausanias as an overlooked genius of Greek prose or to claim for him a spot alongside Plato and Demosthenes in the classical canon. Instead, the goal of my work is much more modest: to analyze Pausanias' literary aims and methods and show how they are essential to an understanding of his testimony on any subject, whether we are looking to him for topographical information or for evidence of the attitudes and mentalities of the time in which he lived.

My study of the way Pausanias constructs his account benefits from a number of recent developments in the study of travel literature and the literature of landscape. One distinctive thing about the *Periegesis* that gets little attention is that it is the longest and most detailed narrative in classical literature in which the author relates the experiences of his own travels.[11] The ancient Greeks have a reputation for being explorers and travelers, but the literature of travel was not a genre in which they excelled.[12] The sunburst of the *Odyssey* at the dawn of Greek literature turned out to be

---

[11] Elsner 1992 (and 1995: 125–155), 1997a, and 1997b, and Hartog 2001 make a good beginning in applying the perspectives of the study of travel literature to Pausanias.

[12] On Greek travel and travel literature, see Friedländer 1921–1923: 2.99–207; Casson 1974; Marasco 1978; Janni 1984; André and Baslez 1993; Hartog 2001: 79–160.

nearly the end, rather than the beginning, of the fruitful exploitation of travel motifs in Greek literature. Not long after the *Odyssey*, travel seems to have joined trade, manufacturing, labor, and cookery in the realm of the banausic, the unkempt closet of mundane things one did to survive and prosper, but found too undignified to make the focus of great artistry. There were, of course, authors who traveled and who wrote about what they saw on their travels. Herodotos, who serves in many ways as a model for Pausanias,[13] recognized at the dawn of Greek historiography the importance of seeing things for oneself, both for the purposes of ascertaining facts and for claiming the authority to write about them. Herodotos' history of the Persian wars includes ethnographic and historical information about Egypt and the Near East that he presents as the fruits of his own travels in those regions. "Seeing for oneself" (*autopsia* in Greek),[14] was bequeathed by Herodotos to the historiographical tradition as a methodological ideal, and claims of *autopsia* remained an important motif in the later course of classical historiography and geographical writing, though many of the best historians chose to hide whatever first-hand experience they had behind a stance of magisterial omniscience.[15]

Aside from geography and history, there are also citations and fragments of ancient texts that hint at a somewhat more robust literature of travel than what remains today (some of which we will be examining in later chapters). Examples include the entertaining excerpts of the sardonic travel commentary attributed to Herakleides Kritikos, Lucian's *True Story*, a travel parody which implies the existence of a literature that is in many ways better classified as fiction, or, in what may be a fragmentary example of the sort of thing that Lucian lampoons, the credulity-stretching narrative of Iamboulos' journey to the island of fork-tongued people (partially preserved, and presented as fact, by Diodoros Siculus, 2.55.1–2.60.5). With the possible exception of Xenophon's *Anabasis*, however, no surviving text other than Pausanias' is based so fundamentally on the author's own travels.

In this respect, Pausanias is not only unusual in his time, but in Greek literature as a whole. Although he does not habitually present his descriptions of sights in the form of a first-person narrative of his travel experience, the phenomenon of travel, his own travel, is never far beneath the surface

---

[13] Pausanias' relationship with Herodotos will be examined more fully in Chapter 4. In general: Pfundtner 1866; Wernicke 1884; Strid 1976; Gurlitt 1890: 50–52; Frazer 1898: 1.lxxiii.

[14] *Autopsia* is not actually a word used by Herodotos, although the ability to speak either as an eyewitness or on the authority of eyewitnesses is clearly important to him. He does refer to himself as an *autoptês* ("eyewitness") in 2.29.

[15] Dewald 1987; Marincola 1997: 63–86; Clarke 1999: 85–87, 240–242.

of his account.[16] Through Pausanias' unobtrusive but recurring assertions of his eyewitness knowledge of various sites, the reader feels his presence at every stage of the journey.[17] When he tells us that a certain route is "easier for a well-girt man than it is for mules or horses,"[18] he doesn't say that he personally tied his garments up around his waist and trod the difficult path. He doesn't have to say that: the nature of his account prepares us to imagine that he did.

The literature of travel and, more generally, literature that describes landscapes are popular subjects in modern literary and cultural studies.[19] Both bring to our critical attention the notion of space, how one perceives it and how one transforms the experience of it into writing, and for this reason they are attractive subjects in an era when the perception and communication of objective reality are frequently held up as problematic. Travel, moreover, is recognized as an activity in which the question of identity is put in play, either by coming to terms with oneself and one's mortal limitations, or by coming to terms with "the Other." Writing about travel, whether fiction or non-fiction, is in turn the expression of that process of self-definition, and is a form of discourse that can both communicate and problematize concepts of self and other, nature and culture, civilization and savagery.

The trend toward studying these sorts of issues in travel writing is one that has mostly bypassed the field of classical literature, not just because of the supposed crusty conservatism of classical scholars but, more importantly, because of the scarcity of ancient Greek or Latin representatives of the genre.[20] With few exceptions,[21] Pausanias' ability to contribute to such inquiries has been overlooked. Study of the *Periegesis* as travel literature can provide for the classical world the same sorts of cultural insights that the travel literature of other societies affords. In particular, the interrogation of identity that is involved in the study of travel literature can be especially informative in the case of Pausanias, who, as we have already mentioned, inhabited an era when the notion of ethnic identity, particularly that of the Greeks, was in a state of ambiguity. Part of what constituted a sense of

---

[16] Alcock 1996: 260–1.   [17] For assertions of autopsy in Pausanias, see Heberdey, 1894.

[18] 10.32.2; cf. 2.15.2, 10.5.5, 10.32.7.

[19] On space, landscape, and "cognitive mapping": Cosgrove 1984; Jackson 1984; Cosgrove and Daniels (eds.) 1988; Folch-Serra 1990; Deutsche 1991; Rodaway 1994; Tilley 1994; Clark 1996; for ancient Greece in particular: Alcock 1993; Alcock and Osborne (eds.) 1994; Shipley and Salmon (eds.) 1996. On travel and travel accounts: Culler 1981; Eade and Sallnow (eds.) 1991; Eisner 1991; Cohen 1992; Morinis (ed.) 1992; Pratt 1992; Larner 1999.

[20] The discursive construction of geography in classical literature has been a topic of recent scholarship, e.g.: Janni 1984; Hartog 1988, 2001; Jacob 1991; Nicolet 1991; Romm 1992; Clarke 1999.

[21] E.g. Elsner 1992, 1994, 1995, 2001b. Hartog 2001.

identity for Greek-speaking people in general and Pausanias in particular
was religion; and as Elsner has pointed out, Pausanias, who not only shows
a deep interest in sanctuaries, temples, and religious artworks but also
records his own participation in certain cult rituals in the places he travels
to, can usefully be considered a pilgrim.[22] An especially fertile field of
research within the realm of travel literature in recent years has been on the
literature of pilgrimage,[23] and Pausanias can play a role in that field in a
way few other ancient Greek (or Latin) authors can.

At this point, some disclaimers are in order: while my analysis depends
on the premise that an author's observation and recording of space is not a
matter free from complications and ambiguities, I do not contend, in the
manner of the jejune caricature of the postmodern critic, that there are no
real landscapes to which Pausanias' text refers. Nor do I argue that Pausanias
is a disingenuous reporter or an unreliable source for the reconstruction
of Greek antiquity. Like most scholars who concern themselves with the
topography and monuments of Greece, I believe Pausanias to be a more
trustworthy and conscientious reporter of the realities of Greece than we
have any right to expect. One of the things I will try to show, in fact, is that
this quality of Pausanias' account – its meticulous and accurate relation of
the realities of Greece as they actually existed in the author's own day – is
one of the distinguishing features that must be studied and understood in
context.

What will be an important premise of this work, however, is that
Pausanias is not merely a passive recorder of information. Even the most
guileless description of a place does more than record the shape of the
landscape; it also has a shape of its own that arises from the confluence of
a number of factors: the physical contours of the landscape; the cognitive
predilections of the mind that perceives the landscape, and the structure of
the narrative form in which the author chooses to communicate his perceptions. Study of how this process works in the case of Pausanias involves
the consideration of how his outlook is influenced by the various social
economies in which the author partakes. As a result, this approach can be
rewarding not only for our understanding of Pausanias, but also for our

[22] Elsner 1992: 8; 1995: 130. Cf. Rutherford 2001; Hutton 2005b pp. 291–299. Some examples of
Pausanias' participation in cult or expressions of religious belief (often taking the form of an obser-
vance of ritual silence about certain topics in his writing): 1.37.4; 2.3.4; 2.17.4; 2.30.4; 2.35.8; 2.37.6;
5.15.11; 8.37.9; 8.42.11; 9.25.5; 9.39.5–14. The issue of Pausanias as "pilgrim" will be examined in greater
detail in the final chapter.
[23] Eade and Sallnow (eds.) 1991; Morinis (ed) 1992, and for classical Greece, Dillon 1997. Naturally,
a good deal of the literature on this topic for antiquity deals with early Christian pilgrimage and
pilgrimage literature: Turner and Turner 1978 Hunt 1982, 1984; Campbell 1988; Sivan 1988a, 1988b;
Holum 1990; MacCormack 1990; Westra 1995; Leyerle 1996; Frank 2000.

understanding of the period in which he wrote. Pausanias' literary aims and methods are not only essential things to understand as background for an interpretation of his account; those aims and methods are, in their own right, illuminating artifacts of the time in which Pausanias lived.

WHAT WE KNOW ABOUT PAUSANIAS

Pausanias is an obscure enough figure that each major study of his work is compelled to rehash the few things we know about him.[24] Pausanias does not talk about himself very much, and even when he does it is rarely for the purpose of giving us biographical details. The earliest datable events and artifacts he ascribes to his own period are from the 120s CE, and the latest are from the 170s.[25] Most – if not all – of his adult lifetime, therefore, fell within the reigns of Hadrian (117–138 CE), Antoninus Pius (138–161), and Marcus Aurelius (161–180).

Pausanias never explicitly tells us where he was born or where he resided, but the most likely candidate for his place of origin is the city of Magnesia-on-Sipylos (modern Manisa in Turkey) in the ancient Anatolian land of Lydia.[26] We surmise this primarily from his statement that certain monuments on Mt. Sipylos relating to the mythical figures of Tantalos and Pelops are located "among us."[27] This reference hardly guarantees that Pausanias was born near Mt. Sipylos, nor that he resided there for most of his life, but it is the only clue that he gives us as to what land he considered home. The only reason for denying the obvious inference of this passage has stemmed from a fruitless effort to identify our Pausanias with one of a handful of contemporary Pausaniases that were known to have come from places other than Magnesia.[28] In the course of his account, Pausanias reveals more familiarity with the area of Magnesia than with any other place outside of the

---

[24] Basic discussions of biographical issues: Gurlitt 1890: 1–55; Frazer 1898: 1.xiii–xcvi (esp. xv–xxii); Regenbogen 1956: 1012–1014; Habicht 1998: 1–27; Arafat 1996: 8–12; Bowie 2001: 20–25.

[25] Gurlitt 1890: 58–61; Frazer 1898: 1.xv–xviii; Comfort 1931: Habicht 1998: 9–12. Bowie 2001: 20–24; 120s: addition of the tribe Hadrianis in Athens (1.5.5); 170s: Marcus Aurelius' victory over German tribes (8.43.6 [dating uncertain but see also 5.1.2, 10.34.5]). Habicht has a useful discussion of Pausanias' use of the phrase "in our time" and similar expressions (ibid.: 176–179; cf. Musti 2001). Nothing to which Pausanias so refers can be dated outside of what would be a plausible life span, although one must still be aware of the fact that such expressions can connote "in the modern era" rather than "while I have been alive." See Pothecary 1997.

[26] For some thought-provoking observations about what it meant to be a "Lydian" in this period, see Spawforth 2001.

[27] παρ' ἡμῖν (5.13.7).

[28] For a survey of the possibilities, see Diller 1955, also Gurlitt 1890: 56–57; Frazer 1898: 1.xix; Regenbogen 1956: 1012; Habicht 1998: 13–17; Arafat 1996: 8. Pausanias is one of the more common personal names in Greek, so the existence of two or more contemporary writers of that name would hardly be surprising.

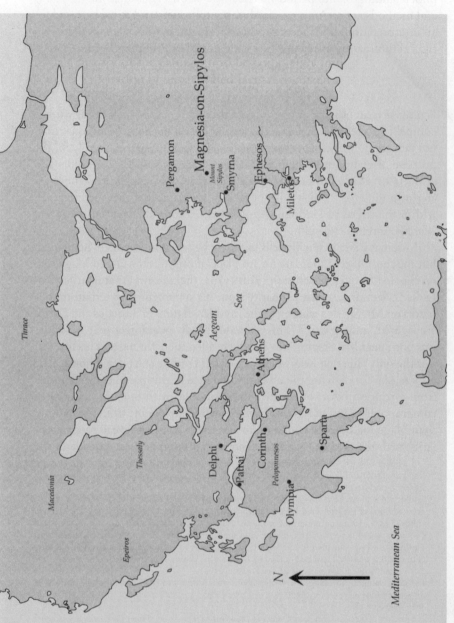

Figure 1.2. Map showing the location of Magnesia-on-Sipylos, in relation to other major cities of Roman Greece and Asia Minor.

territory covered by the *Periegesis*, and in one passage he lets it be known that he was in the vicinity long enough (or often enough) to have witnessed the destruction of three separate generations of locusts (1.24.8). Regardless of the precise location of the place Pausanias called home, it seems generally safe to assume, from these and similar indications, that he was a native of one of the Greek-speaking communities of Asia Minor. This point will be important for understanding Pausanias' relationship with the territory that he does include in his description of Greece.

Pausanias tells us nothing about his background, his family, or his profession. Higher education (of which he manifestly partakes) and travel both required a certain amount of wealth, so it is probably safe to say that Pausanias was a member of the wealthier portion of society. One passage where he praises the generosity of a boon granted to provincial citizens by Antoninus Pius (8.43.5) has been taken to imply that he was himself a Roman citizen,[29] but this ambiguous reference is no sort of proof one way or the other. Many other writers of the period make their Roman citizenship plain, both directly and indirectly. The fact that we have to guess with Pausanias is characteristic of his self-effacing personality and of his relationship with the elite society of the empire, two topics that we will return to on numerous occasions in subsequent chapters.

Anything further we might say about Pausanias' personality, his attitudes, and his predilections, gets us into territory that is even more uncertain. Although on rare occasions Pausanias does express what he represents as his own personal opinion, we have the problem of determining whether the sentiments on display belong to the author himself or to the personality he feels obliged by his literary project to adopt. Even in the case of lightly regarded prose authors, the problems of distinguishing personality from persona cannot be overlooked.[30] Pausanias' religious attitudes, a topic we will touch on in several subsequent chapters, are a case in point; he presents himself as a very pious individual, devoted to the traditional gods and to the traditional religious customs of old Greece.[31] There is no particular reason to doubt that this attitude is sincere, and some very good reasons to think that it is. Yet even if we grant Pausanias' sincerity, it is also true that the religiosity of Pausanias' persona functions well for furthering his literary aims. Literary effect is not necessarily the same as literary affectation, and it is the literary effect and the literary functionality of Pausanias' self-expression to which we will confine ourselves.

---

[29] Swain 1996: 332.   [30] Cf. Veyne 1988: 100–102.
[31] The most complete survey of Pausanias' religious views is in Heer 1979: 127–314.

INTRODUCTION TO THE *PERIEGESIS*

To call Pausanias' account a "topographical" one, one that describes places, is something we cannot do without qualification, or at least without defining our terms carefully. The work does not consist merely of a physical description of the landscapes and monuments of Greece. At least one half of the text is devoted to the presentation of history, mythical traditions, and other information pertinent to the places Pausanias visited. An interesting problem, one that is probably beyond settling, is the question of which was more important to Pausanias, the stories or the monuments, or, to use the author's own terms, the *logoi* (stories, accounts) or the *theôrêmata* (sights);[32] but the question of which was given precedence in the structuring of his text is far more clear: from beginning to end, Pausanias' account is organized around his narrative of the places through which his travels took him. The sites and monuments he mentions are linked together in the landscape by a series of itineraries, and his disquisitions on other topics, historical, mythical, cultural, and religious, are nearly always introduced in connection with some place or monument encountered along these routes. The sights lead Pausanias to stories; the stories do not lead Pausanias to sights. This is, of course, a generalization; in a number of instances, which we will consider in due course, Pausanias allows a *logos* to guide the ordering and classifying of the sights,[33] but in general the itineraries that Pausanias traces from one place to the next provide the structure upon which both the *logoi* and the *theôrêmata* are organized and presented.

To call Pausanias' work a "description of Greece" is also somewhat misleading. First of all, one must choose between various conceptions of what "Greece" was in his time, and to any of these concepts Pausanias' text will prove incongruous to some degree. The problem of how Pausanias defines the boundaries of his "Greece" is a topic that will be discussed in detail in Chapter 3. What we can say for the present is that the territory covered systematically in the text constitutes an integral part of the peninsular Greek mainland, more specifically the entire Peloponnese and a portion of central Greece running from Athens in the east to Phokis and Ozolian Lokris in the west.

The territory that Pausanias includes in his description includes many of the oldest and most famous Greek cities – Athens, Sparta, Corinth, Argos and Thebes, for instance – and some of the most popular destinations for

---

[32] Pausanias 1.39.3.
[33] One example is his reference to the Philopappus Monument (1.25.8). The monument, along with the entire sector of Athens around the Mouseion hill, is mentioned only as an appendage to a historical account relating to Cassander and his fortification of the city.

visitors, such as Delphi, Olympia and Eleusis. Yet this represents only a small part of the Greek-speaking world in Pausanias' time. Pausanias' own homeland in Asia Minor, though it had been Greek for centuries, receives only passing references. Likewise, the Greek cities and communities of the more northerly mainland (Thessaly, Aitolia, Akarnania, Macedonia, Thrace), the Aegean islands, Crete, and the myriad other places where Greek communities persisted, are left out. Each of the ten volumes of the *Periegesis* deals with one of the traditional divisions of the mainland: Book 1 is devoted to Attica, for instance, Book 3 to Lakonia (the territory of Sparta), Book 9 to Boiotia, and so on. There are minor exceptions to this rule – Book 1, for example, also includes the territory of Megara along with Attica – but the only major exception is the committing of two books, 5 and 6, to the territory of Elis. The explanation in this case is the presence of the Shrine of Zeus at Olympia, home of the Olympic games. Olympia was a site that simply offered too much noteworthy material for Pausanias to confine to a single scroll.

The *Periegesis* begins in a manner so abrupt that some have suggested that the original beginning of the work has been lost. In Chapter 6 I will discuss why I agree with those who find such a suggestion unnecessary. The text as we have it starts by putting the reader in the perspective of someone approaching the mainland by sea from the east (1.1.1):

τῆς ἠπείρου τῆς Ἑλληνικῆς κατὰ νήσους τὰς Κυκλάδας καὶ πέλαγος τὸ Αἰγαῖον ἄκρα Σούνιον πρόκειται γῆς τῆς Ἀττικῆς.

Of the Hellenic continent, in the direction of the Cycladic islands and the Aegean sea, the headland of Sounion projects from the land of Attica.

Mention of the first landfall, Cape Sounion in Attica, serves as Pausanias' sole means of introducing the subject of the first book, Attica and Athens. The perspective from which the work begins may well reflect the way Pausanias himself saw the mainland for the first time, perhaps as a young man making the voyage from Asia Minor to Athens for the purpose of studying philosophy and rhetoric. Yet we see in the opening passage a characteristic that recurs throughout the work: movement from place to place in the text is accomplished not by the author's description of his own motions but by means of quasi-impersonal generic participles: "*For one sailing* past the cape [of Sounion] there is a harbor and a temple of Athena Sounias on the peak of the headland. *For one sailing onward* there is Laurion, where the Athenians once had silver mines . . ."[34] (1.1.1, emphasis

[34] καὶ λιμήν τε παραπλεύσαντι τὴν ἄκραν ἐστὶ καὶ ναὸς Ἀθηνᾶς Σουνιάδος ἐπὶ κορυφῇ τῆς ἄκρας. πλέοντι δὲ ἐς τὸ πρόσω Λαύριόν τέ ἐστιν, ἔνθα ποτὲ Ἀθηναίοις ἦν ἀργύρου μέταλλα.

added). More frequently, even this minimal amount of personal focaliza-
tion is absent and Pausanias furthers the progress of his itineraries simply
by saying that one monument is "near" (πλησίον), "not far" (οὐ πόρρω),
"beyond" (ὑπέρ), etc., the next monument. This is a further example of
what was alluded to before: Pausanias' tendency to mask his first-person
experience in third-person or impersonal narrative, a self-effacing affectation that is undercut just often enough by the occurrence of first-person
pronouns and verbs to make the artifice apparent (e.g. 1.23.7: καὶ ἄλλα ἐν
τῇ Ἀθηναίων ἀκροπόλει θεασάμενος οἶδα; "I know of other things on the
Acropolis of the Athenians, having seen them"). The opening sea voyage
seems to transport the author, his impersonal traveler, and the reader across
a threshold to a separate realm within which the cognitive journeys of the
text will be played out. With the exception of a handful of brief coastal
voyages and ferryboat trips to islands that are hard by the shore, the rest of
the *Periegesis* is confined to dry land.

As a more substantial example of Pausanian description, the following is
a passage that occurs a little bit later in Book 1, where Pausanias is tracing
his first series of sights within the city walls of Athens, starting from the
Peiraieus gate and proceeding toward the center of the city (1.2.4):

ἐσελθόντων δὲ ἐς τὴν πόλιν οἰκοδόμημα ἐς παρασκευήν ἐστι τῶν πομπῶν, ἃς
πέμπουσι τὰς μὲν ἀνὰ πᾶν ἔτος, τὰς δὲ καὶ χρόνον διαλείποντες. καὶ πλησίον
ναός ἐστι Δήμητρος, ἀγάλματα δὲ αὐτή τε καὶ ἡ παῖς καὶ δᾷδα ἔχων Ἴακχος·
γέγραπται δὲ ἐπὶ τῷ τοίχῳ γράμμασιν Ἀττικοῖς ἔργα εἶναι Πραξιτέλους.
τοῦ ναοῦ δὲ οὐ πόρρω Ποσειδῶν ἐστιν ἐφ᾽ ἵππου, δόρυ ἀφιεὶς ἐπὶ γίγαντα
Πολυβώτην, ἐς ὃν Κῴοις ὁ μῦθος ὁ περὶ τῆς ἄκρας ἔχει τῆς Χελώνης· τὸ δὲ
ἐπίγραμμα τὸ ἐφ᾽ ἡμῶν τὴν εἰκόνα ἄλλῳ δίδωσι καὶ οὐ Ποσειδῶνι.

As one goes into the city there is a building for the preparations of the festival
processions that they perform in some cases yearly and in other cases at intervals.
And nearby is a temple of Demeter; statues are herself and the child, and Iacchus
holding a torch. It is written on the wall in Attic script that they are works of
Praxiteles. Not far from the temple is Poseidon upon a horse, hurling his spear at
the giant Polybotes, about whom the Coans tell a story concerning Cape Chelone;
but the modern-day inscription gives the statue to someone else and not Poseidon.

In this passage, a number of noteworthy characteristics of Pausanias'
methods are on view. We had occasion earlier to mention the piousness
of Pausanias' persona, and the religious nature of the first several sights
he mentions within the city is a good example: the *Pompeion*, in which
sacred processions, chiefly that of the Panathenaia, were prepared, a temple
of Demeter with its statuary, and a separate statue of Poseidon. More of
Pausanias' propensities are on display here as well: interest in art history

is reflected in his report that the Demeter group is ascribed to Praxiteles, and the caution or skepticism that causes him to specify his source for the attribution suggests that his interest is not a passive one. His active processing of the sensory data that he perceives in his visits to Athens is also noticeable in his treatment of the statue of Poseidon. Poseidon's identity shines through to him (presumably from the iconographical attributes of the now-lost statue), despite the inscriptional evidence to the contrary. This passage shows us something significant about the way Pausanias conceived of his role as author: he presents himself not just as a recorder of facts and images but as an authority, one who can get behind deceiving appearances and present his audience with a closer approximation of the truth. Through passages such as this, Pausanias asserts his status not only as an eyewitness but as a connoisseur of what is worth knowing about his subject.

One of the most well-known aspects of Pausanias' work is its selectivity.[35] On more than one occasion he cautions the reader that it is not his intention to mention everything he possibly can in his descriptions (e.g. 1.39.3; 3.11.1). While he is rarely explicit about his criteria for selecting what to include, he has a noticeable fondness for artworks (particularly cult statues), temples, shrines, and tombs of heroes. In addition to the predilection for religious items, his preference for ancient artifacts over contemporary ones is even more pronounced. The one passage where he comes closest to expressing his criteria outright is in the introduction to his description of the city of Corinth, a passage that we will have occasion to return to in a later chapter (2.2.6):[36]

λόγου δὲ ἄξια ἐν τῇ πόλει τὰ μὲν λειπόμενα ἔτι τῶν ἀρχαίων ἐστίν, τὰ δὲ πολλὰ αὐτῶν ἐπὶ τῆς ἀκμῆς ἐποιήθη τῆς ὕστερον. ἔστιν οὖν ἐπὶ τῆς ἀγορᾶς – ἐνταῦθα γὰρ πλεῖστά ἐστι τῶν ἱερῶν . . .

Worth mentioning in the city are those of the antiquities that still remain, but most things were made in [the city's] latter heyday. Along the agora, then – for that is where most of the shrines are . . .

Corinth had been destroyed by the Romans in 146 BCE and refounded as a Roman colony in 44 BCE. It is the city's contemporary life as a colony that Pausanias refers to as its "latter heyday." Corinth's unusual circumstances inspire Pausanias to take the unusual step of explaining why he begins his description of the city the way he does. *Archaia*, remnants of antiquity, are in short supply, so Pausanias proceeds directly to a description of the

---

[35] Frazer 1898: I.xxxiii–xxxvi; Regenbogen 1956: 1090; Habicht 1998: 23–24.
[36] See below, pp. 147–149.

next best thing, the *hiera*, the shrines, or, more literally, the "holy things." In cities other than Corinth, where *archaia* were still plentiful, Pausanias seems to feel no need to defend his rationale. As we shall see in Chapter 2, Pausanias' antiquarianism is one of the things that bind him most closely to the culture of his contemporaries. The second century CE was a period in which Greeks were particularly mindful of their independent, pre-Roman and even pre-Hellenistic past, and philhellenic non-Greeks shared that interest. Accordingly, Pausanias seems to take for granted an audience who will accept an antiquarian topography with no need for explanations or justifications on the part of the author.

Recently, Karim Arafat, while acknowledging this archaizing tendency, has prudently cautioned against overemphasizing it.[37] Pausanias does mention a number of buildings, artworks, and monuments that are contemporary with his own time, and in light of the prevalence of archaism and antiquarianism in the contemporary imperial culture, the thing that needs explaining is why Pausanias includes as many references to recent things as he does. Despite his taste for antiquities, Pausanias does not usually attempt to re-create the world of Greece as it was in the pre-Roman past. Instead, he reports to us the past as it is in his present. He tells us of deserted cities, burnt temples, missing statues and even, as in the case of the Poseidon statue mentioned in the passage above, of divine statues that have been reinscribed to suit some more worldly purpose.[38] The contemporary perspective that the author adopts even as he is focusing on the past is one way in which he establishes his authority as an ever-present witness.

Certain other features of the *Periegesis* reveal important things about the nature of the author's project. First of all, the work as we have it was carefully planned and deliberately executed. Crucial insight into the design and composition of the work comes from cross-references within the text: promises to cover certain subjects later in the work, or references to topics already covered in a previous part. These cross-references make it clear that the order of the books and, probably, the divisions between books were part of Pausanias' original plan.[39] They also show either that Pausanias was already planning the later books when he was writing the earlier ones or that at some point he subjected his writings to a redaction that allowed him to conceptualize the entire work synoptically.

---

[37] Arafat 1996: 1–42.

[38] Frazer 1898: I.xiv–xv and n. 6 (a detailed listing of several such passages). Pritchett 1999: 195–222.

[39] A comprehensive catalogue of cross-references can be found in Settis 1963: 61–63. Also Gurlitt 1890: 69; Frazer 1898: I.xvii, n. 5; Habicht 1998: 11, n. 57.

As Mario Moggi has pointed out, Pausanias includes far more cross-references between different parts of his work than authors of comparable works such as Strabo and Diodoros.[40] Some have speculated either that the work remained unfinished at the author's death or that the text preserved in the manuscripts is only part of what Pausanias wrote. As evidence for the former, it is pointed out that Book 10, the last book, seems somewhat rushed and ends abruptly; a single promise to cover something later on (9.23.7) is left unfulfilled, and the land Pausanias' account covers does not correspond (as was mentioned before) to any preconceived notion of "Greece."[41] Some of these same arguments, along with the lack of any prologue at the beginning of the work, have been used to speculate on the possibility that "missing" parts of Pausanias might be waiting to be discovered on papyri in the sands of Egypt. Unfortunately, none of the arguments advanced in support of this possibility is compelling. A fuller treatment of these problems will have to wait until a later part of this book.[42] For now, it is enough to say that the cross-references show that if Pausanias had plans to write more books than we now possess, those plans were decidedly more nebulous than his plans for the ten books we do possess. The consistency of the topographical framework Pausanias uses to structure his account also suggests a carefully worked-out plan into which it would not necessarily be easy to accommodate the addition of many other territories. The introductory route traced in each book (except the first, of course) continues an itinerary begun in a previous book – in most cases (Books 2, 3, 4, 7, 10), in the book immediately previous. By beginning and ending his topographical accounts in these books at the borders between territories, Pausanias succeeds in imparting unity and cohesiveness to the work as a whole.

Pausanias spent a great deal of time bringing his work to completion. This is something we might suspect in any case, but a look at the datable references in the text removes all doubt. The most unequivocal dating of any part of the work comes in Book 5 (5.1.2), where Pausanias states that he is writing 217 years after the foundation of the Roman colony at Corinth. Since the colony at Corinth was founded in 44 BCE, Pausanias is speaking to us from the year 173 CE. A less precise but certainly much earlier date is provided by a later passage, 7.20.6, where the process of describing the odeion in Patras apparently puts Pausanias in mind of the similar odeion

[40] Moggi 1993: 402–403.
[41] Gurlitt 1890: 2–4 and 68, n. 13. Robert 1909: 261. Meyer 1954: 19. Habicht 1998: 5–6. Bearzot 1988: 90–112. Cf. also Heberdey 1894: 2.
[42] See Chapter 3.

in Athens built by the Athenian millionaire celebrity Herodes Atticus. Pausanias explains to the reader that he did not mention the Athenian structure in his book on Attica for the simple reason that construction of it had not begun at the time he was writing that book. Since Herodes had the Odeion constructed in memory of his wife, who died around 160 CE, Pausanias would thus seem to have written Book 1 some time before or shortly after that date.[43]

From these two datable references, we can be sure that the composition of the *Periegesis* spanned a period of at least ten years, and probably took considerably longer. Frequent references to the emperor Hadrian, particularly in the first book, have led one of Pausanias' modern editors, Domenico Musti, to suggest that a large part of the work was conceived during or soon after that emperor's reign (117–138 CE), a thesis that would stretch the total composition time into the vicinity of forty years.[44] This thesis is far from unassailable; the prominence of Hadrian in Pausanias' account may simply reflect the fact that Hadrian left more of a visible impact on Greece, in the form of religious dedications and infrastructural improvements, than any other emperor. Still, a period of research and composition that lasted over twenty years or more is certainly conceivable. Of course, it is not necessary for Pausanias to have been at work on his project continuously during any particular period. There are a number of reasons for thinking that at least the first book, the book on Athens and Attica, was published separately from the others: it is the only book for which we have a *terminus ante quem* as early as 160 (the reference to the Odeion of Herodes mentioned above), and, as we shall see in subsequent chapters, the way in which Pausanias handles the description of Athens and Attica exhibits certain methodological differences from what we can observe in most later books.[45] On the other end of the time frame, some of the later datable references, including the one that dates the writing of Book 5 to 173, may well have been added in a later redaction of material that was already substantially complete some time before. Despite these uncertainties, however, we can safely say that the *Periegesis* possesses the characteristics of a work a long time in the making.

Another measure of the effort Pausanias put into his work is the extent of the travels he pursued in the course of his research. Pausanias leads his readers to all the celebrated tourist spots of Greece, shrines like Delphi and Olympia, and major cities like Athens and Corinth, places that were well equipped with decent roads, inns, and tour guides to accommodate

[43] Frazer 1898: 1.xvi–xvii; Habicht 1998: 9–12.   [44] Musti and Beschi 1982: 1.xii–xix.
[45] Gurlitt 1890: 2–3; Frazer 1898: 1.xvii–xviii; Meyer 1954: 18–19. Skeptical of the notion of separate publication are Regenbogen 1956: 1010; and Habicht 1998: 7–8.

visitors. But he also wanders far from the well-worn roadways between these first-class sites. He ventures into unpopulated wastelands and over steep and narrow mountain tracks in search of things that only the most adventuresome tourists would put on their list of obligatory sights: ghost towns, abandoned temples, caves through which Herakles was reputed to have descended to the Underworld, the tombs of obscure local heroes, and other *recherché* attractions. Pausanias was an energetic explorer of places that few ever bothered to visit in his time.[46] W. K. Pritchett has recently demonstrated something that provides additional insight into the energies Pausanias devoted to this effort: the distance measurements in *stadia* that Pausanias frequently gives between sites are not taken from any known written source, but instead seem to be estimates that Pausanias himself made based upon the time it took him to walk from place to place.[47] Though he never mentions his means of transport explicitly, we can assume that he traveled a good deal of the time on foot. Many of the roads that he traveled (such as the road fit for a "well-girt man" mentioned above) were unsuitable for wheeled traffic, and were too rough for making swift headway on the expensive and relatively delicate hooves of a horse. In mainland Greece, walking – with or without the accompaniment of a plodding pack-animal – was often the quickest and most efficient means of travel.[48]

Finally, the ultimate index of the remarkable effort and diligence that Pausanias put into his *Periegesis* is the precision and vividness with which he records the state of Greece in his own time. Despite his reticence, despite his tendency toward the impersonal, despite the archaizing focus and selectivity of his account, Pausanias projects an unfalsifiable authenticity to which every season's archaeological results only seem to add further confirmation. The proof of Pausanias' ability to record an accurate picture of second-century Greece can sometimes be stunning. In 1892, for instance, a large chunk of a stone statue base was found in a field south of the Lakonian site of Amyklai.[49] On it are inscribed the many honors and offices of a member of the Spartan elite of the Roman period, a certain Sextus Eudamos, son of Onasikrates and descendant of Herakles. The positions listed include the hereditary priesthood in a large number of cults: that of the *Sebastoi* (the Roman emperors), of the Dioskouroi, of Poseidon Asphalios,

---

[46] Friedländer 1921–1923: 2.99–107 comments on the tendency of upper-class travelers of this era to stick to the well-worn tourist itineraries, and on the lack of taste for adventure travel.

[47] Pritchett 1999: 17–36, esp. 20–22.

[48] On the identification and study of ancient roads in the area covered by Pausanias, the work of Pritchett is fundamental, esp. Pritchett 1980. In recent years, Yiannis Pikoulas has set a new and exacting standard for the identification and study of ancient Greek roads (see esp. Pikoulas 1995).

[49] *IG* V.1.559 (= Sparta Museum inventory no. 544; cf. Tod & Wace 1906 *s.v.*; Wide 1893).

Athena Chalkioikos, Athena Poliouchos (along with the other gods who shared her shrine), Tyche Sopatro, Artemis Patriotis.[50] Demeter and Kore in Phrourion, Sostratia in Egeila,[51] Aphrodite Ourania, Tyche Toichagetos, Hermes Ouranios, Demeter and Kore in Diktynna, Mnemosyne and the Muses,[52] and Zeus Hypatos. In all, Eudamos served as priest for the cults of at least eighteen gods and goddesses, and he held the position of *agonothetes* (Master of the Games) for two important athletic competitions, the Dioskoureia and the Leonideia. Pausanias, in the course of his description of Sparta, makes mention of both of these festivals, and of the cults that Eudamos was involved with, Pausanias mentions temples, shrines, or at least the names of all but five: the two Tyches, Artemis Patriotis, Hermes Ouranios and Demeter and Kore in Phrouria.[53] As with most Greek cities of the time, the religious life of Sparta was a complex collection of cults from various places and times in which traditional gods, new gods, traditional gods in new guises, heroes and divinized rulers were worshipped. Pausanias reproduces that intricate religious milieu with remarkable fidelity. The effortlessness with which he seems to do so belies the effort and time that must have gone into it.

PAUSANIAS IN THE MODERN WORLD

The purpose of dwelling on the time and the physical exertion Pausanias had to devote to the writing of the *Periegesis* is not to portray Pausanias as extraordinarily hardworking, meticulous or productive. The point is rather that the *Periegesis* is not a hastily produced work, or one that was written upon a brief and superficial acquaintance with the sights of Greece. This is an elementary observation, perhaps, and one with which few would likely argue when stated as such, but it is still an observation to which much of the scholarship on Pausanias, even some of the most recent work, seems to give insufficient regard. This brings us back to the topic first raised at the beginning of this chapter, the history of the modern scholarship on Pausanias. Some comments on the genealogy and the sociology of the modern study of Pausanias are necessary in order to understand the tenor

---

[50] The epithets of Tyche and Artemis here are poorly preserved on the stone. I transliterate here (and throughout) the readings adopted in *IG*.

[51] = Aigila? (Paus. 4.17.1).

[52] All that remains on the stone are the first two letters of Mnemosyne's name; "and the Muses" is conjectural.

[53] Pausanias does mention a temple of Artemis without epithet in the place known as Phrouria (3.12.8), and a statue of Artemis (again without epithet) in the agora of Sparta (3.11.9). Perhaps one or both of these could pertain to the unaccounted-for cults in the inscription.

of current scholarship and to define the new areas in which this book hopes to make a contribution.

In the late nineteenth century, scholarly attitudes toward Pausanias generally split into two camps: one camp saw Pausanias as an honest and reliable guide to the antiquities of Greece; the other, inspired by the great German philologist Wilamowitz,[54] believed him to be a literary fabricator and an armchair topographer who cobbled together much of his account from earlier written sources. Of these two opposing views, the former fared considerably better over the course of the twentieth century, and with good reason: it was the one supported by the majority of scholars who were familiar with the actual topography and archaeology of Greece. The contrasting view never had much in its favor, aside from a general prejudice against Greek authors of the Roman era, an overly positivistic faith in the powers of source criticism,[55] and the personal *auctoritas* of Wilamowitz. Supporters of the "liar school" of Pausanias[56] never managed to find a single topographical passage in Pausanias that they could convincingly attribute to a surviving previous text. Meanwhile, in contrast, each year brought new archaeological reports out of Greece confirming the general, and sometimes very specific, accuracy of Pausanias. Archaeological and topographical researches also demonstrated that the picture Pausanias gave of Greece was a contemporary one: it refers to the state of sites and monuments as they were in Pausanias' own day, not as they were in the earlier periods, in which his alleged sources were writing. The Eudamos inscription discussed above is a case in point.

In fact, while it is always tempting to cast such scholarly differences in terms of Manichaean struggles between equally potent foes, this particular quarrel was never really much of a fight. Wilamowitz himself never published a full defense of his views, and apart from a single little-read book by August Kalkmann,[57] it is hard to find anything but half-hearted and highly qualified support for the view of Pausanias as a chimney-corner topographer in any of the published literature. The final nail in the coffin for the present generation came with Habicht's entertaining demonstration that the origin of the discredited notion lay more in the pettiness and personal animus of Wilamowitz than in anything resembling evidence or rigorous analysis of the text. Wilamowitz, it seems, had become embarrassingly confused while trying to use the *Periegesis* as a guidebook for shepherding a

---

[54] Wilamowitz 1877: 326–367, esp. 344–347.   [55] Cf. Whitmarsh 2001: 41–45.
[56] The phrase "liar school" is borrowed from Pritchett 1993 (who uses it in reference to Herodotean studies).
[57] Kalkmann 1886.

party of German noblemen around Olympia, and subsequently blamed his guide, Pausanias, in preference to blaming himself.[58]

Long before Habicht, though, even as early the 1930s,[59] the liar school was already mostly defunct, apart perhaps from the sort of isolated recrudescences that merely illustrate the principle that no bad idea ever completely dies.[60] It is therefore somewhat curious to observe the influence that the struggle against it has had on the scholarship of subsequent decades. Battling Wilamowitz and his fellow source-critics is a major theme of Habicht's work and also of the authoritative Pauly–Wissowa encyclopedia article on Pausanias written by Otto Regenbogen in 1956. The Wilamowitzian thesis was both outrageous and demonstrably wrong, and such theses tend to draw fire long after their demise.

This prolonged shadow-boxing on the part of Pausanias' champions is in itself neither unusual nor particularly pernicious, but the defense of Pausanias has traditionally been accompanied by another attitude that has had some unfortunate effects. It is here we arrive at the notion introduced at the beginning of the chapter, the tendency to view Pausanias as a "dependable dullard." Even before Wilamowitz was born, the idea that Pausanias was an honest and reliable source was frequently coupled with a low estimation of his intelligence and sophistication. The great British topographer William Leake, an early nineteenth-century pioneer in the use of Pausanias for the recovery of the lost landscapes of ancient Greece, put the two ideas together quite nicely:[61]

. . . at this distance of time, in the absence of all other authority of the same kind, one cannot but value [Pausanias'] work the more, from his having been deficient in that ardour of genius, which often makes travellers the dupes of their own feelings, and leads them to exaggerate and misrepresent.

Pausanias is thus the historian's favorite kind of source: a congenial, plodding workhorse who is too dull to lie and too unimaginative to distort the facts in pursuit of literary artifice. One finds traces of this attitude in much of the scholarship that purports to be pro-Pausanias, even in the work of Wilamowitz's formidable contemporary, J. G. Frazer, whose six-volume commentary on the *Periegesis*, first published in 1898, is still an essential reference. Frazer once complained to his colleague A. E. Housman about

[58] Habicht 1998: 165–167.
[59] The decade in which the last substantial expression of the Wilamowitzian viewpoint was published: Deicke 1935.
[60] E.g. Jacoby 1944: 40–41, n. 12; Fehling 1988.
[61] W. M. Leake, *The Topography of Athens, with Some Remarks on its Antiquities* (London, 1831) xxxiv. On Leake's use of Pausanias, see now Wagstaff 2001.

the way Wilamowitz used to belabor "my poor old friend Pausanias *and no doubt many a better man.*"[62] In Frazer's commentary itself, one finds a number of jovial but condescending remarks like the following in regard to Pausanias' writing style:[63]

> The author bestrides his high-horse; he bobs up and down and clumps about on it with great solemnity; it is not his fault if his Pegasus is a wooden hobby-horse instead of a winged charger . . . Pausanias cannot be blamed for trying to write well; the pity is that with all his pains he did not write better.

We can see in this statement, as elsewhere, an unresolved tension; Pausanias' attempts at literary sophistication are obvious, but to preserve his notion of Pausanias' congenial simplicity Frazer must characterize them as unsuccessful and negligible. More recent scholarship tends to refrain from expressing such unflattering opinions of Pausanias, and indeed it is possible that few still hold such opinions, yet the habit of thinking of Pausanias as a dependable dullard has deep roots, and it continues to exert influence in a number of ways. We have already mentioned the extent to which literary study of the text has been retarded as a result, and this lack of attention probably accounts for a further gap: though scholarship on Pausanias himself is on the rise, there remains a tendency to ignore him in broader studies of the literary and cultural history of the period. For instance, a collection of essays on "Antonine Literature" refers to Pausanias once, in passing, in the course of 219 pages;[64] a general study of the phenomenon of the Second Sophistic contains only a handful of brief references, and confuses our Pausanias in the index with the sophist Pausanias of Cappadocia and with Pausanias the lexicographer.[65] Thomas Schmitz's perceptive study of "education and power" in the period likewise pays little attention to Pausanias, perhaps because Schmitz considers the *Periegesis* as an example of the sort of *Fachschriftstellerei*, which, to his mind, provides little evidence for his prime concern, the public role of literature in this period.[66] Finally, Tim Whitmarsh's excellent new study of Greek literature of the Roman period contains only two brief references to Pausanias,[67] even though (as will be evident in subsequent pages of the present work) many

---

[62] J. G. Frazer, letter to A. E. Housman (1927), quoted in Ackerman 1974: 361 (emphasis added).
[63] Frazer 1898: 1.lxix–lxx.
[64] Russell 1990: 108 (the reference comes in the course of the essay by Anderson).
[65] Anderson 1993: 4–5, 6–7, 105, 122–3; the index reference, which classes all three authors under the heading "Pausanias of Cappadocia," is on p. 301.
[66] Schmitz 1997: 36. The only comment Schmitz makes specifically about Pausanias comes on page 178.
[67] Whitmarsh 2001: 121, 153, n. 75.

of Whitmarsh's insights about the nature of literature in this period are
fundamentally pertinent to the study of Pausanias. Thus, while Pausanias
himself is drawing more favorable attention, that attention remains somewhat isolated. With few exceptions,[68] the extent to which Pausanias can
contribute to the literary and, particularly, cultural history of the second
century remains consistently undervalued in broader studies.

We can see a more specific manifestation of the undervaluation of the
Periegesis in the frequent characterization of it as a "travel guide" or an
"ancient Baedeker."[69] The idea in itself is not what is so problematic; the
phrase "travel guide" covers a number of possible types of text, and, as we
shall discuss further in Chapter 7, there is no doubt that *Periegesis* could
be used as a travel guide of some sort. The problem comes in the way the
assertion is made: as if by definition, a "travel guide" is a work of no imagination and no artistry; as if a "travel guide", even a modern one like *Fodor's*
or the *Blue Guide,* cannot be interrogated in terms of its language and style,
its principles of inclusion and exclusion, and its ideological underpinnings;
and as if identifying the *Periegesis* as a "travel guide" answers any question
we might have about its author's aims and methods. The shortcomings of
this view have been well rehearsed, but it continues to show up in modern
scholarship.[70] Often, its more recent exponents rely on the formulation of
Frazer, whose words are worth citing verbatim:[71]

Why was Pausanias at such pains to present everything to his readers in its exact
position? The only probable answer is that he wished to help them to find their
way from one object of interest to another; in other words that he intended his
Description of Greece to serve as a guide-book for travelers. If his aim had been
merely to amuse and entertain his readers at home, he could hardly have lighted
on a worse method of doing so; for the persons who find topographical directions
amusing and can extract entertainment from reading that "this place is so many
furlongs from that . . . ," must be few in number and of an unusually cheerful
disposition. The ordinary reader is more likely to yawn over such statements and
shut up the book.

It is thought-provoking, and indicative of the ideological potency of this
image of Pausanias, that as astute a scholar as Frazer could characterize
so inaccurately and simplistically a text to which he obviously devoted an
enormous amount of study and thought. The answer to Frazer's opening

[68] Most notably Swain 1996: 330–356; I emphasize that my remarks here do not apply to the many
excellent works of recent years that focus particularly on Pausanias, only to general studies of the
period in which Pausanias lived.
[69] Gurlitt 1890: 9–10; Frazer 1898: I.xxii; Habicht 1998: 21–23. *Contra:* Robert 1909: 6–7; Veyne 1988:
3; Elsner 1992: 4 (= Elsner 1995: 128–129).
[70] See, for instance, Arafat 1996: 33.   [71] Frazer 1898: I.xxiv

question is simply that Pausanias was *not* at such pains to present everything
to his readers in its exact location. As we shall see in Chapters 3, 4, and 5,
Pausanias keeps detailed topographical directions and talk of "furlongs"
to a minimum, except where he has nothing he finds more interesting to
say. Also, one does not have to read far in Pausanias before coming to
a place where a topographical sequence that the author is tracing breaks
off. A traveler relying on the *Periegesis* as a guide would often find himself
stranded in the middle of nowhere, with no clue in the text as to how
to get to the next sight. Such pains as Pausanias does take to present the
"exact location" of sites to his readers need not be explained solely as an
attempt to guide the patient traveler on his journey. His efforts can far
more consistently be explained as an organizational tactic that he pursues
for a number of beneficial effects: giving structure to an immense amount of
data, providing readers with a vivid image of the landscape being described,
and, by replicating in prose the physical and visual perspective of the traveler, reminding the reader that the text has the authority of eyewitness
experience.

A related and even more common misconception is that the *Periegesis*
is a more-or-less immediate record of a single grand tour through the sites
and territories of Greece. The classic statement of this is the 1894 monograph by Rudolph Heberdey, *Die Reisen des Pausanias in Griechenland.*
Heberdey attempted to distinguish between places Pausanias visited and
those he didn't on the basis of two main criteria: explicit claims of autopsy
on the part of Pausanias (which Heberdey generally accepted as genuine)
and places where Pausanias used past-tense verbs to describe things (on the
theory that such references represented the way things "were" at the specific time of Pausanias' unique visit, whereas places Pausanias didn't visit
could be described in the time-indeterminate present tense). Heberdey
manifested the results of his investigation in a series of maps showing
"traveled" and "untraveled" routes. The "traveled" routes were unified,
and the gaps in them filled, by the assumption that the author accomplished his researches on a single grand tour. Though useful in many ways,
there are serious problems with nearly all of Heberdey's basic assumptions.
Like many Germanophone scholars of the time, Heberdey, was influenced
by Wilamowitzian notions of Pausanias' truthfulness: for Heberdey, the
places where there is explicit evidence that Pausanias visited are to be taken
as the *only* places he visited. The "untraveled" routes Pausanias presents
as his own are allegedly drawn from previous sources. For present purposes, however, the most important assumption Heberdey made was that
of the single grand tour. There are numerous indications in the text that

Pausanias' travels were more prolonged and complex. To turn once more to
the passage mentioning the Odeion of Herodes (7.20.6), that passage alone
guarantees that Pausanias visited Athens at least twice before writing Book 7:
once before and once after Herodes' auditorium was built. Likewise,
Pausanias' itineraries lead the reader from Attica to both Boiotia (Book 9)
and the territory of Corinth (Book 2); from the territory of Argos (Book 2)
to both Lakonia (Book 3) and Arkadia (Book 8). The routes so described
would be impossible to follow on a single tour without a ludicrous amount
of backtracking. Pausanias never mentions such return-journeys, and even
supposing what is hardly likely, that Pausanias' travels include *only* the
backtracking necessary to allow the itineraries he describes to unfold in the
order that we have them, that in itself would have afforded him at least two
looks at a number of the places he describes.

These are all truths that most present-day scholars would probably
acknowledge. Nevertheless, the habit of thinking of Pausanias' itineraries
as the transcript of a single continuous tour persists in the scholarship.
Nowadays, it is not so much Pausanias' travels as a whole that are thought
of that way but his experience of individual sites. Occasionally, scholars talk
of Pausanias as if they viewed his text as little more than a transcript of the
author's impressions as he walked through a place, impressions recorded
perhaps by a faithful servant who followed behind him, stylus and wax
tablets in hand. Here, for instance, is how R. E. Wycherley constructs part
of Pausanias' movements on his visit to the Agora of Athens (emphasis
added):[72]

> *Pausanias entered* at the northwest corner [of the agora]. From this point *he would
> have had an impressive view* up the Panathenaic Street. . . . *Without hesitation he
> turned* along the street to the right and concentrated first on the ancient shrines
> and buildings of the west side. . . . *Pausanias now doubles back* northwards and
> describes the Eponymous Heroes, Amphiaraos . . . and other remarkable statues,
> leading on to the Temple of Ares. *He is now in the middle of the square . . .*:

In reality, unless one assumes that Pausanias made one and only one visit
to the agora, there is no reason to suppose that he actually performed any of
the actions that Wycherley ascribes to him here, at least not in this specific
sequence. Pausanias' description of the agora is likely to be the product of
several sojourns in Athens, if not a long-term residency, with prolonged
and repeated visits to at least some of the monuments described in the
passage in question. Now it is probable that Wycherley, one of the more

---

[72] Thompson and Wycherley 1972: 205. This passage is in reference to Pausanias 1.3.1–1.8.2. See Figure
5.1 for a diagram of the agora with Wycherley's reconstruction of Pausanias' route indicated.

astute scholars of the twentieth century when it comes to the use of literary texts for the interpretation of archaeological remains, was fully aware of this. It is convenient and almost irresistible to talk about Pausanias' text in this way as a shorthand for what would otherwise have to be expressed in a much more cumbersome fashion: "Pausanias chooses to begin his description of the Agora from the point of view of someone entering it from the northwest . . ." As long as one is aware that this is a conceit, it is a rather harmless one. The problem comes when the conceit is taken seriously; erroneous readings of the text frequently result. In a way, this misreading of Pausanias is a tribute to Pausanias' proficiency in producing a clear and effective organization of the material in his work: without referring explicitly to his own movements, he succeeds in conveying to the reader the cognitive impression of a journey from point to point. The result is a much more vivid and comprehensible image of a site than a mere list of monuments and artifacts could provide. Pausanias' success in this area, however, should not distract us from the fact that the travels upon which the *Periegesis* is based were most probably conducted at various times over the course of the long period of the work's composition, and they probably involved several different visits to many of the sites and monuments that he includes in his account. Consequently, when Pausanias sat down to compose his topography of any particular landscape, he potentially had a great number of different perspectives from which to choose.

This is not to say that there may not be some passages in the *Periegesis* that record the author's first and only trip to a place. This is particularly likely to be the case with some of the more remote places Pausanias visits. Conversely, there are cases where Pausanias treats a place he almost *had* to have visited more than once as if he knows it primarily from a single visit. One of the places we can be fairly confident in saying Pausanias visited often is the city of Megara, which stands on the Isthmus of Corinth athwart the major land routes between the Peloponnesos and the rest of Greece. Yet at one point in his account of Megarian territory, he describes very specifically what seems to be a one-time experience (1.41.2): ἐντεῦθεν ὁ τῶν ἐπιχωρίων ἡμῖν ἐξηγητὴς ἡγεῖτο ἐς χωρίον Ῥοῦν ὡς ἔφασκεν ὀνομαζόμενον (from here our guide to local matters led us to a place called, according to him, Rhous). No other single sentence in the entire *Periegesis* gives us more insight into how Pausanias traveled. His use of the word "our" (ἡμῖν) suggests that he traveled with company rather than alone (although the possibility that he is employing a "literary we" is not to be excluded); he availed himself of local guides and depended on them for some of the information he imparts, and the casual and matter-of-fact way

Figure 1.3. Megara. The modern town is centered on the distinctive twin acropoleis of the ancient city.

that he refers to "the guide" suggests that he did not expect his audience to find it strange that he did so.[73] The way Pausanias expresses himself in this passage does make it seem like he only made one visit to Rhous in the company of a particular guide. It would be hazardous, however, to assume that the rest of his account was likewise based on a single journey. He may well have visited Megara a number of times but only made one journey to that particular part of the Megarian territory. It could also be the case that while he visited some places several times, he did not do so with the intent of collecting data for his *Periegesis* on every occasion. Unlike a simple travel diary, in which the form of the work tends simply to follow the physical movement of the traveler, the structure of Pausanias' *Periegesis* is a result of deliberate decisions on the author's part about how a description of Greece is best constructed.

An assumption of simplicity of compositional technique, that is, viewing the *Periegesis* as a travel diary or a travelogue of a single journey, is one of the most prevalent effects that remain from decades of thinking of Pausanias as a dependable dullard. Another effect is a tendency to think of Pausanias' text as an undifferentiated mass, where what is important about each passage

[73] On Pausanias and his guides, see now Jones 2001.

can be understood in isolation rather than in context. In recent articles, John Henderson and Mary Beard have pointed out how some of the most avid and innovative readers of Pausanias at the turn of the twentieth century, including L. R. Farnell and Jane Harrison, viewed Pausanias' text chiefly as a treasure trove of priceless information that could be dismembered and amputated at will in an effort to uncover the embedded gem of a recondite artwork or a rare religious practice.[74] In more recent times, scholars have routinely had more respect for the integrity of the work, but there remains a certain scholarly tunnel vision that focuses on the individual elements of the text without a comprehensive view of the whole. One author, for instance, introduces us to Pausanias' description of the temple of Hera at Olympia and invites us to think of it as a typical example of "Pausanian description,"[75] when in fact many elements of the description that the author points out specifically, such as the architectural order of the columns, are *not* a usual part of Pausanias' methods of description and occur only in the case of a few temples. The article in question offers many insightful comments about particular phenomena in Pausanias' text, but it also makes the mistake of viewing the phenomena out of context and assuming that the characteristics observed in discrete parts of the text are present in the text as a whole. The analogy of the blind men and the elephant comes to mind again, although it goes without saying that the main issue is not the "blindness" of these scholars (whose mental, if not visual, acuity is something the current author can only envy) but rather the nature of the elephant. The *Periegesis* is a large work, a complex work, a multifaceted work; and one of the theses I will advance about it is that it is a work that regularly, perhaps even by design, defies generalization. In the end, I cannot claim to have produced anything more than my own blind-man's view of this literary pachyderm; what I do hope to accomplish is a description of those parts of the elephant that are not as prominent and which have not received as much attention – the vast gray body that connects the legs, the tail, the trunk, the tusks, and other more conspicuous and sensational body-parts – in hopes that such a perspective will combine with others to give a more coherent picture of the animal as a whole.

[74] Henderson 2001; Beard 2001.   [75] Calame 1990: 227–229.

CHAPTER 2

Pausanias' world

That the longest travel narrative in ancient Greek comes to us from an author of the second century is not just a matter of chance. Following the expansionary activities of Trajan, the three emperors whom we can name as Pausanias' contemporaries reigned over a period of retrenchment and consolidation. This was the high point of the *pax Romana*, an unprecedented period of peace and stability. Until the German incursions that took place in the reign of Marcus Aurelius, the empire's borders were relatively stable and calm, and its interior calmer still. At the center lay the Mediterranean Sea, historically the main avenue of transport and trade for the peoples whose communities sat around its shores like ants or frogs around a pond.[1] There had been a time when this sea was a hostile one, made perilous by piracy and by the competing political and military interests of dozens of independent states. In Pausanias' day, however, it was the serene center of a peaceful and unified world. At no time in the recorded history of the Mediterranean had travel been as safe and convenient, and in the society that developed within the safety of the empire's borders, the act of traveling took on a particular cultural significance.

TRAVEL AND SOCIETY

While moving from place to place was easier for everyone in this period, it was especially easy for those who had wealth and connections. The people who were most likely to take advantage of the expanded opportunities for travel were accordingly the more privileged elements of society. Members of the imperial elite traveled for a number of motives, including education, recreation, adventure, and religion. Political concerns may have been the last thing on most travelers' minds as they made their journeys, but the majority of people whose movements have left some trace belonged to the class that

---

[1] The image is Plato's: *Phaedo* 109b1.

30

held what passed for political power under Rome's domination. Their traveling, therefore, cannot be divorced from the power structures within the
society of the time. Inevitably, the journeys of the elite, particularly those
undertaken for pleasure and personal enrichment, were more than simple movements from place to place; they were also acts that symbolized
the confidence in the very system that kept the elite in their privileged
position. Traveling from one part of the empire to another and being
greeted with pomp and ceremony at every stopping-place was one way in
which the emperor and the officials of the Roman state manifested their
sovereignty and made themselves a concrete part of their subjects' lives.[2] A
similar social and political dynamic operated on a smaller scale when the
rest of the Roman and non-Roman elite went traveling. To travel was not
only to take advantage of the order that Roman domination brought to
the Mediterranean but also to participate in its perpetuation. By passing
freely from Britain to the Black Sea and from the Pyramids to the Pillars of
Herakles, the upper-class travelers of this era mirrored the movements of
their rulers and contributed to the cultural homogenization of the territories under Rome's control. Well before Pausanias' time, travel had become
a marker of upper-class identity, and the grand-tour experience that took
both Roman and provincial aristocrats on secular and spiritual pilgrimages
to Greece, Egypt, Rome itself, and the other culturally iconic spots under
Roman hegemony, had become an ever more popular rite of passage.[3]

This habit of travel cooperated with a long-standing trend toward cos-
mopolitanism among the elite of the empire, a trend that gradually eroded
the old distinctions between people based on membership in a locally
defined ethnicity. Though imperial subjects continued to identify themselves proudly with traditional ethnic epithets, and some obsolete designa-
tions such as "Phrygian" and "Mysian" were even revived,[4] the differences
marked by these terms had ceased to have the same political or cultural
importance that they had before the Roman conquest. Philopappus,
the "Syrian man" we encountered in the previous chapter, claimed to
be descended from Macedonians but was a citizen of Rome and could
serve as her consul. He was equally at home in Athens, and was deemed
Athenian enough to qualify for selection as one of the archons of the city,
a position once open only to those of unmixed Athenian ancestry. In this
respect, Philopappus was not an anomaly. Arrian (Flavius Arrianus) from

[2] Millar 1977: 28–40.
[3] Friedländer 1921–1923: 2.107–131; Casson, 1974: 229–291; Marasco 1978: 77–85; André and Baslez
1993: 119–168; Chevallier 1998.
[4] Gurlitt 1890: 57.

Bithynia was granted the same honor at Athens after retiring there from a long career that included imperial service in the form of a consulship and a proconsulship.[5] Mestrius Plutarchus, better known as Plutarch, a proud citizen of Chaironeia in Greece, served as both Priest of Apollo at Delphi and, perhaps, as procurator for the Roman government in the province of Achaia. He addressed his immense output of philosophical and historical reflections to friends and acquaintances of various national and linguistic backgrounds, including both Philopappus and the imperial courtier Sosius Senecio.[6] The empire-wide network of elite associations that is reflected in the writings of Plutarch and other authors was both a product of and an incentive for the habit of travel that the elite freely engaged in during this era.[7]

The role of Hellenism in this cultural environment is also important. In recent years, scholars have learned to be cautious in using words like "Hellenism" and "Romanization," since these are modern terms that do not necessarily match up with ancient categories of thought. When, for instance, we find physical and intellectual artifacts we think of as "Roman" in "non-Roman" contexts, labeling the phenomenon "Romanization" may reflect more on the way we classify things than on how the people of the time did.[8] In a subsequent chapter, for instance, we shall see that even for Pausanias, something as quintessentially Roman (in our eyes) as a bath building or an aqueduct can contribute to a Hellenizing construction of landscape. At the same time, similar difficulties bedevil the concept of Hellenism itself: the extent to which particular manifestations of "Hellenism" had a genuine pedigree in traditional Greek culture is not always an easy matter to discern. Nevertheless, if we keep such complications in mind and focus on perception rather than actual origins, we can usefully address Hellenism as the tendency to place high value on things *perceived* as being Greek, whether in the field of language, literature, art, or architecture.

---

[5] On Arrian's career in general: Bosworth 1980–1995: 1.1–7; Stadter 1980: 1–18; Tonnet 1988: 1.9–59; Swain 1996: 242–246.

[6] Jones 1972: 3–64; Puech 1991: 4831–93. On the question of whether or not Plutarch was procurator, see Swain 1996: 171–2, who is skeptical, but the larger point that Greek intellectuals of the period frequently sought and served in imperial positions is hardly in doubt; see Bowersock and Jones 1974: 35–40; Quass 1982. On the suggestion that Sosius Senecio was of Eastern, rather than Roman, extraction, see Swain 1996: 426–427, who finds the evidence unconvincing. It is symptomatic of the trend under discussion that one can tell nothing about Sosius' ethnic origins just from his name.

[7] See, in general, Bowersock 1969: 43–58 and 76–88; Schepens 1998; Galsterer 1998.

[8] On the problematic nature of "Romanization," see, for instance, Yegül 1991: 345–355; Freeman 1993: 438–445; Woolf 1994 and 1997; Webster and Cooper 1996; Alcock (ed.) 1997: 1–7. On the parallel problems in "Hellenism," see Bowersock 1990; Bowie 1991; and the articles in Saïd 1991, especially, for the Roman period, those of Dalimier: 17–32; Frézouls: 125–149; Hartog: 149–168; Bowie: 183–204; Jacquemin: 217–232.

So defined, Hellenism can be recognized as one of the most important cultural trends in the second-century Roman Empire. People who are new to the study of antiquity are often surprised to learn that the dominant language of cosmopolitan imperial society of this period was not Latin but Greek. In the eastern part of the empire, knowledge of Latin, beyond the few words needed for dealing with the realities of imperial administration, was rarely more than rudimentary. In contrast, the mastery of Greek was a mark of a well-educated individual, a *pepaideumenos*, from one end of the empire to the other.[9] From a broader historical perspective, there is nothing surprising in this. Greek was already the *lingua franca* in the Hellenistic East long before Rome's sway extended in that direction, and Rome herself had developed in a milieu steeped in cultural influences from nearby Greek colonies in Sicily and southern Italy. "Conquered Greece conquered Rome," as the Roman poet Horace is sometimes paraphrased,[10] yet the cultural influence of Hellenism over Rome began long before the political hegemony of Rome was even conceivable. From the time of the earliest preserved Roman literature, and assuredly for some time before that, a thorough grounding in Greek language, literature, and cultural ideology was a cornerstone of erudition for the Roman elite.

As Rome's power expanded, the geographical scope of her Hellenizing tendency was bound to expand as well. This development has some important manifestations in the time of Pausanias. The most prominent and successful cultural figures of his day were performing intellectuals who took advantage of the ease of travel to tour the cities of the empire, winning fame, status, and considerable wealth by delivering extemporaneous oratory in Greek to appreciative audiences. These orator-philosophers were styled "sophists" in homage to the itinerant wise men of classical Greece, and the period of their ascendancy, beginning in the mid-first century and extending through the second, is commonly referred to in modern scholarship as the "Second Sophistic."[11] The stars in this intellectual firmament,

---

[9] Bowersock 1969; Swain 1996: 43–51; Schmitz 1997: 83–91; on the social importance of *paideia* more generally, see Kaster 1988: 32–134; Morgan 1998: 240–273.

[10] Horace, *Ep.* 2.1.156–7: Graecia capta ferum victorem cepit et artes intulit agresti Latio. More literally, "Captive Greece captured her savage conqueror and brought the arts to rustic Latium."

[11] The phrase "Second Sophistic" belongs to the chronicler of this "movement," Philostratos, and he uses it not to refer to the period but to the type of oratory practiced by these men. Nevertheless, the phrase "Second Sophistic" has come to be applied to the entire period beginning in the middle of the first century CE (the date of Niketes of Smyrna, whom Philostratos identifies as the first important representative of the species in the Roman era) to Philostratos' own time in the early third century. It is worth noting, however, that Philostratos uses the phrase "Second Sophistic" only once, and in reference to a rhetorical tradition he sees as beginning with the fourth-century BCE orator Aischines (*Lives of the Sophists* 507). Brunt (1994) argues that current studies in the "Second Sophistic" follow

in addition to being empire-wide celebrities, frequently served as political leaders in their own communities and on the broader imperial scene. Men like Herodes Atticus of Athens[12] and Polemon of Laodicea[13] used their wealth, reputation, and connections to attract interest and favors for their native cities and for other communities who sought their patronage. The characteristic combination of oratorical, economic, and political potency possessed by the masters of this craft is suggested by the sophists' biographer Philostratos when he says the following of the earliest Roman-era sophist, Niketes of Smyrna (*VS* 511):

Niketes, inheriting a science [i.e. the science of oratory] that had been left in a straitened condition, endowed it with avenues (παρόδους) far more glorious than the ones he himself had built for Smyrna, connecting the town with the Ephesus gateway, and making his works, in their magnitude, equal to his words.

Many of the sophists, including Herodes and Polemon, were also active participants in the imperial system of government, performing not only local liturgies and magistracies and funding, like Niketes, local building projects, but also serving the empire as consuls and proconsuls, as provincial officials, as secretaries to the emperor, as tutors for the families of the Roman elite, and as priests in the cult of the Roman emperors.[14]

Although the Second Sophistic was primarily a phenomenon of the eastern half of the empire, it had an impact in the West as well, and the cosmopolitan appeal of its Hellenism was also exhibited in other, non-sophistic literary and cultural endeavors. This was a time when a man from Syria, not Philopappus this time but Lucian, and Favorinus from Arelate in Gaul (modern Arles in France) could both aspire to being virtuosi in the Greek language and in the expression of Hellenic culture.[15] The ease

---

Philostratos' epochal construction of the first-century CE rebirth of sophistic rhetoric too uncritically; the sort of declamation practiced in the "Second Sophistic" arose long before (see also Russell 1983 for a broader view of the history of Greek declamation). As Schmitz rightly points out, however, sophistic declamation in this period takes on an importance in the social context of the mature empire that it never had previously (Schmitz 1997: 14–17), so treating this as a unique period is justifiable, and "the Second Sophistic" is as good a name for the period as any. See also Swain 1996: 2, n. 2.

[12] Philostratos *Lives of the Sophists* 545–566. On the activities and international euergetism of Herodes, see Ameling 1983; Tobin 1997; Galli 2002.

[13] Philostratos *Lives of the Sophists* 530–544; Gleason 1995: 21–54; Boatwright 2000: 157–162.

[14] Bowersock and Jones 1974: 35–40; Quass 1982. Bowie (1982) wisely cautions against overemphasizing the role played by the careers these men had as sophists in their acquisition of imperial clout. Many would have been prominent figures otherwise by virtue of their wealth and family background. This was a period when wealth, travel, education, literary notoriety, and political influence were inextricably linked, and distinguishing which of these threads were most important can be a frustrating, if not futile, task. On this topic, see also Schmitz 1997: 21–25; Saïd 2001.

[15] Jones 1986; Gleason 1995: 3–20; Swain 1996: 43–51; Schmitz 1997: 67–91; Holford–Strevens 1997.

Figure 2.1. A portrait bust of the sophist Herodes Atticus, found near his family estate at Kifisia, outside Athens.

of movement and the empire-wide network of contacts made possible by the Roman peace encouraged the advancement of Hellenism as a common cultural standard.

HELLAS, HELLENISM, AND PHILHELLENISM

Many of the emperors themselves, beginning especially with Nero and continuing later with Hadrian and Marcus Aurelius, were enthusiastic advocates of Hellenism. Hadrian, who seems to have been the emperor of Pausanias' youth, was extraordinarily attentive not just to the ideal of Greek culture but also to Greece itself. As a youth in Spain, he earned the nickname "Greekling" (*Graeculus*) for his devotion to Greek studies,[16] and as emperor he visited Greece on at least three occasions, each time lavishing on the Greek cities, especially Athens, a number of dedications, both ornamental and infrastructural, that went some way toward repairing the relative neglect into which the physical appointments of Greece had fallen in the previous centuries.[17] On the last of his visits, in 131–132 CE, Hadrian presided over the establishment of a league of Greek cities, the Panhellenion, which had its headquarters in Athens and which restricted its membership to cities in two categories: cities of the old Greek world – chiefly mainland cities like Athens and Sparta – and cities that could make a convincing case for having originated as colonies of the cities in the first category.[18] Through the founding of the Panhellenion, Hellenism was given a certain measure of institutional substance, and the high status of the mainland in the cultural hierarchy of the Greek world – an important thing to keep in mind in the case of a non-mainlander like Pausanias – was given official validation.

In important ways, Hadrian's philhellenism was emblematic: while the spirit that propagated Greek cultural sensibilities in this era was no mere affectation, it did not always spring from Greece itself. In fact, most of the people in this era who admired Greek culture were not born into it; instead, like Hadrian, who was born in Spain, and like many of the other philhellenes of the period, they experienced Hellenic culture as something distinct, though inseparable, from their own, something to which their first significant exposure came in the course of their education, and as a result was learned culture rather than native culture. One result of this is that the expressions of Hellenism in this period are remarkably detached from

---

[16] *H. A. Hadrian* 1.5.

[17] For Hadrian's travels, see Halfmann 1986: 40–47, 188–212. On Hadrian's "building program" in Greece, gsee: Adams 1989; Clinton 1989a and 1989b; Willers 1990; Boatwright 2000. Assuming Pausanias was native to the area of Magnesia on Sipylos (see previous chapter), he would have grown up in proximity to the city of Smyrna, one of the main focal points, alongside Athens, for Hadrian's generosity. See Boatwright 2000: 157–162. Pausanias was also a (probably younger) contemporary of the sophist Polemon, another great benefactor of Smyrna (see also Chapter 6 below for further discussion of this point).

[18] Spawforth and Walker 1985 and 1986; Willers 1990: 26–52; Boatwright 2000: 147–50. There is some controversy over whether the initiative for founding the Panhellenion came from Hadrian or from the Greek cities. Jones (1996: 30–31) interprets the main literary text, Dio 69.16.1–2, as indicating the latter. Regardless, the foundation certainly met with Hadrian's approval and can therefore be taken as some indication of the proper role the emperor envisioned the Greeks playing within the empire.

the contemporary reality of Greece.[19] With some exceptions, the image of Greece one finds in the surviving literature of the age is the Greece of the history books, the classical Greece of Themistokles and Socrates, a land that provided the fodder for the imaginary set speeches that rhetorical trainees were instructed to compose, a country that ceased being interesting with the Macedonian conquest.

It was this sort of Hellenism, an abstract Hellenism rooted in the distant past, that captured the imagination of the imperial intelligentsia, not one that arose from Greek soil or from the continuing, contemporary culture of the old mainland. Likewise, the Greek language that was learned, written, and paraded as a marker of elite status was not contemporary Greek as spoken by everyday people but a punctilious recreation of classical literary diction, chiefly the Attic dialect of classical rhetoricians like Demosthenes, who had flourished upwards of five hundred years earlier.[20] Greece, as constructed in the collective imagination of the Hellenizing Roman Empire, was a place where such a language was still spoken, where Pan still roamed the hills of Arcady and where the fall of Troy and the victory at Salamis were still fresh and exciting news. This is the image of Greece that educated citizens of the empire brought with them as they landed in Patrai to begin their grand tour of the famous classical sites, or as they arrived in Athens to study philosophy. It is a conception of Greece against which the image Pausanias constructs of it must be measured and defined. It is plausible to suggest that one of the things Pausanias was trying to accomplish was to produce a corrective to such overly idealized notions of Hellenism by portraying accurately, and with eyewitness authority, the contemporary (and often parlous) state of the physical symbols of Hellenic tradition. Yet the historical perspective Pausanias himself displays is sometimes strikingly abstract. For instance, at one point in the first book he prefaces a discussion of the antiquity of cults of Demeter with the following observation: "Those of the Greeks who compete most frequently with the Athenians over the issue of antiquity and over the gifts they say they have received from the gods are the Argives; just as among the barbarians the Egyptians

---

[19] Bowie 1970; Anderson 1993: 101–132; Arafat 1996: 43–79; Swain 1996: 65–100. Schmitz 1997:18–26 objects to the characterization of Greek discourse in the Second Sophistic as *weltabgewandt* (detached from the real world), and in the sense that the sophists and their contemporaries, by propagating a certain construction of the Greek past, were active and engaged participants in a contemporary social *habitus*, his objections are completely valid. Nevertheless, under the construction of Greek history that was deemed to have social value at the time, very little of importance had happened in Greece since the classical period, and in that sense the construction, not the individual who partook of it, was detached from the real, or at least the contemporary world.

[20] On this "Atticism," see Chapter 6 below.

compete with the Phrygians."[21] It is by no means unlikely that in the game of jockeying for image within the province of Achaia, the contemporary Argives and Athenians did indeed vie with one another to be known as the possessors of the earliest and most holy. The same may be true in some sense for contemporary "Egyptians" and "Phrygians" (whatever meaning these "barbarian" ethnic terms had in the context of the empire); but what Pausanias is obviously referring to here is the story told nearly six centuries earlier by Herodotos about the Egyptian pharaoh Psammetichos, and how, in an attempt to bolster Egyptian claims of primacy, Psammetichos had two newborn babies isolated from contact with other people. To the chagrin of the pharaoh, who expected the babes to utter his own language spontaneously, the first word out of their mouths was the Phrygian word for bread (Hdt. 2.2.1–5). This episode, as transparently fictitious as it may seem to us, created in the collective educated consciousness of imperial culture a perpetual state of rivalry between the "Egyptians" and the "Phrygians," regardless of whether the actual contemporary inhabitants of Egypt or the inhabitants of what used to be Phrygia had any knowledge of or interest in the issue.

There are a number of interesting parallels between Hellenism in this period and Hellenism of the modern age. The creation of the modern Greek nation-state was fostered by educated Westerners, who revered an image of Greece rooted in the classical past but who frequently displayed what was at best indifference for the present-day inhabitants of the country. The modern Greek people, like their ancient Greek counterparts in Pausanias' day, have had the burden of dealing with powerful neighbors and benefactors who have often seemed more concerned about the welfare of the Greek antiquities than about the people of Greece themselves. Like their modern descendants, the Greeks of Pausanias' era probably felt tremendous pressure to make their land and their culture what non-Greek philhellenes wanted them to be, and to accept the attention and support of their admirers while somehow preventing their country from becoming what the poet Seferis called "a boundless hotel."[22]

Some parts of second-century Greece were indeed in the process of becoming boundless hotels and on-site museums, or at least of altering their identity significantly to fit Greece's role as the geographical cynosure of the educated empire's Hellenized imaginary. The Agora at Athens, which in classical times was an open plaza at the heart of the city and a central

---

[21] Ἑλλήνων οἱ μάλιστα ἀμφισβητοῦντες Ἀθηναίοις ἐς ἀρχαιότητα καὶ δῶρα, ἅ παρὰ θεῶν φασιν ἔχειν, εἰσὶν Ἀργεῖοι, καθάπερ βαρβάρων Φρυξὶν Αἰγύπτιοι.

[22] ἕνα ἀπέραντο ξενοδοχεῖο, G. Seferis, *Thrush* 1.21. Cf. Leontis 1995.

gathering-spot for government, commerce, and community life in general, was in Pausanias' day overgrown with an enormous lecture hall, a temple transported from the countryside, numerous honorary statues, and dedications by wealthy individuals, Greek and non-Greek, Athenian and non-Athenian.[23] The focal space of classical Athenian democracy had become a showground where the philhellenic elite of the empire could display their wealth, power, and cultural pretensions. Elsewhere in the shrines and cities of Greece, the venerable decay of the older buildings and monuments was offset and sometimes overshadowed by prominent new monuments, like the tomb of Philopappus, and dedications memorializing the largess of powerful outsiders.[24]

On a broader scale, the political divisions which had both kindled and suffocated the dynamism of classical Greece were subsumed under the system of provinces which the Romans had established. The part of mainland Greece described by Pausanias lay within the province of Achaia, and was administered by proconsuls dispatched by Rome. Within Achaia, and within the other provinces that encompassed Greek communities, the old city-states by and large maintained their borders and their individual governments, and some were granted special privileges, such as freedom from taxation, that other cities of the province were not. But external affairs were generally funneled through the imperial administrative superstructure. Quarrels between Greek cities, which were once occasions for bloodshed, were now conducted mostly by rhetoric and by petition to the imperial authorities. These verbal battles were, in addition, frequently over issues of a nature that exemplified the extent to which Greece's former ideals of autonomy and self-sufficiency had been altered, issues such as which city would be granted the right to build a temple for the cult of the emperors, or would be the site of the proconsul's provincial court.

As we have already mentioned, many Greeks, particularly the elite, were active and willing participants in such transformations. Rome was a gentle mistress, who demanded of the Greeks no wholesale changes in religion or language, and who allowed a great deal of self-determination in local affairs. Rome provided peace, stability, and physical improvements, and for all these benefits many Greeks seem to have felt the loss of absolute

---

[23] Cf. Thompson and Wycherley 1972: 111–116, 160–167, 204–207; Camp 1986: 181–214.

[24] Pausanias himself mentions several buildings and monuments of his own period dedicated either by non-Greeks or by citizens of Greek cities outside of their home cities. In addition to the numerous building efforts undertaken by Hadrian (see note 17 above), there are the activities of Herodes Atticus at Isthmia (2.1.7), Olympia (6.21.2), and Delphi (10.32.1); the baths built at Corinth by the Spartan Eurykles (2.3.5). Among Greeks, the career of Herodes probably represents the best-documented case of this sort of trans-political euergetism; cf. Philostratos, *VS* 551.

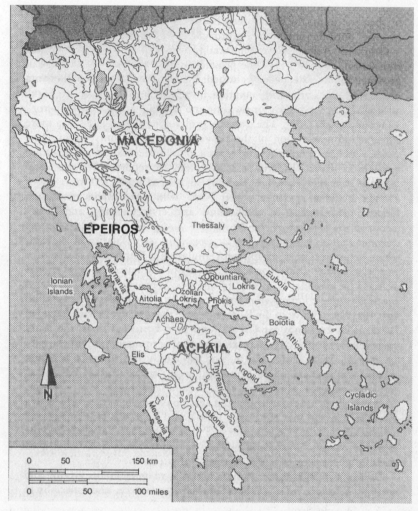

Figure 2.2. The Roman provinces in mainland Greece in Pausanias' time.

autonomy and the occasional depredations of corrupt provincial administrators a price worth paying. There was a lot to be gained by individuals and communities from playing along with the imperial political structure. By pleasing Rome, one could rise in the ranks of the political and social hierarchy. One could accrue power, wealth, and empire-wide prestige, and, less selfishly, steer lucrative imperial beneficence back to one's home city. Literature and inscriptions of the period are full of examples of Greeks doing just this, and some of the names of people who did so have already been mentioned. Conversely, there is no evidence whatsoever of any serious organized resistance to Roman rule among the Greek communities in Pausanias' day. Moreover, while Greeks may have regretted their own loss of independence, the Greek sense of tragedy, engrained in them for centuries (or at least revived in this period, along with the rest of classical style and sensibility), prevented them from overlooking the role played by the Greeks themselves in allowing Rome's domination to overtake them. By the time of Pausanias, there is little clue that anyone in the literate classes thinks that Roman rule was anything but an inevitable fact of life.

HELLENISM VERSUS ROME

Despite this lack of overt opposition, it would hardly be surprising to find a certain amount of remorse among Greeks of this period, and nostalgia for the days when the Greeks, not the Romans, were the most powerful people along the Mediterranean seaboard. After all, the classical past of Greece celebrated in the Hellenized culture of the empire was a Greece of stubborn autonomy, and the contrast between the spirit of Demosthenes and that of the present-day leaders of the Greek world was an obvious one. Consciousness of this contrast is expressed a number of times in writings of the period, including Pausanias' comment that after the death in 182 BCE of Philopoimen, one of the last major Greek leaders to resist the intrusion of Roman influence, "Greece ceased producing worthy men" (8.52.1).[25]

In his recent study of the relationship of Greek authors to the imperial power structures in the period of the Second Sophistic, Simon Swain has argued that there is a persistent pattern of subtle resistance in Greek writings of this period, a jaundiced attitude of recalcitrance and alienation that coexists alongside praise of Rome and alongside conciliatory tendencies in the treatment of Romans and Greeks. Plutarch, for instance, in his most famous work, the *Parallel Lives*, pairs prominent figures from Greek history with comparable Romans. Far from presenting a chauvinistic argument for Greek superiority through these comparisons, Plutarch does his best to portray the vices and virtues of his Greek and Roman subjects as being commensurate. In its integration of Greeks and Romans under the same moral framework, the *Parallel Lives* stands as one of the most effective literary embodiments of the contemporary cosmopolitan ideal. In other works, however, Plutarch betrays an attitude that is less conciliatory toward

---

[25] καὶ ἤδη τὸ μετὰ τοῦτο ἐς ἀνδρῶν ἀγαθῶν φορὰν ἔληξεν ἡ Ἑλλάς.

the Romans. For instance, in the essay known as *Political Advice*, he offers frank and starkly realistic counsel about how a politically active Greek can survive in what is often a corrupt and hostile Roman system.[26] Swain sees this dichotomy in Plutarch's attitude as being symptomatic and typical of the time. Greek writers seem to have one mode of expressing their feelings toward Rome when addressing the Romans themselves (or the empire's educated elite that included Romans) and another when their addressees were fellow-Greeks. Even Pausanias' contemporary, Aelius Aristeides, whose oration *On Rome* is probably the most effusive surviving laudation of the benefits of Roman rule written by one of Rome's subjects, speaks very differently about the empire in some of his orations addressed to Greek audiences.[27]

Swain's observations draw attention to the complexity of Greek attitudes in this period, but it is safe to say that the situation is even more intricate and conflicted than Swain's analyses might lead one to suspect. Recent studies of cultural expressions in the context of colonialism and neocolonialism have taught us that when it comes to the interactions between dominant and subject peoples, currents run deep and the eddies within the currents are particularly difficult to trace. Even the most impassioned expression of a spirit of independence has a hard time avoiding the hegemony of discourse exercised by the dominant culture, and even the most authoritarian and oppressive imperial powers are affected by the sometimes subtle influence of the people they control. To take the example of the Greek writers just mentioned, one must keep in mind that we are already dealing with the unusual circumstance in which the culture that is dominant politically, Rome, willingly accepts the influence and cultural preeminence of the "foreign" culture of Hellenism. In that context, the role that the Greeks end up playing can be quite paradoxical. This becomes evident when one considers that while many sophistical orations, such as those of Dion of Prusa and Aristeides, may have initially been delivered to all-Greek audiences, there is no reason to suppose that they were, or could have been, confined to a Greek audience when they were *published*. Neither Dion nor Aristeides, who surely had a hand in deciding which of their orations would be published and in what form they would be disseminated, would ever have imagined that copies of their less pro-Roman works could be kept from the hands of the non-Greek members of the widely traveled and intensively networked cosmopolitan elite. Similarly, Plutarch, who spent considerable

---

[26] Swain 1996: 161–183.

[27] Swain 1996: 284–297. For a reading of *To Rome* that does not view it as abjectly pro-Roman propaganda, see Stertz 1994.

efforts and achieved considerable success in appealing to both Greek and non-Greek readers, could scarcely have thought that his non-Greek audience would refrain from discovering what he had written in his *Political Advice*. Rather than imagine such unlikely scenarios, it is better to suppose that the anti-Roman (or less pro-Roman) sentiments that Swain identifies in all the authors of this period were not separate from the cross-cultural discourse between Greek and non-Greek but were instead an integral part of it. "Greeks addressing Greeks" was perhaps a mode of literary expression from which Greek and non-Greek alike could derive satisfaction.

More specifically, when Swain says that Aristeides' *To Rome* ". . . tells us a good deal about what the imperials wished to hear about themselves" in contrast to what Aristeides himself might have felt,[28] we can agree. The question, however, is whether the same could be said for other works that are less overtly encomiastic. The Romans may have derived some measure of self-validation from seeing the Greeks express an independent spirit in their literature. Having tamed a lion, after all, is a more satisfying accomplishment than having tamed a lapcat. The *parrhesia* (freedom of speech) allowed to the Greeks is also likely to have enhanced the Romans' own self-image as moderate and merciful rulers.[29] Dion of Prusa is probably relying on that attitude when he opines, in a speech delivered at Rhodes but later published (to a wider audience that doubtlessly included Romans), "do not imagine that the Romans would be so obtuse and ignorant as to choose that nothing that they rule be free and noble, but to prefer instead to hold sway over slaves" (31.112).[30] Moreover, elite Romans, with their Hellenized upbringing, were conditioned to respond to the stereotype of the "tragic warner." The tragic warner, a character type one finds frequently in Greek literature, especially in Athenian drama and in Herodotos, is a person who acts as spokesman for the gods and for traditional Greek morality on the subject of the variability of fortune and of the necessity for caution and moderation. Examples include the old servant who, at the beginning of Euripides' *Hippolytos*, warns his brash young master not to ignore any of the gods, or like kings Croesus and Demaratos in Herodotos' histories who, after falling from their own exalted positions, remain on the scene to advise the Persian kings and to remind them how precarious their perch on top of fortune's wheel can be. Often, figures who serve as tragic warners to rulers

---

[28] Ibid. 275.

[29] Cf. Ahl 1989; Habinek 1990. In the fourth century CE, Julian (*Caesares* 326a–b) found it plausible to portray Augustus as taking pride in the *parrhesia* he allowed to Greek philosophers in his retinue.

[30] μὴ γὰρ οἴεσθε Ῥωμαίους οὕτως εἶναι σκαιοὺς καὶ ἀμαθεῖς ὥστε μηδὲν αἱρεῖσθαι τῶν ὑφ᾽ αὑτοῖς ἐλευθέριον εἶναι μηδὲ καλόν <κἀγαθόν>, ἀλλὰ βούλεσθαι μᾶλλον ἀνδραπόδων κρατεῖν.

are fallen rulers themselves, like Croesus and Demaratos, so the parallel between them and the Greeks in relation to the Romans would have been particularly apposite.

Many Greek authors of the Roman period, insofar as they addressed issues of Greek–Roman relations, can be thought of as playing just such a role. Far from being offended by their criticisms, the Romans could congratulate themselves on the fact that they, in contrast to Xerxes and Hippolytos, were prudent enough to listen to the lessons they were being offered.[31] The Romans were happy to have the Greeks be stern schoolmasters, but in both Greek and Roman culture the position of schoolmaster was a socially inferior one. This point is exemplified by some of the earliest preserved orations of the period of the Second Sophistic, those of Dion of Prusa (Dio Chrysostom). In the first of Dion's series of four orations *On Kingship*, probably delivered in the presence of Trajan early in his reign,[32] the orator portrays himself as a vagabond philosopher who spent years in lonely exile, wandering around in beggar's garb and becoming personally acquainted with the vicissitudes of human fortune (Dion 1.50). While this self-presentation may have a grounding in fact – Dion actually did spend several years in exile during the reign of Domitian – it is also a convenient persona through which to offer the new emperor moral instruction. The attitude of the philosopher to the monarch is that of tutor or pedagogue to a youthful charge.[33] He can describe the emperor to his face as "lacking an abundance of confidence and an abundance of refinement" (1.5) and refer to the favor of the gods not as something that is already manifest but as something that the emperor must strive to earn (1.45). But this freedom to be frank should never be confused with social equality, or with an empowerment of the Greeks that posed the slightest threat to the dominant position of Rome. By lecturing and criticizing the emperor, Dion is playing the role that the emperor has allowed him to play, and is fulfilling a function within, rather than opposed to, the imperial power structure.[34] Tolerating, and even fostering, a visibly free-thinking Greek intelligentsia could even play a role in the way the emperor and other Romans of authority

---

[31] It should be pointed out here that "listen to" is not synonymous to "follow"; I am making no claim about the extent to which Roman behavior was influenced by the lectures of philosophical Greeks, merely that the Greek philosophers and sophists had a role to play in a social dialogue with the Romans that had at least as much impact as the actual philosophical and ethical arguments they were making. See Rawson 1989.

[32] Jones 1978b: 115–119.

[33] See Moles 1990, and again cf. Julian's description (*Caesares* 326b) of how Augustus looked upon the philosopher Athenodoros as a sort of pedagogue, and therefore tolerated his outspokenness.

[34] See Whitmarsh 1998 on Dion; and Rawson 1989, Fein 1994, and Whitmarsh 1999 more generally.

positioned themselves in their own society, a process that could be starkly independent from anything the Greeks actually said for good or ill about the Romans. Illustrative are the words Trajan, eager to rehabilitate the image of the principate by distinguishing himself from the philosopher-banishing Domitian, is reported to have said to Dion, as he rode through the streets of Rome on his gilt triumphal chariot with Dion at his side: "I do not know what you are saying but I love you as I love myself."[35] The substance of Dion's lectures was insignificant in comparison to the mere fact that he was being allowed to lecture and be seen at the emperor's side.

None of this is to diminish the capacity of the Greeks to think, and express, genuinely uncharitable thoughts toward the Romans and their rule, or even to engage in a form of double-sided diction that would deliver one message to a Roman audience and a different, more subversive one appreciable to fellow-Greeks. But in the final analysis, even things that on the surface appear to be critical of Rome can, in the social context of the second century, actually support the ideology upon which the elite power in the empire rests. The very usefulness of the terms "pro-Roman" and "anti-Roman" is questionable in such a context. The least we can say is that no statement, from Pausanias or any other Greek author of the period, should be so characterized without careful historicization and contextualization.

A similar complexity prevails in the dialogue between Greek and Roman in other areas. Susan Alcock has recently argued that both Greek and Latin literature of the period present an exaggerated image of the decline of Greece.[36] In comparison to pre-Roman days, the territory of mainland Greece actually was in a state of decline by most measurable standards: in population, in economy, and in the physical state of some of its most sacred monuments and sites. Pausanias attests to this decline, as does the archaeological record.[37] The portrait one gets in the literature, however, is consistently that of a country in a more advanced state of decrepitude than was objectively the case. After serving as the proconsul of Achaia in 46 BCE, for instance, Servius Sulpicius Rufus wrote to Cicero describing his impressions on arrival in the province he was to govern (Cicero, *Ad Fam.* 4.5.4):

ex Asia rediens cum ab Aegina Megaram versus navigarem, coepi regiones circumcirca prospicere. post me erat Aegina, ante me Megara, dextra Piraeus, sinistra

[35] Philostratos *Lives of the Sophists* 488. See Whitmarsh 1998: 207–209.   [36] Alcock 1993: 24–32.
[37] For an examination of the economic state of Roman Greece that relies (rather too much) on Pausanias, see Kahrstedt 1954. See also Alcock 1993: 33–92, with references to recent archaeological surface surveys that attest to declines in population, or at least to a change in settlement patterns that led to the draining of population from large tracts of countryside and many smaller cities.

Corinthus, quae oppida quodam tempore florentissima fuerunt, nunc prostrata et
diruta ante oculos iacent. Coepi egomet mecum sic cogitare: "hem! nos homunculi
indignamur, si quis nostrum interiit aut occisus est, quorum vita brevior esse debet,
cum uno loco tot oppidum cadavera proiecta iacent?"

Returning from Asia, as I was sailing from Aegina toward Megara, I began to gaze
at the lands all around me. Behind me was Aegina, in front of me Megara, to my
right Piraeus, to my left Corinth. Towns that at one time were at the height of
prosperity; towns that now lie flattened and ruined before one's eyes. I began to
think to myself as follows: "Ha! We tiny humans are upset if one of us, who are
destined for a shorter life, has died or been killed, while in this one place so many
towns lie discarded like corpses?"

Of the places mentioned by Servius, Corinth had been destroyed in
146 BCE and in 45, when Servius was writing, had yet to be refounded as a
Roman colony. Thus, the description of it as "flattened and ruined," and
the likening of it to an unburied corpse, could well be literally accurate.
None of the other places mentioned by Cicero's friend, however, were
actually in ruins at that time, though without doubt all of them had seen
better days. While there is no need to browbeat Servius for what amounts
to a modest rhetorical exaggeration, it is important to recognize it as an
exaggeration and to recognize the ideology that makes it effective. The
physical and political mortality of cities had, before Servius got a hold of it,
a long history in classical thought as an *a fortiori* argument for the fragility
of human happiness (cf. Hdt. 1.5.3–4).

The contrast between Greece's glorious past and its abject present was
a powerful motif in the convoluted negotiation of status that went on
between Greeks and non-Greeks in the imperial elite. For the Romans,
contemplation of the fate of Greece served as a *memento mori*; for the
Greeks, the decline in their national fortunes was a badge of insight-bringing
experience – as in the case of Croesus or Sophocles' Oedipus, being the
victim of tragedy tends to increase one's reputation for wisdom. Alcock
has further argued that so much ideological capital was invested in this
concept of Greece's fate that it might have had a concrete effect on how
Greece developed in the first few centuries of Roman rule.[38] Any impulse
that a wealthy Roman or Greek might have had to invest money or effort
in the rehabilitation of Greece from its downtrodden state might have
been impeded by the expectation that Greece *should* be downtrodden. A
prosperous Greece would clash with the ideology of decline and fall that
was promulgated by Hellenism itself.

[38] Alcock 1997: 103–115.

To turn to Pausanias specifically, the question of his attitude toward Roman rule has long been a subject of debate,[39] a debate perpetuated by the fact that Pausanias evidently makes statements that can be interpreted as both "pro-Roman" and "anti-Roman." Too often, however, the proponents on one side or the other have taken these statements out of context and argued without due regard for the complexity of the very issue of what it meant to be "pro-Roman" or "anti-Roman" at this time. Pausanias has unabashedly positive things to say about the emperors of his own time, particularly Hadrian, and little overt criticism of any emperor, contemporary or prior.[40] At the same time, he does have harsh words for those Romans who were responsible for the destruction and despoliation of various sites in Greece, and at one point, in a passage where the manuscript reading is in dispute, seems to refer to Roman rule as a "misfortune" (συμφορά) for the Greeks (8.27.1).[41] Rome and Roman rule is an everyday reality for Pausanias, one that intersects the axes of his topographical and historical efforts at every level, and Pausanias has a multiplicity of responses to it that defy simple characterizations. We will see Pausanias occupying not a single position on Rome but numerous positions. And for each of these positions, a consideration of where Pausanias stands in relation to his contemporaries will be more meaningful than a description of his stance in isolation.

PAUSANIAS THE CONFORMIST

In its general outlines, Pausanias' ambiguous attitude toward Rome is quite harmonious with the outlook of other authors of the day. As mentioned before, the Greeks were acutely conscious of the complicity of their own ancestors in their downfall; by the time of Pausanias, tragic fractiousness had come to be seen as a national character trait. An author in whom this

[39] Gurlitt 1890: 87; Regenbogen 1956: 1069–1070; Palm 1959: 63–74; Forte 1972: 419–427; Habicht 1998: 117–140; Arafat 1996: 106–215; Swain 1996; 330–356; Jacquemin 1996; Steinhart 2002a and 2002b.

[40] Such criticism as Pausanias does direct in the emperors' direction tends to be delivered obliquely, as for instance in his stern disapproval of the attempt of a portentiously unnamed emperor (Nero) to dig a canal through the Isthmus of Corinth (2.1.5), who proved by his failure "how difficult it is for a human to do violence to things that the gods have arranged" (2.1.6).

[41] In this passage, Pausanias, according to the manuscript tradition, refers to population movements within Greece that occurred κατὰ συμφορὰν ἀρχῆς τῆς Ῥωμαίων (as a result of the misfortune of Roman rule). An early editor, Etienne Clavier, suggested an emendation: κατὰ συμφορὰν ἐπὶ ἀρχῆς τῆς Ῥωμαίων (as a result of a misfortune *in the period* of Roman rule). Scholars who have favored the emendation include: Palm 1959: 72–74; Habicht 1998: 119–120; Arafat 1996: 202 and Rocha–Pereira, who adopts the emendation in the latest Teubner edition. Others, including Swain 1996: 353–354, and Steinhart 2002, prefer to keep the manuscript reading (though these two scholars differ on the implications of the reading). I hope to publish an article examining this issue in the near future.

view had been inculcated could easily refer to the Roman conquest as a "mis-fortune" and refer to Philopoimen as the last worthy Greek, but could also cite without objection the emperor Vespasian's judgment that the Greeks "had forgotten how to be free" (7.17.4),[42] and show no enduring bitterness in references to the current Roman rulers, or to the contemporary Roman system of imperial control. Likewise, as was mentioned in the previous chapter, Pausanias' predominant interest in the pre-Roman past of Greece is consonant with the prevalent preoccupations of the day. While one might be tempted to read into his silence about Roman and contemporary affairs a certain disdain or disapproval, the fact is that when it came to the sorts of subjects that Pausanias' text regularly covers – artworks, monuments, and history – his predilections are very similar to other Greek authors of the day, and, more importantly, similar to the tastes of the Romans themselves when it came to Greek matters.[43] In this respect, Pausanias is the opposite of subversive.

Aside from the Roman question, there are other areas in which Pausanias can be seen as reflecting trends of the day. His emphasis on religious monu-ments and artworks and the religious bent of the personality he projects are, in general, nothing unusual at this point in history. Greco-Roman polythe-ism was still going strong as a civic religion, one through which worshipers not only satisfied their individual spiritual needs but also affirmed their membership in a community of worshipers. Since religious customs were among the most traditional parts of society and were one thing that the contemporary Greeks shared in nearly unadulterated form with their clas-sical ancestors, religion could stand as one of the mainstays of Hellenism. Alongside this emphasis on the traditional there was, paradoxically, a con-tinuation of a long trend of supplementing the ancient Pantheon with mystical and soteriological cults of a non-Greek and non-Roman origin: Isis from Egypt, Mithras from Persia, and Christ from Judea, for example. The coincidence of these factors, among others, resulted in the appear-ance in this period of some of the most religiously oriented texts writ-ten in Greek and Latin by non-Christian authors, works such as Aelius Aristeides' *Sacred Tales* (the story of his long-time devotion to the healing god Asklepios) and Philostratos' biography of the first-century CE mystic Apollonios of Tyana. Pausanias' religiousness, in itself, is quite at home in this era.[44]

---

[42] ἀπομεμαθηκέναι . . . τὴν ἐλευθερίαν τὸ Ἑλληνικόν. Nero had granted "freedom" to Greece, but when internecine strife broke out during Vespasian's reign, the emperor revoked the privilege.

[43] This is a point well made by Arafat 1996: *passim*, but esp. 43–79.

[44] Cf. Behr 1968; Anderson 1994.

Another feature that Pausanias shares with other writers of the period is an interest in description. No other contemporary writer engages in the description of physical objects to the extent that Pausanias does, but the presence of a descriptive impulse is discernible in many other works of the period.[45] In part, this is an outgrowth of the literary technique of *ecphrasis* (description) that goes all the way back to the beginnings of Greek literature in passages like the description of Achilles' shield in Homer's *Iliad* (18.478–608). It also owes something to the emphasis in contemporary rhetorical training on the *sapheneia* (clarity) and *enargeia* (vividness) that description was thought to lend to oratorical expression. *Ecphrasis* was one of the types of *progymnasma* (preliminary exercise) that the teacher of rhetoric would have his students compose, and was designed to give the student practice in producing these very effects.[46] More specifically, though, the connection of the description of a physical object with a historical or mythical *logos* was yet another thing that appealed to the contemporary fascination with the past: a physical monument can lend to a narrative a more tangible foothold in the privileged past than it would otherwise have. In the first three centuries CE, we see a number of works in which visible monuments are not only described and associated with *logoi*, but are used, as in Pausanias, as a frame that gives order and unity to a complex or disjointed narrative. Examples include the *Imagines* by Philostratos,[47] which purports to be a series of lectures inspired by paintings that the narrator and his ten-year-old interlocutor encounter on a tour of a portrait gallery. Another example is the *Tabula* of Cebes, which, although fictionally ascribed to the Cebes who appears as an acquaintance of Socrates in Plato's writings, was probably a product of the first or second century CE.[48] The philosophical narrative that occupies the bulk of this work is cast as the interpretation of an allegorical painting which the narrator, a stranger to the place in which the painting resides, learns from a wise old native. Similarly, one of the earliest of the surviving Greek novels, Longus' *Daphnis and Chloe*,

---

[45] On this point in general, see Bartsch 1989 (esp. pp. 3–39), who, however, does not mention Pausanias in this regard. On Pausanias specifically, see Elsner 1994, 1995: 125–155.

[46] Cf. Dion. Hal. *Lys.* 7; Theon, *Progymnasmata* 118–119; [Demetrius], *Peri Hermeneias* 209–220; Nicolaus *Progymnasmata* 67–70; [Hermogenes] *Progymnasmata* 10; [Cornutus] 96 and 111. It should be noted that the specific term *ecphrasis* is not used solely, or even primarily, by the Greek sources to refer to the description of physical objects such as artworks and monuments. See also: Lausberg 1973: 339–401; Zanker 1981: 297–311; Leach 1988: 1–24; Bartsch 1989: 7–10; Fowler 1991; Becker 1992: 8–14; Walker 1993: 353–375; Kennedy 1999: 26–28.

[47] Whether this Philostratos is the same as the author of *Lives of the Sophists* is not completely clear. Cf. Bryson 1994; Elsner 1995: 28–39. A second book of *Imagines* by a younger Philostratos could also be adduced here, as would the *Ecphrases* of Kallistratos of the late third or early fourth century.

[48] Cf. Elsner 1995: 39–48.

is framed as the interpretation of a painting found in a cave-shrine of the Nymphs on Lesbos. Once again, the narrator presents the *logos* not as his own reading of the painting, but as what he was told by a local ἐξηγητής (interpreter):[49]

Ἐν Λέσβῳ θηρῶν ἐν ἄλσει Νυμφῶν θέαμα εἶδον κάλλιστον ὧν εἶδον· εἰκόνα γραπτήν, ἱστορίαν ἔρωτος. Καλὸν μὲν καὶ τὸ ἄλσος, πολύδενδρον, ἀνθηρόν, κατάρρυτον· μία πηγὴ πάντα ἔτρεφε. καὶ τὰ ἄνθη καὶ τὰ δένδρα· ἀλλ' ἡ γραφὴ τερπνοτέρα καὶ τέχνην ἔχουσα περιττὴν καὶ τύχην ἐρωτικήν· ὥστε πολλοὶ καὶ τῶν ξένων κατὰ φήμην ᾖεσαν, τῶν μὲν Νυμφῶν ἱκέται, τῆς δὲ εἰκόνος θεαταί . . . Πολλὰ ἄλλα καὶ πάντα ἐρωτικὰ ἰδόντα με καὶ θαυμάσαντα πόθος ἔσχεν ἀντιγράψαι τῇ γραφῇ· καὶ ἀναζητησάμενος ἐξηγητὴν τῆς εἰκόνος τέτταρας βίβλους ἐξεπονησάμην, ἀνάθημα μὲν Ἔρωτι καὶ Νύμφαις καὶ Πανί, κτῆμα δὲ τερπνὸν πᾶσιν ἀνθρώποις.

While hunting on Lesbos in the grove of the Nymphs I saw the most beautiful sight I had ever seen, a painted image, a story of love. The grove was a fine one, rich in trees, full of flowers, well watered; one spring fed everything, both the flowers and the trees. But the painting was more pleasurable; it exhibited outstanding craftsmanship and a romantic adventure, so that on account of its reputation many people, even foreigners, came both to worship the Nymphs and to see the painting . . . As I was looking with wonder at these and other things, all of them romantic, a desire overcame me to copy the painting in writing, so I found an interpreter of the painting and wrote four books as an offering to Eros and to the Nymphs and to Pan, and as a pleasing possession for all mankind.

The grand-touring elite of the empire probably had ample experience in encountering obscure and cryptic monuments and having the pertinence of them to their history and cultural heritage decoded by local guides.[50] This alone may be sufficient to explain the appeal of such motifs, and may be an important part of the cultural environment that encouraged Pausanias to envision an audience for the sort of work he was writing.

The idea of anchoring and adding resonance to a *logos* by connecting it with a monument from the past is in itself nothing new in Greek literature; Herodotos likewise refers to physical monuments of figures whom he mentions, like the costly dedications of Gyges and Croesus at Delphi (Hdt. 1.14.1–3; 1.50–51), and thereby lends some substance and validity to the folklore-like tales he recounts about the figures. For Herodotos, though, the *theôrêma* is usually secondary, mentioned for purposes of corroboration and illustration after the *logos* is through, while in Pausanias and his

---

[49] *Daphnis and Chloe*, Prologue 1.1–3; cf. Jones 2001.
[50] The issue of Pausanias' relation to local tour guides and to authorities in local history will be examined further in Chapter 3. His alleged *generic* relation to these guides, as a written analog of what such guides might have said on site, has already been alluded to in Chapter 1 and will be addressed further in Chapter 4.

near-contemporaries, the *theorema* serves as the means of access to the *logos*, and hence becomes part of the background against which the *logos* is interpreted as it is read. In both Herodotos and the later writers, then, the reference to the physical contributes to *enargeia*, and *sapheneia* but beyond that the function toward which it serves tends to differ.

PAUSANIAS THE NON-CONFORMIST

In more ways than one, Pausanias seems to be an author who is characteristic of the period in which he lived. But there are also a number of ways in which he is unique, and even apparent similarities seem superficial on closer inspection. With regard to the fondness for description exhibited by him and his contemporaries, for instance, the sheer extent to which Pausanias engages in physical description sets him apart. One might add to this the fact that while Pausanias' contemporaries allow the *theorema* to introduce the *logos* and to give the *logos* substance and local associations, for most of them the *logos* clearly remains the primary focus. This is obviously true for *Daphnis and Chloe* and for the *Tabula* of Cebes, where the paintings that are used as an entrée to the narrative fade into the background as soon as they have discharged their introductory and tone-setting duty. For Pausanias, the sight and the story have a more nearly equal importance, and the interaction between them is more of a mutual exchange. The story explains the monument and its importance; the monument embodies the story and centers it incontrovertibly in a particular place.

In the area of religion, likewise, Pausanias' piety, though by no means out of place in the second century, has a contour of its own that is hard to parallel precisely. As befits the journeys he makes to the most tradition-laden parts of the Greek world, his devotion to the traditional gods and heroes of classical Greece is remarkably exclusive for the period. As mentioned before, he has little to say about cults of Isis or Serapis (though he occasionally makes brief mention of the existence of their shrines and statues), and nothing at all to say about Christ, and he also seems to be at best disinterested and at worst disdainful towards the most important and widespread imported cult in Greece in his time, the "imperial cult" of the deified emperors. His attitude toward this last development in the religious life of Greece is one thing that sets him solidly apart from many of his contemporaries, a good number of whom vied earnestly to serve as priests and benefactors of the emperors' cult.[51]

---

[51] On the imperial cult and the response to it in the Greek east, see: Bowersock 1973; Price 1984a and 1984b; the articles in Small, ed. 1996. On religion in general, and on the imperial cult in particular, see Chapter 8 below.

Lastly, in the area of literary form, Pausanias stands almost completely alone, not only in terms of the subject-matter and the methodology of his work but in the very language in which he casts it. This is a subject that will be addressed in detail in the chapters that follow, but it is apposite to make some introductory comments here. The most prominent writers of Pausanias' day aspired toward a literary language that resurrected the diction of the great authors and orators of classical Athens. They followed the lead of Demosthenes, Isocrates, Plato, and Xenophon in matters of style, and even went so far as to put back into use Attic vocabulary and orthography that had long since become obsolete. This "Atticism" was prevalent enough to become something of an industry: handbooks and lexica of Attic vocabulary and morphology were compiled, and to a remarkable extent the ability to write in a hypercorrect Attic manner became a mark of membership in the educated elite.[52] Despite the fact that he lived during the high point of the Atticizing movement – the most proficient and punctilious Atticizer was his contemporary, Aelius Aristeides – Pausanias shows no interest in Atticizing whatsoever. As we shall see, the language in which he couches his description is itself a literary creation, far different from the vernacular Greek of the time, but it displays an avoidance of Attic style and forms that can scarcely be anything other than deliberate for someone educated, as he surely was, on a steady diet of classical Attic masters. Since this was an era in which "style made the man" more than many, Pausanias' choices are more than arcane academic preferences; they reflect the way that he relates to the contemporary cosmopolitan elite.

In the same vein, there is the matter of Pausanias' self-presentation. Pausanias' reticence about himself, which goes hand-in-hand with certain other features of his work, such as the lack of any introductory prologue and the lack of specific addressees for the work, stands out in this era when Hellenized education and literary production were among the emblems by which the elite identified itself and recognized members of its own. Most authors of the period spend a good deal of effort in their works positioning themselves in relation to their audience, in relation to the social echelon they belong or aspire to, and to their rivals in the same field of literary endeavor. Pausanias does very little of that, except insofar as his failure to do so might be construed as some sort of positioning statement in its own right. The possible motives for his self-effacement, or more accurately, lack

---

[52] Anderson 1993: 86–100; Swain 1996: 43–64; Schmitz 1997: 67–96. For further references and discussion, see Chapter 6 below.

of self-promotion, will also be one of the main topics in later pages of this work.

In conclusion, certain features of the *Periegesis* make it a work that is hard to imagine as a product of any other age. Pausanias' antiquarian predilections, his eagerness to catalog the physical manifestations of the Greek past, his fascination with visual evocations of cultural ideas, and the religious and nostalgic tint of his entire work are perfectly at home in the time of Hadrian, Lucian, and Aristeides. At the same time, the *Periegesis* cannot simply be classified as a typical product of the time. In many respects, it is a completely unparalleled work that represents a very individual reaction to the social and historical circumstances that the author found himself in. I have mentioned here how that individual viewpoint is manifested in certain specific areas; it remains to be demonstrated how it is communicated by the very structure and texture of his topographical construction of the physical and cultural landscapes of Greece. This will be the subject of the next three chapters.

CHAPTER 3

Designing the Periegesis

A modern reader, particularly one who has been to Greece and has studied the antiquities of Greece, brings a lot of baggage along when he or she sets out to read Pausanias. We know the shape of Greece; we see it in our mind's eye spreading along the Aegean like a bony, outstretched hand. As Pausanias leads the reader from place to place, we imagine the rocky path and the blue sky and the rough scrub-covered hills. We know where the sites are (the main sites anyway) on a map; we can imagine Pausanias' routes between them traced in two-dimensional space. We think of myths, heroes, and historical events associated with each place. All of these images affect our cognition of the text, the way we interpret what Pausanias says and the way we fill in the gaps left by what he doesn't say. On the other side of the author–reader transaction, Pausanias' translation of his experience of the landscape into words on paper is similarly conditioned by the unique way that he sees things. The accounts of all writers who describe journeys or places reflect the authors' cognitive mapping;[1] that is, they reflect the intersection of the physical landscape and the cognitive landscape of personal and cultural preconditioning that resides in the observer's mind. Part of understanding the methods of a writer like Pausanias is learning to understand his internal landscape; to do so, we must, as best we can, look beyond our own preconditioned expectations. Too often the principles by which Pausanias organizes the whole of his topography are assumed to be self-evident ones that any writer of a travel guide or any person who set about describing Greece could have chosen, but in fact they are the result of choices that Pausanias made consciously or unconsciously. An attempt to understand the nature of the *Periegesis* must therefore begin with some very basic questions: why Pausanias chooses to cover the area that he does; how

---

[1] For the phrase "cognitive mapping," see Tolman 1948. On studying the formation and communication of spatial perceptions as discursive processes, see, e.g.: Culler 1981; Cosgrove 1984; Pratt 1992; Rose 1993; Golledge and Stimson 1997. For the application of similar perspectives to classical literature, see: Hartog 2001; Nicolet 1991; Romm 1992; Clarke 1999.

54

he divides that area into smaller units for the purposes of his description; the various methods he employs in addressing the task of description in different parts of his work, and the means by which he attempts (if indeed he does) to combine these separate parts into a coherent whole.

THE SCOPE OF THE *PERIEGESIS*

Our present text of Pausanias comprises a systematic description of the entire Peloponnesos and a continuous portion of central Greece reaching as far west as Naupaktos. The area described is predominantly continental, the only islands included being small ones close to shore. I shall argue in this chapter that Pausanias' choice of territories to describe is determined by the coincidence of a number of factors. The most obvious of these factors are the degree to which any given region was involved in the history and mythology of pre-Roman Greece, and the extent to which physical reminders of ancient times were remaining in Pausanias' day. Less obvious, but just as important, are the extent of Pausanias' firsthand familiarity with the topography, monuments, and traditions of the various regions and the ease with which a description of any particular region can be incorporated into the topographical design of his composition.[2] It will be necessary to deal with these matters at some length; an attempt to understand the topographical limits that Pausanias set for himself involves consideration of some fundamental tendencies which affect his operating procedures at every level.

Many scholars have considered the problem of why Pausanias includes the territories he does in his description and why he excludes other territories, but until fairly recently their efforts were sidetracked by the misinterpretation of a single sentence in the first book which, in the absence of any specific programmatic statement, was taken as an indication of the work's intended scope. In 1.26.4, Pausanias breaks off his discussion of a certain monument on the Athenian acropolis, saying that the vastness of his subject will not allow him to dilate further: δεῖ δέ με ἀφικέσθαι τοῦ λόγου πρόσω, πάντα ὁμοίως ἐπεξιόντα τὰ Ἑλληνικά (it is necessary for me to get on with my account, as I am dealing with all Greek matters in like fashion). Even though they were long recognized as a direct echo of Herodotos (1.5), the words "dealing with all Greek matters in like fashion" were interpreted by many as an earnest promise to describe "all of Greece," a promise which, under standard geographical conceptions of Greece, does

---

[2] For a similar but slightly different set of criteria, see Bultrighini 1990b.

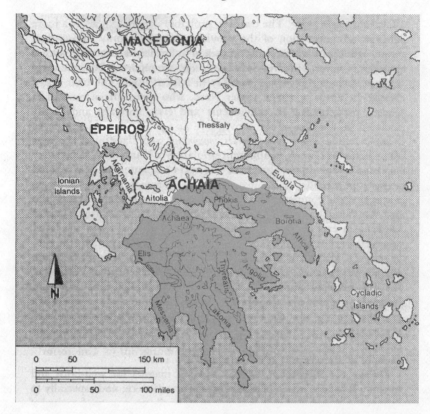

Figure 3.1. Mainland Greece; the shaded area represents the territory covered
in Pausanias' *Periegesis*.

not seem to be fulfilled; one should at least expect the inclusion of such
areas as Thessaly, Euboia, and Doris, or even Aitolia, Akarnania, Epeiros,
and the Greek islands of the Aegean and Ionian seas.[3] Attempts to explain
the absence of these territories were sometimes quite elaborate. Some took
refuge in the hypotheses that either Pausanias left his work unfinished or
that certain parts of it had been lost. Others suggested that Pausanias confined himself to a more limited concept of Ἑλλάς based on the boundaries
of such entities as the Roman province of Achaia or the classical Delphic
Amphictyony.[4]

[3] Gurlitt 1890: 2–4 and 68, n. 13; Robert 1909: 261; Trendelenburg 1911: 8; Meyer 1954: 19; Habicht
1998: 5–6; Bearzot 1988: 90–112. Cf. also Heberdey 1894: 2.
[4] For Achaia, cf. Meyer: 1954: 20; Habicht: 1998: 5, n. 27. For the Amphictyony, Bearzot 1988: 108–112.

In reality, none of these explanations is necessary since Pausanias never claims that he intends to describe "all of Greece." In the passage in question, he does not say that he must move on to describe πᾶσαν . . . τὴν Ἑλλάδα ("all of Greece") but πάντα . . . τὰ Ἑλληνικά (all Greek things). τὰ Ἑλληνικά is used in one other place by Pausanias (9.6.1), but in this case and in the several cases where forms of τὸ Ἑλληνικόν appear, the connotation is always social or ethnic, never geographical. For Pausanias, the term does not denote primarily a place, but a cultural community and tradition.[5] Moreover, on a more practical level, the term could not possibly function as a geographical delimiter for Pausanias' account. Since Pausanias is aware that τὸ Ἑλληνικόν and Ἕλληνες existed in places as far-flung as Libya, Sicily and Thrace,[6] a true effort to deal in equal measure (ὁμοίως) with πάντα τὰ Ἑλληνικά would have taken him far beyond the geographical aims that anyone has ascribed to him. For these reasons, a growing number of scholars nowadays seem to understand this passage in one of two ways: either as a somewhat casual rhetorical exaggeration (one that also provides Pausanias with an opportunity to give a nod to Herodotos) or as a cultural rather than a geographical promise.[7] To borrow the words of Elsner, Pausanias may be saying that he intends to treat "all that was interesting to the Greek-speaker about Greece at the height of the Roman Empire."[8] This reading would be more satisfying, though, if it weren't for the fact that

[5] The passage in 9.6.1 deals with the alleged Medizing of the Plataians in 480 BCE: δοκοῦσιν δὲ ἑλέσθαι τὰ βασιλέως Ξέρξου πρὸ τῶν Ἑλληνικῶν ("They seem to have chosen [literally] the things of King Xerxes in preference to those of the Greeks"). Here τὰ Ἑλληνικά no more means "Greece" than τὰ βασιλέως Ξέρξου means "Persia". Meyer translates the sentence in 1.26.4 correctly: ". . . ich all griechischen Dinge gleichermaßen behandeln will" (Meyer 1954: 80), yet elsewhere interprets it as a promise to describe "ganz Griechenland" (p. 19). Frazer, on the other hand, translates "I have to describe all of Greece" (Frazer 1898: 1.38; cf. 1.xxii), but he also recognizes that "all things Greek" is a more literal translation (1.xxv), and nowhere does he attribute any particular geographical significance to the passage.

[6] τὸ Ἑλληνικόν refers to: a) The Greek people as a whole, without any clear regard for their geographical situation (e.g. 7.3.1, 7.7.6, 8.52.2, 10.8.2, 10.11.6); b) a certain portion of the Greek people, in contrast to barbarians, in contexts of invasion or colonization. Use of the term in this sense occurs frequently in reference to the Greeks who resisted the Gallic invasion (e.g. 10.8.3, 10.22.13; cf. 7.6.7, where it becomes clear that in this case τὸ Ἑλληνικόν did not include the majority of the Peloponnesians), and in the narration of the colonization of Ionia, where it refers to the Greek colonizers as opposed to the indigenous inhabitants (e.g. 7.2.9, 7.3.6). Similarly, the Greeks in Cyrenaica are referred to as part of [τὸ Ἑλληνικὸν τὸ] ἐν Λιβύῃ (10.13.5). Parallel to these usages is that of γένος Ἑλληνικόν in reference to the Greek element in predominantly non-Greek areas or among populations of mixed ethnicity; cf. 5.27.12 (the Mendaians in Thrace), 7.3.7 (Pamphylians). As for Ἕλληνες, as one might expect, they occur all over the map; cf. 1.11.5 (Corcyra), 1.23.4 (Crete), 1.34.2 (Thracian Chersonese), 4.5.3 (Asia Minor), 4.23.9 and 5.25.6 (Sicily). Note also the πόλεις Ἑλληνίδες in Sicily (1.12.5), Italy (5.26.5), and Ionia (6.24.2).

[7] Regenbogen (1956: 1011) was one of the first to express any skepticism toward the idea that this "promise" should be taken completely at face value.

[8] Elsner 1992: 5.

there were certainly Greek things of interest to Greek-speakers at this time
outside of the territory that Pausanias covers. Pausanias mentions some of
these himself: Delos,[9] for instance, and the shrine of Zeus at Dodona in
Epeiros.

The issue of Pausanias' concept of Greece is worth pursuing, since the
title of the work, *Periegesis Hellados* (assuming for the moment that it
is Pausanias' title), does seem to promise something. What is it that the
"Description of Greece" is intended to be a description of? If we look into
Pausanias' usage of terms relating to *Hellas* (the Greek term for "Greece"),
a curious fact emerges: Pausanias seems to have no fixed idea at all as to
what constitutes Hellas. Actually, this fact is hardly surprising when one
considers the remarkable geographical fluidity of this term throughout the
history of Greek literature. Even among the geographers, whose business
it was to distinguish Hellas formally from the rest of the inhabited world,
there is a fair amount of disagreement. Pseudo-Skylax defines what he
calls Ἑλλὰς συνεχής ("continuous Greece", as opposed to "Greek cities"
[πόλεις Ἑλληνίδες] in non-Greek territories) as beginning in the northwest with Ambracia and ending in the northeast with the Peneios river
in Thessaly (33, 65). These boundaries may ultimately be derived from
the classical Athenian geographer Phileas, to whom they are attributed
by Dionysios son of Kalliphon (31 ff.).[10] Herakleides Kritikos (pseudo-
Dikaiarchos), who also seems to have followed Phileas, says that there
were those who, incorrectly in his opinion, excluded all of Thessaly from
Hellas (fr. 3 Müller). There was also disagreement early on about the north-
western border. Pseudo-Skymnos, citing Ephoros, sets it at the Acheloos
(470), thus including Aitolia but not Akarnania and Epeiros. Closer to
Pausanias' time, Strabo, who also cites Ephoros, names Akarnania as the
westernmost territory of Hellas (8.1.3), but instead of stopping at the
Peneios in the northeast he also includes Macedonia (8.1.1). Dionysios
the Periegete goes even further, defining the whole peninsula south of
Oricia and Thrace as Hellas (398 ff.), thereby encompassing both Epeiros
and Macedonia.[11] Ptolemy defines Hellas as coterminous with that part

---

[9] On which, see the brilliantly conceived article by Jacquemin (2000): "Pausanias à Delos . . ."
[10] This Dionysios' Ἀναγραφὴ τῆς Ἑλλάδος in trimeters is transmitted in manuscripts ascribed to
Dikaiarchos. He is occasionally referred to in earlier scholarship as pseudo-Dikaiarchos, and should
not be confused with the author of the more famous prose work once attributed to "pseudo-
Dikaiarchos", now generally ascribed to Herakleides Kritikos. The author of the Ἀναγραφή gives
us his name in an acrostic in the opening lines of his poem. He refers, like pseudo-Skylax, to Ἑλλὰς
συνεχής, confirming the impression that Phileas served as a source for pseudo-Skylax as well.
[11] See also the commentary of Eustathios *ad loc.*, which makes Dionysios' labored hexameters a bit
more clear.

of the Roman province of Achaia which was north of the Isthmus, thus
excluding Akarnania, Epeiros, Macedonia, Thessaly, and, surprisingly, the
Peloponnesos (3.15.1; cf. 3.15.14). It is likely that such discrepancies arose
not so much from the shifting of official borders from one era to the next as
from the fact that "Greece" never had borders that were more than hypothetical. In a land that was never politically unified in any meaningful sense,
whether a particular territory or people belonged to Hellas was largely a
matter of ethnic aspirations and prejudices. The ambiguity of this concept
could even be exploited for political advantage, as when Philip V responded
to Roman and Aitolian demands that he withdraw his armies from "all of
Hellas" by asking "how do you define Hellas?"[12]

It is hardly surprising, then, that authors who are less concerned with
presenting a systematic geography are far from consistent in their use of
the term Hellas. For instance, Pausanias' model Herodotos employs it in
a number of usages that vary from one context to the next. Lists of the
dedications of barbarian kings to religious sanctuaries "in Greece" (ἐν τῇ
Ἑλλάδι) can include places as diverse as Ephesos in Anatolia (1.92.1) and
Cyrene in northern Africa (2.182.1), and Greek envoys sent to seek aid from
Gelon of Syracuse can flatter the tyrant by saying that his Sicilian empire
gave him power over "no small portion of Hellas" (7.157.2). Other places
which Herodotos, at one time or another, considers to be in Hellas include
Thessaly (7.132.1; 7.172), Perrhaibia (7.132.1), Eretria (6.94.1, 6.106.2),
Dodona (2.56.1), Ionia as a whole (3.39.3), Cyzicus (4.76.5), Rhodes, Samos
and the other Aegean islands (1.27.2; 2.182.1; 6.49.1–2), Zankle (6.24.1) and
Magna Graecia (3.136–7). Yet in the narration of Xerxes' climactic campaign, Hellas shrinks to the point that it comprises only the area where the
barbarians will meet concerted Greek resistance. After marching through
the Greek territories of Asia Minor, through Thrace, Macedonia, and
Thessaly, Xerxes has still not reached "Greece"; Thermopylai and the infa-
mous footpath from Trachis have become the "entrance to Hellas" (7.175.2:
τὴν ἐσβολὴν . . . ἐς τὴν Ἑλλάδα; 7.176.2: ἡ . . . ἔσοδος ἐς τὴν Ἑλλάδα;
7.176.5, 177; 8.15.2). Here we see the flexible connotation of Ἑλλάς being
used to contribute to the drama of this crucial point in Herodotos' narrative. In addition to encompassing a large portion (but not the entirety) of
the original Greek homeland, the area south of Thermopylai housed the
final line of defense for the Hellenic nation as a whole. The Greek states
to the north and east of the pass had already fallen under Persian domination, while those to the west, in the views ascribed by Herodotos to the

[12] Polyb. 18.5.7. On the general problem of the emergence of the term *Hellas*, see Lévy 1991.

participants and onlookers, would succumb soon after the allied resistance failed (7.157.2–3; 7.168.1).

Pausanias' use of the term is quite comparable to that of Herodotos, and in some cases the similarities are far from being coincidental. In his narrations of the invasions of the Persians and the Gauls, Pausanias uses Herodotos' very words to portray Thermopylai as the "entrance to Hellas" (1.3.5: τὴν ἐς τὴν Ἑλλάδα . . . ἐσβολήν; 1.4.2: τῆς ἐσόδου τῆς ἐς τὴν Ἑλλάδα; cf. 3.4.8). One might be tempted to see these passages as indicating what Pausanias truly thinks Hellas to be, especially since the territory covered in the present text would correspond fairly closely to the area south of Thermopylai, were it not for the absence of eastern Lokris (including Thermopylai itself), Doris, and, perhaps, Aitolia.[13] Yet the fact that this "definition" is a direct echo of Herodotos, occurring in a narrative that parallels Herodotos' account of the Persian invasions, makes it questionable as an indication of Pausanias' own general outlook, and in any case it is not a definition to which Pausanias consistently adheres. Even in the narration of the Gallic invasion he refers once to the area south of the pass as "Greece within Thermopylai" (τὴν ἐντὸς τῶν Θερμοπυλῶν Ἑλλάδα), suggesting that there was something "outside Thermopylai" which he considered part of Hellas (10.20.9).

Elsewhere we see that for Pausanias, as for Herodotos, the inclusion of any particular region in Hellas depends to some extent on the context; for example, Hellas is more extensive in opposition to barbarian lands, and more restricted when it comes to a distinction between different parts of the Greek mainland. Pyrrhos is called the first Greek (Ἕλλην, 1.11.7) "to set out from Hellas across the Ionian sea to do battle with the Romans": ὁ πρῶτος ἐκ τῆς Ἑλλάδος τῆς πέραν Ἰονίου διαβὰς ἐπὶ Ῥωμαίους (1.12.1). This passage may or may not imply that there was some part of Hellas which was not πέραν Ἰονίου from the point of view of the Romans (perhaps Pausanias had in mind the Tarantines, who invited Pyrrhos to aid them in their war with their northern neighbors). More certainly, this passage places Pyrrhos' Epeirote kingdom in Hellas; but in other cases, where there is no contrast with a non-Greek power like the Romans, Epeiros and the Epeirotes seem to be distinguished from Hellas proper (1.11.5, 5.14.2). Similarly, Pausanias often distinguishes between Hellas and the Greek states of Anatolia (7.5.13, 8.43.4, 8.45.5), but can refer to the battle of Mykale (in Anatolia), obliquely and somewhat loosely, as a "sea battle in Greece" (8.46.3). In presenting a moralistic catalog of betrayals of the common Greek cause for the sake of

---

[13] Cf. Bearzot 1988: 93.

private gain, a disease which he claims has afflicted Hellas from the beginning of time (7.10.1: οὔποτε τοῦ χρόνου παντὸς τὴν Ἑλλάδα ἐκλιπόν – cf. 7.10.5), the first example he gives is from Ionia, the treachery of the Samian trierarchs during the Ionian revolt (7.10.1). His second example, the betrayal of Eretria to the Persians by a pair of prominent Eretrians, also pertains to an area not covered in the present text.

In sum, Pausanias' variable usage of the term Hellas makes it questionable whether he had any firm opinion as to its geographical connotation, and there is no reason to suppose that he expected his readers to have one either. Therefore, the answer to the question of what the *Periegesis Hellados* describes is in a very real sense answered by the text itself: read the *Periegesis* and you will find out what Greece is. That being the case, it is interesting to note that Pausanias' text does come close to corresponding to the limits of the Roman province of Achaia (see Figure 3.1).[14] Despite Pausanias' decidedly antiquarian tastes and his overall lack of interest in matters of imperial administration, this resemblance cannot be dismissed out of hand; to a certain extent, it would be in line with Pausanias' general tendency to portray the antiquities of Greece as they existed in his day. Moreover, there is some evidence that in the second century CE *Hellas* could be used as a synonym for the province of Achaia. Pausanias himself at one point makes a reference to the Roman proconsuls of Achaia, calling them "the ones governing Hellas" οἱ τὴν Ἑλλάδα ἐπιτρεπεύοντες (5.15.2), and in a later passage (7.16.10) he takes pains to explain why the province is called Achaia and not Hellas.[15] Yet Pausanias' coverage of the province of Achaia, if that was his intent, is not complete: a comprehensive topography of the Roman province would include at least Aitolia and Opuntian Lokris. Rather than assume a missing book or more expansive original intentions on Pausanias' part, however, I would suggest the possibility that Pausanias may have been aware of the resemblance of his *Hellas* to the province of Achaia and also aware that the resemblance was not perfect. His decision to set the borders of his topography where he did may have been a subtle commentary on the difference between what Rome defined as "Greece" and "what was interesting to a Greek-speaker about Greece." This would be congruent to a pattern we will recognize elsewhere in Pausanias: a tendency to distance himself from the realities of the Roman Empire without divorcing himself

---

[14] As noticed by Meyer 1954: 19.

[15] In 5.15.2, Pausanias' use of Hellas may also be conditioned by his desire to avoid confusion between the Roman province and the Peloponnesian district of Achaea, which is what he means by Ἀχαία everywhere except 7.16.10. By way of contrast, Ptolemy calls the old Peloponnesian district ἡ ἰδίως καλουμένη Ἀχαία (3.16.10).

from them altogether. Be that as it may, the idea that Pausanias must be attempting to cover some sort of "Greece" that exists independently of his own devising has little to recommend it and is, I would argue, an assumption carried over from the world of modern travel guides, where authors are assigned a fixed territory such as "Greece" that they are responsible for covering. Even if there were some stable notion of Greece that could be pinpointed, it would still be within Pausanias' purview to decide whether to cover the entirety of that territory in his account. To explain why Pausanias' text deals with some areas and not others, we must take into account factors which have less to do with the borders of any political or ethnic entity than they have with the author's own sensibilities and methods. In short, we must seek internal motivations rather than external ones.

At the beginning of this chapter, I proposed four criteria which play a role in determining whether any given territory is to be incorporated in the *Periegesis*: the richness of the historical and mythical traditions pertaining to each territory; the quantity and quality of the physical remains of antiquity; the extent of Pausanias' personal familiarity with the territory, and the ease with which the territory can be incorporated into the author's overall design. Naturally, in the absence of any direct statement on the part of the author, any such criteria are completely hypothetical and serve merely to schematize the common general characteristics of the various regions included in the text. I will not speculate on the extent to which Pausanias was conscious of these criteria, but I will show that the scope of the text as we have it is completely understandable through a consideration of these factors, and thus that the search for a single comprehensive "program" for the work is as unnecessary as it is fruitless and methodologically questionable.

The first two criteria which I have proposed deal with Pausanias' interest in the history and mythology of the ancient Greeks and in the physical monuments visible in the Greece of his time. These criteria obviously emerge from the content of the work, and are suggested by Pausanias himself in such passages as 1.39.3, where he claims as his goal the reporting of all that was "most noteworthy in both stories (*logoi*) and sights (*theôrêmata*)." Of course, by themselves this passage and others like it (cf. 2.13.3; 3.11.1) tell us nothing about the territorial scope of his work; they address the question of how he intends to deal with the territories he has chosen to describe, but not why he chose those territories in the first place. Nevertheless, a consideration of the sorts of *logoi* and *theôrêmata* Pausanias found most noteworthy may have a bearing on the problem of why he deemed certain areas worthy of being included in his periegesis. I shall begin with the *logoi*.

An integral part of Pausanias' treatment of each territory or major city is the narration of the highlights of its history, beginning with the earliest heroic legends and continuing sometimes even to Hellenistic times and beyond. In later books, in addition to local histories, Pausanias also emphasizes the participation of each city or *ethnos* in a series of panhellenic or quasi-panhellenic military efforts, including the Trojan war, the Persian wars, the battle of Chaironeia, the Lamian war, and the resistance to the invasion of the Gauls. From the fifth book on, this canon of cooperative Greek activities is gradually standardized to the point that the record of involvement or non-involvement becomes almost a formulaic element in the history of each region and major city, as in the case of the following example, from the history of Arkadia which introduces the eighth book (8.6.1–3):

> For the Arkadians in common the earliest noteworthy event was the war at Troy, and next was the fighting that they did in support of the Messenians against the Spartans. They also took part in the war against the Medes in the affair at Plataiai. More by compulsion than out of good will for the Spartans they joined in fighting the Athenians, crossed over to Asia with Agesilaos, and finally went along with the Spartans to Leuktra in Boiotia. But they showed their mistrust toward the Spartans often, and especially after the defeat of the Spartans at Leuktra, when right away they deserted them and went over to the Thebans. They were not among the Greeks who fought against Philip and the Macedonians at Chaironeia and later in Thessaly against Antipatros, but then they didn't fight against the Greeks either. When the Gauls threatened at Thermopylai, they say that they did not take part because of the Spartans who, they feared, would have ravaged the land while their youth were away. As for the Achaean League, the Arkadians took part in it more eagerly than all the other Greeks.

As was the case with the Arkadians, not every nation took part in all of these defining campaigns, but for each of the peoples whose history Pausanias narrates participation was at least plausible, and where they abstained their non-participation is something that has to be explained.[16] This shared history, seen in opposition to the idiosyncrasies in the local histories of individual communities, is one factor which unites the various regions Pausanias includes in his *Periegesis*, and this gives us some insight into the historical sensibilities which contributed to making any given region "worth mentioning" (ἄξιον μνήμης) in Pausanias' eyes.

More evidence of this sort might be drawn from such passages as 7.6.8, where Pausanias discusses the power vacuum that existed in the early third century BCE that would pave the way to the eventual rise of the Achaean

---

[16] Alcock 1996: 251–260.

League: at this time, he says, nobody was strong enough any longer to dominate the Greek world (προεστήκεσαν κατ' ἰσχὺν οὐδένες ἔτι τοῦ Ἑλληνικοῦ); the Spartans, Thebans and Athenians had all failed to recover sufficiently from their reverses in the previous century. Here, his list of states which *might* have held preeminence is tellingly limited (absent are the Aitolians, Epeirotes, and Macedonians, for instance), and reveals once again that Pausanias' historical interests are oriented first and foremost toward the Greece which existed before the Macedonian conquest permanently altered the traditional patterns of internecine rivalries and uneasy alliances. Chaironeia was, for Pausanias, "the beginning of evil for all Greeks" (1.25.3, 9.6.5); another Herodotean statement, but one which testifies to a fairly narrow conception of who was "Greek" in the truest sense. Extended narratives of subsequent events, including the activities of the Achaean League and the careers of Aratos and Philopoimen, stand as illustrations of the process of decline which began in 338 and culminated in Roman domination.[17]

In Chapter 8, I will argue that the precise nature of Pausanias' historical sensibilities and the way in which he saw his historical narratives interacting with his descriptions of sights are things that did not remain static throughout the period in which he was composing the *Periegesis*. One corollary to this argument that must be mentioned at this juncture is that generalizations about Pausanias' historical interests are hazardous. Nevertheless, in general this sort of nostalgic attitude toward the volatile days of self-determination was not uncommon in Greek writers of Pausanias' era, and it is at least plausible to suggest that such an outlook on history was one of the causes, and not the result, of Pausanias' choice of subject-matter. One of Pausanias' aims may well have been to describe the present state of those territories which, in his view, were closely involved in the most important events of Hellenic history, events including the catalogue of panhellenic campaigns mentioned above. It is hardly surprising that the three cities mentioned in 7.6.8 as potential leaders of the Greek world are among the most thoroughly described in the whole work. If Pausanias' historical predilections provide a basis for the inclusion of certain territories in the *Periegesis*, they may also help to account for the exclusion of others. The Greek states in Cyprus, Libya, and Sicily, for example, were certainly parts of τὸ Ἑλληνικόν, but their effect on what Pausanias saw as the main sweep of Greek history was perhaps too marginal and intermittent to warrant inclusion. At the same time, however, this criterion is obviously not sufficient in itself to explain fully the extent of Pausanias' topography, since no firm line can

---

[17] Cf. Ameling 1996.

be drawn between the territories that were relevant to Pausanias' historical predilections and those that were not. There is no evident historical rationale for including regions such as Messenia, Achaea and Ozolian Lokris – the inhabitants of which did not play much of an active role for the bulk of the period in question – while excluding Aitolia, Thessaly, Akarnania, and such islands as Euboia and Crete.

What one might call Pausanias' mythological interests can also be adduced in this regard. Whether or not Pausanias recognized any essential distinction between history proper and the quasi-historical traditions of Greece's heroic age,[18] some of these legends were very important to the Greeks for their own sense of cultural and national identity, and as such they appropriately play a large role in his narration of the histories of the various regions. Among these traditions, Homer and the legends pertaining to the return of the Heraklids (which brought the Dorian Greeks into the Peloponnesos, according to tradition) play a conspicuous role; like the events of panhellenic history just mentioned, they involved most of the territories with which Pausanias deals, and provide them with a common traditional background. They served in large measure, moreover, as the basis for the historical and ethnic geography Pausanias follows in describing these regions. The extent to which deference to these legends, most notably those of the Dorian invasion, influenced Pausanias' methods will be considered in more detail below. Here, one need only note that his interest in these heroic traditions is likely to have provided an additional impetus toward focusing his efforts on the regions and peoples most directly involved in them, particularly on the homelands of the leaders of the Trojan expedition and the regions affected by the Dorian migrations. Conversely, those areas which became Greek only in later times, namely the majority of the overseas colonies, would have been less likely to attract Pausanias' attention; they had no part in this common tradition, except insofar as they traced their descent to part of the original motherland. This hypothesis thus helps to explain the inclusion of certain territories in the *Periegesis* at the expense of others, but, once again, it does not offer a comprehensive explanation. For instance, it provides no justification for the exclusion of the homelands of Odysseus, Meleager, Tydeus, Achilles, Jason, Idomeneus, and the original Dorians, to name a few examples. In sum, a consideration of Pausanias' historical and mythological interests can be used to explain why the later and more distant additions to the territory of τὸ Ἑλληνικόν do not make

---

[18] On Pausanias' attitude toward myth in relation to history see Veyne 1988: 95–102. This topic will be discussed further in Chapter 8.

it into his *Periegesis*, but in order to account for the scope of his work with greater precision, one must look for other factors.

The second of my proposed criteria is the condition of the *theôrêmata*, the material remains of antiquity which existed in Pausanias' day. This may seem at first glance to be the most obvious and important factor, yet its significance for the overall structure of the work has generally been overemphasized. It has long been recognized that Pausanias' archaic tastes in art and architecture have influenced his choice of things to describe, causing him, for example, to omit from his descriptions all but the most conspicuous monuments of the period subsequent to the Roman conquest. In the same way, his preference for artifacts related to cult, myth, and important historical personages allows him to pass over the vast majority of secular structures and monuments. As a large proportion of Pausanias' efforts are devoted to the description of extant physical objects, it is quite appropriate that his most thorough treatments are of places which had a large supply of the kinds of remains that interested him most, as did Athens, Olympia, and Delphi, for example.

It is possible, if not probable, that Pausanias embarked on his work with the intention of describing all those areas which had the most notable antiquities, and, as we will see in subsequent chapters, in many cases the quality of the material remains of any given site has a definite effect on the topographical methods he employs. For the question of why he chose to describe certain regions to begin with, however, it is difficult to advance this criterion as a consistent principle. In most of the territories Pausanias includes in his *Periegesis*, the monuments he finds most noteworthy tend to be concentrated in one or two sites, such as Athens in Attica, Sparta in Lakonia, Olympia in Elis, and Delphi in Phokis. In such cases, the comparatively barren landscape of the surrounding countryside, while it is treated more cursorily, is still not ignored. Other territories, Achaea, Messenia, and Arkadia for instance, lack even the attraction of these major cultural centers. The fact that Pausanias devotes an entire book to each of these territories shows clearly that the possession of impressive monuments, thriving cities, or important sanctuaries was not an absolute prerequisite for inclusion in the *Periegesis*. Pausanias dutifully records the *theôrêmata* that any territory has to offer, but his interest is not completely predicated on their quality or quantity. As we shall see, Pausanias had a number of techniques for producing a substantial account of a territory which had scanty monumental marvels. Hence, attempts to explain the absence of such territories as Aitolia and Thessaly with reference to their depopulation or lack of significant monuments do not account for the fact that a very large part of the territory which *is* covered was in a similar state in the second century CE. Had he wanted to write an *Aitolika* or a *Thessalika*, he would not have been prevented by their lack of visible antiquities.[19]

The third criterion is a thoroughly practical one: the extent of Pausanias' personal autopsy. Although it is fashionable nowadays to put great faith in Pausanias' autopsy, there is danger in going too far in that direction and ascribing to Pausanias an almost unlimited ability to gather firsthand information, far beyond what the author himself claims or implies. Autopsy is one of the main elements by which Pausanias' work is distinguished from that of his predecessors and contemporaries; he attempts to describe the country as it exists in his day, a goal which can only be accomplished through personal inspection. His ability to produce the sort of description he wanted is thus directly tied to the depth of his personal familiarity with any given territory, and while it is impossible to tell how much autopsy was necessary before Pausanias felt prepared to write about a major site or territory, one gets the impression that it was somewhat more than a single brief visit. Although Pausanias was doubtlessly a well-traveled man,[20] there is a limit to the amount of territory with which he could become sufficiently familiar to suit his own purposes, and hence there is a practical limit to the extent of his *Periegesis.* We will see below that even within the boundaries of the present text, there seem to be areas where Pausanias' familiarity is less profound than it is in other areas, and at the end of the work, in his description of Phokis, there are numerous anomalies that might well be a sign of limitations in his personal acquaintance with the terrain. It could be that at this point Pausanias was coming near to the frontiers of his usable knowledge. There is no reason to suppose that he had acquired a sufficient degree of firsthand familiarity with any region outside of the present text, with the possible exception of his native Asia Minor. The fact that Pausanias visited Thessaly (9.30.9) and (perhaps) Dodona (1.17.5), does not mean that he envisaged including them in his *Periegesis*, and even if he did have that intention at some point, he may never have had the opportunity to investigate them thoroughly enough.

The fourth and final criterion is the relation of a region to Pausanias' overall topographical design. The existence of this overall design and its precise nature are the subjects of the rest of this chapter. For the present, we may briefly note the obvious fact that Pausanias does not leap in

---

[19] As for Aitolia, the area seems to have suffered depredations in the Roman period due to forcible relocations to Nikopolis and Patrai, although "some large settlements in Eastern Aitolia show evidence of extensive habitation in Roman times" (according to Bommeljé, Doorn, Deylius, et al. 1987: 23).

[20] For a discussion of Pausanias' wide-ranging travels, see Frazer 1898: 1.xx–xxi.

desultory fashion from one tourist attraction to the next, but tries to present his material in a coherent topographical framework that is more or less continuous from beginning to end. On the large scale, he strives for topographical coherence and comprehensiveness: the territory he covers may not correspond to anyone's concept of "Greece," but it is at least a complete and coherent portion of Greek territory. Regions such as Messenia and Achaea, which were weak in regard to the other criteria, may have been included more for the sake of this sense of topographical completeness than for any other particular reason. Conversely, in addition to whatever other reasons there might have been for excluding such territories as Epeiros, Sicily, and any of the Greek islands that were more than a short sail from shore, it would have been more difficult to incorporate them into his topographical scheme.

So far, I have attempted to explain the scope of Pausanias' *Periegesis* as a function of the author's own interests, experiences, and methods. Of the four proposed criteria, the topographical design of the work will concern us most in the present study. Once Pausanias settled on this design as his organizing principle, it had a substantial effect on the types of information and the amount of information he decided to include in (or exclude from) his account.

DIVISION OF THE WORK

Each one of Pausanias' ten books describes a discrete and well-defined territory, and in most cases these territories correspond to the traditional ethnic, linguistic, and intermittently political divisions of ancient Greece. Hence, Book 3 is devoted to Lakonia, Book 4 to Messenia, Book 7 to Achaea, Book 8 to Arkadia and Book 9 to Boiotia. From the third book on, the description of each of these regions is prefaced by an ethnic history tracing the lineage of the inhabitants back to the migrations and eponymous heroes of mythical times, thus giving each book an ethnic as well as a geographical focus. Most of the exceptions to this pattern are relatively minor: Elis, owing to the lengthy description of Olympia, is covered in two books, 5 and 6. Book 10 is largely concerned with Phokis, but includes in the manner of an appendix a single chapter on the contiguous region of Ozolian Lokris (10.38). Similarly, Attica serves as the subject for all of Book 1, except for a few final chapters on the neighboring territory of Megaris, which Pausanias believes to have belonged to Athens in the Heroic Age (1.39.4).[21]

---

[21] Cf. Strabo, 9.1.6–7.

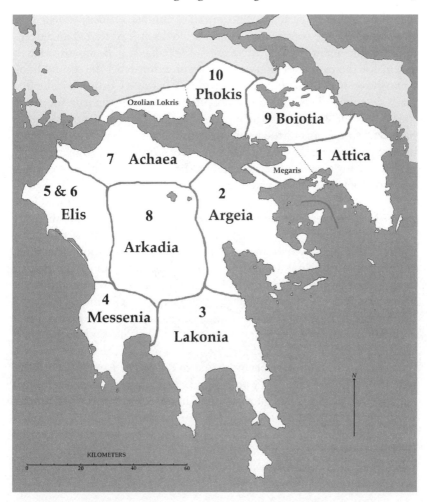

Figure 3.2. The regions of Greece covered in each of the ten books of the *Periegesis*.

The one major departure from the norm comes in Book 2, and the nature of this exception provides an interesting study in the interplay between Pausanias' topographical and historical interests.[22] Book 2 is unusual in that it comprises the description of many states which are normally thought of as being distinct and independent, including Corinthia, Sikyonia, Phliasia, Argolis, Epidauria, Aigina, Troizenia and Hermionis. Other books,

---

[22] See Musti 1988 and, for a contrasting interpretation, Piérart 2001.

including Books 7, 8, and 9, encompass a number of independent peer city-states, but the communities of those books at least shared an agreed-upon ethnic identity (i.e. "Achaeans," "Arkadians," "Boiotians" that is absent for the people of Book 2. The manuscripts label the second book Κορινθιακά (Corinthian matters), obviously because Corinthia is the first place described. This should not obscure the fact that the true subject of the book is the Argolid, of which, according to Pausanias, Corinthia was a part. The first words of the book make this clear: "The Corinthian land, being a part of Argeia . . ." This assignment of Corinthia to Argive territory is, as we shall see, quite idiosyncratic, and the rationale behind it is revealed, at various points in the second book, to lie in the realm of traditional geography. Most of these territories, Corinthia, Sikyonia, and the others, were parts of the Homeric kingdoms of Argos and Mycenae, and all of them are associated by their Doric heritage, which they owed directly or indirectly to the Argive dynasty of Temenos.[23] Following these traditions, Pausanias considered most, if not all, of this corner of the Peloponnesos to be part of the larger Argive territory, which he alternately, and without apparent distinction, calls ᾿Αργεῖα or ᾿Αργολίς.[24] That the determining factor in this for Pausanias was the history of these areas as parts of the Dorian lot of Temenos is indicated by his statement at 2.7.1, that Sikyon became a part of ἡ ᾿Αργεῖα from the time of the Dorian conquest of the city.

Pausanias may not have been the first to define the Argolid so broadly, but there were certainly other possible schemes. In fact, the concept of an Argolid that encompasses all the lands Pausanias ascribes to it is difficult to document without the testimony of Pausanias himself. Pausanias' reference at the beginning of Book 5 (5.1.1) to "those of the Greeks who say that the Peloponnesos has five parts (μοῖρας) and no more" may imply that there were others, like Pausanias, who divided it into six parts.[25] However, in the preserved literature, Pausanias is the only one to do so. Strabo, at one point,

---

[23] Piérart 2001.

[24] As Roux (1958: 85) points out, after the Roman sack of Corinth in 146 BCE, Corinthian territory was portioned out to Argos and Sikyon, but this redistribution probably did not remain in effect after the refounding of Corinth, and in any case does not explain why Pausanias considered such places as Sikyon and Phleious as parts of ἡ ᾿Αργεῖα (2.7.1, 2.25.2, 8.1.1–2). For other parts of this territory being Argive, see: 2.24.7 and 8.54.7 (Hysiae); 2.38.5–7 (Thyreatis). Pausanias does seem aware that some of the various lands he includes in his Argolis have more of an independent existence than the minor divisions of the other Peloponnesian territories. When he enumerates the several peoples of the Peloponnesos at the beginning of Book 8 (8.1.1–3), he lists separately the Corinthians, Epidaurians, Troizen, Hermione, and the Sikyonians, although these last are still considered to inhabit part of Argolis.

[25] I am not convinced that "those of the Greeks" are merely straw men constructed by Pausanias on a misunderstanding of Thucydides 1.10 (cf. Frazer 1898: 3.465; Hitzig–Blümner 1896: 2.282).

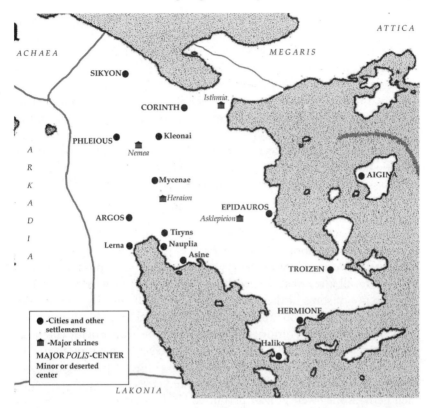

Figure 3.3. The territory covered by Book 2, an area with many independent *polis*-centers.

seems to conceive of the entire northeastern coast of the Peloponnesos, from the Lakonian border to the Isthmus, as belonging to Argeia,[26] but elsewhere he treats Corinth and Sikyon as separate. More influenced by Homeric geography than by tales of Dorian migrations, Strabo generally seems to visualize Argeia as corresponding to the kingdom of Diomedes as delimited by Homer in the *Iliad*, a realm that includes Asine, Hermione, Troizen, Epidaureia and Aigina, but not Corinth or Sikyon (8.6.1, 3, 4, 10, 19).[27] Pseudo-Skymnos, who claims to follow Ephoros, also treats Sikyon and Corinth separately from the Argives (516 ff.), and the distinction between the peoples of Pausanias' Book 2 and those of the other books is seen most clearly in Pseudo-Skylax (37–54), who speaks of the "nations" (ἔθνη) of the Achaeans, Eleians, Arkadians, Spartans, Lokrians, Phocians, Boiotians, and

[26] Strabo 8.2.2; cf. Pliny *NH* 4.1.1.   [27] Cf. Homer *Il.* 2.559–569.

Megarians, but not of the Argives. Instead, he refers to Corinth, Sikyon, Argos, Nauplia, Hermione, Troizen and Epidauros with the terms "city" and "territory" (*polis* and *chôra*). Pausanias' decision to treat these separate city-states as parts of a larger entity defined by traditional geography allows the second book to conform to the pattern of the others: the territories described in each separate book are not only coherent geographical entities but are also unified in some sense by a common background in the legendary tradition.

Pausanias' decision to devote an entire book to each of these territories (two books in the case of Elis) must also be recognized as one of his most basic organizing principles. The suitability of this scheme, both in terms of the physical, cultural, and political geography of the country and with regard to the author's particular antiquarian interests, cannot be taken for granted. Not every region provided the same quantity or quality of antiquities and local traditions. Where material of primary interest to Pausanias was less rich, he was obliged to engage in special efforts to produce enough material to fill a reasonably sized book.[28] This need may help to explain the presence of some of the extended *logoi* which frequently occur in the description of areas poor in *theôrêmata*. These include the twenty-nine chapters on Messenian history in Book 4,[29] and the history of the colonization of Ionia in Book 7 (7.2.1–5.13). If such passages were not motivated in part by a desire to flesh out the descriptions of antiquity-poor regions, and thereby to maintain an approximate balance between the separate books, then perhaps they were at least permitted by the scarcity of more relevant material. There are also more subtle ways in which this concern for balance between the individual books helped to shape Pausanias' account, and we will return to these later on.

---

[28] Of course, there is no standard length for a Pausanian book, and between the shortest, Book 6 (81 pages in Spiro's Teubner edition), and the longest, Book 8 (133 pages), there is a considerable difference. Book 8, however, is an anomalous book in many respects, some of which will be discussed below. If one disregards Book 8, and Books 1 and 10, which contain the exhaustive descriptions of Athens and Delphi, the lengths of the remaining books are remarkably similar (108 for Book 2, 85 for Book 3, 104 for Book 4, 86 for Book 5, 81 for Book 6, 88 for Book 7, and 98 for Book 9). It may be worth suggesting that Books 5 and 6, which contain the description of Olympia, were a single book at some point in the history of the text. Book 6 proceeds seamlessly from the method of description begun in Book 5, and if a division between the two was originally intended, Pausanias certainly takes no pains to point it out. If the Pausanian corpus were originally nine books instead of ten, it would have the same number of books as the histories of Pausanias' revered Herodotos. Of course, the division of Books 5 and 6 must have occurred before the time of Stephanos of Byzantium, who cites the book numbers as we have them today. Perhaps, then, a more likely hypothesis would be that the description of Elis began as a single book in Pausanias' mind, but was split when he found that Olympia offered him too many things to write about.

[29] On the balance between *logoi* and *theôrêmata* in Book 4 specifically, see: Alcock 2001; Baladié 2001.

Finally, it is difficult to say to what extent the traditional ethnic divisions of the Greek mainland around which Pausanias structures his account correspond to recognized and meaningful political divisions within the Roman province that existed in his day. However, in cases where comparative evidence exists, it seems that Pausanias defines his territories using contemporary boundary lines rather than those of Greece's independent past. In some instances, this is hardly surprising or significant. For instance, it is hard to know what to make of the fact that Kromyon, the northernmost town encountered in Pausanias' description of Corinthia, is said by Strabo (8.6.22) to have belonged at one time to Megaris.[30] It may be that the explanation for this assertion lies partly in Strabo's tendency to schematize political geography on the basis of physical geography;[31] in fact, this tendency causes Strabo elsewhere (9.1.1) to assert firmly that "Kromyon belongs to [the Megarians] and not the Corinthians," simply by virtue of the fact that it lies north of the Isthmus.

In other cases, Pausanias' boundaries reflect a situation that is more recent than the classical age, but one that has nonetheless been long established. Thyreatis, on the frontier between Argolis and Lakonia, was in his day (ἐπ᾽ ἐμοῦ) cultivated by Argives (2.38.5), and is accordingly described in the second book together with the rest of the Argive possessions. Argive control of the territory was established once and for all only after the battle of Chaironeia in 338 BCE.[32] Prior to that time, the Spartans had maintained a hegemony that dated from the fabled Battle of Champions. A similar but more troublesome example is that of Oropos on the borders between Attica and Boiotia (see Figure 4.2). Pausanias claims that in his day (ἐφ᾽ ἡμῶν) this frequently disputed territory belonged to Attica and had belonged to Attica since the time of Philip II (1.34.1). Pausanias has certainly misread history in this case, since there is ample evidence that Oropos changed hands several times after 338 BCE.[33] Yet it is also clear that at least in the mind of Pausanias

[30] See also Strabo 9.1.6.   [31] Cf. Baladié 1980: 1–2.
[32] Phaklares 1990: 36–39.
[33] For literary evidence, see Frazer 1898: 2.463–4, and, more recently, V. Petrakos 1968: 17–44, who takes advantage of epigraphical evidence that has come to light more recently. Frazer may be incorrect when he states that "in Strabo's time . . . Oropus was still reckoned to Boiotia," since Strabo himself seems to be unsure about the matter. In 9.1.3 he does refer to Ὠρωπὸν τῆς Βοιωτίας, but this comes in the same section where he assigns Kromyon to Megaris. The emphasis here is on physical geography, and from the standpoint of physical geography, the territory of Oropos does have more in common with Boiotia than with Attica. Moreover, earlier in this passage Strabo cites Eudoxos of Knidos as a source, and although we cannot be sure that this reference to Oropos was taken from Eudoxos, Eudoxos was active in a time when Oropos may well have been Boiotian politically as well as geographically (mid-fourth century). Strabo deals with the territory of Oropos both in his description of Attica (9.1.22) and in his description of Boiotia (9.2.6).

Athens' hold on Oropos had been secure for several centuries; hence it appropriately finds its place in the first book rather than the ninth.

Of greater interest are the cases where Pausanias' text seems to reflect border changes that are more recent. For Pausanias, the contemporary (ἐφ' ἡμῶν) border between Elis and Achaea was the river Larisos, and this river serves as the topographical boundary between the sixth and seventh books (6.26.10; 7.27.5). He also tells us, however, that the border previously lay farther north at cape Araxos, and this older border was still operative in the time of Strabo (8.3.4). The town of Prasiai, on the coast of the Argolic gulf south of Thyreatis, was once independent enough to be a member of the Calaurean league, but at some point their membership was expropriated by the Spartans, and classical sources refer to Prasiai as a Lakonian city.[34] Later sources, however – including Polybios (4.36) and Strabo (8.6.2) – call it Argive, and it is possible that Prasiai was yet another part of the territory detached from Lakonia after Chaironeia.[35] For Pausanias, this city, which he calls Brasiai, is once more Lakonian and is included in the third book as the northernmost of the Free Lakonian territories on the Argolic gulf (3.24.3).

On the western frontiers of Lakonia, Strabo set the border with Messenia at the promontory called Thyrides (8.2.2; 8.5.1). Pausanias' Lakonia extends considerably farther to the west, and includes a number of cities, including Pephnos, Leuktra, Kardamyle, Gerenia and Alagonia, which he says were originally Messenian and in some cases were still inhabited by Messenians (3.25.9–26.11).[36] In the case of Kardamyle, Pausanias claims that it was detached from Messenia and annexed to Sparta by Augustus. Of the rest of these cities, Gerenia and Alagonia are members of the Free Lakonian League, which, at least in Pausanias' mind, was also a creation of Augustus.

By including these cities in his description of Lakonia, Pausanias reveals that his concern for portraying the present-day state of things can override considerations of traditional ethnic identity, at least when he deals with such minor localities as these. The antithesis of this situation can be found, however, in the case of Stymphalos and Alea in Arkadia. Pausanias claims that both of these cities had at some point joined τὸ Ἀργολικόν and were no longer numbered among the Arkadians (8.22.1; 8.23.1). Since these cities occupied territory contiguous to Pausanias' Argolis, he could have

---

[34] For membership in the Calaurean League, see Strabo 8.6.14. Classical references to Prasiai being Lakonian include Thuc. 2.56 and Aristophanes *Peace*, 242–5.
[35] Phaklares 1990: 37.   [36] On this passage, see Le Roy 2001: 232–237.

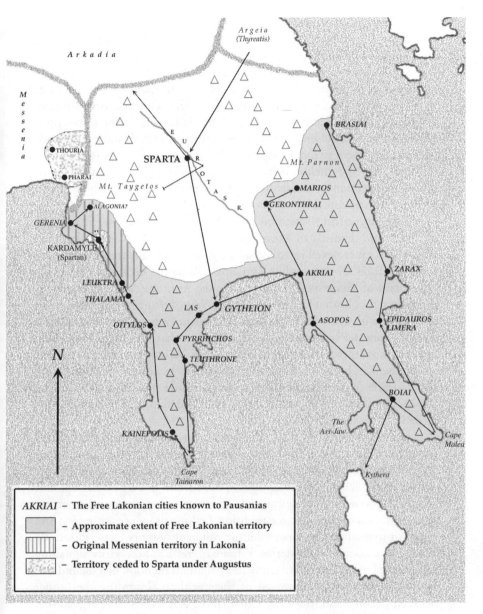

Figure 3.4. The territory of Lakonia covered in Book 3, showing the routes Pausanias traces from Sparta to the Free Lakonian cities. Of the Messenian cities put under Spartan control by Augustus, Pausanias describes Kardamyle in Book 3 but places Pharai and Thouria in Book 4.

accordingly included them in the second book, but instead they form part of his description of Arkadia. Here, one might argue that in contrast to the minor border states between Lakonia and Messenia, the traditional connection between Stymphalos, Alea and the rest of Arkadia was too strong for Pausanias to ignore. The legendary eponymous founders of these cities were descendants of the mythical kings of Arkadia, whose history Pausanias investigates in detail and uses as a unifying traditional theme throughout the eighth book. Pausanias prefaces the history of each of these cities with reference to, respectively, Stymphalos the grandson of Arkas (8.22.1) and Aleos the son of Apheidas (8.23.1), thereby providing both cities with an explicit connection to this common Arkadian tradition which stands in contrast to their contemporary political allegiances.

Another interesting exception to the general pattern comes at the sites of Pharai and Thouria in Messenia (4.30.2–31.2). Like Kardamyle, these cities had been annexed to Lakonia by Augustus and apparently remained so in Pausanias' day, yet unlike Kardamyle Pausanias includes them in his description of Messenia and not of Lakonia. As in the case of Stymphalos and Alea, it may be that Pharai and Thouria were too intrinsically Messenian to be dealt with apart from the rest of the territory, but another important factor to consider is that along the coastal route that Pausanias is following in this section, these cities were separated from Lakonia by territory that was still Messenian, both officially and traditionally. In order to include Pharai and Thouria in the third book, Pausanias would have had to break the topographical continuity of his description and skip over territory which he had not yet described.

In sum, Pausanias generally – but not always – sets the boundaries of his territories in accordance with contemporary borders, and this is consistent with his desire to present an accurate portrayal of the present-day state of the antiquities of Greece. The exceptions to this pattern reveal a certain amount of tension between this desire and Pausanias' other aims and interests, particularly his concern for the traditional ethnic unity of each region and his effort to maintain a topographically coherent system of description. By using contemporary boundaries, Pausanias was not necessarily signalling his approval of the boundaries, any more than his mention of a dilapidated temple meant that he approved of their neglect. Regarding the border between Lakonia and Messenia, Christian Le Roy has recently argued that the emphasis Pausanias puts on the ethnic identity of the inhabitants of these towns – Messenians living in Lakonia, Lakonians living in Messenia – is an implicit criticism of the changes to the traditional borders executed by Augustus.[37] This is not unlikely, and would be congruent with what I suggested above about the discrepancy between Pausanias' *Hellas* and the Roman province of Achaia.

THE TOPOGRAPHICAL SEQUENCE

Pausanias' *Periegesis* begins with Attica, proceeds through the Peloponnesos and then returns to central Greece for the descriptions of Boiotia and Phokis (see Figure 3.2). Since Pausanias had already planned the latter part of his work by the time he was writing the first book, this ordering cannot be taken for granted as fortuitous or natural. It is interesting to note, for instance, that the general east-to-west trend of Pausanias' account is in contrast to most of the other extant descriptions of Greece, which proceed west-to-east.[38] The reasons why Pausanias chose this particular sequence are not completely clear, although some general observations and speculations can be made. In light of Pausanias' antiquarian tastes, his decision to begin his *Periegesis* with Athens is understandable because of the richness of that city's literary and historical tradition and its large quantity of preserved antiquities. From Attica, his account proceeds directly toward the Peloponnesos, which even for Strabo was the most illustrious (ἐπιφανεστάτη) part of Greece (8.1.3),[39] and which must have been a major center of attention for anyone, like Pausanias, interested in the early myth and history of the Greeks. Only after he has described the whole Peloponnesos does he turn north and deal with Boiotia and Phokis, once again taking Attica as his point of departure.

For the Peloponnesos, Pausanias' interest in the geography of the Dorian invasion, which, as we have seen, was instrumental in his definition of the territory in Book 2, may also have influenced the order of his description. His treatment of the main divisions of the Peloponnesos proceeds in a clockwise spiral, beginning with his Argolid and continuing with all the coastal districts – Lakonia, Messenia, Elis, Achaea – before turning to landlocked Arkadia. The guiding role given here to the littoral regions may in part be inspired by the practices of previous writers, both *periplous* ("coastal voyage") writers and more standard geographers, who tend to

---

[37] Le Roy 2001: 235–237, Le Roy (p. 237, n. 35), discussing my previous expression of ideas similar to the ones I express here (Hutton 1995: 91) calls my ideas "diamétralement opposée" to his own. That was no doubt due to unclear language on my part, which I have tried to rectify here.

[38] For an author like Strabo, based in Rome, this is no surprise, but it is apparently also true of Ephoros (cf. Strabo 8.1.3 and Ps.-Skymnos 470 ff.).

[39] See also Pliny *NH* 4.4.9, on the Peloponnesos: "paeninsula haut ulli terrae nobilitate postferenda."

describe Greece from a seaborne perspective and to define its various parts in relation to points on the coast. This was naturally the case for the *periploi*, but the intricate contours of the Greek coastline and the relative isolation of much of the hinterland made it an attractive method for geographers as well. Strabo, for instance, speaks explicitly of the wisdom of making the sea one's "counselor" in organizing a description of Greece.[40] But for Pausanias, whose work is based on the experience of his own travels, and who shows only a superficial and sporadic interest in the sea itself, this pattern was by no means predetermined. One reason for his decision to treat the Peloponnesian territories in the order in which they lay along the coastline (and to do it clockwise, whereas Strabo, Pliny, Ptolemy, and others did it counter-clockwise) may have been to allow him to deal with the three Dorian districts of the Peloponnesos (Argolis, Lakonia, Messenia) without interruption, before turning to the non-Dorian lands. Pausanias nowhere makes this intention explicit, but at the beginning of his description of Elis, the first non-Dorian territory he treats in the Peloponnesos, he does make the distinction between the three non-Dorian regions, Arkadia, Achaea and Elis, and "the [regions] of the Dorians" (αἱ Δωριέων [μοῖραι]) (5.1.1).

For whatever reason, the fact that Pausanias' treatment of the territories of Greece follows any order at all is worth noting in itself. As was mentioned previously, the topographical description of the territory in each book (with the obvious exception of Book 1) begins at or near the border at a point contiguous with one that was mentioned in a previous book, in most cases the book immediately preceding. Thus, Pausanias ends the first book at the boundary between the Megarians and the Corinthia (1.45.10), and begins the second book at Kromyon (2.1.3), which lay north of the Isthmus along the line of the coast road from Megara and Athens. The transition between Books 2 and 3 is even more direct. The former ends on Mount Parnon, where Hermai stand marking the border between Argolis and Lakonia (2.38.4), while the first words of the latter are "after the Hermai." The transition between Lakonia in 3.26.11 and Messenia 4.1.1 is similarly immediate. This pattern of topographical continuity from each book to the next is not broken until the beginning of Book 8, where Pausanias presumably could have begun his description of Arkadia by following a route from Achaea, but instead decides to pick up the two routes to Mantineia from Argos, the Argive sections of which he described in Book 2 (8.6.4, cf. 2.25.1–6).

---

[40] Strabo 8.1.3 ff., where he cites Ephoros as an authority for this practice. See also Ptolemy 3.16. Outside of the Peloponnesos, Pausanias' own comments on the extent of Phokis (10.1.2) make an interesting comparison, as he defines the territory in terms of where it touches the sea on the south and where it does not touch the sea on the north.

He ends the eighth book by describing the Arkadian end of the third route from Argos to Arkadia (toward Tegea this time) that he describes in Book 2 (8.54.7, cf. 2.24.5). Obviously, there was no direct route between Arkadia and Boiotia, but Pausanias begins Book 9 on the road from Eleutherai to Plataia, a route which he began in Book 1 (1.37.8). The topography of Phokis begins where Book 9 leaves off, between Chaironeia and Panopeus (10.4.1, cf. 9.40.12).[41]

Recently, a growing number of scholars have begun to realize that the sequence of Pausanias' books is hardly haphazard, and reflects a good deal of thought about large-scale design. Walter Ameling has noted that Pausanias' reference to the Gaulish invasion of 279 BCE in Book 1 is balanced by a longer narrative of the same invasion in Book 10, effecting a sort of ring-composition.[42] Other correspondences between the two books might be noted: the abrupt opening of the former and the abrupt ending of the latter.[43] The extra-territorial coda on Megara on the former and the extra-territorial coda on Ozolian Lokris on the latter. Long descriptions of paintings by Polygnotos in both books,[44] carried like the Gallic narrative to much greater length in the later book (1.22.6–7, 10.25.1–31.12). Of the sites that Pausanias describes in Greece, two of the most splendid were no doubt Athens (Book 1) and Delphi (Book 10), and, as Elsner has noted, the most splendid site of all, Olympia, straddles the mid-point of the work, standing between the two poles of Athens and Delphi as a "grand metonym for all of Pausanias' Greece" with its panhellenic monuments and associations.[45] Domenico Musti has suggested even more parallels: in addition to pairing Books 1 and 10 (Athens and Delphi), Musti would associate 2 and 9 (Argos and Thebes, linked by the tradition of the Seven against Thebes), 4 and 7 (extended historical narratives on the Messenian and Achaean wars) and of course 5 and 6 (Olympia).[46] Missing from Musti's scheme are Books 3 (Lakonia) and 8 (Arkadia), but one could easily suggest a link between these two books in the extended royal histories that begin both books.

---

[41] Compare also 6.26.10 with 7.17.5, the topographical transition here being interrupted by the extended λόγοι on Achaean and Ionian history. On the boundary between Messenia and Elis (Books 4 and 5), see below.

[42] Ameling 1996: 146–147.

[43] On the ending, see Nörenberg 1973; Alcock 1996: 267. The abrupt beginning will be discussed further in Chapters 6 and 7.

[44] Cf. Elsner 2001b: 7.   [45] Elsner 2001b: 17.

[46] Musti, personal correspondence to Mario Moggi reported by Moggi 1993: 403. Musti, to my knowledge, has not published this suggestion anywhere, though he does discuss the link he perceives between 2 and 9 in Musti 1988.

CONCLUSION

In sum, the overall structure of Pausanias' topography is neither haphazard nor illogical. The elements of that structure which we have examined in this chapter form a discernible plan that is sophisticated enough to suggest a high degree of authorial control over the subject-matter. That the author nowhere states this plan specifically does not negate its existence, and is in keeping with his well-known reluctance to allow his own personality to intrude into his work. A proper evaluation of Pausanias' testimony must take into account the author's concern for carrying out this design. For example, I have mentioned that the desire for balance between the accounts in each separate book may have had an effect on the amount of non-topographical information included. On a smaller but more pervasive scale, this concern for balance may also affect the types and amounts of topographical information which he gives within the descriptions of territories, sites, and monuments. Many types of information of interest to modern topographers and archaeologists are only given sporadically by Pausanias, such as the names of mountains and rivers, the courses of rivers and their tributaries, the quality of roads, the distances from each site to the next, compass directions, industry and land use, the population of individual cities, the character of the local inhabitants, non-religious architecture, and the architectural order of buildings. The intermittency of such data was at one time explained by Pausanias' use of written sources: where the source provided this information, Pausanias copied it; where it did not, he was not bothered by the lack.[47] All of this information, however, could have been gained or verified by attentive autopsy, so there is no reason to speculate about a previous source at all.

One obvious explanation is that such items, which might be called items of secondary interest to Pausanias, were included more often where the things he was most interested in were scarce. To take the example of distances between sites, they are most often given between minor sites, ones with few or no monuments to antiquity, or between major sites and points in the depopulated countryside. Pausanias does not bother to give us the distances between, for instance, Athens and Megara, Megara and Corinth, Corinth and Argos, Argos and Epidauros, Argos and Tegea, Tegea and Sparta. A likely reason for these omissions is that he has too much else he wants to say about these places. His description of Arkadia, a territory with few thriving cities, many depopulated ones, and no major panhellenic religious centers, contains a far greater number of stadion measurements than

---

[47] See Meyer 1954: 41 for a relatively recent incarnation of this argument.

any other book. Book 8 also contains more information on rivers, compass directions, the sizes of statues, and the borders of the territory with all its neighbors than is normal for the rest of the work. The secular buildings of Megalopolis, a city which was in decline in Pausanias' day, are described with unusual completeness.

Pausanias does not tell us all that he knows and sees. Where certain information is not given in his text, no conclusions can safely be drawn about lacunae in his sources or about the extent of his own ability and diligence. Not long ago, the eminent archaeologist Anthony Snodgrass devoted an essay to the shortcomings of the descriptions of Boiotia by a number of classical authors, including Pausanias.[48] Snodgrass' chief contention, that modern archaeologists should not confine their interests to the types of information supplied by written sources, is incontrovertible. What is less compelling is the estimation he presents of Pausanias' methods and abilities. Pausanias' main limitation, in Snodgrass' view, is a lack of awareness of the countryside which he traverses, apart from the cities and sites he seeks out and the narrow corridors of the roadways between them.[49] In this regard, he compares Pausanias unfavorably with Strabo, since Strabo does a more systematic job in providing information about such things as stadion measurements, the sizes of towns, compass directions, and lateral spatial relationships between sites (as opposed to linear relationships along the lines of separate roadways).[50]

If Pausanias has less to say on these matters, however, it may be because his aims and interests were different. For Strabo, such information is the very essence of his work, as he sought to present as complete a geography as possible, encompassing the physical, mathematical, political, and historical aspects of that discipline. Strabo relied more on written sources than on personal inspection for his knowledge of Greece; hence he was encumbered neither by the overwhelming amount of data provided by extensive autopsy nor by the exigencies of Pausanias' specific interests and methods. Although Strabo is a more useful source for certain types of evidence, no one could argue that his account of Boiotia, or of any part of Greece, is more coherent and accurate overall than that of Pausanias.[51] There are few sorts of

[48] Snodgrass, 1987: 67–92.
[49] Snodgrass 1987: 77–79; cf. 86: "rural settlement, population and agriculture are passed over in silence, requiring as they do an awareness of rural space."
[50] Snodgrass 1987: 86–92. The "linearity" of Pausanias' descriptions will be discussed more fully in the following chapters, as will Snodgrass' comments on Pausanias' choice of routes and possible topographical sources.
[51] P. W. Wallace, who is generally favorable to Strabo, says, "Strabo writes as if he were more familiar with the Boiotia of the Homeric Catalogue than with the real Boiotia of the Aonian plain" (Wallace 1979: 171).

information found in Strabo or in other topographical writers for which Pausanias does not show an interest and aptitude, at least from time to time.[52] It seems reasonable to suggest that he often inserts such observations where it would be conducive to producing a substantial account for each territory. This is one example of how consideration of Pausanias' overall design may affect one's appreciation of his testimony, and in subsequent chapters we shall see the same concern for balance and topographical coherence at work on a more detailed level.

[52] E.g.: for lateral spatial relationships, see 2.25.5, 10.5.1, 10.33.12 (Book 10 seems particularly rich in this regard). For agriculture and land use: 10(!).33.7, 6.26.6, 2.38.4–5. Pausanias of course gives *stadion* distances and compass directions frequently, albeit not systematically. As for population, he often speaks of deserted cities and areas (see especially 2.28.2), and the various words he uses for cities and towns (πόλις, κώμη, πόλισμα, χωρίον, etc.) may perhaps reflect a sense of varying size and development (see the requisites for a *polis* he lists at 10.4.1). These aspects of Pausanias' description will be discussed in greater detail in the following chapters.

CHAPTER 4

Marking territories

Now that we have examined the design and structure of Pausanias' work as a whole, we must proceed to an analysis of the methods he uses in describing the territories that provide the subject-matter for each of the ten books. It is at this level that we first encounter the one topographical principle of the *Periegesis* that is universally recognized, the so-called "radial plan." The best description of this method in English continues to be that of Frazer:[1]

> After narrating in outline the history of the district he is about to describe he proceeds from the frontier to the capital by the nearest road, noting anything of interest that strikes him by the way. Arrived at the capital he goes straight to the centre of it, generally to the market-place, describes the chief buildings and monuments there, and then follows the streets, one after the other, that radiate from the centre in all directions, recording the most remarkable objects in each of them. Having finished his account of the capital he describes the surrounding district on the same principle. He follows the chief roads that lead from the capital to all parts of the territory, noting methodically the chief natural features and the most important towns, villages, and monuments that he meets with on the way. Having followed the road up till it brings him to the frontier, he retraces his steps to the capital, and sets off along another which he treats in the same way, until in this manner he has exhausted all the principal thoroughfares that branch from the city. On reaching the end of the last of them he does not return on his footsteps, but crosses the boundary into the next district, which he then proceeds to describe after the same fashion.

As we shall see, the number of times that Pausanias follows this scheme to any degree of detail are actually quite few. Still, Frazer's characterization does embody a number of recurring topographical motifs, and it cannot be disputed that this radial plan is chief among Pausanias' methods for handling large areas of land. The trouble is that in modern scholarship this technique has come to be regarded as the only identifiable technique, and in some ways the schematization of it has come to take precedence over

[1] Frazer 1898: I.xxiii–xxiv.

serious consideration of the text itself, as if once a glimmer of regularity is perceived in the midst of apparent amorphousness it becomes permissible to ignore all that does not conform to the pattern. Hence, if one looks at the maps made to accompany modern studies of Pausanias (including this one), one finds the "routes" of Pausanias drawn in neatly, all connecting with one another forming orderly spokes radiating from the various "capitals," complete with arrows showing the direction in which the author walked. Once one begins reading the text, however, one finds that not all lines connect and that some of the routes drawn on the map are not even mentioned by the author. This is a classic case of cognitive stereotyping: we expect Pausanias to follow a pattern that we have recognized, and this causes us to overlook the fact that he frequently deviates from it. We therefore miss some of the subtle ways that Pausanias varies his approach to the territories. In part, these variations in Pausanias' approaches are dictated by terrain, by the quality of roads, and probably by a number of other mundane factors that we cannot possibly recover at this point. But there are also times when the texture of the topographical network he constructs seems to follow the contour of his own cognitive mapping, a contour that bends around a number of complex junctures of present and past, and of landscape and tradition. In this chapter, we will take a brief look at the different varieties of organization that Pausanias employs in each of the ten books, and then take a closer look at one book, Book 2, in order to see in detail how and why Pausanias makes some of the choices he does in arranging his territorial descriptions.

VARIETIES OF THE RADIAL PLAN

The first thing to recognize is that the radial plan itself is not as simple as one might think from reading Frazer's description of it. For one thing, not all of the "capitals" play an equal role in Pausanias' scheme. There are what I will henceforth call "primary hubs", which are usually major cities or sanctuaries. Primary hubs are sites from which Pausanias traces numerous routes in different directions, and from which Pausanias does not return to a previous point in his itinerary. Below this on the hierarchy are the "secondary hubs," which also serve as the starting-point for one or more excursions branching off from the main route. But after Pausanias is through with a secondary hub, he returns to the primary hub from which he started out. Aside from primary and secondary hubs, there are a number of minor centers that fulfill special roles in the topographical network. These include places located on Pausanias' main route into or out of a territory which serve as the point of departure for one or two side-routes. Finally, there are hubs from which Pausanias does not "retrace his steps," but which lie on the course of a major route from a primary hub and are clearly subordinate to it. In the following sections, we will see that the way Pausanias deploys his radial scheme between these different sorts of hubs varies significantly from book to book. Quite often it is clear that the choices Pausanias makes in assigning primary or secondary status to particular hubs and in organizing the topography of each territory in general reflect his personal vision of what the landscapes of Greece should communicate.

TERRITORIES WITH ONE PRIMARY HUB

In five of the nine territories Pausanias covers, Attica, Lakonia, Elis, Boiotia, and Phokis, Pausanias organizes his topography around a single primary hub. In some cases, his decision to do so was probably heavily influenced by the road network emanating from the main city, but in some cases there seem to be other factors at work. In Book 1, all routes lead from Athens, and when we turn to the description of Elis, we find that the topographical framework of Books 5 and 6 is focused squarely on Olympia. After describing two routes to the sanctuary, one from the south, with Samikon serving as an introductory hub for a side-trip to Lepreos (5.5.3–5.6.7) and one along the course of the Alpheios from the boundaries of Arkadia (6.21.3–22.6),[2] the rest of Elis is described on a pair of routes leading from Olympia to the city of Elis. First, a mountain route that leads through Pylos to Elis (6.22.5), and then a route farther to the west that passes Letrinoi (6.23.1). After the description of the city of Elis, this route continues to the port of Kyllene, and from there to the boundaries of Achaea (6.24.6).

An interesting case to consider is the description of Lakonia in Book 3, where all major routes lead to and from Sparta (see Figure 3.4). After the initial route from the frontiers of Argolis into the city (3.1.1, 10.6–11.1), Pausanias traces a number of routes from Sparta to the various parts of Lakonia: first, a route to Amyklai (3.18.6); then one which proceeds southeast to Therapne before turning abruptly west to end along the slopes of Taygetos (3.19.7–20.7); then one following the course of the Eurotas in a northwesterly direction toward the boundary with Arkadia (3.20.8–21.3), and then one down to Gytheion, the main port of Sparta (3.21.4). Gytheion

---

[2] This is the passage that embarrassed Wilamowitz. He assumed that after the introductory route, all subsequent routes proceeded away from Olympia; hence he tried to read this itinerary *from* Heraia as though it were describing a route *to* Heraia (Habicht 1998: 170).

then serves as a secondary hub for a pair of extended routes which circum-
scribe the peninsulas of Malea and Tainaron, the latter terminating at the
boundary with Messenia and Book 4. The way Pausanias centers his network of roads in Book 3 on Sparta reflects the traditional preeminence of
Sparta over the whole of Lakonia,[3] and it is by no means improbable that
he intended it to do so. However, Pausanias' choice of Gytheion for the
starting-place for his itineraries through the southern reaches of Lakonia
may reflect an additional motive. While this decision makes a certain
amount of geographical sense, at least as a means of describing the coastal
regions of Lakonia, Pausanias also includes a certain number of inland sites,
including the cities of Geronthrai and Marios. These communities lay far
inland in the Parnon range to the east of Sparta, and could have been easily
included in an itinerary from the city itself. Instead, Pausanias reaches them
on a side route that branches off from the coastal village of Asopos on the
route around the Malea peninsula that he traces from Gytheion. This is an
extremely unlikely route for a traveler to take to get to these cities, and one
might rightly question whether it is the route Pausanias himself ever took.
Pausanias' motive seems clear in this case: as we have already seen, many
of the coastal cities of Lakonia, including Gytheion, were members of the
Free Lakonian League established (or re-established) by Augustus. Before
beginning his itineraries from Gytheion, Pausanias lists the members of
the League (3.21.7). Pausanias has literally gone out of his way to accord a
certain unity in his topographical plan to the Free Lakonian cities and a
certain distancing from Sparta. Pausanias' artful design of his itineraries in
Book 3 manages simultaneously to acknowledge the traditional power of
Sparta and to respect the relatively new autonomy of the Free Lakonians.

   In the tenth book, more than two thirds of which is devoted to the
description of Delphi, the situation is somewhat more complex. Many
Phocian sites are used by Pausanias to anchor a complex series of itineraries.
Delphi, however, serves as the only primary hub. Pausanias begins his
description of Phokis where he left off in the ninth book, on the road
from Chaironeia. This road continues past Panopeus to Daulis to Delphi
(10.4.9–5.5). After the extended description of Apollo's shrine at Delphi,
the rest of Phokis is traversed on a series of routes beginning from Delphi:
the first route heads to the heights of Parnassos and the Corycian cave
(10.32.1). Then another one proceeds north across the mountain to Tithorea

---

[3] In line with a widespread phenomenon of the Roman period, rural depopulation had probably led to
a significant increase of the dominance of the city over countryside of Lakonia by the time Pausanias
was writing. Cartledge and Spawforth 1989: 127–142. For sites in Lakonia, see: Shipley 1996a and
1997; Kennell 1999; Hutton 2005a.

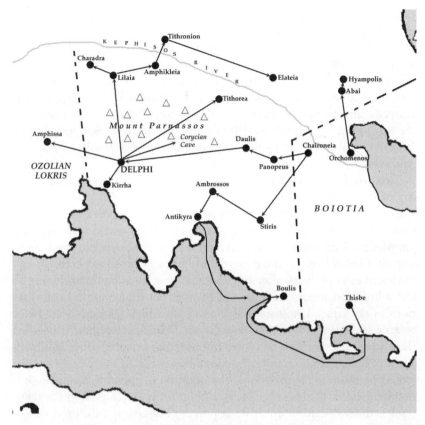

Figure 4.1. Pausanias' routes through Phokis in Book 10.

and to the deserted city of Ledon (10.32.12–33.1). The third route from Delphi also takes a mountainous path northwest to Lilaia (10.33.3), whence a pair of routes are traced to Charadra (10.33.6) and Amphikleia (10.33.9). Amphikleia serves in turn as a secondary hub for routes to other sites in the valley of the Kephisos, ending finally at Elateia (10.34.1). The final two routes from Delphi head south, the first one only as far as the harbor of the Delphians at Kirrha (10.37.4), and the second one to the Lokrian city of Amphissa (10.38.4), which serves as the starting-point of his brief and sketchy tour of Ozolian Lokris (10.38.4–13).

Alongside these relatively normal itineraries, the description of Phokis has one oddity that is worth noting. In addition to the initial route into the territory, near the end of his Phocian account Pausanias mentions three other routes leading into Phokis from the direction of Boiotia. After describing Elateia, Pausanias eschews the "mountain road" from Elateia to the final Phocian cities in that region, Abai and Hyampolis, preferring instead to approach those cities on a road from Boiotian Orchomenos (10.35.1). Subsequent to his description of Abai and Hyampolis, he describes yet another road from Chaironeia in Boiotia down to the Phocian city of Stiris (10.35.8), and thence to Ambrossos and Antikyra. Finally, he approaches the semi-Phocian city of Boulis[4] on a sea route from Boiotian Thisbe (10.37.2), while mentioning that one can also approach Boulis by sea from Antikyra.

Two possible explanations for this unprecedented violation of the sanctity of Pausanias' territorial borders suggest themselves: 1) perhaps we are witnessing an example of what was envisioned in the previous chapter: a place where Pausanias is coming to the end of his useful topographical knowledge. Pausanias may approach these Phocian sites on routes from outside Phokis because these are the only routes he knows well enough to describe; 2) perhaps, after ten books, Pausanias is finally beginning to feel a little too strongly the discord between his topographical constructions of the Greek landscape and the ways in which his readers are likely to experience the sites in their own travels. While he could have included these sites on extensions of routes from Delphi or some other landmark within Phokis, he chose instead to describe a way that the average traveler would be more likely to follow. The question is probably insoluble, but despite these difficulties the salient feature of Pausanias' plan in the tenth book is the way that the entire description of Phokis, with the exception of these oddments near the end of the book, is centered ultimately on Delphi as the primary hub for all routes. Elateia, by Pausanias' own estimate the territory's second largest city (10.34.1), serves merely as an end-point on the longest of the routes traced from Delphi.

Another highly unusual situation prevails in Pausanias' description of Boiotia in Book 9.[5] Here, after the introductory routes to Thebes from the Attic frontier, not only do all the main routes begin from the city of Thebes, but they are integrated with the topography of the city itself to an uncommon degree. As we shall see in the next chapter, when Pausanias uses

---

[4] Pausanias apparently believes that the Boulioi were not considered Phocians, but the text, which suffers from corruption at a crucial point, may have once indicated that they were at one time members of the Phocian assembly (the text reads λέγονται δὲ οἱ Βούλιοι Φιλομήλου καὶ Φωκέων σύλλογον τὸν κοινόν). If this is true, it may explain why Pausanias included Boulis in the tenth book, rather than the ninth. Cf. McInerney 1999: 74–76, 329–332; Bommelaer 2001.
[5] Well described by Musti 1988.

a city as a hub, he usually finishes the description of the city itself before tracing routes from the city to more remote parts.[6] This distinction between city and countryside is not maintained in Book 9. As Pausanias reminds us, the citadel of Thebes, the Kadmeia,[7] was famous for its seven gates (9.8.4–7), and these gates serve as important landmarks in his description of the city. After describing the vicinity of the gate of the Proitidai, he begins a route from there that leads toward Euripos and the cities of Tanagra and Anthedon (9.18.1–22.7). Then he returns to the Proitidaian gate and, surprisingly, begins to describe more monuments, including a stadium and a hippodrome, immediately outside it (9.23.1–4). From there, he initiates a second route from the Proitidai (9.23.5–24.5). Later, a third route departs from the gate of the Neistai. Pausanias traverses the rest of Boiotia on his third itinerary, and once again it begins with a description of objects directly outside the gate (9.25.1–4).

The description of Boiotia includes a number of important sites as secondary hubs: the strait of Euripos serves as crossroads where the aforementioned routes to Tanagra and Anthedon diverge (9.19.6, 22.5); Akraiphnion plays the same role for the routes that end at Larymna and Halai (9.23.7, 24.4); in the long final itinerary, roads branch off from the Kabeirion to Onchestos (9.25.5) and Thespiai (9.26.6). Thespiai in turn serves as intermediate hub for routes to Mount Helikon and the Valley of the Muses (9.28.1), Kreusis (9.32.1) and Haliartos (9.32.5), and beyond Haliartos the itinerary proceeds toward the Phocian border on a direct route. This complex of secondary centers makes the description of Boiotia seem less unified than the descriptions of Lakonia and Elis, or even of Phokis, but the fact remains that in the overall structure of the book, Pausanias makes his description of the Boiotian countryside almost an appendage of his description of the city of Thebes. Although Thebes in his day was a poor remnant of its former glorious self, it still served as the center of Pausanias' attention in Book 9.[8]

The descriptions of all the territories we have looked at so far share the common feature of having a single primary hub. Even so, Pausanias adapts this one pattern to the individual requirements of each territory, and as a result there is significant variation in the way he links the description of the territory to the primary site. We will encounter still greater variation as we go on to consider the rest of the territories in the *Periegesis*.

---

[6] This phenomenon will be examined more fully in the next chapter.

[7] Pausanias states that in his day the acropolis was the main area of habitation, and that the people called it "Thebes" rather than "Kadmeia."

[8] On Pausanias' description of Thebes and on the condition that the city was in when he visited it, see Symeonoglou 1985: 148–154, 173–202.

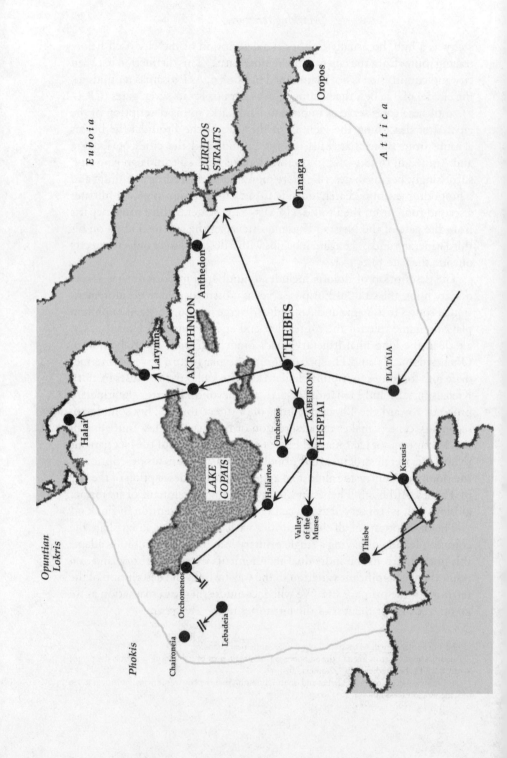

TERRITORIES WITH NO MAJOR HUBS

In stark contrast to territories dominated by a single site, there are territories that possessed few major centers of population or cult, and in these cases, the traces of Pausanias' radial plan are at best faint. In Book 4, where only six chapters are devoted to the description of the Messenian territory, the only sites that come close to serving as a hub of any kind are the cities of Thouria and Messene. Pausanias approaches Thouria on a continuation of the seaboard itinerary he had begun in the third book (4.1.1, 30.1–31.1). From Thouria, he takes a brief side-route to Kalamai and Limnai (4.31.1–3), and then a second route to Messene (4.31.4). From Messene, he also takes two routes, one that passes the Stenyklaros plain on the way to Andania and Dorion (4.33.4), and a second which returns to the sea at the mouth of the Pamisos and proceeds from there along the coast, around the cape of Methone and all the way north to the borders of Elis (4.34.1–36.7), where the fourth book ends. Thus, Messene does serve as a hub of sorts for much of the descriptive material in the fourth book, but the two routes that are traced from Messene hardly constitute a well-developed radial plan.

In the seventh book, the radial scheme is even less evident. In his description of Achaea, which also comprises a small portion of the book (after the extended histories of Ionia and the Achaean League), Pausanias does not use any single site as a primary hub. Instead, the chief point of topographical reference is the main highway which runs along the narrow coastal plain between the mountains and the gulf of Corinth. Such inland sites as are mentioned are accessed by separate side-routes from this main thoroughfare. In Achaea, the geography of the territory has as much to do with the absence of the radial scheme as does the paucity of important sites.

TERRITORIES WITH MULTIPLE HUBS

The radial plan is most fully developed in those territories that possess a number of noteworthy sites, none of which is especially preeminent over the rest. In Book 2, which will be examined in greater detail below, Corinth and Argos serve as primary hubs for a well-demarcated radial plan, with Sikyon, Troizen and Hermione among the secondary hubs. It is in Arkadia, however, that Pausanias comes closest to following the idealization of the radial plan consistently from beginning to end. This territory was rich in tradition and history, and filled with a number of renowned locales. In contrast to this venerable image, however, many of the sacred and celebrated

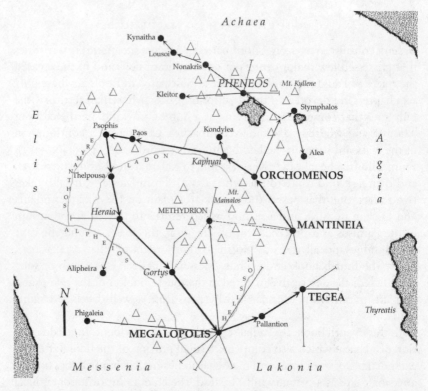

Figure 4.3. Pausanias' routes through Arkadia in Book 8. The dotted lines indicate places where the central site of Methydrion is referred to in the course of Pausanias' itineraries.

spots of Arkadia had fallen victim to neglect and abandonment in Pausanias' day.[9] Where he finds the human monuments lacking, Pausanias responds by treating the land itself with greater respect and attention than anywhere else in his *Periegesis*. Pausanias spends more effort here than in any other book in describing the mountains, the major rivers and their tributaries, and other items of physical geography that give shape to the land his narrative traverses. It can hardly be coincidental that Arkadia is also the territory in which the topographical pattern of his itineraries is laid out most explicitly and in the greatest detail.

Pausanias begins the description of Arkadia by tracing not one but two paths from Argolis into the territory of Mantineia (8.6.4–6). These routes are both continuations of a route that he had already described in the second

---

[9] For excellent discussions of Pausanias' account of Arkadia, see Jost 1973, 1992, 1998.

book (2.25.1–3).[10] The first primary hub is the city of Mantineia, and from Mantineia Pausanias traces a number of routes to the boundaries of the Mantineian territory (8.10.1), including two toward the south where the Mantineians had borders with Tegea and Pallantion (8.10.2–12.1), and one to the west toward Methydrion (8.12.2–5). Finally, he describes two routes north toward Orchomenos, the first of which he follows only to the border of Orchomenian territory; on the second route north, he finally crosses the boundary of Mantineian territory and proceeds to Orchomenos itself, his next primary hub (8.12.5–13.1).

From Orchomenos he first mentions one road leading northwest toward Kaphyai, then takes a second road north (8.13.4). He soon comes to a fork in this road, which presents him with the choice of heading either to Stymphalos or Pheneos (8.13.5–6). Choosing the latter route he proceeds north-west to Pheneos, which he uses as a secondary hub on his Orchomenian itinerary. He traces four roads from Pheneos, the first toward the boundaries between Arkadia and Achaea (8.15.5). The next road leads east to Mount Kyllene and the frontier between the territories of Pheneos and Stymphalos (8.16.1). He then traces two longer routes to the west, the first to the city of Kleitor, the second to Nonakris and the waters of the Styx (8.16.6–19.1). Then, having explored the territory of Pheneos in every direction, he returns to Mount Kyllene, where he resumes the route he began previously and follows it into the territory of Stymphalos (8.22.1). From Stymphalos, this route continues to the site of Alea.

Pausanias' itinerary now returns to the primary hub of Orchomenos, where he once more picks up the westbound route he had mentioned leading to Kaphyai, following it this time all the way to Kaphyai (8.23.3). From Kaphyai, he takes a single side-route to Kondylea, and then proceeds upon his main route, following the watersheds of the Ladon and Erymanthos rivers toward the west and the south. He passes Paos, Psophis, Thelpousa and a number of lesser sites, until he ends up in Heraia (8.25.12). Heraia, lying in the far west of Arkadia, serves as a minor hub for excursions west toward the Eleian border (8.26.3) and south to Alipheira (8.26.5). Then Pausanias resumes his main route in a southeasterly direction toward Megalopolis. Upon reaching the border between Heraia and Megalopolis, Pausanias pauses to give an outline of Megalopolitan history (8.27.1–17), then continuing his progress along the main road he comes to the village of Gortys (8.28.1) which serves as hub for a brief side-trip to the Arkadian

---

[10] See Pritchett 1980: 1–53 and Pikoulas 1995: 293–297 for the location of the passes, which Pausanias calls the Prinos and the Klimax, and for confirmation that they are both likely end-points for the route Pausanias describes in Book 2.

Figure 4.4. The site of the remote village of Methydrion, which Pausanias mentions from three different points on his itineraries. Some ruins of walls can be discerned in the left mid-foreground.

interior in the direction of Methydrion (8.28.4), a place he has already mentioned in his Mantineian itineraries (8.12.2).

When Pausanias finally reaches Megalopolis, it becomes the third primary hub in the description of Arkadia. From Megalopolis, he traces a total of seven roads: the first two proceed south to the border between Megalopolis and Messenia (8.34.1–35.1). The third follows the Alpheios and its tributaries to the boundaries of Lakonia (8.35.3). The fourth proceeds north, to Methydrion, which is mentioned here for the third and last time in Pausanias' description. This time, Pausanias finally traces the route all the way to Methydrion itself and describes what there is to see there, and then follows the route beyond Methydrion to the borders Megalopolis shares with Kaphyai and Mantineia (8.35.5). The fifth route from Megalopolis follows the course of the river Helisson toward the north-east and brings us once again to the frontiers of Mantineia at Mount Mainalon (8.36.5). Next, Pausanias takes an extended journey west toward Phigaleia and Bassai (8.36.9–43.6), then a final route from Megalopolis heads east toward Pallantion and Tegea (8.44.1). Tegea serves as a final hub for routes exploring the Tegeans' borders with Lakonia (8.54.1), Thyreatis (8.54.4), and Argos (8.54.5). The end of Book 8 comes on this route at the Argive border, where he links up with the Argos–Hysiai route he had begun to describe in Book 2 (2.24.5–7). Overall, Pausanias' itinerary of Arkadia traces an immense number of different routes in all directions, but by focusing all routes on the hubs of Mantineia, Orchomenos, Heraia, Megalopolis, and Tegea, Pausanias manages to describe an orderly counter-clockwise circuit of the territory. He ends up near where he began, and in much the same way as he began, at the juncture with a route which he had visited in a previous book. No other book has a topographic organization more sophisticated or more explicitly expressed.

THE RADIAL PLAN RECONSIDERED

From this overview of Pausanias' uses of the radial plan we can see that he is capable of varying the scheme in order to make his description suit each territory. His topographical networks serve not only to organize the myriad sites in his *Periegesis*, but also to place them in a sort of hierarchy. By choosing a certain site to use as a primary hub, Pausanias places the focus of an entire region on that site and emphasizes its importance or noteworthiness. Usually, these primary hubs are the cities which are the preeminent economic and political centers of the region, although in the case of Thebes, which was in a poor state in Pausanias' day, the conclusion is inescapable that mythological and historical considerations play a major role.[11] In the case of Delphi and Olympia it is clearly a religious preeminence, instead of – or in addition to – a secular one, that makes them the focus of Pausanias' scheme.

Although we have seen that the shape Pausanias' topography takes can occasionally be influenced by the physical geography of the region he is describing, as in Achaea, just as often Pausanias constructs his network of routes in a way that disregards geographical barriers and natural paths of communication. We saw this with the routes to the inland Free Lakonian cities in Book 4, but the best example comes in the description of Phokis, a territory split into two essentially separate parts by the huge massif of Parnassos. Nothing could make less sense from the point of view of geography or ease of travel than to tie the description of the entire territory to a single center at Delphi, yet that is precisely what Pausanias does, since for his intents and purposes Delphi *is* the center of Phokis, and it is the

---

[11] Cf. Musti 1988.

connection to Delphi that gives the various cities and peoples of Phokis the unity that nature would deny them.

SUB-TERRITORIES

A different sort of obstacle that Pausanias' itineraries must negotiate is the pattern of sub-territories (or "districts," to use Frazer's terminology) within the larger territories each book comprises. These smaller territories are usually those of an ancient or contemporary *polis*, and their boundaries usually (though not always) limit the extent of Pausanias' itineraries from any given hub. As we saw above in the description of the Mantineian sub-territory, for instance, Pausanias carefully traces each route from the city and stops when he gets to the boundary of the neighboring sub-territory. It is only when he intends to leave Mantineia for good that his description finally crosses the boundary line on its way to the next hub. This is the radial plan in its most pristine form, covering the sub-territory comprehensively, and prudently refraining from taking on anything beyond the borders before that task is finished. Another important effect these sub-territories have on the shape of Pausanias' itineraries, however, occurs at the transition between one sub-territory and the next. Frequently, Pausanias will trace a route up to the border of the land of a *polis*, and then interrupt the topographical series he has been following to introduce and discuss the new territory as a whole. It is often here that he inserts a *logos* outlining the history of the city, and sometimes he mentions important monuments, sites, and shrines in separate parts of the territory, with no topographical connection between them. For instance, in the ninth book he traces a route from Thebes to the Euripos, and then turns to the east and mentions a shrine of Mykalessian Demeter and the site of Aulis (9.18.3.–19.6). This brings him to the frontier of the territory of Tanagra. The next site, Delion, he introduces with the following words (9.20.1): "There is in Tanagran territory on the sea a place called Delion" (ἔστι δὲ τῆς Ταναγραίας ἐπὶ θαλάσσῃ καλούμενον Δήλιον). The only topographical indication he gives is that Delion is "by the sea"; he does not mention the fact that Delion lies at the opposite end of the Tanagran coast from the last site mentioned, Aulis.[12] After Delion, Pausanias mentions some other sites in Tanagran territory – the tomb of Orion, Mount Kerykion and a place called Polos – again with no topographical transitions (9.20.3). Pausanias does not resume the topographical thread until he is describing a series of shrines within the city itself (9.22.1).

[12] Delion is usually identified with the modern Delesi; see Pritchett 1980: 27–30; J. Fossey 1988: 62–66.

Such interruptions of the topographical sequence are not uncommon at the boundaries of sub-territories. To take another example from Book 9, the only topographical transition that Pausanias makes between his descriptions of Orchomenos and Lebadeia is that their territories are contiguous to one another (9.39.1), and at the same time he defines the territory of Orchomenos in relation to Phokis: "In the direction of the mountains the Phocians live beyond the Orchomenians; but in the plain Lebadeia shares a border with them" (τὰ μὲν δὴ πρὸς τῶν ὀρῶν Φωκεῖς ὑπεροικοῦσιν Ὀρχομενίων, ἐν δὲ τῷ πεδίῳ Λεβάδειά ἐστιν αὐτοῖς ὅμορος). These examples serve to show that the sub-territory is an important organizational unit for Pausanias, and that at the beginning of his description of a sub-territory, unusual things can happen. Particularly at such points in Pausanias' itineraries, no topographical sequence can be assumed if none is expressly stated.

A CASE-STUDY: BOOK 2

To illustrate better how various factors can combine to influence the way Pausanias designs his itineraries, we will now take a more detailed look at a single book. Book 2 is ideal for this purpose, since the territory it describes is not dominated by a single site, nor is it void of famous and flourishing cities and sanctuaries (see Figure 3.3). It contains a combination of just about every type of itinerary (and every type of problem) that we can observe in the other books.

As was mentioned in the previous chapter, Book 2 presents Pausanias with special problems of its own. The major cities of the territory, Corinth, Argos, Sikyon, Aigina, Troizen, etc., had a tradition of independence, and most of them, at one point in history or another, were among the leading cities of Greece. If, as we observed in the cases of Book 3 and Book 9, Pausanias uses his networks of itineraries to establish hierarchies between sites as well as to connect and separate cities for historical or cultural reasons, how can he construct a network of routes that respects the distinct identities of the cities of Book 2 while maintaining a sense of order and structure to his narrative?

THE WAY TO CORINTH

As we saw in Chapter 3, the subject of Book 2 is, strictly speaking, the territory Pausanias calls Argeia.[13] The first sentence of the book tells us

---

[13] See above, 69–72.

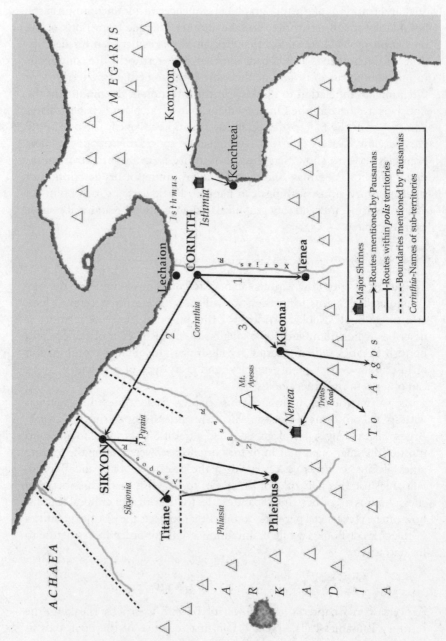

Figure 4.5. Pausanias' routes from the primary hub of Corinth in Book 2.

that Pausanias is about to embark upon the description of one of the sub-territories of this region, namely Corinthia: ἡ δὲ Κορινθία χώρα μοῖρα οὖσα τῆς Ἀργείας . . . (2.1.1). After a brief mythological and historical introduction (2.1.2–3), he begins describing sites in Corinthia, starting with the first village in Corinthian territory on the road from Athens: "in Corinthian land is a place called Kromyon" (2.1.3). From Kromyon, the place where Theseus killed the sow Phaia on his way to Athens, he begins a brief topographical thread comprising a pine tree and an altar of Melikertes. Thanks to the mythological associations, and to references to Kromyon in other sources, we can locate these places along the coast of the Saronic gulf, and thereby determine that Pausanias is in fact continuing the coastal road from Megaris.[14] After reaching the altar of Melikertes, we have apparently arrived at what Pausanias considered to be the Isthmus; the next item in the description, the place where Sinis (another one of Theseus' adversaries) used to attach his victims to bent pine trees in order to rend them asunder, is introduced with the words "at the beginning of the Isthmus" (ἐπὶ τοῦ ἰσθμοῦ τῆς ἀρχῆς) (2.1.4). At this point, however, whatever topographical sequence Pausanias is following, whether implicit or explicit, is broken temporarily. The mention of Sinis elicits from Pausanias a single sentence describing in general the deeds of Theseus. This sentence seems to round off and conclude this brief introductory stretch of coastal sites, and Pausanias next turns his attention to the Isthmus itself.

The Isthmus, in a peculiar way, seems to function almost as a sub-territory in its own right. Pausanias first delimits its extent on both sides: "the Isthmus of the Corinthians extends on the one side to the sea at Kenchreai, on the other to the sea at Lechaion, for this is what makes the land within it part of the continent" (2.1.5). Then, as he had done for the Corinthian territory as a whole, he adds a brief digression on the history and myth of the Isthmus, including the effort to drive a canal through it (by Nero, although Pausanias does not deign to mention his name) and the legendary competition for Corinthia between Poseidon and Helios, a competition which ended with Poseidon being awarded the Isthmus (2.1.5–6). This latter story provides a transition to Pausanias' description of the sanctuary of Poseidon at Isthmia.[15] The beginning of the description of the sanctuary is an odd one in many respects. After telling about the adjudication of the quarrel between Poseidon and Helios, he says: "They say that from this point the Isthmus was Poseidon's; worth seeing here are a theater and a

---

[14] For the location of Krom(m)yon, see Wiseman 1978: 17–19.

[15] I should point out that "Isthmia" as a toponym seems unknown to Pausanias; he describes the famous sanctuary as merely part of the "Isthmus."

stadium of marble. As one goes up to the shrine (ἱερόν) of the god . . ."
(2.1.6–7). The theater and the stadium are doubtless the ones connected
with the shrine, but they are presented in no particular topographical order
and in no explicit relationship to the shrine itself.

After his description of what there is to see in the shrine of Poseidon, Pausanias then turns his attention to the harbors of Corinthia, and once again
deals with them out of topographical sequence. First, he mentions Lechaion
and some points of interest there, then Kenchreai (2.2.3). In introducing
his description of the sights of Kenchreai, he does give a topographical
location for a temple of Artemis, not from the point of view of one coming
from Lechaion, but instead for those arriving "on the road to Kenchreai
. . . from the Isthmus" (2.2.3). After this section on the harbors, Pausanias
finally approaches the city of Corinth itself with the words "for those going
up to Corinth" (ἀνιοῦσι δὲ ἐς Κόρινθον) (2.2.4).

As we can see, this approach to Corinth from the Megarian frontier is a
good deal more complicated than one would expect from Frazer's characterization of the standard method. Pausanias may well have "proceed[ed] from
the frontier to the capital by the nearest road," but he gives no explicit indication of following any particular road consistently. As we have seen in cases
from other books, the beginning of a sub-territory is a place where Pausanias
frequently allows other considerations to take precedence over topographical precision. Here at the beginning of his treatment of Corinthia, these
other considerations include mythological and historical associations of the
territory, and a desire to illustrate its unique and significant geographical
situation. This, I take it, is the point of treating both of the Corinthian
harbors together instead of as points on separate itineraries: Corinth's out-
lets to both seas constitute one of the city's most essential and remarkable
features. This introduction to Corinthia is further complicated by the presence of the Isthmus, a noteworthy geographical feature in its own right,
one that has its own connections to myth and history and serves as home
to an important religious sanctuary. In all, Pausanias' introduction to the
sub-territory of Corinth is one of the best examples of the difficulties that
can occur when Pausanias' desire to give an overview of an important region
conflicts with the linear progression of his standard itineraries.

Given this as an introduction, when it comes to Pausanias' approach
to the city itself, one might legitimately ask the following question: When
Pausanias says "for those going up to Corinth," from what place is Pausanias'
itinerary "going up" toward the city? It is usually assumed that he is arriving
from Kenchreai, since that is the last place he mentions before coming
to the city; but Pausanias does not state that this or any other place is

his starting-point, and by this time the topographical thread, which was never very strong to begin with, has been broken twice by sections of non-linear description, first of the Isthmus, and then of the harbors. There is no reason to assume that Pausanias has suddenly decided to begin a topographical ordering from this spot. If Pausanias has any sense that his readers might expect him to proceed to the capital by the shortest route, then perhaps we should understand Pausanias to describe a direct route to the city from the Megarian border. The most convenient route from the eastern side of the Isthmus to Corinth in antiquity may well have joined the road to Kenchreai before reaching the city,[16] but correlation of this passage with archaeological remains need not be constrained by the premise that Pausanias was following either of these two roads. On his route up to the city, Pausanias mentions a number of monuments, including the tomb of Diogenes the Cynic, and a grove called Kraneion (2.2.4). So far, no solid evidence of these monuments has been uncovered, and one reason may be that archaeologists have typically focused their attention on the south-eastern portion of the city, where the road from Kenchreai is believed to have crossed the lines of the city walls.

ROUTES FROM CORINTH

After his description of Corinth itself, which ends on the citadel of Acrocorinth (2.5.1–4), Pausanias describes three itineraries departing from the city. The first apparently remains within the sub-territory of Corinth, while the second passes beyond the borders of Corinthia and encompasses the territories of Sikyon and Phleious. The third route quickly heads out of Corinthia toward the next primary hub at Argos.

The first road from Corinth is a "mountainous" route (ὀρεινήν), starting from the Teneatic gate, apparently on or near Acrocorinth, and leading to the place called Tenea which Pausanias says is 60 stadia distant. Tenea has not been identified with certainty, but is often linked to a site with some ancient remains lying near the modern town of Klenia, south of Corinth in the upper valley of the Xerias river.[17] If this identification is correct, then Pausanias' figure of 60 stadia is fairly accurate. It is interesting to note

---

[16] The complete courses of ancient routes in the area of the Isthmus cannot be known for sure, but extrapolations can be made from the location of ancient settlements and monuments, traces of roadway uncovered in excavation (such as those at the Isthmian sanctuary; see *Isthmia* II, 87–89), and the position of city gates at Corinth. Some of this evidence will be examined more closely in the next chapter. In general, see Wiseman 1978: 64–74.

[17] Wiseman 1978: 92.

that this is the first stadion measurement Pausanias has given in the second book. Characteristically, he gives it for the route which the fewest readers are likely to follow. The route up the Xerias valley actually continues over the mountains to provide an alternative route to the area of Argos,[18] but Pausanias betrays no knowledge of the route beyond Tenea.

The next route from Corinth accommodates "those going from Corinth not to the inland but on the road toward Sikyon" (2.5.5).[19] In his city description of Corinth, Pausanias had already described things to see on this road within the city limits (2.3.6–4.5). He returns to it now to describe its extra-urban course on the way to Sikyon, which is the next important hub. After mentioning a burnt temple "not far from the city" (οὐ πόρρω τῆς πόλεως), he brings the reader directly to the boundary of Sikyonia and begins his introduction of the new sub-territory: "The Sikyonians – for they are the Corinthians' neighbors in these parts . . ." (2.5.6). There follows a long excursus on the mythical and historical background of the Sikyonian land and people (2.5.6–7.2) – an excursus much longer than the one devoted to Corinthia – after which he apparently picks up the same route (2.7.2). Strabo says that the border between Sikyonia and Corinthia was the Nemea river (8.6.25), and we have no reason to suspect that this was not true in Pausanias' day.[20] For his part, Pausanias does not mention what forms the actual border, but the first monument he describes in Sikyonia, a tomb of a certain Lykos the Messenian (2.7.2), must have been well beyond the Nemea river, as the subsequent itinerary shows. The next item on the route is the Olympion, which is located "on the right for those who have already crossed the Asopos after the tomb of Lykos" (2.7.3). The Asopos is parallel to the Nemea river, and runs along the eastern side of the site of Sikyon itself. The sights beyond the Asopos follow a clear and (as far as we can tell) straightforward topographical ordering: a little bit beyond the Olympion on the left of the road is the tomb of the Athenian comic playwright Eupolis; this is followed by another private tomb and a communal tomb for Sikyonian war heroes (2.7.4), and finally, next to the city gate is a spring called Stazousa.

In contrast to the route to Corinth, a single route leads up to the city of Sikyon, with landmarks along the way carefully located in relation to one another. Here, the boundary of the sub-territory does not notice-ably interrupt the topographical sequence, despite the length of the myth-historical introduction that the border-crossing inspires. In these respects,

---

[18] The so-called *Kontoporeia*; cf. Pikoulas 1995: 276–283.
[19] ἐκ Κορίνθου δὲ οὐκ ἐς μεσόγαιαν ἀλλὰ τὴν ἐπὶ Σικυῶνα ἰοῦσι . . .
[20] On the borders of Sikyonia, see Lolos 1998.

the approach to Sikyon is far more straightforward than the approach to Corinth. There are, however, some anomalies worth noting. As we have seen, the tomb of Lykos and the Olympion were on the city side of the Asopos, and consequently so were the other monuments which Pausanias seems to locate in its vicinity. Since the last monument Pausanias mentions in Corinthia, the burnt temple, is also not far from its city, we can conclude that for most of the journey between the city walls of Corinth and those of Sikyon, a distance of some 15 kilometers, Pausanias does not mention a single site or monument, nor does he give any indication of the distance.

At this point, the description of the city of Sikyon intervenes. When Pausanias resumes his investigation of the countryside, he begins with two routes to the south (2.11.3): first comes the road which he says is the direct one from Sikyon to Phleious (ἐκ Σικυῶνος ... τὴν κατ᾽ εὐθὺ ἐς Φλιοῦντα), which he follows for an unspecified distance to a grove called Pyraia. The second route, the route to Titane, is one that Pausanias describes in great detail. He says it is 60 stadia to Titane and the road is "impassable to yoke-teams because of its narrowness." Each of the two routes to the south heads in the direction of the neighboring territory of Phleious, but Pausanias follows neither of them beyond the border at this time. After describing Titane and its sanctuary of Asklepios, Pausanias begins a third route at Sikyon which proceeds northward toward the sea, and leads him to the Sikyonian harbor. From the harbor, he turns "toward Aristonautai, the harbor of the Pelleneans," which is the first significant settlement beyond Sikyonian territory to the west. This route ends at the Sythas river. In Book 7, we learn that the Sythas river was the border between Sikyonia and Achaea (7.27.12). Pausanias does not mention that fact here.

Pausanias' exploration of the Sikyonian sub-territory is now complete, and at this point he turns to the territory of Phleious. Immediately upon completing his route to the Achaean frontier, he begins a new section as follows (2.12.3): "Phliasia borders upon the land of the Sikyonians." Instead of tracing a completely new route from Sikyon, Pausanias informs us that the two routes to the south, the ones whose courses within Sikyonia he has already explored, lead to the city of Phleious: "The city [of the Phliasians] lies about forty stadia from Titane, but there is a direct road to it from Sikyon." Phliasia is the last of the places that Pausanias visits from the secondary hub of Sikyon. On the whole, the Sikyonian itineraries follow the classic radial plan to a high degree. All the routes within the sub-territory of Sikyon are exhausted before the *Periegesis* moves on to Phliasia. The manner in which Pausanias first mentions the routes to Phleious but does not follow them beyond the border is similar to the examples we noted in the itineraries at Pheneos and Orchomenos in Arkadia.

THE WAY OUT OF CORINTHIA

Immediately after the description of Phliasia we find Pausanias back at the primary hub, Corinth, tracing another route, this time to Argos. This is the route by which Pausanias' *Periegesis* leaves Corinthia for good. There was more than one way to get to Argos from Corinth. The route Pausanias chooses to describe on this occasion passes through the small city of Kleonai, west of Corinth: "For one proceeding from Corinth to Argos there is Kleonai, a city of no great size" (2.15.1). From Kleonai, there are two routes south toward Argos, and Pausanias comments on the quality of both (2.15.2): "The one is for well-girt men and is short, the other, upon [the mountain] called Tretos, is also narrow, surrounded as it is by mountains, but is nevertheless better suited for vehicles." Pausanias' next directions are slightly vague but apparently refer to the second of these two routes: "In these mountains," he says, the cave of the Nemean lion is still shown to visitors, and "the place called Nemea is about 15 stadia distant." The lion's cave cannot be located with certainty, but Pausanias' pass through the Tretos is usually identified with the Dervenaki pass, through which a modern highway also travels.[21] Having detoured from this route to Nemea, Pausanias briefly describes the dilapidated sanctuary there, the traditional home of the panhellenic Nemean games,[22] and comments on a nearby natural landmark: "Mount Apesas is above Nemea; here they say Perseus was the first to sacrifice to Zeus Apesantios." It is interesting that Pausanias chooses to mention Mt. Apesas (modern Foukas), a prominent table-topped mountain, at this point. From several earlier spots in Pausanias' itinerary, it would have been a prominent site, and in fact the site of ancient Kleonai is located on its eastern flanks. The reason that Pausanias delays mention of it until his description of Nemea may be that from the floor of the Nemea valley the view of Mt. Foukas is particularly impressive. It may also be because the mountain, like the sanctuary, is sacred to Zeus. Pausanias tells us that Perseus was the first to sacrifice to Zeus Apesantios, and we know from other sources that there was a cult of Zeus located on the summit.[23]

---

[21] See Frazer 1898: 85–87; Pikoulas 1995: 56–59, 273–276.
[22] On Pausanias' description of Nemea, see Sutton 2001.
[23] *Etym. Mag. s.v.* ἀφέσιος; St. Byz., *s.v.* ἀπέσας.

After his description of Nemea, Pausanias gives the first clear indication that his itinerary is following the route over Tretos: "For those ascending to Tretos and going again on the road to Argos. . ." (2.15.4). Then, without indicating that the road has come out of the pass or reached the Argive plain, he says that the ruins of Mycenae are on the left. The first mention of Mycenae launches Pausanias on a lengthy narration of traditions relating to the foundation of the city and the fifth-century destruction of it by the Argives (2.15.4–16.5). To some extent, this passage, inserted at the point where Pausanias' itinerary makes its entrance into the Argive plain, serves as an introductory *logos* for the entire Argolid. It includes the stories of the eponymous heroes Inachos and Argos, as well as that of Danaos, Akrisios, and Perseus. A brief description of the ruins of Mycenae follows (2.16.5).

At this point, Pausanias adopts the point of view of someone proceeding from Mycenae toward the plain. First, a side-route takes him to the Argive Heraion: "On the left of Mycenae the Heraion is 15 stadia away" (2.17.1). The fact that Pausanias describes the Heraion (located south of Mycenae) as being "on the left of Mycenae" shows that the general direction of his itinerary has shifted toward the west. When he is done describing the sanctuary of Hera, Pausanias begins another route from Mycenae toward Argos, or perhaps more likely continues the same route from which he diverged to visit the Heraion (2.18.1). In the course of this route, Pausanias lists a series of sites and monuments in an explicit topographical sequence: "for those going from Mycenae to Argos on the left beside the road," there is a shrine of Perseus; "a little beyond this shrine . . . on the right" is the grave of Thyestes; "for those going a little further," past the grave, "there is on the left" a place called Mysia and a shrine of Demeter Mysia; "for those going further," there is the river Inachos; "for those who have crossed" the river there is an altar of Helios, and finally "from here you will come to a gate named after the nearby shrine; the shrine belongs to Eileithyia" (2.18.1–3).[24] Having thus arrived at the city wall, Pausanias presents the traditional history of Argos down to the last of its kings (2.18.4–19.2), and then begins the city description with the sanctuary of Apollo Lykios in the Agora (2.19.3).

In its careful enumeration of the monuments one encounters on the way to the city, Pausanias' approach to Argos is similar to his description of the route toward Sikyon. However, it also shares certain characteristics with

---

[24] It is interesting to note that the last site Pausanias mentions in the city of Corinth is another shrine of Eileithyia near the Teneatic gate (2.5.4). If Pausanias' reputation for literary subtlety weren't so low, one might be tempted to call this some form of ring-composition.

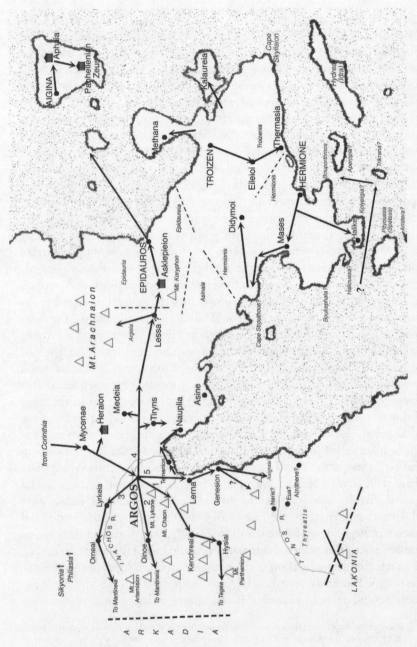

Figure 4.6. Pausanias' routes in the Argolid. The boundaries that Pausanias mentions between *polis*-territories are indicated with dotted lines.

the beginning of the description of Corinthia. In Corinthia, the Isthmus and its attendant antiquities stood directly athwart Pausanias' introductory route, and his efforts to do justice to the Isthmus bring about some complications in his itinerary. Here on the way to Argos, Pausanias is similarly faced with a site of major interest to him, Mycenae, at the very beginning of his treatment of the Argive territory. In this case, the topographical thread is not completely broken by the side-trip to Mycenae, but the route Pausanias traces to Argos is not direct, and his narrative of Mycenaean history seems to take the place of a more general treatment of Argive history. It also seems to cause him to omit any reference to the fact that his itinerary has entered Argive territory.

ROUTES FROM ARGOS

When he has finished the city description, Pausanias begins a new section of his *Periegesis* with the following sentence: "There are roads from Argos leading to many places in the Peloponnesos, including, in the direction of Arkadia, to Tegea" (2.24.5). With this sentence, Argos is being announced as the second and final primary hub in Book 2. In all, Pausanias will describe five routes from Argos to various parts of Argolis, beginning with a route toward Tegea to the southwest, then proceeding in clockwise fashion to describe a westerly route and a northwesterly route (both leading to the frontier of Arkadian territory) then a route to the east which encompasses the entire eastern Argolid, and finally a route to the south which passes through Lerna and heads to the frontier of Lakonia. This last route, which brings the Argive itineraries to an end, also takes us to the end of Book 2.

The fact that Pausanias begins this network of roads with the route toward Tegea may be no accident. Of all the roads that led to and from Argos in Pausanias' time, the two most important and heavily traveled were doubtlessly the highway heading north toward Corinth and the Isthmus (the route upon which Pausanias entered the Argive plain), and the highway heading south toward Tegea and beyond Tegea to Lakonia, Megalopolis and Olympia. The evidence for the course of this latter road has been collected and discussed by Pritchett and Pikoulas.[25] It probably departed from the southern part of the city, turned inland near the springs of Kefalari, crossed the easternmost reaches of the Ktenias range, descended into the valley of the modern Xavrio river and went by the dilapidated hinterland

---

[25] Pritchett 1980: 54–77; Pikoulas 1995: 134–49, 297–299.

town of Hysiai near present-day Achladokampos. In describing this route, Pausanias draws an unusual amount of attention to the mountains that the route passes directly south of the city. First Mt. Lykone, directly south-west of the Argive citadel, which had a sanctuary of Artemis Orthia on it (2.24.5). The second mountain, Chaon, is "a little farther away on the right of the road" (2.24.6). At its foot, Pausanias notes some cultivated trees and says: "Here the water of the Erasinos comes up to the surface." The Erasinos river is generally identified with the modern Kefalari, which issues from the base of a mountain some 5 kilometers south of Argos.[26]

The next two routes Pausanias traces from the city also head inland toward Arkadia.[27] The first heads in a roughly westerly direction toward Mantineia, and Pausanias carefully specifies that this is not the same road as the one to Tegea, and that it departs from the gate beside the Deiras (2.25.1). This gate probably stood on the saddle between the Larissa (the Argive acropolis) and the lower round hill to the north of the city commonly (and incorrectly) referred to as Aspis.[28] After describing what there is to see on that route, Pausanias returns to Argos and describes a second route from the Deiras gate toward Lyrkeia and Orneai, sites which apparently lie in the Inachos valley northwest of Argos (2.25.4–6). Lyrkeia was in ruins in Pausanias' day. All Pausanias finds there, besides some things that he considers "not worth mentioning" (οὐκ ἀξιόλογα), is a single sculpted stele. Almost as an afterthought, Pausanias tells us that Lyrkeia is 60 stadia from Argos, the first distance figure he has included since 2.15.2, where he tells us how far it is from Mycenae to the Heraion. This information also serves as a transition from Lyrkeia to Orneai; Pausanias says that Orneai is a further 60 stadia from Lyrkeia (2.25.5). Having described the handful of shrines and sanctuaries that were in Orneai, Pausanias concludes this section by locating Orneai in a more extended geographical context: "the lands beyond Orneai are Sikyonia and Phliasia" (2.25.6), an observation that also serves to round off his exploration of the western and northern limits of Argive territory through his first three itineraries from the city. The eastern and southern parts of the territory remain.

---

[26] See Frazer 1898: 3.210–211 for description and references from earlier travelers.

[27] For the location of these routes and the sites along them, see Pritchett 1980: 1–53; Pikoulas 1989; Pikoulas 1995: 288–296.

[28] For arguments that the "Aspis" was located elsewhere, see Lambrinoudakis 1969–1970: 47–72; Croissant, 1972: 137–154. Piérart 1982: 139–152.

GRAND TOUR OF THE EASTERN ARGOLID

At this point, we arrive at one of the more peculiar features of the organization of Book 2. Most of the eastern Argolid is traversed by a single extended itinerary which Pausanias now embarks upon, following the road "from Argos to Epidauria" (2.25.7). The first sight he mentions on this route is a pyramidal monument alleged to be a common tomb for those who died in the legendary battle between Akrisios and Proitos. This monument is apparently quite close to the city, for after it Pausanias mentions a side-road to Tiryns heading off to the right of the main road (2.25.8).[29] After commenting on Tiryns' history and its Cyclopean walls, Pausanias continues this side-route toward the sea (καταβάντων . . . ὡς ἐπὶ θάλασσαν) and notices a monument which he identifies as the bedrooms (θάλαμοι) of the daughters of Proitos (2.25.9). At this point, Pausanias must be quite close to the site of Nauplia, but he refrains from mentioning Nauplia for the time being. From Tiryns, Pausanias' route returns to the main road (λεωφόρος) and brings the reader past the conspicuous bronze-age citadel of Medeia, which lies on the left side of the road. After mentioning Medeia, which was in ruins already in his day, Pausanias returns again to his original route, the straight road to Epidauros (τὴν ἐς Ἐπίδαυρον εὐθεῖαν), and comes next to the village (κώμη) of Lessa (2.25.10). Pausanias makes mention here of the massive mountain that looms over the eastern Argolid, Mount Arachnaion, saying that it lies "above Lessa," and on Arachnaion are altars of Zeus and Hera where the natives sacrifice when they need rain. In going from Medeia to Lessa, Pausanias' itinerary has once again made something of an unheralded leap. Medeia lies on the eastern edge of the Argive plain, and while Pausanias' Lessa has not been identified, the best candidate is the site of the modern town of Ligourio, where numerous signs of antiquity have been found. Just by reading Pausanias' description, one might expect to find oneself in Lessa soon after leaving Medeia, but in fact Ligourio is over twenty kilometers from Medeia over complicated terrain.

THE EPIDAURIAN SUB-TERRITORY

On arriving at Lessa, Pausanias identifies this spot as being the boundary between Argeia and the land of the Epidaurians (2.26.1). Once again,

---

[29] For adequate refutation of the highly unlikely notion (Kelly 1976: 85–86) that the monument mentioned by Pausanias is the pyramidal structure near modern Ligourio (some 25 kilometers east of Tiryns), see Pritchett 1980: 69–74.

Pausanias finds himself in a complicated situation as he enters a new sub-territory: what interests him most about the territory of Epidauros is not the city itself but the famous Asklepieion which lies within it, and which anyone following the natural course of Pausanias' itinerary would encounter before arriving at the city: "Before reaching the city itself you will come to the sanctuary of Asklepios" (2.26.1). At this point, Pausanias delivers a *logos* which begins with narration of the traditions about the early inhabitants of Epidaureia down to the arrival of the Dorians under Deiphontes (2.26.1–2). Soon, however, the focus of the narrative shifts to how the land became sacred to Asklepios, and this *logos* serves as a more specific introduction to the god's sanctuary (2.26.3–10), which Pausanias then proceeds to describe (2.27.1–7). The description of the Asklepieion ends with a mention of the mountains which surround it, Titthion and Kynortion, the latter being the site of the sanctuary of Apollo Maleatas (2.27.7). Finally, Pausanias takes the reader up toward yet another mountain, Koryphon, and on the way points out the so-called "Twisted Olive," and a sanctuary of Artemis on the peak of the mountain. About the Twisted Olive, Pausanias adds the intriguing information that he tried to discover whether Herakles set it there to mark the boundary of the Asinaians, but could not find the answer due to depopulation and the resulting scarcity of reliable informants. This passage attests to Pausanias' curiosity about boundaries and matters of pure geography, an interest he rarely expresses directly. Also, this passage serves as an engaging coda to round off Pausanias' description of the Asklepieion and its environs.

Immediately after this, Pausanias resumes the main road leading down to the city. First, he comes to "a place (χωρίον) where wild olives have grown" called Hyrnethion (2.28.3). This place is named after Hyrnetho, the daughter of Temenos and wife of Deiphontes, who was responsible for Doricizing the territory. Pausanias takes this opportunity to relate the story of her sad fate and how she came to give her name to the place (2.28.3–7). This tale recalls and continues the introductory *logos* of the territory from where he had left it before describing the Asklepieion (2.26.2), and thus provides an effective introduction to the city of the Epidaurians. This approach to Epidauros provides the third example of what seems to be a recurring pattern in the second book: a major point of interest lying within the sub-territory of a city directly in line with Pausanias' main route to the city. In this case, the attraction of the Asklepieion prevents Pausanias from proceeding directly to the "capital" of the territory, and it causes a fragmentation of his introductory *logos*, much as Mycenae did in the case of the territory of Argos.

AIGINA

After the brief city description of the city of Epidauros itself (2.29.1), Pausanias turns to the island of Aigina, which he locates "opposite Epidaureia" (2.29.2: ἀπαντικρὺ τῆς Ἐπιδαυρίας). Aigina is the most important island that Pausanias includes in the *Periegesis*, and the only one he describes in any detail. Following a myth-historical introduction (2.29.2–5) and the description of the city (2.29.6–30.2), Pausanias sketches a single route through the island. On this route he seems to make a slight error or misstatement: the temple of Aphaia, is "on the way to the mountain of Zeus Panhellenios" (2.30.3). Zeus Panhellenios is without doubt the conical peak, nowadays called simply "Oros" (Mountain), which towers above the southern half of the island. Remains of the sanctuary of Zeus Panhellenios are easily visible on its northern face. Meanwhile, the well-known temple of Aphaia, which has been identified by inscription, stands in the northeast corner of the island. The only way that the temple could be considered "on the way" to the mountain of Zeus from the city is if the route encompassed the entire circuit of the island on the north and east sides. This may indeed have been the way Pausanias traveled, but it is certainly not the most direct way to the mountain. Either Pausanias' description is exceedingly opaque, or he misremembered the route when he was writing his final account. One might suspect that Pausanias was writing without personal knowledge of the terrain, but he claims to have performed a sacrifice at the sanctuary of Zeus (2.30.4), and if he actually traveled up to the mountain he most likely would be aware that he did not pass a temple dedicated to Aphaia along the way.

THE SUB-TERRITORY OF TROIZEN

The side-trip to Aigina seems to have interrupted the topographical thread of Pausanias' main route. When Pausanias moves on to Troizenia, the territory which lies on the northern side of the eastern tip of the Argolid, he does not describe it from the perspective of one sailing there from Aigina, nor does he explicitly trace a land route from Epidauros; instead, he simply says: "The Troizenians are adjacent to Epidaureia" (2.30.5: τῆς δὲ Ἐπιδαυρίας ἔχονται Τροιζήνιοι). At this point, we can see that Pausanias has, for the time being, abandoned his practice of tracing routes from hub to hub. The entire territory of Epidaureia serves as a reference point, first for the location of Aigina and now for Troizenia. As we have seen, this is a method that he does use elsewhere, as when he locates the territory of

Lebadeia with respect to that of the Orchomenians in Boiotia (9.39.1), but it is a fairly rare practice. It is difficult to say why Pausanias treats Troizenia in this unorthodox way. Perhaps it is simply to introduce some variety into what has become a very extended itinerary from Argos, or perhaps it reflects on the limits of Pausanias' personal familiarity with the territory. It could be, in other words, that Pausanias does not describe a land route from Epidauros to Troizen (or a sea route from Aigina to Troizen) because he never traveled that way when he went to Troizen. This idea, of course, could never be more than speculation, but we shall soon see other cases in the eastern Argolid where the degree of Pausanias' personal familiarity with the area is at issue.

Continuing with unusual methods of description, Pausanias follows no route at all into the city of Troizen; after a complete myth-historical introduction (2.30.5–10), he launches directly into his city description, beginning with the agora (2.30.10–31.1). After the city description, Pausanias' treatment of the sub-territory proceeds without topographical ordering, in a manner reminiscent of the way he treated the demes, mountains, and islands of Attica: first, the islands Hiera and Kalaureia (2.33.1–2), then the peninsula of Methana, which Pausanias describes as "an isthmus in Troizenian territory sticking out into the sea a long way" (τῆς . . . Τροιζηνίας γῆς . . . ἰσθμὸς ἐπὶ πολὺ διέχων ἐς θάλασσαν) (2.34.1). Although it is the last of the land-forms Pausanias describes in Troizenia, Methana is actually closer to Epidauria than anything he has mentioned so far. With the territory of Troizenia, Pausanias has reached the easternmost point on his grand tour of the eastern Argolid, and the methods he uses in describing this sub-territory are as unusual as any in the *Periegesis*.

THE SUB-TERRITORY OF HERMIONE

The next territory Pausanias deals with on his eastern Argolid tour is Hermionis, which occupies the southern part of the eastern tip of the Argolid and the small peninsula projecting south toward the island of Spetses.[30] At first, it seems as though Pausanias intends to continue using entire territories as reference points rather than tracing individual routes: "Within[31] the isthmus [of Methana], Hermione shares a border with the

---

[30] Pausanias seems to use the terms Hermionis and Hermione to refer to the territory of the *polis*, while he consistently calls the city itself Hermion.

[31] In this context, "within" (ἐντός) can only mean "on the far side of" (cf. Pausanias' usage in 2.1.5). This implies that Pausanias is visualizing the geographical situation from a western perspective – perhaps that of someone in Epidauros or Argos.

land of the Troizenians" (2.34.4). But then, after a relatively brief introductory *logos*, Pausanias does trace a route from the Rock of Theseus in
Troizen toward Hermionian territory. Here, Pausanias has actually reversed
his usual order of doing things; instead of tracing a route up to the border and then presenting the historical narrative for the new territory, he
locates the new territory using broad geographical reference points (within
the isthmus of Methana, bordering on Troizenia), tells its *logos*, and only
then begins tracing a route, most of the items of which are still, apparently, within Troizenian territory. On this route he ends up at a sanctuary
of Demeter Thermasia, which he locates "by the sea" (πρὸς θάλασσαν)
and "on the boundaries of Hermionis" (ἐν ὅροις τῆς Ἑρμιονίδος) (2.34.6).
Having finally arrived at the territory he introduced in the previous section, instead of turning west and continuing on to the city of Hermione,
Pausanias mentions that Cape Skyllaion is about 80 stadia away from the
shrine of Demeter (2.34.7). Skyllaion is apparently the same as the modern
Cape Skili, the easternmost point in Argolid territory, and by Pausanias' own
reckoning would be located in Troizenian territory (2.34.7). Quite unex-
pectedly, Pausanias next begins to describe a seaborne journey to Hermione
from Cape Skyllaion. This brief stretch of seagoing itinerary is fraught with
problems which will be discussed further at the end of this chapter.[32] For
now, it is suffices to say that Pausanias' approaches to the city of Hermione,
both by land and by sea, are somewhat unusual.

FROM HERMIONE TO ASINE

After his description of the city of Hermione, Pausanias proceeds to explore
the western part of the Hermionian peninsula and the coast of the Argolic
gulf. Here, in a territory that was largely deserted in his day, Pausanias'
descriptions of roads and distances become exceptionally precise: "for those
going along the direct road to Mases about 7 stadia and turning to the left
there is a road to Halike . . . mid-way between the Pron [mountain] and
another mountain called Thornax in ancient times" (2.36.1); "Beside [a
temple to Apollo by Mt. Thornax] there is a road to Mases for those who
have turned aside from the main road" (2.36.2). Mases was apparently
the western harbor of the Hermionians. Having reached the coast of the
Argolic gulf at Mases, he continues his rapid progress in a general westerly
direction: "From Mases there is a road on the right leading to a headland
called Strouthous" (2.36.3); "From this headland it is 250 stadia along the

peaks of the mountains to the place called Philanorion and to Boleoi . . .
and another place called Didymoi is 20 stadia distant from here" (2.36.3).

Pausanias' sudden propensity toward supplying information on distances
and direction is countered by a lack of almost any other details about what
there was to see in these places. His treatment of the western reaches of
Hermione is so sketchy that one might legitimately wonder if Pausanias is
describing these places from firsthand experience. A possible response to
such a suggestion might be that there was little to comment upon in these
remote and sparsely populated places; but then the question becomes, or
rather remains, why Pausanias includes them in his account in the first
place. It may be that he felt a need to enlarge upon the description of
Hermione, in order to make the description of the territory seem worthy
of the city. Or perhaps he simply wanted to add material that would bring
him closer to the next spot on his itinerary. In any case, Pausanias passes
on to the next sub-territory with the following words: "From here there
is the land once called Asinaia, which belongs to the Argives" (2.36.4).[33]
Pausanias has little to say about Asinaia, other than how it was conquered
and annexed by the Argives. The only topographical clue Pausanias gives
us as to the location of the deserted capital Asine is that it is "on the sea".
He does not mention the fact that in reaching Asine his itinerary has gone
full-circle and has, in fact, almost made it all the way back to the Argive
plain.

THE GRAND TOUR OF THE EASTERN ARGOLID: OBSERVATIONS

So ends this unusually long and complicated itinerary from the city of Argos.
There are other routes that cover a comparable amount of territory, as for
example the routes around the Malea and Taenaric peninsulas in Book 3,
but those routes are through territory that was generally sparsely inhabited
and void of major sites. By contrast, the eastern Argolid, though parts of
it were barren and depopulated, contained a major active sanctuary and
numerous important cities (Aigina, Troizen, Epidauros, Hermione) that
were important mythically and historically even if they were not politically
or economically significant in Pausanias' own day. Pausanias displays a
remarkable range of techniques along this route. While the description of
Epidaureia is fairly straightforward (aside from the complication caused by
the Asklepieion), and the treatment of Aigina hardly less so (aside from the

---

[33] τὸ δὲ ἐντεῦθέν ἐστιν Ἀργείων ἥ ποτε Ἀσιναία καλουμένη . . .

confusion over the location of the Aphaia temple), the descriptions of the remaining territories become progressively more idiosyncratic.

If we search for reasons why Pausanias chose to cover such a large and complex territory in a single extended route, we might surmise that he did it to emphasize the traditional preeminence of Argos.[34] All the territories on the route received the Dorian element of their population thanks to the activities of the Temenid dynasty of Argos. Perhaps even more importantly, all of the major and some of the minor cites on the itinerary, including Tiryns, Hermione, Asine, Troizen, Epidauros, Aigina, and Mases, are listed as being subject to Argos in Homer's Catalogue of Ships (*Iliad* 2.559–563). Another more mundane factor influencing the design of Pausanias' routes in this part of the Argolid may be the physical geography and the road patterns. The various sites on the western fringes of Argolis are serviced by separate roads running up the valleys which lie perpendicular to the main axis of the Argive plain. For nearly all the sites in the eastern Argolid, however, there is only one practical land route to take from the city, and that is the route that Pausanias describes (this would not, however, explain the inclusion of Asine on this route). If such practical considerations influenced the layout of Pausanias' itineraries, then perhaps we can see the variety of creative and unusually different methods he employs along this route as a strategy to make the extended succession of site after site seem less monotonous and predictable. One final possibility is that this is a faithful record of the route that Pausanias used the one and only time he ever traveled to these sites.

THE LAST ROUTE

There remains the final route from Argos, one that heads south toward Lerna and points beyond (2.36.6). Rivers predominate in the first part of this itinerary; as Pausanias heads down toward the sea he crosses first the Erasinos (2.36.6), whose sources he had visited earlier at the foot of Mt. Chaon, then the Phrixos, then the Cheimarros (2.36.7), and finally he reaches Lerna "by the sea" (πρὸς θαλάσσῃ). After describing the complex of springs, lakes, and sanctuaries associated with Lerna (2.36.8–37.6), Pausanias describes routes from Lerna leading along the seaboard in both directions. The first route runs along the northern shore of the Argolic gulf toward Temenion (2.38.1–2). When he reaches Temenion, he states that Nauplia is, in his opinion, 50 stadia away (2.38.2). Pausanias might have mentioned at this

[34] This is suggested by Piérart 2001.

point that Nauplia was also just a handful of stadia away from both Tiryns and Asine, which he had mentioned on his great route through the eastern Argolid, but he doesn't. The second route from Lerna heads south into Thyreatis.[35] Along the way, Pausanias encounters the site where the fabled Battle of the Champions was fought between the Argives and the Spartans; then he mentions three villages (κῶμαι), Anthene, Neris and Eua, in no explicit topographical order.[36] "Stretching beyond the villages," he says, is Mount Parnon and on it are the "borders of the Spartans in the direction of the Argives" (2.38.7). This sets the topographical stage for the beginning of Book 3.

SUMMATION OF BOOK 2

From this synopsis of the second book we can get some idea of the range of methods Pausanias can employ in his descriptions. On the large scale, the radial plan is quite in evidence: all roads lead to or from the primary hubs of Corinth and Argos. But the closer we look at any individual section of the *Periegesis*, the more variation we see. Topographical order may be abandoned for the description of sites within a sub-territory, as in Corinthia and Troizenia, or may be indicated with only vague connections, as in the case of the transition between Hermione and Asinaia. We should especially note the general lack of the monotonous litanies of sites and monuments that Frazer seems to envisage in his description of the radial plan; in only a few places, such as on the roads leading up to Argos and Sikyon, does Pausanias present a thick topographical chain of sites and objects. In his descriptions of sub-territories and individual routes, Pausanias is free to vary his methods and his focus, and he does so to great effect, emphasizing in one area the mountains, in another area the rivers and springs, and in other places the quality of the roads or the species of trees. He also varies the deployment of the mythical and historical *logoi* pertinent to the regions he is describing. In some places, as with Sikyon and Troizen, he

---

[35] Pritchett (1980: 102–142) proposes an emendation in the text at this point which would have Pausanias describing not one but two routes from Lerna into Thyreatis, the first the "narrow and . . . difficult" one along the coast and next one further inland over Mt. Zavitsa, which is where Pritchett would locate the site of the "Battle of the Champions." This suggestion makes good sense of the topography, and is completely consistent with Pausanias' practice as we have seen it in this book. Where Pausanias gives information on road quality, as he did for the roads from Sikyon to Phleious and from Kleonai to Argos, he is often distinguishing between two alternate routes. Cf. also Phaklares 1990: 209–212.

[36] For ideas about where these villages may have been located, see Pritchett 1980: 138–142; Phaklares 1990: 47–55, 96–104.

appends a full narrative to the first mention of a city or its territory. In other cases, such as in Corinthia, Argeia and Epidaureia, the *logoi* are postponed or fragmented in a way that allows them to be correlated to specific sites within the region. Also, the second book provides some excellent examples of the different ways sub-territories can operate as elemental units of the structure of the book: the Sikyonian sub-territory is handled in classic fashion, while that of Troizen is wholly idiosyncratic, and in Corinthia and Epidaureia we see variations on the standard pattern that can be explained as Pausanias' response to unique features that those territories possess.

Finally, it is worth emphasizing that Pausanias' arrangement of his itineraries and his presentation of information are not designed for the utmost benefit to travelers. Advice on "furlongs" is exceedingly rare, and there are many places where the most astute traveler would find himself lost if he had only Pausanias' text to go by. Considerations of balance, variation, history, and mythical traditions all go in the layout of his routes. At various places, Pausanias takes the time to mention springs, mountains, distances, road quality, vegetation, etc., but in what must be a deliberate attempt to avoid redundancy never gives the same ancillary information for two consecutive sites or places. In contrast, the fragmentary description of Athens and Boiotian cities by Herakleides Kritikos (which was mentioned in Chapter 1 and will be discussed further in Chapter 7), consistently supplies stadion measurements and road conditions for the approach to each of the cities that the author visits.

Rather than conforming to the exigencies of a practical guide, the *Periegesis* reflects Pausanias' capacity for seeing the landscape as an embodiment of mythistoric traditions. Marcel Piérart has commented on how the itineraries Pausanias traces through the Argolid replicate and respect the traditional dominance of Argos over the region, and also reflect the fact that most of the cities connected by the routes that emanate from Argos have traditional ties to that city; either they were subject-cities to the heroic kings Agamemnon and Diomedes or they acquired their Doric dialect and identity as Dorians from invaders or colonizers from Argos.[37] In a different but not incompatible reading, Domenico Musti has also drawn a parallel between the way Pausanias plans his routes from Argos in the latter half of Book 2 and the way his routes through Boiotia are appended (as we have seen, to an unusual degree) to the description of the city of Thebes. Musti suggests that this similarity reflects Pausanias' respect for the traditional tie between the two cities embodied in the myth of the Seven against Thebes,

---

[37] Piérart 2001.

in which a number of Argive heroes come to Thebes with the Theban royal claimant Polyneikes and battle for the city outside the same seven gates on which Pausanias anchors his Boiotian routes.[38]

From what we have seen so far, we can tell that Pausanias did not view his task to be as simple as fitting the information from each territory into a perfunctory and mechanical scheme. If we consider the amount of effort that he must have expended in putting together a description that was appropriate to each territory, perhaps we can look with more sympathy on certain aspects of his methods that seem odd or deficient from our perspective. One curious characteristic of Pausanias' methods, visible in the second book and elsewhere, is a noticeable tendency he has to focus his attention squarely on the itinerary he is following and to pay little regard to the surrounding countryside. Anthony Snodgrass vividly characterizes this element of Pausanias' itineraries: "The image that springs to mind is that of a man crossing a morass on lines of duckboards who does not venture on short cuts."[39] This tendency leads to some peculiar effects that deserve to be commented upon. In what might be called a sort of topographical tunnel vision, Pausanias rarely betrays any sense of spatial relationship *between* separate itineraries. It's as if each of the routes he traces in exploring the countryside of any given region exists in its own universe, completely isolated from other routes. This is in spite of the fact that the routes he traces often pass through adjoining territories and occasionally come within a few kilometers of each other. There are a number of curious examples of this in the second book. For instance, the sites of Phleious and Nemea lie less than 10 kilometers from each other, with only a modest mountain range between them. As we have seen, Pausanias approaches the former via a route originating from Sikyon to the north (2.12.2 ff.), while his visit to Nemea occurs as a detour from the main route he follows between Corinth and the Argive plain (2.15.2). Nowhere in his description of the two sites does he betray the slightest awareness of their proximity to each other. An even stranger example comes later in the book: Tiryns, Asine, and Nauplia are described in the course of what are essentially three different routes; Tiryns comes on a detour near the beginning of the route that encompasses the entire eastern Argolid (2.25.8), and Asine is the final site on that same

---

[38] Musti 1988. It must be noted, however, that Pausanias was strongly of the opinion that there were more than seven Argive heroes (2.20.5, a passage that will be discussed further in Chapter 8).
[39] Snodgrass 1987: 84.

Figure 4.7. From the site of Tiryns, the acropolis of ancient Nauplia – modern Nauplion –
is clearly visible (the lower of the two hills in the background). The site of Asine is a few
kilometers to the left of this photograph. Pausanias mentions the three sites at the
end-points of three separate routes.

extended route (2.36.4). Nauplia is the end-point of a completely separate
route starting from Lerna (2.38.2). Nowhere in Pausanias' text is there the
slightest indication that Asine is less than 10 kilometers from Nauplia, or
that Nauplia is less than 5 kilometers from Tiryns, or that the peninsula on
which Nauplia sits is clearly visible from the site of Tiryns. Imagine some
trusting ancient traveler using Pausanias as a guide and following his routes
carefully; he works his way through to the end of Book 2, diligently traces
the route from Lerna along the coast, and finds himself in the same lonely
corner of the Argive plain that he has already been in twice before. Then
imagine him tossing all ten scrolls of the *Periegesis* into the Argolic gulf. He
could hardly be blamed.

These examples typify what Snodgrass aptly calls Pausanias' "relentless
linearity."[40] From Pausanias' account, one gets a very detailed view of the
points of interest that lie within a narrow corridor along each roadway,
but often no view of how these slices of the landscape fit together to form
the larger landscape of the territory as a whole. Snodgrass, in commenting

[40] *Ibid.* Snodgrass himself produces another example of this tunnel vision from Book 9, involving the
sites of Haliartos and Onchestos (9.26.4; 9.32.5).

on this characteristic of Pausanias' narrative, rightly points out that this is a serious limitation on Pausanias' usefulness for anyone interested in getting a true picture of that larger landscape. Yet it would be a mistake to assume that because we want to find such information in Pausanias, he would certainly have given it to us had he been able. Snodgrass cites a suggestion by Christian Jacob that "Pausanias may have habitually used, not a proper two-dimensional map, but an itinerary of the kind of which one precious example is preserved for us in the Peutinger Table."[41] That Pausanias consulted such itineraries is not hard to believe, and at the very least, the lack of concern they exhibit for two-dimensional proportionality may reflect contemporary habits of viewing and representation that Pausanias also partook of. Nevertheless, it is scarcely imaginable that such itineraries played a substantial role in determining for Pausanias the routes he would choose to describe. A large number of the sites Pausanias visits – remote sanctuaries, tiny settlements, deserted ruins on dead-end roads – would appear on none but the most comprehensive of itineraries. The Peutinger Table itself includes only a small fraction of the places covered by Pausanias' text.[42] Moreover, the very purpose of charts like the Peutinger Table is to show the best and most convenient routes from one place to the next, whereas there are many occasions where Pausanias avoids the best and most convenient routes. Even if Pausanias consulted such visual aids (a supposition which is plausible but unsupported by any evidence), there is no reason to suppose that they set his agenda for him.

One could argue that the existence of such representations of space as the Peutinger Table, which radically distorts and stretches all the routes and landforms out along the horizontal axis in order to accommodate the entire Roman Empire on the width of the surface on which the diagram is written, may have conditioned Pausanias to be satisfied with a representation of space that is less three-dimensional than a modern author would be comfortable with. But then again, there are plenty of times when Pausanias resists the supposed urge to confine himself to two dimensions. Frequently, he shows himself quite capable of perceiving and describing more complex spatial relationships between routes and sites. In the first book, he does not tell us how far it is from Athens to Marathon, or which road to take to get there, but he does tell us that Marathon is equidistant

---

[41] The words are those of Snodgrass 1987: 85–86; Jacob, 1991–2: 41.
[42] On the Peutinger Table, see Miller 1916; Pritchett 1980: 197–288.

from Athens and Karystos in Euboia (1.32.3).[43] He tells us that Salamis "is situated alongside Eleusis and stretches all the way to Megarian territory" (1.35.2). In Lakonia, while describing a route that leads from Therapne to the opposite side of the Eurotas valley (3.20.2–3), he mentions that the route passes by Amyklai, a site he has already described on a different route (3.18.6). Even in the second book, Pausanias shows that his geographical bearings are quite sound when, at the minor site of Orneai in north-western Argolis, he observes that the lands on the other side of Orneai (τὰ ἐπέκεινα Ὀρνεῶν) are Sikyonia and Phliasia (2.25.6). It is highly unlikely that any graphic itinerary of the day would have given Pausanias so accurate a sense of the location of a very unimportant place. This alone should be sufficient to suggest that there was no deficiency in Pausanias' feel for the wider geographical relationships of the regions he traveled in, and that his failure to mention the proximity of Nemea to Phleious was not due to ignorance.

The entire eighth book is a masterful demonstration of how sophisticated Pausanias' sense of space can be. The first thing Pausanias does in this book is to orient the reader geographically by locating Arkadia in relation to the other regions of the Peloponnesos he had been talking about in the previous six books (8.1.1–3). Then, after the narration of the traditional history of Arkadia, Pausanias delimits the eastern boundaries of the territory by mentioning three routes in from Argolis: one into Tegean territory over Mount Parthenion, and two into the Mantineian land over the Prinos and Klimax passes (8.6.4). Throughout the subsequent topographical description, Pausanias is continually relating parts of the Arkadian territory to previously mentioned territories of the Peloponnesos: to Achaea (8.15.8; 16.5), to Elis (8.26.3), to Messenia (8.34.1; 35.1), to Lakonia (8.35.3; 54.1), and again to Argolis (8.54.4–5). It might be that Pausanias designed the eighth book to provide a fitting summation to his description of the Peloponnesos as a whole. He slides Arkadia like a jigsaw puzzle piece into the interlocking geographical framework he has constructed in the previous books. Moreover, his topography of Arkadia itself, as we have seen, is quite deliberately designed to follow a circular path beginning and ending on the eastern side with the contiguous territories of Mantineia and Tegea. At the center of this circle is the city of Methydrion, a small town apparently subordinate to Megalopolis in Pausanias' day, located in the

---

[43] Remarkably, this statement is correct within 10 kilometers or so, as the crow flies. The three sites do not lie on the same line, however.

central highlands of Arkadia between the waters of the Maloitas and Mylaon rivers. Pausanias mentions this relatively insignificant locality no less than three separate times in the course of Book 8, at three separate stages of his itinerary (8.12.2; 28.3; 35.5).[44] By repeatedly referring to this central reference point, Pausanias conveys to the reader a sense of where any given site lies within the totality of Arkadian territory. The wheel-like course of Pausanias' Arkadian itinerary, however, is probably not designed solely to give a sense of the broad picture of Arkadian topography. As the last book in Pausanias' description of the Peloponnesos, the counter-clockwise momentum of Pausanias' progress counters the clockwise manner in which he covered the other Peloponnesian territories. As he passes each territory again and mentions roads leading into it from Arkadia, he recapitulates the themes of Books 2 through 6 in reverse order, bringing a satisfying conclusion to his handling of this major segment of his description of Greece.

All these examples show that Pausanias was quite capable of accurately visualizing and clearly describing complex geographical relationships between sites in the lands his itineraries traversed. The reason for his apparent tunnel vision is therefore not ignorance, and certainly not his blind adherence to some pre-set map, chart, or list of sites. Most instances can simply be ascribed to his lack of interest in providing such information, or, perhaps better, to his interest in other matters which take precedence over keeping the reader fully oriented in the physical landscape at every step along the journey. Through his daisy-chains of cities, towns, and sanctuaries, Pausanias maintains a descriptive narrative that is varied and unmonotonous, one that balances present-day as well as traditional identities and relationships. These, I suggest, are Pausanias' main goals. Helping the traveler find his way and giving a vivid sense of the three-dimensional lay of the Greek landscape are things he is capable of, but evidently considers secondary to his main tasks.

PAUSANIAS AT SEA

While much of the foregoing has been devoted to defending Pausanias from charges of error or incompetence, the time has come to admit that there are some cases where he is completely wrong. Pausanias' mistakes are also worth looking at because they can often tell us as much about his aims and methods as the things he gets right. One of the most obvious

---

[44] The actual description of the city of Methydrion is at 8.36.1–3.

and puzzling errors comes (as was mentioned briefly above) near the end of Book 2, where Pausanias purports to be describing an approach to the city of Hermione by sea from Cape Skyllaion, the easternmost point of the Argolid (2.34.7–10):

> To one sailing from Skyllaion toward the city there is another promontory Boukephala and after the promontory, islands: First, Halioussa – and this one provides a harbor suitable for ships to anchor – then Pityoussa, and third the one they call Aristera. To one sailing past these there is once again a promontory Kolyergia sticking out from the mainland, and after it an island called Trikrana and a mountain jutting into the sea from the Peloponnesos, Bouporthmos . . . In front of Bouporthmos lies an island called Aperopia, and not far from Aperopia is another island Hydrea. After this [island] a crescent-shaped beach lies along the mainland, and after the beach a headland extends up to the shrine of Poseidon . . . Here is where the Hermionians had their earlier city.

There are few passages in Pausanias where the physical topography of a stretch of territory is presented in such detail, and this detail allows us to identify the islands and headlands Pausanias lists with a high degree of certainty. Unfortunately, when we do so we find that what Pausanias is describing is a journey to Hermione not from Skyllaion but from some point in the opposite direction. Halioussa, for instance, is evidently an island-like peninsula near the modern town of Porto Heli and the ancient Halike. Pityoussa is obviously Spetses (which was formerly known as Petses) and Hydrea can hardly be anything but the long, narrow island of Hydra (Idra), which would have been the first landmark on a westbound voyage from Skyllaion rather than one of the last.[45] Two explanations suggest themselves for how Pausanias might have made this error: he may have misremembered or misread his notes when he sat down to write about this stretch of territory, or he might have adapted the description from some other written account, mistaking the orientation and the starting-point of the original.[46] A couple of indications make the second alternative somewhat more likely: first, the bare listing of physical landmarks of which this passage mostly consists, with passing references to towns and monuments, is hard to parallel elsewhere in Pausanias' text. Second, as a seaborne description that contains apparent errors, it is not alone in Pausanias' text. Nearly every time that Pausanias

---

[45] Pausanias' error was recognized early on by Bursian (1872: 86); cf. Lolling 1879: 107–113; Frazer 1898; 3.290–293. Papachatzes 1974: 2.264–271. More recently, see Jameson, Runnels, and van Andel 1994: 573–582. Some attempts have been made to rescue Pausanias from the charge of error, all of them rather desperate. See, for instance, Levi 1971: 1.214, n. 201, and earlier suggestions canvased by Frazer (loc. cit.).

[46] As suggested by Kalkmann 1886: 181–182; Heberdey 1894: 46–48.

begins to describe things from sea, he seems to get something wrong.[47] For instance, in the course of what seems to be an east-to-west journey around Cape Tainaron at the southern end of Lakonia, he reverses the order of two ports near the cape, Achilleion and Psamathous (3.25.4).[48] Similarly, in Book 9, while describing coastal sites in Boiotia from a seaborne perspective, he inverts the order in which one would pass by Tipha (Siphai) and the port of Thisbe on an east-to-west journey (9.22.2–4).[49] In all three of these cases, while Pausanias is ostensibly following a clockwise route in his description of coastal sites, some of the sites he names are in counter-clockwise order. Most surviving geographies and *periplous* (coastal voyage) accounts deal with the coast of the Greek mainland in counter-clockwise fashion. The conclusion therefore seems clear: either Pausanias' wits got addled in a remarkably similar fashion every time he stepped on board a boat or he was borrowing – somewhat carelessly – information from a previous geography or *periplous* on these occasions.

If, in the case of the coast of the eastern Argolid, Pausanias supplemented his autoptic testimony with material from an earlier source, an important question to ask is why. Strictly speaking, there was no need for him to do so, since he had already traced a land route from Troizen into Hermionian territory, and there were no major sites on any of the islands or headlands that appear in this part of the account – none major enough that any topographer would have to fear criticism for omitting them. The most plausible explanation would seem to be a literary one: Pausanias seems to have felt that this part of his itinerary through the eastern Argolid needed a

---

[47] Pausanias' initial approach to Attica by sea is a special case, since he is hardly likely to have relied on a previous source for his observations on that journey, but it may be worth noting that here too he makes an error: he mentions only a temple of Athena on the promontory at Sounion (1.1.1), when in fact the most conspicuous temple there was (and is) the temple of Poseidon. Cf. Dinsmoor 1974.

[48] Psamathous is located by most scholars on the eastern side of the narrow cape (at modern Porto Kayo), and Achilleion directly behind it on the west (modern Marmari), yet Pausanias names Achilleion first. Le Roy (2001: 225–228) has recently come to Pausanias' defense by suggesting that Achilleion may actually be another harbor to the north of Psamathous on the east side, but this theory ignores the testimony of Pseudo-Skylax (46) who vividly describes the two ports as being "butt-to-butt" (ἀντίπυγος). This is a perfect way of describing the relationship between Marmari harbor and Porto Kayo.

[49] Pausanias sails west from Kreusis and puts in to shore near Thisbe. After describing Thisbe itself, he proceeds to Tipha (= Siphai) with the words "for one sailing along from there . . ." παραπλέοντι δὲ αὐτόθεν . . . See Fossey 1988: 172–173. Fossey points out that the fortified coastal settlement of Siphai lay in the easternmost recess of the bay of Dhomvreni, and would not necessarily have been the most convenient landfall for a westbound voyager visiting the bay. Pausanias does not specify the direction in which he sails from the harbor of Thisbe, and Leake, assuming that Pausanias was continuing his westerly journey, located Tipha farther west, at a site now known from an inscription to be the site of Chorseia, a town which Pausanias never mentions (Leake 1835: 2.514–516).

bit more substance, perhaps to emphasize the fact that with the territories of Hermione and Troizenia he had reached the easternmost limit of his grand tour of the peninsula.

CONCLUSION

Now that we have studied the intricate and complicated considerations that went into the arrangement of Pausanias' work, we can look at his "tunnel vision" and his occasional lapse into topographical confusion with greater understanding. Pausanias set an enormous task for himself. Not only did he have to engage in extensive travel and research to collect the massive amount of information in his account, but when it came to writing it all down, instead of concatenating all his data haphazardly, and instead of tying it together in a repetitive and mechanical radial scheme, he carefully structured the presentation of his information with due regard for clarity, variety, balance between sections, and respect for historical and mythological traditions.

A consideration of Pausanias' methods within the individual books shows that while the radial plan is undoubtedly the most important and consistent organizing principle in the *Periegesis*, Pausanias' application of it is not as simple a matter as is commonly supposed. There are frequently gaps in the topographical sequence, and places where the organization is topical or associative rather than spatial. Also, a glance beneath the surface reveals other organizing principles in operation instead of, or in combination with, the radial scheme. Underlying the topographical descriptions in each book, and to a certain extent determining the shape of the schemes Pausanias employs, are the numerous sub-territories into which the major territories are divided, largely on the basis of the limits of ancient *poleis*. It is at the boundaries between these sub-territories that Pausanias is most liable to shift or widen his topographical focus, and where the sequence of spatial connections from one site to the next is most likely to encounter a discontinuity. Altogether the schemata by which Pausanias presents his description of territories are very complicated, and recognition of this fact bears a number of important implications for the interpretation of Pausanias' testimony: first, one cannot assume that Pausanias is following a topographical sequence when there is nothing in the text that specifically indicates it. Another thing to note is that, as in the examples of topographical tunnel vision we have discussed, odd effects can sometimes result from the way Pausanias operates. We should recognize the source of such anomalies and not be quick to convict Pausanias of incompetence or deficiency. In the next chapter, Pausanias' methods of organizing and presenting his descriptions of cities will be examined. We will find that many of the methods discussed in this chapter are repeated on a smaller scale in Pausanias' treatment of urban landscapes. Many of the difficulties that these methods entail will recur as well.

CHAPTER 5

City descriptions

Most of Pausanias' topographical efforts are devoted to the description of cities and sanctuaries. It would not be going too far to say that the large-scale structures of the work serve mainly as a framework for connecting the more detailed descriptions of the major centers of population and religion in the territory Pausanias covers. It is in the cities and great shrines that the things that interest Pausanias most, the religious artifacts and the monuments reminiscent of ancient times, occur in the greatest concentration. This proliferation of *theôrêmata*, together with the corresponding proliferation of *logoi*, presents Pausanias with an enormous problem of information management. This chapter will address the question of how Pausanias defines and delimits a city, and will survey the various methods he employs in constructing his description. Then the city of Corinth will serve as the object of an in-depth case-study of how Pausanias handles particular problems in urban topography. We will find that, in addition to organizing and reporting information about the state of the Greek cities in his day, Pausanias' city descriptions reflect the author's attitudes about Hellenic identity and about what the Greek cities represent, or ought to represent, in the context of the Roman world.

WHAT IS A CITY?

In order to understand how Pausanias approaches the business of describing a city, it is necessary first of all to gain a sense of what his concept of a city was. Pausanias is one of a handful of authors, including Strabo and Stephanos of Byzantium, who are major sources for the history and geography of the distinctive Greek institution of the "city-state", so this problem is one with implications that go far beyond the study of Pausanias.[1] The word

---

[1] Cf. Alcock 1995, who provides an overview of Pausanias' use of the term *polis* and other terms for population centers, focusing on the cities and near-cities in Boiotia. She also makes prudent observations on Pausanias' strengths and weaknesses as a source for the history of the institution of the *polis*.

used by Pausanias that is most frequently translated as "city" is, as one might expect, *polis* (πόλις), but this is not the only word he uses to refer to areas of concentrated human habitation. In Pausanias' vocabulary there exists a range of terms, including *khôrion* (χωρίον),[2] *kômê* (κώμη), *polisma* (πόλισμα), and *polis*, which seem to stand in a somewhat flexible hierarchy, with *polis* reserved for the largest and most important settlements. His usage of these terms can convey some sense of the size and character of the various inhabited places he mentions in the *Periegesis*, a sense that is often lacking in the work otherwise.

The difference between a *polis* and a *polisma* seems chiefly to be one of size. Pausanias never uses the latter term to refer to a town of more than middling size,[3] and in the case of many *polismata* he specifies that they are not large, or gives a precise description of their situation in the landscape as though their expanse was capable of being comprehended in a single glance.[4] This is something he rarely does in the case of a *polis*.[5] As the distinction is mainly one of size, inevitably there are places that lie on the cusp and escape easy classification, such as Kaphyai in Arkadia (8.23.3) and Tithorea in Phokis (10.32.11), which are called both *polisma* and *polis* in the course of Pausanias' account.[6] While there seems to be a vague upper limit

[2] It might be argued that *khôrion* should be left off this list, since it has a semantic versatility similar to that of the English word "place," and unlike the other terms is not restricted in its application to currently or formerly inhabited places. There are instances, however, where *khôrion* is apparently used as a synonym with other terms for settlements. Pausanias also uses *dêmos* (δῆμος) in the specialized sense of "town" or "township" particularly in Attica (e.g. 1.26.6), but also in Elis (e.g. 5.9.6, 6.24.5), Achaea (7.27.8), and Arkadia (8.45.1).

[3] The list of *polismata* includes Methana in Argolis (2.34.1), Aigiai (3.21.5), Marios (3.22.8), Zarax (3.24.1), Kardamyle (3.26.7) in Lakonia; Ampheia (4.5.9), and Kolonides (4.34.8) in Messenia; Kerynia (7.25.5) and Phelloe (7.26.10) in Achaea; Alipheira in Arkadia (8.26.5); Akraiphnion (9.23.5), Kopai (9.24.1), Kyrtones (9.24.4), Korseia (9.24.5), Halai (9.24.5), and Tipha (9.32.4) in Boiotia. In this section, I have omitted from consideration *polismata* that are mentioned by Pausanias only in historical or mythical narrative.

[4] "Not large" (οὐ μέγα): Methana (2.34.1); Ampheia (4.5.9); Tiphai (9.32.4); for descriptions of location, the most complex is that of Kaphyai (8.23.3): τὸ μὲν δὴ πόλισμα ἐπὶ τοῦ πεδίου τῷ πέρατι ὀρῶν οὐκ ἄγαν ὑψηλῶν παρὰ τοῖς ποσίν ἐστι ("the *polisma* is on the edge of the plain at the foot of mountains that are not very tall"). Other *polismata* are ἐπὶ λόφου ("upon a hill": 4.5.9), ἐπὶ ὑψηλοῦ ("upon a height": 4.34.8; 10.38.8), ἐπὶ λίμνῃ ("upon a lake": 9.24.1) or ἐν ὄρει ("on a mountain": 7.25.5; 9.23.5; 9.24.4).

[5] One example is his depiction of the situation of Hermione (2.34.11), cf. also his remarks on Messene (4.31.4). Contrary to the implication of Cohen 2001: 97, this sort of synoptic description of a *polis* is hardly common in Pausanias.

[6] Cf. also Alipheira (8.26.6), Akraiphnion (9.23.5), Myonia (10.38.8). Also, the Lakonian *polismata* of Marios, Zarax, and Alagonia are listed among the *poleis* belonging to the Eleutherolakones (3.21.7). Zarax is also called a *polis* in 1.38.4. In the case of Kaphyai (see the quotation in n. 4 above) and Akraiphnion, Pausanias may be using the term *polismata* to distinguish the physical structure of the city from the *polis* as a political and cultural entity (cf. the first meaning for πόλισμα given by LSJ: "the buildings of a city"; in the same entry, one is referred to the distinction in Latin between *urbs* and *civitas*). I should emphasize that this is not a distinction that seems to operate in most of Pausanias' uses of the word.

to the size of a *polisma*, there is definitely a minimum standard as well. In discussing the site of Letrinoi in Elis (6.22.8), Pausanias says that it was once a *polisma*, but that in his day nothing was left of it but a few buildings (οἰκήματα) and a temple (apparently still in use) of Artemis. Clearly, to Pausanias these assets are not enough to allow Letrinoi to maintain its former status as a *polisma*.

While the distinction between *polis* and *polisma* is based mainly on a physical size, a distinction of a different sort exists between these two types of places and a *kômê*. In addition to indicating a settlement that is small in size, the term *kômê* can also connote a certain degree of political subordination. Pausanias tells us, for instance, that Methydrion in Arkadia was once a *polis*, but is now a *kômê* subject to the Megalopolitan state (τὸ Μεγαλοπολιτικόν) (8.12.2; cf. 8.27.5).[7] Conversely, we are told that Pallantion was transformed from a *kômê* into a *polis* by the emperor Antoninus Pius (8.43.1). Pausanias does not tell us exactly how the emperor effected this change, but he does add that among the benefits granted to the Pallantians were independence (ἐλευθερία) and exemption from tribute (ἀτέλεια). Perhaps this was all that was required. Elsewhere, Pausanias tells us that Pallantion, like Methydrion, had once been subject to Megalopolis, so the "freedom" and "exemption" he refers to may have included autonomy from Megalopolis in addition to immunity from obligations to the Roman authorities, as it is usually interpreted.[8] In any case, one might surmise that this new status brought increased prosperity and population,[9] but on this point Pausanias is silent. The only change he cites explicitly is an end to the town's political dependency.

From the evidence presented so far, we can already see that when Pausanias refers to a settlement as a *polis* he is saying something significant about its status. In a frequently cited passage in the tenth book, he expresses his minimum standards for a *polis* even more explicitly. The subject here is the Phocian town of Panopeus (10.4.1):[10]

---

7 Another village in the same situation is Gortys (8.28.1; cf. 8.27.5), which is classified as a *kômê* despite the fact that it houses an operational shrine of Asklepios. We are also told that Teuthis, also in Arkadia, was once a *polisma*, but is now a mere *kômê* (8.24.8). No explanation of the transition is given. Other κῶμαι include Ereneia in Megaris (1.44.5), Lessa in Argolis (2.25.10), Anthene, Neris, and Eua in Thyreatis (2.38.6), Amyklai (3.19.6), Krokeai (3.21.4), Palaia (3.22.6), Glyppia, and Selinous (3.22.8) in Lakonia, Herakleia in Elis (6.22.7), Nestane in Arkadia (8.7.4), and Alalkomenai in Boiotia (9.33.5). Other κῶμαι that are explicitly stated to be dependent on other cities include Olmones and Hyettos in Boiotia, which were towns nearby to one another in Orchomenian territory (9.24.3).
8 See, for instance, Alcock 1993: 22–23.
9 So far, no archaeological evidence has been reported that attests to such an upswing in the Antonine period. See Jost in Casevitz, Jost and Marcadé 1992: 268–269.
10 See Alcock 1993: 22; 1995: 326.

στάδια δὲ ἐκ Χαιρωνείας εἴκοσιν ἐς Πανοπέας ἐστὶ πόλιν Φωκέων, εἴγε ὀνομάσαι τις πόλιν καὶ τούτους οἷς γε οὐκ ἀρχεῖα οὐ γυμνάσιόν ἐστιν. οὐ θέατρον οὐκ ἀγορὰν ἔχουσιν, οὐχ ὕδωρ κατερχόμενον ἐς κρήνην, ἀλλὰ ἐν στέγαις κοίλαις κατὰ τὰς καλύβας μάλιστα τὰς ἐν τοῖς ὄρεσιν, ἐνταῦθα οἰκοῦσιν ἐπὶ χαράδρᾳ. ὅμως δὲ ὅροι γε τῆς χώρας εἰσὶν αὐτοῖς ἐς τοὺς ὁμόρους, καὶ ἐς τὸν σύλλογον συνέδρους καὶ οὗτοι πέμπουσι τὸν Φωκικόν.

It is twenty stadia from Chaironeia to Panopeus,[11] a city of the Phocians, if, that is, anyone would give the name of city to those for whom there are no government buildings, no gymnasium, who have no theater, no market-place, no water conducted into a fountain, and who live in hollow shelters, quite similar to the huts used in the mountains, right at the edge of a ravine. Still, they at least maintain boundaries of their land with their neighbors and they even send representatives to the Phocian assembly.

The uncharacteristically blunt manner in which Pausanias registers the deficiencies of Panopeus should not distract us from the fact that in the end he does decide to call it a *polis*, and what the Panopeans are given credit for in this passage is as interesting to consider as what they lack. The reason that Pausanias considers Panopeus a *polis* is, as far as he tells us, chiefly the town's political status: it maintains borders with neighboring cities and sends its own representatives to the Phocian assembly. It is, therefore, recognized as an independent peer by neighboring states, and it is this that makes it more than a *kômê*, despite its lack of impressive civic structures.[12] This is additional evidence that a *polis* for Pausanias was not exclusively, or even primarily, a collection of buildings, temples and monuments.

Nevertheless, this passage also reveals that certain tangible elements contributed to Pausanias' concept of what a *polis* should normally be. It is not necessary to take too seriously the roll of features that Panopeus lacks, and assume that Pausanias carefully examined each city he visited to make sure that it lived up to these specific standards before calling it a *polis*. Still, the passage makes clear that in Pausanias' eyes any self-respecting *polis* could be expected to have attained a certain degree of development in its physical facilities and infrastructure. In fact, the case of the people of Ledon, also in Phokis, proves that autonomy and recognition by one's neighbors

[11] A literal translation would seem to be, "It is 20 stadia from Chaironeia to the Panopeans, a city of the Phocians . . ." This is the only case to my knowledge where Pausanias puts the name of the people of the city in direct apposition to the word *polis*. There are some ambiguous cases, such as at Parapotamioi in Phokis, where the usual name of the city is the same as the plural ethnic adjective (10.33.7–9). For the city of the Panopeans, Pausanias elsewhere uses the singular *Panopeus* (Πανοπεύς).

[12] It is interesting to note in this regard that Pausanias seems to have been unimpressed by the formidable city walls that are still visible on the site of Panopeus (for illustration, see Papachatzes 1981: 5.278). He does mention them (10.4.2), but they are not enough to make the place unequivocally a *polis*.

were not enough to make a community a *polis* (10.33.1). Pausanias says that Ledon "was once considered a city" (πόλις δέ ποτε ἐνομίζετο) but that "the Ledontians had abandoned their city" (ἐξελελοίπεσαν οἱ Λεδόντιοι τὴν πόλιν) and gone to live in a small settlement by the Kephisos. In Pausanias' day, some seventy people lived in this settlement, which he does not even dignify with the name of *kômê*, referring to it instead as merely a collection of "dwellings" (οἰκήσεις). Nevertheless, the Ledontians "are eligible to participate in the common assembly of the Phocians, just like the Panopeans." Clearly, Pausanias classes Ledon and Panopeus together as borderline πόλεις, with Panopeus managing to remain just above the line that Ledon has dropped below. It seems significant in the case of Ledon that the people have abandoned the physical site of the old city, which still remains to be seen "40 stadia upland from the people who dwell by the Kephisos," and which stands as a reminder of the community's more impressive status in days gone by.

Thus, although a very modest community could still be deemed worthy of being called a *polis* by Pausanias, there is a certain expectation of visible, tangible substantiality that goes along with the concept of a *polis*. This perhaps explains why the features Pausanias found wanting in Panopeus (offices, a gymnasium, a theater, a market-place, public fountains) frequently appear in his description of many cities, even if as individual monuments they do not possess the qualities that most readily attract Pausanias' attention, namely artistic distinction, advanced age, and connections to cult, myth, or history.[13] These physical symbols of city life, all of them manifestations of a sense of community among the inhabitants, add an element of vitality to Pausanias' descriptions. Of course, Pausanias did not feel obligated to include each of these elements in his account of each city; he mentions no theater at Megara, for instance, no gymnasium or office buildings at Patrai, and no fountain at Sikyon. But in most of the larger city descriptions he does include a reference to at least one example of each of these types of structure. Though Pausanias rarely makes them the subject of extended discussion, their presence in the account does add an important complement to his depiction of the city as a whole.

In answer, then, to the question of what a *polis* is to Pausanias, we can say that it is can be different things in different contexts. He can use the term loosely of an unimpressive settlement in isolation, but can also be

---

[13] Gogos 1988 has analyzed Pausanias' references to theaters in particular. His conclusion that with a few conspicuous exceptions Pausanias uses theaters merely as convenient topographical reference points seems to me to be a bit too reductive, though theaters can certainly serve that function for Pausanias.

highly particular in his application of the term in context where he is comparing cities or contrasting a city's present state with its former state. While size, physical attributes, or numerous attractive buildings can help to determine whether or not he will use the term, the most consistent criterion would seem to be one of political status; a *polis* is an autonomous community in control of itself and its borders.[14] At the same time, the word *polis* also seems to carry with it the connotation of a certain level of civic development and vitality, and Pausanias does make an effort to provide evidence of such development in his descriptions, where it exists. His acknowledgment of theaters, fountains, gymnasia, and other indices of a healthy contemporary communal life in the πόλεις he visits compensates somewhat for the tendency to which his dominant interests incline him, namely portraying the cities he visits as repositories of antiquities or open-air museums populated more by the ghosts of myth and history than by living human beings. Finally, one more observation we can make about the word *polis* is that when Pausanias uses it in his topographical descriptions, it seems generally to refer to the actual physical city and not to any entity like a "city-state" which encompasses both the city and the non-urban territory it controls.[15] In other words, when Pausanias employs expressions like "for one going into the *polis*" (εἰσελθόντι εἰς τὴν πόλιν), he is talking about going into the city itself and not just into the territory controlled by the city. As we shall see in the next section, this distinction is an important one for the structure of Pausanias' account.

CITY AND COUNTRYSIDE

How does Pausanias integrate his descriptions of cities into the large-scale structures that we have examined in previous chapters? The territory belonging to any *polis*, even one as lowly as Panopeus, can stretch far beyond

[14] This definition is consistent with almost all the evidence, but as with almost any single word in Pausanias, no generalization of its meaning can be made that is universally valid. Pausanias does, infrequently, use the word to designate communities that were not, as far as we know, autonomous, large, or well appointed, as in the case of Pagai and Aigosthena in the territory of Megara (1.44.4). Pausanias also uses the term *polis* for the Achaean towns of Pharai and Triteia, both of which he says are subject to the authority of Patrai (7.22.1, 6). One might attempt to explain this by pointing out that the subordinate position of both of these towns was a relatively recent development: Pausanias says they were gifts of Augustus to the people of Patrai, and probably constituted part of his program to develop Patrai as a Roman colony. Admittedly, this is not as recent a development as the actions of Antoninus on behalf of the Pallantians, but perhaps Pausanias was more ready to allow that *polis* status could be granted by imperial fiat than that it could be taken away.

[15] This distinction is made explicit in 1.29.2; 1.26.6; 1.14.7; 1.30.2. See, however, n. 6 above for possible exceptions.

the limits of the central conurbation. Pausanias has various ways of referring to this extra-urban territory, including the terms *khôra* (χώρα),[16] *gê*
(γῆ), and *moira* (μοῖρα), and it seems, as was mentioned above, that Pausanias maintains a distinction in terminology between this territory and the
urbanized area of the *polis* proper. We encountered these extra-urban territories in the previous chapter, where they were referred to as sub-territories,
and we saw how they served as important segments in the structure of
Pausanias' large-scale topographical schemes.[17] The descriptions of these
sub-territories can often be viewed as distinct units, the integrity of which
Pausanias strives not to violate in the laying-out of his itineraries: Pausanias
typically traces routes from the city to various parts of the sub-territory
without crossing its boundary until he is ready to move on to the next
sub-territory. We have also seen that the point of transition between one
sub-territory and the next is often the site of a topographical discontinuity
in Pausanias' account: upon reaching the boundary of a sub-territory he is
about to describe, Pausanias frequently begins describing things within the
sub-territory that have no explicit topographical connection to the route
he was following up to that point. In the case of city descriptions, this
pattern is repeated on a smaller scale: as we shall see, the beginning of
the city description is not necessarily connected topographically with the
route upon which Pausanias' itinerary approaches the city, and once the
city description has begun, the routes traced within the city do not cross
over the boundary between the city and the countryside. In this manner,
the city descriptions mark out a space in the landscape for the city itself
that is separate from the surrounding *khôra*. The urban area is thus isolated as a topographical unit, just as the sub-territories serve as isolated and
autonomous features within the topographical plan of each book.

The initial approach to a city and the transition from a territory description to an urban description occur in a manner that varies from place
to place. Frequently, Pausanias traces a single route through the territory
in the direction of the city proper (what we might call an "introductory
route"), and then proceeds to describe the city. This is the way he operates
at Argos (2.18.3–19.3), Sparta (3.11.1–2), Megalopolis (8.27.11–30.1), and in
numerous other cities,[18] and this is also the characteristic manner which

---

[16] It seems to have become accepted practice nowadays to use the term *khôra* (*chora*) to designate the
non-urban territory belonging to a *polis*. I have avoided that practice here so as not to give the
impression that Pausanias uses *khôra* in this sense exclusively or consistently. In Pausanias, *khôra* can
refer to any stretch of land, and is basically synonymous with *gê*.

[17] See pp. 96–97 above.

[18] For instance, Sikyon (2.7.5), Argos (2.18.1–19.3), Hermione (2.34.4–10), Patrai (7.18.2–8), Mantineia
(8.8.1–2), Tegea (8.44.7), Thebes (9.8.7), and Elateia (10.34.1–6).

Frazer identifies in his description of the radial plan: "He proceeds from the frontier [of the territory] to the capital [i.e. the *polis*] by the nearest road, noting anything of interest that strikes him by the way."[19] This is not his method in every case, however. Sometimes, as in the case of Megara (1.39.4–40.1), Phleious (2.12.3–13.1) and Troizen (2.30.5–31.1), Pausanias leaps to the description of the city immediately upon reaching the boundary of the sub-territory. At other times he will mention sites within the sub-territory in no topographical order before beginning the city description, as at Tanagra (9.19.5–20.3).

We now come to the question of how the city description itself begins, and it is here that we encounter one of the most important points to understand about Pausanias' city descriptions. Even in cases where Pausanias gives a precise and detailed description of a route leading up to the city, his account of the city will usually not begin as a simple continuation of the same route. Instead, upon reaching the city limits Pausanias chooses some prominent point within the city, often the agora or the acropolis, and begins his urban itineraries from that point. In other words, there is in most cases a topographical discontinuity between the introductory route and the beginning of the city description. We have already had a brief look at an excellent example of this in the description of Sikyon (2.7.4–5): Pausanias traces his introductory route up to a gate in the city wall (πρὸς τῇ πύλῃ), then immediately shifts to the present-day acropolis of the city (ἐν δὲ τῇ νῦν ἀκροπόλει) and begins his description of the sights of the city from this point. This is typical of the way that Pausanias begins his city descriptions, and as a normal feature of Pausanias' methods it reveals once again that Pausanias conceives of the city descriptions as being discrete elements of his account that are not dependent on the topographical structure of his description of the region at large. Exceptions to this practice are very rare; only in Athens, Plataia, Thebes, and Pellene does Pausanias continue an inter-urban itinerary past the city gate into the center of town.[20]

The recognition of this as a recurrent principle of Pausanias' city descriptions was one of the more important insights of Carl Robert.[21] Robert classifies the city descriptions according to the place Pausanias chooses for his starting-point, the most numerous type being the *Markttypus*

---

[19] Frazer 1898: I.xxiii.
[20] Athens: 1.2.4–6; Plataia: 9.2.5; Thebes: 9.10.1; Pellene: 7.27.1–4. An analogous situation may exist at the island of Aigina, where Pausanias begins his description of the city at the harbor (2.29.6).
[21] Robert 1909: 116–118.

("agora-type"), examples of which include Corinth, Troizen, Sparta, Messene, and Megalopolis.[22] The next most frequent place for Pausanias to start is the acropolis, as he does at Sikyon, Phleious, Patrai, and Pheneos.[23] More difficult to categorize are the numerous descriptions where Pausanias begins with a single prominent shrine or building, as he does at Argos (where Pausanias begins with the shrine of Apollo Lykios: 2.19.3), Tegea (the temple and shrine of Athena Alea: 8.45.4), and Megara (the fountain house of Theagenes: 1.40.1). In these cases, we can characterize Pausanias' practice by saying that he begins with whatever he considers the "most illustrious" (ἐπιφανέστατον) site in the city. Sometimes, as at Argos, it becomes clear that the "most illustrious" site happens to be in the agora or on the acropolis,[24] and the description becomes in effect an "agora-type" or an "acropolis-type," but Pausanias leaves that for the traveler or the archaeologist to discover for him- or herself.[25] Once he has chosen his starting-point, Pausanias' procedures differ greatly from one city to the next and are consequently difficult to categorize. Nevertheless, Robert's basic observation is valid: that the city description can be, and in fact usually is, topographically independent of the description of the countryside is a principle that is crucial to an understanding of Pausanias' account. This isolation of the beginning of the city description from the description of the surrounding countryside continues throughout the city description. Regardless of where it starts, once an urban description begins, it tends to stay within the confines of the city itself until it has covered everything in the city that it is going to. None of the routes that Pausanias traces within the city pass beyond the boundary of the city into the countryside, and in general his account does not return to any point in the countryside until the city-description is complete. Any further exploring of the surrounding χώρα is done after the city description is finished, usually by means of routes that start at the city limits and branch outward.

[22] Corinth: 2.2.6; Troizen: 2.31.1; Sparta: 3.11.2; Messene: 4.31.6; Megalopolis: 8.30.2.

[23] Sikyon: 2.7.5; Phleious: 2.13.3; Patrai: 7.18.8; Pheneos: 8.14.4.

[24] At Argos, we know from other ancient sources that the shrine of Apollo Lykios was in the agora. See, for instance, Thuc. 5.47.11; Soph. *Elektra* 6–7 and scholia *ad loc.* Vollgraff 1907: 173–184.

[25] Beyond the typological distinctions discussed here, Robert goes on to posit some additional characteristics of each of the types, most of which are poorly supported by the evidence. One such observation that does seem to have some validity is that agora-type descriptions usually end on the acropolis, thereby framing the account with the two most prominent parts of the city (Robert 1909: 119). This is true of Corinth, Sparta, Messene and Argos (which is in effect an agora-type), but not of Megalopolis. At Megalopolis, Pausanias employs a different framing device: he begins by mentioning the river Helisson and how it divides the city, and he ends with mention of a spring (8.32.5), the waters of which flow into the Helisson.

The next question, then, is what constitutes the city limits. What is it that demarcates the city from its surrounding territory and forms a boundary which Pausanias' urban itineraries do not cross? What *precisely* does Pausanias mean by such phrases as "upon entering the city" (ἐσελθόντων [*vel sim.*] ἐς τὴν πόλιν)? In most instances, as one might expect, the city walls are what provide this boundary, as we can tell in the case of Argos: after tracing an introductory route from the direction of Mycenae and mentioning various objects along it, Pausanias comes·to a gate in the city wall (2.18.3). At this point, his itinerary comes to a halt; he pauses to relate some information about the traditional kings of Argos (2.18.4–19.2), and then commences his urban itinerary with the words: "For the Argives in their city . . ." Ἀργείοις δὲ . . . ἐν τῇ πόλει (2.19.3). He does a very similar thing at Athens, where the last object he mentions before beginning his city description is a monument "not far from the gates" (οὐ πόρρω τῶν πυλῶν) (1.2.3); immediately after this, he continues with the words "for those who have entered the city (ἐσελθόντων δὲ ἐς τὴν πόλιν) (1.2.4). Finally, at Sikyon, he ends his introductory route up to the city with a mention of a spring in a cave "by the gate" (πρὸς τῇ πύλῃ), and the urban itinerary commences immediately after this, beginning at the acropolis (2.7.5).[26] In most places, however, Pausanias is not so explicit at the beginning of his description about where he marks the transition between the *polis* and land outside it; he merely breaks off his description of the introductory route and abruptly begins his account of things within the city.[27] In some of these cases, however, it becomes clear at the end of the city description that the boundary is indeed the city wall, since routes traced away from the city take their starting-point from a gate in the wall. For instance, after completing the city description of Messene, Pausanias begins a route toward the hinterlands of Messenia which begins "from the gates" ἀπὸ τῶν πυλῶν (4.33.3).

From such evidence, we might suppose as a general rule that the city walls mark the boundary of the *polis* for Pausanias and provide a physical limit for his urban itineraries, and indeed for the vast majority of cities there is nothing in Pausanias' account that is inconsistent with that hypothesis. In the description of at least one major city, however, there appears to be a possible exception. In tracing an introductory route toward Corinth "for those going up to Corinth," among the last items he mentions before beginning his description of the city proper is a grove called Kraneion,

[26] See also the description of Thebes (9.8.4–7).

[27] As is the case with Sparta (3.11.1–2), for instance, Megalopolis (8.30.1–2), and Hermione, Patrai, Mantineia, Tegea, and Elateia (see note 18 for references).

which, he says, lies "before the city" (πρὸ τῆς πόλεως [2.2.4]). The trouble here is that before mentioning Kraneion, Pausanias mentions the tomb of Diogenes the Cynic, which he locates "by the gate" (πρὸς τῇ πύλῃ). As long as Pausanias can be understood to be continuing the itinerary "for those going up to Corinth," the natural expectation is that anything he mentions after Diogenes' tomb will be within the gate and hence within the wall.[28] Even if this is the case, however, it may just represent Pausanias' response to certain particular features of the layout of Corinth. The circuit of city walls at Corinth was extraordinarily long, and it encompassed much more territory than was ever covered by concentrated urbanization.[29] In this instance, then, Pausanias may have considered the land immediately within the wall as essentially part of the open countryside, and still distinct from the *polis* proper.

In addition to the case of Corinth, there are other instances where Pausanias' description proceeds in an unusual fashion at the boundary between city and countryside. At Thebes, where the description of the entire territory of Boiotia is connected with the famous seven gates of the Kadmeia, the distinction between extra- and intra-urban itineraries is occasionally blurred for items in the vicinity of these gates.[30] At Athens, an initial approach is made to the city from Phaleron, at which time Pausanias' itinerary enters the city (ἐσελθόντων δὲ ἐς τὴν πόλιν) and encounters a monument to the Amazon Antiope (1.2.1). Then Pausanias shifts

[28] An episode in Xenophon (*Hellenica* 4.4.2–5) reveals that Kraneion lay within ear-shot of crowd noise from the theater and the agora of fourth-century Corinth. This implies a certain (though admittedly vague) limit to the distance between Kraneion and the city center. For more testimonia on the location of the Kraneion (none of it conclusive) see Wiseman 1978: 86.

[29] See Carpenter and Bon 1931: 80: ". . . it is apparent that the enclosed area [within the wall] greatly exceeded in size the actual needs of the city . . . the great wall girdle enclosed the most extensive city domain in mainland Greece." Carpenter estimates the course of the wall to run approximately 10 kilometers. Its length impressed even Strabo (8.6.21). Another factor that may have influenced the way Pausanias used the walls in his account of Corinth is their state of disrepair. They surely sustained some damage during Mummius' sacking of the city, and Strabo (*loc. cit.*), writing from autopsy, finds only traces along the slopes of Acrocorinth. Nevertheless, it is likely that around the lower town at least the stone socle, which by itself still presents a formidable aspect along some stretches of the wall, remained largely intact, and as Pausanias' account suggests, there were still things that could be identified as πύλαι (see Carpenter and Bon 1931: 82–83; A.W. Parsons, *Corinth III.ii*, 124–5). Surveys of the site of Corinth have revealed that the Roman colony was laid out on a grid that covered a relatively small space within the circuit of the walls: Romano 1993; Walbank 1997; Romano 2003.

[30] See Symeonoglou 1985: 182–185. An interesting possibility in the case of Thebes is that Pausanias' account reflects his awareness on some level of an outer circuit of walls that ran around the lower city in classical times (see Symeonoglou 1985: 118–122). Although it is questionable whether any significant stretch of the wall was visible in his day, the previous existence of the wall may have had an effect on the layout of buildings, roads and other features directly outside the Kadmeia, such that it impressed Pausanias as having more the character of the *polis* than of the *khôra*.

abruptly to a second introductory route, this one from Peiraieus, and enters the city again from a different direction (1.2.2–4). Later, in the midst of his city description of Athens, he passes beyond the walls to describe the area beyond the Ilissos and the Panathenaic Stadium (1.20.2). Otherwise, most urban itineraries seem to treat the city wall as their limit.

THE RADIAL PLAN

Once he has chosen the starting-point for his urban itinerary, Pausanias frequently constructs some sort of radial organization for his account, using the starting-point (agora, acropolis or ἐπιφανέστατον) as a hub. If he chooses the agora as his starting-point, for instance, he will usually describe fully what he finds interesting in the agora, then trace routes from the agora in several directions without actually revisiting the agora itself. In this way, the hub of his urban description functions analogously to the role that the city as a whole plays in relation to the surrounding territory. Quite often, however, the execution of the pattern is not so simple. At Argos, for instance, Pausanias begins (as was mentioned above) at the shrine of Apollo Lykios, which is in or adjacent to the agora (2.19.3), and proceeds to describe a long series of monuments in close proximity to it (2.19.3–20.7). Presumably, these monuments are likewise in or near the agora.[31] Pausanias then shifts to a description of the area behind (ὄπισθεν) these monuments, which comprises the Kriterion, the theater, and a shrine of Aphrodite. Of these items, the theater can be located with certainty on the slope of the acropolis to the west of the agora, hence Pausanias' itinerary has moved well away from the agora and his original starting-point. But then, after mentioning the shrine of Aphrodite, a likely candidate for which has been located south of the theater,[32] he proceeds back toward the agora: "for those descending from there and turning again toward the agora" (κατελθοῦσι ἔνθεν καὶ τραπεῖσιν αὖθις ἐπὶ τὴν ἀγοράν) (2.21.1) and, after cataloging another extended sequence of buildings and monuments, he ends up at a memorial for Pyrrhos which, he says, is "just about at the middle of the

---

[31] For archaeologically informed discussions and tentative reconstructions of Pausanias' itineraries in the area of the agora: Piérart and Thalmann, 1978: 777–790; Piérart 1982: 139–152; Croissant 1972: 137–154; P. Aupert 1987: 511–517; Pariente 1992: 195–225; Marchetti 1993: 211–223; Marchetti and Rizakis 1995. So far, little has been recovered that can definitely be correlated to Pausanias' account, but there are some remains found in the agora which Pariente (*op. cit.*) believes can be associated with the fire of Phoroneus and the statues of the "Seven against Thebes" mentioned by Pausanias (2.19.5; 20.5). See also Pariente 1987: 591–597.

[32] See Croissant 1972: 137–8. Piérart 1982: 140.

agora" (κατὰ μέσον μάλιστα τῆς ἀγορᾶς) (2.21.4). It seems, then, that Pausanias' itinerary has described a rough circle and has come back to a spot near its starting-point. At Argos, Pausanias indicates the location of almost every one of the multitude of *theôrêmata* with respect to neighboring monuments, so the topographical sequences here are as continuous and explicit as they are anywhere in the *Periegesis*. Yet the routes that these topographical chains mark out seem to employ something decidedly different from a radial plan. A possible reason for this irregularity is that Pausanias was simply overwhelmed by the sheer number of antiquities that Argos possessed, and could not find a way to reduce them to his usual scheme, but a different solution has been proposed by Marcel Piérart.[33] Piérart suggests that the irregular path of Pausanias' account is due in part to the irregular shape of the Argive agora, which seems not to have been a well-defined, orthogonal space, but instead a place with irregular contours which was, moreover, divided into two sections by a large, pi-shaped stoa. Perhaps the complexity of the agora at Argos led Pausanias to formulate a complex strategy for dealing with both the agora itself and its relation to the rest of the city. The same might be said for the Agora of Athens, another irregularly shaped agora that in Pausanias' time had its open spaces overgrown with structures. There, too, Pausanias' account follows a highly idiosyncratic path.[34] In Athens, as at Argos, Pausanias takes pains to indicate where each monument stands in relation to the one previously mentioned, but even where he does so, he does not often concern himself with signaling where the path he traces deviates from a straight and predictable course amid the sights. A good sense of this can be obtained from a comparison between Figure 5.1, the Athenian Agora as it has been recovered by archaeologists, and Figure 5.2, the same Agora as imagined by Carl Robert solely on the basis of Pausanias' text. As we shall see again later on, the mental images that Pausanias' topographical descriptions impart to readers are often quite different from the physical reality of what he is describing.

Argos and Athens are not the only places where the design of Pausanias' city description seems to be influenced by local peculiarities. At Megara, a city which has the unusual distinction of possessing two acropoleis (see Figure 1.3), both of the acropoleis serve as foci for Pausanias' description: the description begins at the fountain house of Theagenes, proceeds to the eastern acropolis (Karia), and then descends from that acropolis toward the north (1.40.1–41.8). When he has exhausted the possibilities in that

[33] Piérart 1982: 149.   [34] See Thompson and Wycherley 1972: 204–207.

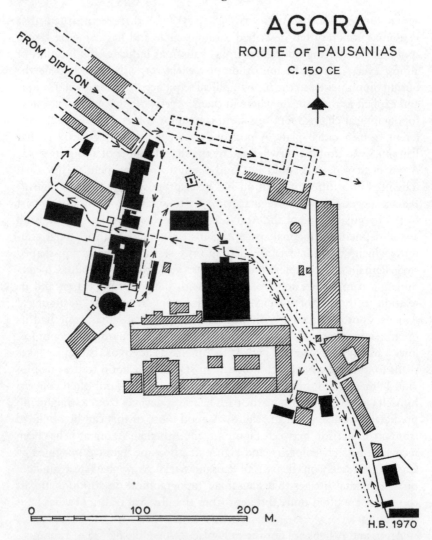

AGORA
ROUTE OF PAUSANIAS
C. 150 CE

Figure 5.1. The Agora of Athens, with the circuitous route that Pausanias' description
seems to follow indicated with arrows (from Thompson and Wycherley 1972).

direction, his description leaps to the western acropolis (Alkathous) and
eventually proceeds toward the agora and the southern part of the city
(1.42.1–43.8).[35] In Megalopolis, a city split into north and south regions by

---

[35] For interpretations of Pausanias' account of Megara and Megaris, see the series of articles by Muller
(1980–1984).

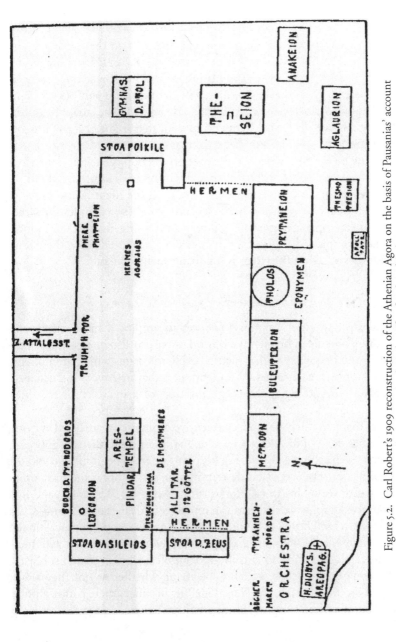

Figure 5.2. Carl Robert's 1909 reconstruction of the Athenian Agora on the basis of Pausanias' account (without benefit of archaeology).

the river Helisson, Pausanias' description is likewise split, and he shows an uncommon penchant for highly detailed indications of position and direction: after telling how the river Helisson divides the city into two parts, Pausanias begins his description "in the part on the north side, on the right side as one looks at it from upstream" (8.30.2). Later, he locates a shrine of Zeus Soter in relation to one of the stoas near the agora: "It is very near to this stoa in the direction of the rising sun" (8.30.8); he then goes on to describe objects "on the other side of the stoa, toward the setting of the sun" (8.31.1). A gymnasium is located "right next to the agora toward the setting of the sun" (8.31.8). Having completed the north side of the city, he starts to describe "the part on the opposite side of the river, toward the south" (8.32.2). Had Pausanias always been as precise about his directions, far fewer problems would remain in the identification of sites and monuments he mentions in his account. All these examples show that Pausanias was capable of great flexibility in composing his city descriptions, and that a simple radial plan cannot be taken for granted when there is no direct indication that Pausanias is following such a scheme.

TOPOGRAPHICAL SEQUENTIALITY

Regardless of whether Pausanias chooses to employ a radial scheme or some other scheme in his city description, there can also be significant variations in the frequency with which he explicitly states where monuments lie in relation to each other. We mentioned that at Argos, for instance, Pausanias scrupulously specifies the location of a majority of the city's numerous sights in this manner. The result is a series of topographical chains where as many as thirty or more consecutive monuments are listed as being "near," "beside," "upon," "beyond" (etc.) with respect to their neighbors.[36] However, even at Argos he does not keep this up from beginning to end. At one point, near the end of his description, he says simply "there are other things worth seeing in Argos" (ἄλλα ἐστιν Ἀργείοις θέας ἄξια), and lists without topographical orientation an underground chamber, a tomb, and a temple of Cretan Dionysos, before beginning another topographical thread with the temple of Dionysos (2.23.7–8). Occasionally, Pausanias will interrupt his catalogs of monuments in topographical sequence and list objects of the same type or class, without specifying whether or not they are in proximity to one another. At Hermione, for instance, there comes a point when Pausanias says simply, "There are three temples and three statues of

[36] See, for instance, the extended stretch between 2.18.3 and 2.20.7.

Figure 5.3. The site of ancient Megalopolis viewed from the south. The river Helisson divides the site in two. Beyond the river, some ruins of the buildings of the agora can be discerned.

Apollo" (2.35.2). Shortly after that, he discusses the fountains in Hermione: "They have one that is very ancient . . . and another that they have built in recent times" (2.35.3). Surely nothing can be inferred from these passages about how close the monuments mentioned are to each other.

Sometimes the transition from one monument to the next is effected by a comparison or a contrast in some feature that they share. At Korone in Messenia, for instance, the material from which statues are made provides the thread with which Pausanias links the items in his narrative (4.34.6):

The gods who have temples here are Artemis, called Paidotrophos, and Dionysos and Asklepios. Asklepios and Dionysos have a stone statue, but for Zeus Soter a bronze statue has been made which stands on the agora. The statue of Athena that stands in the open air on the acropolis is also bronze . . .

No attempt is being made here to locate the monuments with respect to one another, and one cannot draw any conclusions about the relative location from the order in which Pausanias lists the items. The chiasmus between "Dionysos and Asklepios" and "Asklepios and Dionysos" should give pause to those who would assume that Pausanias' word order replicates the order in which he sees things. As we will see in greater detail in the next chapter, Pausanias usually, if not always, chooses the order of words for stylistic effect rather than topographical clarity.

Finally, as with the descriptions of territories, Pausanias tends to vary his focus in the descriptions of different cities, either to highlight some distinctive feature of the city or to adjust for the overabundance or poverty of noteworthy monuments and sights. In his lengthy and detailed treatment of Argos (2.18.3–24.3), a city rich in antiquities and memorials for famous historical and mythical figures, Pausanias hardly mentions a single civic or non-religious building, aside from the customary theater, and a single gymnasium. In Elis, on the other hand, the stoas which border on the agora are described in great detail; Pausanias comments on their position, their internal design and even their architectural orders (6.24.2–6). Similarly in Megalopolis, a city whose decline in fortune Pausanias comments upon (8.33.1),[37] great attention is paid to the stoas and other public structures. In general, Pausanias exercises a noticeable degree of selectivity and adaptability in deciding what to include in his account, and part of his reasons for selecting various things to say about different cities would seem to be a desire to impart an appropriate amount of heft to each of the places he describes. Cities that are famous, like Megalopolis, or capitals of their regions, like Elis, need to have a respectable amount said about them even if there is little of interest remaining to be seen there. This may explain the unusual amount of attention Pausanias pays to mundane civic buildings and other uncustomary topics in these cities. This impulse on the part of Pausanias is parallel to the impulse that leads him to produce a comparable amount of text for each of the territories covered in the ten books of the *Periegesis*.

This brief overview should give some idea of the customary features of Pausanias' city descriptions. The structure of the city description tends to replicate on a small scale the structure we have observed in the descriptions of sub-territories and larger territories. Pausanias treats his city descriptions as independent units within his overall plan, and there is frequently no topographical continuity between his description of things within the city walls

---

[37] Pausanias' comment that the city was mostly ruins in his day should not be taken at face value. He comments upon the city's decline in order to introduce a digression on the vicissitudes of fortune reminiscent of Thucydides' and Herodotos' observations on how even great cities can become small. Pausanias' own description of the place undercuts this, as it is clear that there was much in Megalopolis that was not in ruins. There is, however, evidence for a certain amount of decline in the city's fortunes. See Roy, Lloyd, and Owens: 1989: 146–150.

and his description of the surrounding countryside. As organizational and compositional techniques, Pausanias employs the radial plan and chains of spatial relationships between the monuments he mentions. Neither technique is applied rigidly or mechanically, however. As in the descriptions of territories, Pausanias is quite inventive when it comes to modifying his topographical plan in order to accomplish a variety of purposes: to suit local physical conditions, to accommodate special historical or cultural considerations, or simply to avoid monotony. To illustrate every possible method Pausanias could employ would involve a close analysis of every city description in the *Periegesis*, a task which is far beyond the scope of this chapter. Instead, we shall now look in detail at the description of a single city, Corinth, to see more clearly how Pausanias responds to a particular urban landscape. It is finally at this level of our analysis that we examine closely Pausanias' handling of specific buildings and monuments, and we will see that here, as he works to cope with a myriad of discrete items that have intrinsic cultural importance, the contours of his cognitive dispositions are most easily discernible.

DESCRIPTION OF CORINTH[38]

The choice of Corinth as venue for a detailed examination of Pausanias' methods is close to inevitable. Most of the major cities that Pausanias describes continue to be densely inhabited in modern times (examples include Athens, Thebes, Argos and Sparta), but the site of Ancient Corinth is not so encumbered. Throughout the Middle Ages and the early modern period, the city of Corinth persisted in its original location, but in the mid-nineteenth century an earthquake severely damaged the town, and the bulk of the population moved to the site of the present-day city of Korinthos on the coast. Subsequently, ancient Corinth has become the focus of one of the longest ongoing excavations in Greece,[39] an excavation that has succeeded in laying bare more of the urban center of an ancient *polis* than is the case with any other city that Pausanias describes in detail. Of course, there are still uncertainties in the interpretation of Pausanias' account of Corinth, and the number of uncertainties that remain is sobering, but at Corinth

[38] Work on this section was mostly complete when I became aware of new studies of Pausanias' itineraries in Corinth by Torelli (2001) and Osanna (2001). I am glad to see that the analyses of these scholars, while different from mine, are not incompatible with it, except in matters of detail (to be noted below).
[39] The American excavation in Corinth recently celebrated its centenary (1896–1996); see Williams and Bookidis, eds. 2003.

we are better able than anywhere else to check Pausanias' treatment of an entire city against the archaeological record.

In some ways, however, Corinth is not an ideal city to use for the illustration of Pausanias' usual practices. In Pausanias' day, Corinth was one of the major urban centers of the province of Achaia,[40] and even if that were not the case, as one of the great cities of archaic and classical Greece Corinth would surely have loomed large in the imaginations of Pausanias and his classicizing contemporaries. Yet, as was mentioned in Chapter 1,[41] the city that Pausanias visited in the second century CE was quite different from the Corinth he would have read about in the history books. Some three hundred years earlier, in 146 BCE, the Romans had thoroughly sacked the old city, bringing an emphatic end to the Achaean war and effectively discouraging further resistance to Roman hegemony in Greece. While there is archaeological and literary evidence for continued inhabitation of the city and its territory after 146, there is no evidence for any significant attempt at rebuilding for over a century.[42] Corinth's new life began in 44 BCE, when the Romans established a colony on the site. Non-Greek settlers moved in; the land was resurveyed and redistributed,[43] and while the old city left behind some remnants that the new settlers made use of, including the archaic "Temple of Apollo" and a massive Hellenistic stoa that was reconstructed to serve as the southern limit of the new Roman forum, the majority of the roads, buildings, and temples were thoroughly refashioned or constructed from the ground up.[44] This new version of Corinth was the Corinth Pausanias encountered when he visited.

In the two centuries that intervened between the foundation of the Roman colony and Pausanias' visits, the city underwent significant re-Hellenization. Inscriptions reveal that by the time of Hadrian, Greek had replaced Latin as the most common language for public documents.[45] There

---

[40] For general overviews of the city in the Roman period, see: Wiseman 1979; Engels 1990; Alcock 1993: 156–164; Walbank 1997.

[41] Above, pp. 15–16.

[42] Cf. Walbank 1997; Romano 2003; Gebhard and Dickie 2003.

[43] For a new study of the Roman cadastral survey and urban planning in Corinth and vicinity see Romano 2003 (cf. also Romano 1993). Romano concludes that the earliest Roman centuriation came long before the foundation of the colony, perhaps as early as the late second century BCE.

[44] Discussion of the earliest building activity in the Roman colony can be gleaned from a number of volumes of the official publication of the excavation, though much reevaluation and disputation has occurred in subsequent scholarship. For accounts that are more recent and synoptic, see: Wiseman 1979; Romano 1993; Walbank 1997; Torelli 2001: 135–140.

[45] See Kent 1966: 18–19; the rise of the use of Greek is particularly abrupt during the reign of Hadrian, suggesting that the philhellenism of that emperor did something to encourage the shift. See also Engels 1990: 71–74, and Spawforth 1996 for an onomastic study of the Corinthian population based on inscriptional evidence.

are many probable reasons for this change, including the assimilation of the Italian colonists into their new cultural surroundings and the influx of Greek-speaking immigrants that accompanied the rise in the new city's fortunes. But part of the transformation may also have had to do with the desire among the colony's elite to claim the traditions of classical Corinth for their own community. In Pausanias' own time, the Gallic sophist Favorinus, in a speech to the Corinthians, could flatter them by addressing them as genuine descendents of the famous ancient Corinthians,[46] and could adduce their successful re-creation of a Greek identity for their city as a parallel for his own construction of a Hellenic persona for himself.[47] Despite this Hellenization, both essential and ideological, the Corinth that greeted Pausanias' eyes must have conflicted strongly with what he expected from a city that was prominent in Greece's halcyon days. The scarcity of aged buildings and monuments, the dominance of "Roman" canons of architecture and city planning (more about which will be said later), and the presence of Latin inscriptions on prominent dedications and monuments would all have made an impression, and the dissonance between Pausanias' cognitive expectations and his actual experience of the city surfaces at many points in his account.[48] We have already encountered one prominent example from the beginning of his description of monuments within the city itself. Here, Pausanias' disappointment is almost palpable (2.2.6):

Λόγου δὲ ἄξια ἐν τῇ πόλει τὰ μὲν λειπόμενα ἔτι τῶν ἀρχαίων ἐστίν, τὰ δὲ πολλὰ αὐτῶν ἐπὶ τῆς ἀκμῆς ἐποιήθη τῆς ὕστερον.

The things in the city worth mentioning include the antiquities that still remain, but the majority of them were made in the period of its latter-day prosperity.

Yet Corinth falls short for Pausanias not only because of its architecture and monuments but also because of its inhabitants. At the very beginning of the second book, Pausanias is careful to emphasize the lack of any relationship between the ancient Corinthians and those of his own time (2.1.2):

---

[46] Dion of Prusa 37.1 (this speech by Favorinus is preserved in the corpus of Dion): ὅταν δὲ ὑμᾶς λέγω, τοὺς προγόνους λέγω τοὺς ὑμετέρους καὶ Περίανδρον τὸν Κυψέλου τὸν σοφόν ... ("When I say 'you,' I mean your forefathers as well as Periander the Wise, son of Kypselos").

[47] Dion 37.26: ... παρ' ὑμῖν μὲν ὅτι Ῥωμαῖος ὢν ἀφηλληνίσθη, ὥσπερ ἡ πατρὶς ἡ ὑμετέρα ([there ought to be a statue of Favorinus] in your city because, though he is a Roman, he has been Hellenized, just as your country has been). On this passage and similar ones in the speech, see Whitmarsh 2001: 119–121.

[48] Cf. Piérart 1998b: 150–155.

Κόρινθον δὲ οἰκοῦσι Κορινθίων μὲν οὐδεὶς ἔτι τῶν ἀρχαίων, ἔποικοι δὲ ἀποσταλέντες ὑπὸ Ῥωμαίων.

Corinth is inhabited not by any of the Corinthians – the ancient ones – but by colonists sent out by the Romans.[49]

Later in his description of Corinth, Pausanias makes a rare comment on cult practices that are no longer observed – in this case, sacrificial rites in honor of the children of Medea – and lays the blame for this disruption of the city's religious traditions on the new settlers (2.3.7):

Κορίνθου δὲ ἀναστάτου γενομένης ὑπὸ Ῥωμαίων καὶ Κορινθίων τῶν ἀρχαίων ἀπολομένων, οὐκέτι ἐκεῖναι καθεστήκασιν αὐτοῖς αἱ θυσίαι παρὰ τῶν ἐποίκων οὐδὲ ἀποκείρονταί σφισιν οἱ παῖδες οὐδὲ μέλαιναν φοροῦσιν ἐσθῆτα.

When Corinth was made desolate by the Romans and the ancient Corinthians died, those sacrifices were no longer maintained for [the children of Medea] by the colonists, and their children do not shear their hair, nor do they wear black clothing.

Both of these passages starkly contradict the near-contemporary attitude of Favorinus (or at least the attitude Favorinus projects in his attempt to appeal to the Corinthians), which is probably close to the attitude that the Corinthians (or at least the elite among the Corinthians) had of themselves. Favorinus portrays the resurrection of Hellenic Corinth as so complete that the difference between the ancient inhabitants and the present-day inhabitants is negligible. Even if we had no independent evidence, we might surmise that as astute a sophist as Favorinus would be able to judge his audience's self-image, but the archaeological record confirms that during the time of Favorinus and Pausanias the Corinthians were busily asserting their connection to the very sort of primordial Corinthian traditions that Pausanias accuses them of neglecting. In addition to the re-adoption of Greek as the language of public inscriptions (as mentioned above), Corinthian coinage of the second century has a marked tendency to feature traditional Corinthian gods and cults.[50] In this context, Pausanias' attitude toward the modern version of Corinth seems not only apathetic but antipathetic. One significant effect of Pausanias' attitude is that he expends far fewer words on his description of Corinth than he does on any major city.[51]

[49] In this translation, I have tried to reproduce the potentially significant ambiguity caused by Pausanias' word order. As Whitmarsh (2001: 121) points out, the position in which Pausanias puts the words for "Corinthians" and "ancient" may give readers the momentary impression that he is saying that no Corinthians whatsoever inhabit contemporary Corinth. For more on hyperbaton and other idiosyncrasies of word order in Pausanias, see Chapter 6.
[50] See Walbank 2003. Interestingly, the legends on coins continue to be in Latin throughout this period.
[51] The description of things within the city of Corinth (including historical and mythical *logoi*) occupies approximately nine pages in Spiro's Teubner edition. In contrast, the description of Argos consumes nearly nineteen (2.18.4–24.4); that of Sparta nearly twenty-four (3.11.2–18.5).

This would probably have struck many readers in Pausanias' day as giving pointedly short shrift to the city that Favorinus characterized as "the promenade of Greece" (37.7) and the "prow and stern of Greece" (37.36). The conflicted outlook Pausanias displays makes Corinth problematic as a case-study of his methods of describing a city, yet the opportunity that we have at Corinth for measuring Pausanias' text against solid archaeological data is unparalleled elsewhere, and one could argue that Pausanias' lack of passionate interest in much that he sees in the city leads him to produce a verbal landscape that is less obscured by masses of antiquarian detail than is the case with many other cities. As we have seen already, Pausanias is more explicit about his methodology in Corinth than he is in most other places (2.2.6):

ἔστιν οὖν ἐπὶ τῆς ἀγορᾶς – ἐνταῦθα γὰρ πλεῖστά ἐστι τῶν ἱερῶν – Ἄρτεμίς τε ἐπίκλησιν Ἐφεσία καὶ Διονύσου ξόανα ἐπίχρυσα πλὴν τῶν προσώπων . . .

There is then on the agora – for that is where most of the religious things [*hiera*] are – an Artemis surnamed Ephesia, and wooden images [*xoana*] of Dionysos, which are gilt except for the faces . . .

Cheated of antiquities, Pausanias focuses immediately on the religious monuments of Corinth, and since those come in greatest profusion in the vicinity of the city's forum (which Pausanias calls the *agora*), his description of Corinth will be an example of a *Markttypus* according to Robert's typology. Analogous considerations must have gone into Pausanias' decision of where to begin in other cities, but nowhere does he spell his thinking out more explicitly.

WHERE PAUSANIAS BEGINS

As we saw in the previous chapter, before beginning his description of the city itself Pausanias describes the features of Corinthian territory that lie in the direction of Attica and Megara.[52] This includes the sites on the Isthmus as well as the two ports, Lechaion and Kenchreai. I suggested in my previous discussion that this part of Pausanias' description exemplifies something that frequently occurs when Pausanias reaches the boundary of a new city-territory: a discontinuity in the topographical sequence. I further suggested that this discontinuity was an important thing to take into account when trying to locate the places and monuments that Pausanias mentions in this passage, including the Kraneion and the tomb of Diogenes. Similarly, it is crucial to recognize the discontinuity with which Pausanias distinguishes

[52] See above, pp. 97–101.

his city description from the description of the surrounding countryside. After leading the reader up to the city gate, Pausanias' account leaps to the forum, noting no intervening monuments along the way. The first artifacts he mentions in the forum, the statue of Artemis Ephesia and the wooden statues of Dionysos, are listed in no explicit topographical relationship either to any previous monument mentioned or to each other. They are all simply "on the agora" (ἐπὶ τῆς ἀγορᾶς).[53] Before proceeding, Pausanias devotes several sentences to an explanation of the *xoana* of Dionysos and their provenance (2.2.7). These statues must have been among the items with the greatest claim to antiquity that Pausanias encountered at Corinth: they were reputed to have been made from the tree in which Pentheus was discovered by the outraged maenads in the legend made famous by Euripides' *Bacchae*.[54] It is only after this topographically disembodied beginning, in which Pausanias demonstrates further his determination to ferret out the old and the sacred in the midst of the worldly new city, that he picks up the topographical thread again (2.2.8):

ἔστι δὲ καὶ Τύχης ναός· ἄγαλμα ὀρθὸν Παρίου λίθου· παρὰ δὲ αὐτὸν θεοῖς πᾶσίν ἐστιν ἱερόν. πλησίον δὲ ᾠκοδόμηται κρήνη, καὶ Ποσειδῶν ἐπ' αὐτῇ χαλκοῦς καὶ δελφὶς ὑπὸ τοῖς ποσίν ἐστι τοῦ Ποσειδῶνος ἀφιεὶς ὕδωρ. καὶ Ἀπόλλων ἐπίκλησιν Κλάριος χαλκοῦς ἐστι καὶ ἄγαλμα Ἀφροδίτης Ἑρμογένους Κυθηρίου ποιήσαντος. Ἑρμοῦ τέ ἐστιν ἀγάλματα χαλκοῦ μὲν καὶ ὀρθὰ ἀμφότερα, τῷ δὲ ἑτέρῳ καὶ ναὸς πεποίηται. τὰ δὲ τοῦ Διός, καὶ ταῦτα ὄντα ἐν ὑπαίθρῳ, τὸ μὲν ἐπίκλησιν οὐκ εἶχε, τὸν δὲ αὐτῶν Χθόνιον καὶ τὸν τρίτον καλοῦσιν Ὕψιστον.

There is also a temple of Tyche; upright statue of Parian stone; beside this[55] is a shrine to all the gods. Nearby a fountain has been built, and there is a bronze Poseidon on it and a dolphin under Poseidon's feet emitting water. There is also a bronze Apollo surnamed Klarios and a statue of Aphrodite, the work of Hermogenes of Kythera. There are statues of Hermes, both of bronze and upright, but for one of them a temple has also been built. As for the ones of Zeus, which are also in open air, one of them did not have a surname, but one of the others they call Chthonios, and the third they call Hypsistos.

[53] In the context of the Corinthian forum, a rectangular space bordered by shops, temples, and public buildings on all sides, it might be tempting to suppose that the phrase "on the agora" had some specific meaning for Pausanias, something akin to "along the periphery of the open area," but it is difficult to demonstrate any consistency to his usage in this regard (cf. 3.11.2–9; 6.24.2; 8.30.8; 9.34.3). At Corinth, it does seem that at the very least his use of the phrase serves to set these monuments apart from others that are subsequently mentioned as being "in the middle of the agora" and "beyond the agora" (2.3.1). So "near the periphery of the agora" is a plausible interpretation.

[54] Cf. Osanna 2001: 187–188. One might expect Pausanias to be curious about how such ancient and fragile images managed to survive the Roman pillaging of Corinth, but he makes no mention of that particular problem.

[55] The manuscripts say παρὰ αὐτό, which would have Pausanias saying that the shrine of all the gods was next to the statue (ἄγαλμα) of Tyche. The αὐτό is usually emended to αὐτόν so that the reference is to her temple (ναός) instead.

Once again, where the first item in this list, the temple of Tyche, stands in relation to the statue of Dionysos is not stated, but beginning with the temple of Tyche, we have at least a brief glimpse of a topographical series: the shrine to all the gods is "beside" the temple of Tyche. The fountain of Poseidon is "near" the shrine to all the gods. Here the chain ends, and the Apollo statue, the Aphrodite statue, the two statues of Hermes, and the three statues of Zeus are named without any specific indication of their proximity to the previous monuments. We can also note in this section a continuing emphasis on statuary. Most curious is the manner in which he refers, almost as an afterthought, to the temple that has been built for one of the statues of Hermes. The offhand way Pausanias refers to the temple of Hermes, along with his specification that the statues of Zeus were outside, leaves open the possibility that some of the other statues here, particularly the bronze Apollo and the Aphrodite by Hermogenes, were also housed in temples or shrines that Pausanias does not deign to mention.

The location of the monuments mentioned in this passage has provided one of the more interesting object lessons in the interpretation of Pausanias. Since the original publication of the finds on this terrace by R. L. Scranton,[56] scholars have universally associated this part of Pausanias' text with a suite of ruins at the western end of the Corinthian forum.[57] A low terrace defined the limit of the open area of the forum in this direction, and a number of structures built into or on that terrace were standing in Pausanias' day, including a monumental fountain (undoubtedly Pausanias' Poseidon fountain), a marble "monopteros" (a circular colonnaded monument) and several temple-like structures that are still referred to generically as Temples D, K, G, and F (Figure 5.5).[58] The connection between this group of structures and Pausanias' description seems inescapable, but aside from the Poseidon fountain the exact identity of the monuments has proved more elusive. Scranton suggested that Pausanias' list of monuments began at the south end of the terrace, with the Temple of Tyche (which comes first in the list) to be identified with Temple F, and the other temples and monuments following along in sequence from south to north. Scranton made this suggestion despite the fact that a tympanum block, clearly belonging

[56] Scranton 1951: 3–73.
[57] See, for instance: Meyer 1954: 569–570; Roux 1958: 107–112; Papachatzes 1976: 2.63–66; Musti and Torelli 1986: 217–221, and the references in note 60 below.
[58] Millis 2004 offers a preliminary report of a new analysis of the evidence for the temples of the west terrace, claiming that Temple D seems to have been constructed after the time of Pausanias. Many scholars have suggested Temple D as a likely candidate for Pausanias' temple of Tyche (see note 60 below). If Millis is correct, the temple of Tyche will have to find another home, perhaps Temple K. In any case, this new information does not substantially affect the argument of the next few paragraphs.

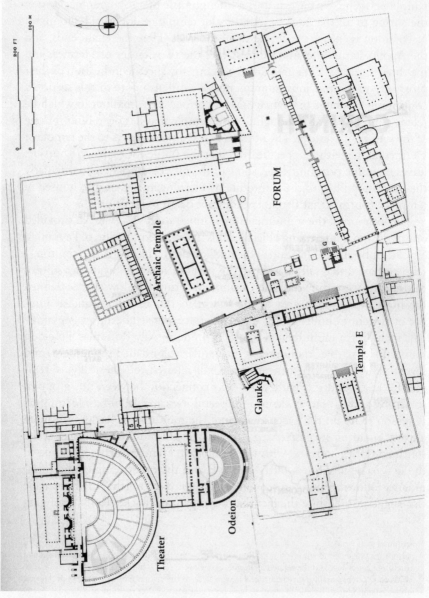

Figure 5.4 Plan of the forum and surrounding areas of Corinth (after Williams and Bookidis, eds. 2003).

to Temple F, bore a Latin inscription dedicating the temple to Venus,[59] a fact that would make the temple seem more appropriate as a home for the statue of Aphrodite that Pausanias mentions at the end of the passage. In spite of this difficulty, Scranton's interpretation was generally accepted for more than twenty years, until Charles Williams pointed out that the tympanum block and other archaeological evidence made it far more likely that Pausanias' description was proceeding from the north to the south rather than from the south to the north.[60] Scranton's suggestion was based on two assumptions: that Pausanias arrived at Corinth from Kenchreai and as a consequence entered the Corinthian forum from the south, and that Pausanias' description of the city was a sequential record of the author's perceptions on a single visit. As we have seen, both of these assumptions are unwarranted. It is likely (though not provable) that Pausanias visited Corinth more than once, and even if he did not, the beginnings of his city descriptions are frequently occasions for topographical discontinuity. When Pausanias begins a *Markttypus* description, the point at which he commences need have no spatial relationship to what he was describing previously.[61] There are few clearer illustrations of the pitfalls of reading Pausanias without due regard for his compositional methods.

The monuments of the west terrace are the last of the sacred monuments that Pausanias locates "on the agora" (ἐπὶ τῆς ἀγορᾶς). He next turns his attention to what is "in the middle of the agora" (ἐν μέσῳ δὲ τῆς ἀγορᾶς) where he records a bronze statue of Athena, and then to what is "beyond the agora" (ὑπέρ . . . τὴν ἀγοράν), a "temple of Octavia, sister of Augustus who ruled the Romans after Caesar, the founder of present-day Corinth" (2.3.1).[62] As we shall see, the identity of this temple is also somewhat controversial, but with regard to what we can glean from Pausanias' text, we can say that when Pausanias uses the preposition ὑπέρ

---

[59] Scranton 1951: 62 (Fig. 44); cf. 68–69.

[60] Williams and Fisher 1975: 25–29 (cf. Williams 1987 and 1989; Williams and Zervos 1990: 351–356). Wiseman 1979: 521–530 and Torelli 2001: 141–155 (cf. Musti and Torelli 1986: 217–221) differ from Williams' interpretation in some respects, but both agree that the description begins at the north end of the terrace rather than the south.

[61] Even if one assumes that Pausanias will begin his description of the forum near a point where a traveler from Kenchreai would enter the forum, it is by no means certain, as Scranton seems to have assumed, that the average traveler from Kenchreai would enter the forum from the south. Streets in Roman Corinth were laid out on a grid plan (Romano 1993, 2003), and there is currently no way of knowing whether a visitor arriving from the east-south-east (the direction of Kenchreai in relation to the forum) would have been routed onto an east–west road or a north–south road as the main avenue of access to the forum.

[62] ὑπὲρ δὲ τὴν ἀγοράν ἐστιν Ὀκταβίας ναὸς ἀδελφῆς Αὐγούστου βασιλεύσαντος Ῥωμαίων μετὰ Καίσαρα τὸν οἰκιστὴν Κορίνθου τῆς νῦν.

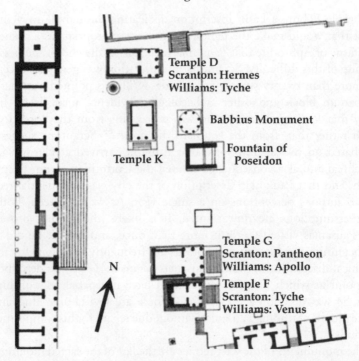

Figure 5.5. The west end of the forum at Corinth, with the diametrically opposed identifications of the temples by Scranton and Williams (after Williams and Bookidis, eds. 2003).

with the accusative case in topographical contexts, he usually (but not always) means something like, "beyond *and at a higher level*."[63] Therefore he is describing the "temple of Octavia" as something that is not strictly speaking "on the agora" or "in the agora," but as something that would be visible from the forum, and hence capable of being treated as a part of the forum and its environs. His reference to a monument "beyond [but visible from] the agora" brings an effective conclusion to his treatment of the sights of the forum. His practice here is similar to the way he proceeds

[63] See Reitz 1891. Reitz was writing before much archaeological evidence was available, and hence could often only distinguish cases where the preposition meant "right over" from those where it meant "beyond." In most places where we can tell, however, "above and beyond" is a workable translation of ὑπέρ with the accusative (see, for instance: 1.14.1; 1.14.6; 1.19.6; 1.41.2; 2.4.6; 2.12.2; 2.15.3; 2.17.7; 2.27.7; 2.38.7; 3.21.1; 7.23.4; 7.25.5; 8.13.6; 8.18.7; 8.44.5; 9.23.7; 9.39.9; 9.41.6; 10.36.7; 10.36.10); compare this with the single case where it means "right over" (2.17.3), and the few instances, including ones we shall encounter shortly, where it means "beyond and at an equal or lower level," e.g. 7.21.14 and 10.38.8.

in the Agora of Athens, where, after describing sights within the Agora, he turns his attention to the Hephaisteion, which he likewise situates "above" the Agora (1.14.6) before moving on to describe the rest of the city. One point we can make in the case of Corinth is that if Pausanias' account of the things ἐπὶ τῆς ἀγορᾶς is confined mostly or completely to the west terrace, then in his eagerness to describe the ἱερά Pausanias passes over in silence three of the four sides of the agora, each lined with stoas, shops, basilicas, and other structures which might have attracted his attention in another city (as they did at Elis and Megalopolis, for instance).

ROUTES FROM THE AGORA: THE ROAD TO LECHAION

Having completed his description of the forum itself, Pausanias now arranges the rest of what he has to say about the city on a series of three routes which depart from the forum in radial fashion. First is the route toward Lechaion (2.3.2): "for those leaving the agora on the road to Lechaion" (ἐκ δὲ τῆς ἀγορᾶς ἐξιόντων τὴν ἐπὶ Λεχαίου . . .). At the beginning of this route, he mentions a monumental gateway (προπύλαια), which supports gilt statues of Phaethon and Helios in their chariots; then he embarks on a string of objects linked topographically to the gateway: a little farther from the gateway and to the right (ὀλίγον . . . ἀπωτέρω τῶν προπυλαίων ἐσιοῦσιν ἐν δεξιᾷ) there is a bronze Herakles, and after him (μετὰ αὐτόν) there is the entrance to the water of Peirene. Upon reaching this spring, one of the more famous landmarks of old Corinth,[64] Pausanias has his best opportunity to launch upon a *logos* since the *xoana* of Dionysos. He tells this story, that of the Nymph Peirene, and then engages in his first architectural description of a building at Corinth: "The spring is outfitted with marble, and chambers have been constructed just like caves, out of which the water flows into an open-air basin" (2.3.3). Next to (πρός) Peirene is "a statue of Apollo and an enclosure (περίβολος)."

From this enclosure, Pausanias returns to the "straight road to Lechaion" (2.3.4). The next thing he mentions is a seated bronze Hermes and after (μετά) it is a statue group of Poseidon, Leukothea, and Palaimon. At this point, Pausanias abruptly begins speaking about baths: "The Corinthians have many baths in many places, some of them built by the public and one of them constructed by the emperor Hadrian . . ." (2.3.5). This turns out to be a rather elaborate introduction to Pausanias' immediate topic,

---

[64] See the testimonia gathered by Hill (1964: 1–4), which include Pindar *Ol.* 12.63–66; Hdt. 5.92.2; Eur. *Medea* 68–69; Strabo 8.6.21 (although Strabo locates Peirene on the acropolis).

the baths constructed or refurbished at the expense of the Spartan grandee Eurykles[65] which were, in Pausanias' opinion, the most renowned (ὀνομασ-τότατον) in the city and which were located "near (πλησίον) the statue of Poseidon." After commenting on the ornamentation of Eurykles' baths, Pausanias mentions statues associated with it: Poseidon "on the left of the entrance," and after him (μετὰ αὐτόν) an Artemis in the pose of a huntress. Here, yet another preamble intervenes: "There are many fountains which have been built throughout the entire city, since they have plenty of flowing water, and there is also the water which the emperor Hadrian had brought in from Stymphalos, but the one that is most worth seeing is the one by the statue of Artemis. On it there is Bellerophon, and the water flows through the hoof of his horse, Pegasos" (2.3.5). With this extraordinary notice, the description of the Lechaion road comes to its end.

Excavations have shown Pausanias' description of the Lechaion road to be highly accurate in a number of respects. The foundations of his Propylaia have been found (Figure 5.6 [B]), and the limestone paving of the Lechaion road itself has been cleared for over a hundred meters as the road heads north from the eastern side of the forum.[66] Just north of the gateway to the right is the entrance to Peirene spring, just where Pausanias places it (Figure 5.6 [C]).[67] Excavations of the interior of the spring have uncovered a plan corresponding closely to Pausanias' description. Adjacent to Peirene to the north is an Ionic peristyle courtyard, identified plausibly (though largely on the basis of Pausanias' account) with his Peribolos of Apollo (Figure 5.6 [D]). Directly to the north of the peristyle are remains of a bath complex which could be the baths of Eurykles mentioned by Pausanias (Figure 5.6[E]). In all, the archaeological corroboration of this itinerary is impressive; in fact, there are few places where the account of Pausanias has been verified so convincingly. From these identifications, however, an interesting fact emerges. All of the monuments which can be linked to Pausanias' description lie within 100 meters of the Propylaia. Therefore, Pausanias' "route" has barely gone beyond the immediate vicinity of the

[65] For discussion of which of the members of the Euryclid clan (a powerful and well-connected family in Roman-era Sparta) this refers to, see Cartledge and Spawforth 1989: 111.

[66] For the archaeological investigations of the road and its monuments, see Fowler (Stillwell) et al. 1932: 159–192 (the Propylaia); 135–141 (the Lechaion road); 135–158 (Baths of Eurykles). For Peirene, Hill 1964: 1–115. For the Peribolos of Apollo, Stillwell et al. 1941: 1–53. For more recent excavation of the "Baths of Eurykles," see Williams 1969: 62–63, and Williams, MacIntosh, and Fisher 1974: 25–33. See also Biers 2003: 305–307.

[67] The statue of Herakles has not been found, although Stillwell et al. 1941: 191, n. 2, mention a possible base for it adjacent to the Propylaia.

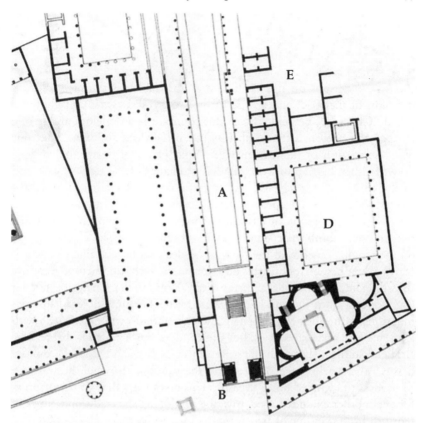

Figure 5.6. The northwest corner of the forum, showing the beginning
of the Lechaion road (A); the Propylaia (B); Peirene (C); a peristyle courtyard, perhaps
Pausanias' Peribolos of Apollo (D); a bath complex, perhaps Pausanias' Baths of
Eurykles (E).

forum itself.[68] There is no hint of this in the text, a fact that is interesting
in light of the high degree of topographical precision Pausanias otherwise
imparts along this stretch.

---

[68] One possibility that would take Pausanias somewhat farther down the road is that the Baths of
Eurykles are not the baths found north of the Peribolos of Apollo, but a larger bath complex, the
superstructure of which is still visible, some two hundred meters farther north and some fifty
meters to the east of the Lechaion road. This would get us about halfway to the city walls.
This idea has been revived by Torelli (Musti and Torelli 1986: 224), but there is some question as to whether these baths would have existed in Pausanias' day. See Biers 1985: 25–26 and
63–64.

THE ROAD TO SIKYON

Pausanias next takes "another road from the agora, the one toward Sikyon" (2.3.6), Sikyon being the next major *polis* to the west of Corinth. The first thing he mentions on this route is a temple and a statue of Apollo on the right of the road, and a little further (ὀλίγον ἀπωτέρω) a fountain called "Glauke's." Beyond (ὑπέρ) this fountain is an odeion, and beside (παρά) the odeion is the tomb (μνῆμα) of Medea's children. After this quick succession of monuments, Pausanias pauses to relate the story of how Medea's children met their end at the hands of the Corinthians, and in the course of this *logos* he asserts that a statue of Deima (Terror) was erected to appease their spirits (2.3.7). Pausanias claims that this statue still exists, but does not indicate its location; one can only assume that it was near the children's tomb. After this, Pausanias branches into an extended *logos* on the various versions of the story of Medea that he was able to uncover (2.3.8–11). When he resumes his description, he picks up the topographical thread again, mentioning a shrine (ἱερόν) of Athena Chalinitis not far (οὐ πόρρω) from the children's tomb (2.4.1). The only object Pausanias mentions in the shrine of Athena is the cult statue, a wooden *xoanon* with a marble face and extremities, but the goddess' epithet at this shrine, "the Bridler," connects her with the story of the Corinthian hero Bellerophon: it was Athena who gave Bellerophon the bridle with which he was able to harness the winged horse Pegasos. This gives Pausanias an opportunity for yet another extended *logos*, this one cataloging the traditional kings of Corinth from the time of Bellerophon down to Kypselos (2.4.2–5).

When he is done with this digression, the next item that he mentions on the route is the theater (2.4.5). The topographical transition he makes at this point is an interesting one: instead of saying that the theater is next to or near the shrine of Athena (locating the new object with respect to the one previously mentioned), he says the shrine of Athena is next to (πρός) the theater. This reversal of his normal order signifies a shift in his topographical focus. From this point, the theater will act something like one of the "secondary hubs" which were discussed in Chapter 4: most of the rest of the items on this route will be located in relation to the theater (2.4.5). Nearby (πλησίον), there is a wooden image of Herakles, said to be the work of Daidalos. Beyond (ὑπέρ) the theater is a ἱερόν of Zeus Kapetolios, and not far (οὐ πόρρω) from the theater is "the old gymnasium" (γυμνάσιον τὸ ἀρχαῖον) and a spring called Lerna. After describing the amenities Lerna has to offer ("columns stand around it and seats have been made for the relaxation of visitors in summertime"), Pausanias then picks up the topographical thread at the old gymnasium. Next to (πρός) the

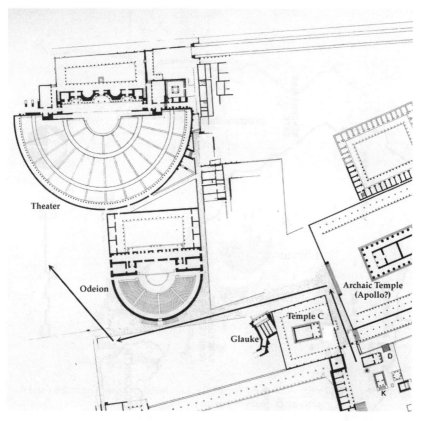

Figure 5.7. The area north-west of the Corinthian forum, showing known landmarks on Pausanias' Sikyon road.

gymnasium are two temples, one of Zeus and one of Asklepios. Pausanias does not specify where these temples are with respect to one another, but he speaks of them as a group: "as for the statues, Asklepios and Hygeia are of marble, but the one of Zeus is bronze."

So ends the route toward Sikyon. Despite the lengthy myth-historical digressions, the topographical sequence is maintained throughout this route, with an interesting variation added in his use of the theater as a hub for the farther reaches of the route. Pausanias employs a city's theater in this way at other places as well, including Patrai (7.20.9–21.6) and Mantineia (8.9.2–6). There are a number of landmarks on Pausanias' Sikyon route that we can locate without doubt. Chief among them are the odeion and the theater, still visible in their position near to one another on the slope leading down from the plateau on which the forum is situated (Figure 5.7).

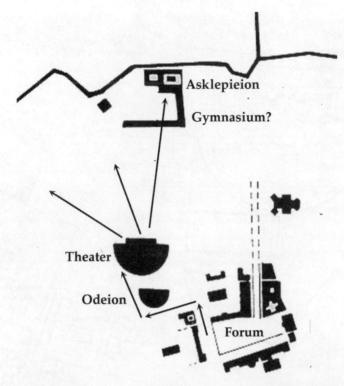

Figure 5.8. The northern side of the city of Corinth, showing known landmarks and the approximate routes of Pausanias' Sikyon road itinerary.

Also, the Asklepieion has been identified by votives and inscriptions as the temple complex lying due north of the theater by the city wall at the very edge of the lower plateau (Figure 5.8).[69] Almost as certain is the identity of Glauke's "spring," which can hardly be anything other than the fountain house carved into a spur of native bedrock south-east of the odeion (Figure 5.7). From these fixed points, the rest of Pausanias' itinerary can be roughly mapped out: the main road from the forum to the north-west begins at the north end of the western terrace, behind the temples on the terrace, and passes between the walls of the precincts of Temple C and the Archaic Temple. If we are to take Pausanias' words utterly literally, then the first item on his itinerary, the temple of Apollo, must be none other than the great Archaic Temple itself. Indeed, the common identification

[69] Roebuck, 1951: 156.

of this temple as the "Temple of Apollo" is based largely on this passage in Pausanias.[70] It is odd that Pausanias should give such brief mention to a temple so large and so markedly ancient in contrast to Roman-era structures in the vicinity. Part of an explanation may lie in the fact that the temple itself and its precinct had been drastically altered in the Roman period.[71] Another peculiarity is that Pausanias seems to omit from his list of sights on this road Temple C, a large Doric temple (larger than any of the temples on the west terrace) ensconced in a rectangular colonnaded enclosure.[72]

Although Pausanias does not say so, the route he is tracing turns sharply left beyond the Archaic Temple, and then passes along the north side of the Temple C precinct and in front of Glauke. The distance between the Archaic Temple precinct and Glauke, Pausanias' ὀλίγον ἀπωτέρω, is a little over fifty meters. In relation to Glauke, the odeion is about the same distance away, and its foundations are on lower ground, so in this case the word Pausanias uses to describe the odeion's situation relative to Glauke, ὑπέρ, must mean simply "beyond" rather than "beyond and at a higher level," and as such is an exception to the most common connotation of the word in Pausanias' usage.[73] Another likely exception will appear soon.

The next items, the tomb of Medea's children and the shrine of Athena Chalinitis, which Pausanias says are near to each other and to the odeion, have not been identified, but from the course of the road we can surmise their general location. It was once thought that the main route turned immediately north from the site of Glauke and went along the eastern side of the odeion and the theater, but more recent excavations in the area east of the theater revealed no major roadway in that vicinity.[74] It therefore seems that the main road continued along the south side of the odeion and only

[70] Stillwell et al. 1941: 132. More recently, see Bookidis 2003: 248–50, 258, with reference to new evidence that provides some support for the traditional identification.
[71] Robinson 1976: 203–239.
[72] On this temple, see Scranton 1951: 131–165. Scranton suggests that the temple is that of Hera Akraia, which is associated by sources aside from Pausanias with the tomb of Medea's children. It is also possible that Temple C is the shrine of Athena Chalinitis, which Pausanias mentions near the tomb (2.4.1), but this would require some backtracking in Pausanias' itinerary. Torelli (2001: 155) suggests that the Hermes statues Pausanias associates with the temples of the western terrace might have been housed in the precinct of Temple C, which would mean Pausanias' itinerary was following an even more convoluted route. While this is not a conclusive objection by any means, it is perhaps preferable to assume that Pausanias simply chose not to mention Temple C.
[73] This has long been noted in the case of Glauke and the odeion (cf. Fowler et al. 1932: 31, n. 1.). See the other exceptions listed in note 63 above.
[74] Williams and Zervos 1984: 83–122.

turned north after passing it. The tomb and the shrine, then, ought to be somewhere to the south or west of the odeion.

As we have seen, the next three items after the Athena shrine, the theater, the shrine of Zeus Kapetolios, and the gymnasium are not linked together in a linear topographical sequence. Instead, both of the shrines and the gymnasium are simply said to be in proximity to the theater. A possible reason why Pausanias employs the theater as a "secondary hub" here emerges when we consider the course that the route to Sikyon must have taken. After passing the odeion and the theater, the main route to Sikyon would probably have made its way through the city's grid with a general northwesterly trend and reached the city wall at a gate more than a kilometer to the west of the theater.[75] The gymnasium, however, which has been associated with remains excavated adjacent to the Asklepieion on the south,[76] lies some 250 meters[77] directly north of the theater. Hence, the gymnasium and the monuments Pausanias associates with it, the spring Lerna, the temples of Zeus and Asklepios, all lie well off the main route to Sikyon. By shifting his point of reference to the theater, Pausanias seems to be indicating, consciously or unconsciously, that his itinerary is no longer linear but is instead dealing with monuments within a space that has at least two dimensions.[78] The shrine of Zeus Kapetolios (apparently the Roman god Jupiter Capitolinus), which Pausanias locates, "beyond the theater" (ὑπὲρ τὸ θέατρον), has not been discovered, but here as well ὑπέρ probably means simply "beyond" rather than "beyond and above." Since the theater sits on ground that slopes down to the north, anything "above" the theater would be in the direction that Pausanias has already covered.[79]

As with the shrine of Zeus Kapetolios, no firm evidence has been discovered for the temple of Zeus mentioned by Pausanias as being "by the gymnasium." One of these structures dedicated to Zeus, however, could possibly be identified with the remnants of a large Doric temple of late archaic date found, not *in situ*, in the area between the theater and the Asklepieion.[80] Roman stucco was found on some of the architectural members, so it is possible that this building survived the Roman sack and

---

[75] Wiseman 1978: 84.

[76] For reports on the excavation of the gymnasium, see: J. Wiseman 1967: 13–41; 1969: 64–103; 1972: 1–42.

[77] This is the distance Pausanias describes as being οὐ πόρρω (actually, the οὐ is omitted in the manuscripts, but is a probable emendation).

[78] See Gogos 1988: 334–5 for Pausanias' use of the theater at Corinth as a topographical reference point.

[79] On Freeman's theory that Pausanias here is referring to Temple E, a theory revived recently by Torelli and Osanna, see n. 92 below.

[80] See: Dinsmoor 1949: 104–115; Roebuck 1951: 5 and 147; Walbank 1989: 382, n. 63; Pfaff 2003: 115–119.

was still in use in Pausanias' day.[81] If so, one of two things is true: either Pausanias ignored completely this temple, which was considerably larger than the "Temple of Apollo,"[82] or he referred to it only very briefly as one of the two sanctuaries of Zeus that he mentions. This is the second time on this route that we have found reason to think Pausanias has paid little notice to a major monument of the pre-Roman era. Pausanias' apparent silence on the topic of the Roman-era Temple C would be a third omission of a major religious structure on this route.

THE ROAD TO ACROCORINTH

Immediately after mentioning the temples of Zeus and Asklepios and their statues, Pausanias begins the final route from the forum, which leads to the citadel of Acrocorinth (2.4.6). As Pausanias tells us, Acrocorinth is "the peak of the mountain beyond the city." Acrocorinth towers so far above the city, and is situated at such a distance from the center of the urban area, that it is almost like a separate *polisma*.[83] Accordingly, Pausanias treats it as a distinct entity. Upon mentioning the citadel, he delivers a brief introductory *logos* about how the peak was awarded to the sun god Helios in arbitration, and how Helios then gave it to Aphrodite. He then engages in an introductory route from the point of view of those going up (ἀνιοῦσι) toward the citadel, noting along the way a series of shrines: first, a pair of precincts (τεμένη) of Isis and another pair for Serapis. After (μετά) these, there are altars for Helios and a shrine of Ananke ("Compulsion") and Bia ("Force"). Beyond and above (ὑπέρ) this shrine is a temple and a θρόνος of the Mother of the Gods (2.4.7). The next monuments are not explicitly given a location in relation to the previous ones: "The [temple] of the Moirai and that of Demeter and Kore do not have statues that you can see." Finally, he says, in this place (ταύτῃ) there is the shrine of Hera Bounaia. Of all these monuments on the road up to Acrocorinth, the only ones that can be located convincingly are those for Demeter and Kore, whose sanctuary has

---

[81] Wiseman (1967: 29–31) believed that some of the elements found in his excavation of the gymnasium were in contexts datable prior to Pausanias, and that therefore the temple was dismantled before Pausanias came to Corinth. As Pfaff notes, however (2003: 119), this is not conclusive evidence. Architectural members were removed from the "Temple of Apollo" in the Roman period, yet the temple remained functional. If a temple so close to the center of the city was still in use in the early Roman period (as indicated by the stucco), there seems little reason to have demolished it later.

[82] New study of the parts of this temple by Pfaff (2003: 116–117) shows that the temple, while colossal, was somewhat smaller than the temple of Zeus at Olympia, so we can no longer call it "the largest temple in the Peloponnese" (as it was dubbed by Dinsmoor 1949).

[83] The summit of Acrocorinth is 571 meters above sea level and approximately 1.5 kilometers from the center of the ancient city as the crow flies.

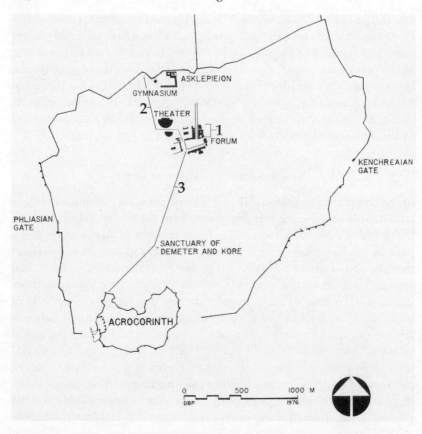

Figure 5.9. Overview of the ancient city of Corinth, with illustrations of the relative lengths of Pausanias' Lechaion road itinerary (1), his Sikyon road (2), and his route to Acrocorinth (3).

been uncovered part-way up the slope of Acrocorinth.[84] Pausanias' vague indications of spatial relationships (μετά, ὑπέρ) give us little information as to whether the other monuments named were also on the slopes or lay further down toward the plain in proximity to the forum.

After completing this introductory route, all Pausanias has left to describe is the citadel itself, and he continues to treat the description of Acrocorinth

---

[84] Stroud 1965: 1–24; Bookidis and Stroud 1997. Within the sanctuary in Pausanias' time there were three temples, and some uncertainty remains as to whether we should assign one to the Moirai, one to Demeter, and one to Kore or one to the Moirai, one to Demeter and Kore, and one to some other divinity.

as a "city" in its own right. As with any city description, he does not begin
the description of the citadel with a continuation of the introductory route.
Instead, he jumps right to the most interesting spot: "For those who have
arrived (ἀνελθοῦσι) at Acrocorinth, there is a temple of Aphrodite" (2.5.1).
Then, behind (ὄπισθεν) the temple is a spring that was said to have been a
gift of the river god Asopos to Sisyphos. Mention of this spring inspires a
multifaceted digression (on the god and the river Asopos) that rounds off
this final route in the description of Corinth.

LEAVING THE CITY

The final thing to consider is how the end of Pausanias' city description ties
in with the routes he takes into the Corinthian countryside and beyond. As
we saw in the previous chapter, Pausanias traces three routes from Corinth.
The first, upon which the nearby town of Tenea is the one and only stop,
is treated as an appendage of the description of Acrocorinth (2.5.4):

ἐκ δὲ τοῦ Ἀκροκορίνθου τραπεῖσι τὴν ὀρεινὴν πύλη τέ ἐστιν ἡ Τενεατικὴ καὶ
Εἰληθυίας ἱερόν· ἑξήκοντα δὲ ἀπέχει μάλιστα στάδια ἡ καλουμένη Τενέα.

For those departing from Acrocorinth on the mountain road there is the Teneatic
gate and a shrine of Eileithyia. The place called Tenea is at most sixty stadia distant.

The second route, the route to Sikyon, is a bit more complex (2.5.5). Here,
the first item Pausanias mentions is the burnt temple, which is "not far from
the city, on the left of the road" (οὐ πόρρω τῆς πόλεως, ἐν ἀριστερᾷ δὲ
τῆς ὁδοῦ). As is the case at the beginning of Pausanias' account, one might
wonder whether by "not far from the city" Pausanias could be referring to
a non-urbanized space that was within the circuit of the city walls. This
would make it plausible to associate the burnt temple Pausanias mentions
here with the large, unidentified Doric temple in the northwest part of the
city that Pausanias would otherwise leave unmentioned. Unfortunately, the
continuation of Pausanias' account leaves little room for that possibility: in
speculating about what caused the fire that burned the temple, he makes
a general observation that during wars dwellings and shrines outside the
wall (τὰ ἔξω τείχους) are often burnt. Pausanias therefore begins this route
outside the city walls, and this route will carry him beyond the territory of
Corinth into that of Sikyon.

The third and final route, the one to Argos, begins after the extended
descriptions of Sikyonia and Phliasia, and with this route there is no specific connection to any point within or near the city. The first point on this

itinerary is the small city of Kleonai, which Pausanias treats as an independent *polis* (2.15.1). In general, Pausanias emphasizes the distinction between city and countryside in his treatment of routes from the city. In fact, one can observe the gap between the two growing with each route: the first route begins right at a gate in the city walls; the second one begins not far outside, and the third one begins in a town, Kleonai, some distance along the route from the city. Once Pausanias has crossed the boundary into Sikyonia on the second route, he seems to regard the monuments of Corinthia as a closed book. Though he anchors the beginning of the third route at Corinth, the first thing he describes along it is the separate *polis* of Kleonai.

THE RECONSTRUCTION OF CORINTH

From the standpoint of methodology, the description of Corinth exhibits many characteristics that seem to be common to Pausanias' city descriptions in general. Just as he does with territories and sub-territories, Pausanias uses his itineraries to produce an impression of the city as a distinct geographical unit. The starting-point of the description is not consequent upon the description of the surrounding territory, and the routes within the city respect the limits that Pausanias sets to the urban area. A consistent topographical plan is even more evident in Pausanias' treatment of Corinth than in other major cities; Pausanias uses the forum as the main hub for his routes that branch to the north, northwest and south. But even in this case, the plan of Pausanias' itinerary is more involved than a simple radial scheme. He employs the theater as a secondary hub for organizing sites in the northern part of the city, and he treats Acrocorinth as something of a city within a city. Through comparison of his account with the archaeological record, we discover that Pausanias omits several major structures, while giving only the briefest of references to others, and there are numerous places where Pausanias' expression of spatial relationships seems incomplete or idiosyncratic.

Elsewhere, I have argued that Pausanias' handling of Corinth betrays a desire on his part to deconstruct the Roman colony and find beneath it something that reflects Corinth's classical identity.[85] He does so by pursuing a number of what I have called "strategies," a term that is appropriate only if we can apply it to motives that are at least partially unintentional or unconscious. In certain ways, the techniques of representation that Pausanias

[85] Hutton 2005b.

employs are incongruous with one another, and this, I would argue, suggests that these "strategies" are outgrowths of a spontaneous pattern of thought rather than a deliberate and carefully planned effort to present Corinth in a Hellenized perspective. The most basic and obvious of these strategies is one that he follows consciously throughout the *Periegesis*: selectivity. Corinth was a large and prosperous city in Pausanias' day, full of impressive structures and monuments, but only a handful of those monuments meet Pausanias' criteria for being "worth discussing" (λόγου ἄξιον).[86] The intention Pausanias makes explicit only at Corinth – to focus on things that are ancient (ἀρχαῖα) and sacred (ἱερά) – reveals this selectivity to be not just a means of reducing the amount of data to a manageable level, but also of identifying and emphasizing particular aspects of the landscape that resonate with Pausanias' cultural expectations.

One effect of this sort of selectivity is the occasional suppression of elements of the landscape that are identifiably modern. But the most interesting of Pausanias' omissions are not the various offices, basilicas, and colonnaded rows of shops that lined the forum and surrounding thoroughfares but features that otherwise might be expected to excite Pausanias' interest. An example of this comes in Pausanias' description of the monuments of the western end of the forum. As we noted, Pausanias mentions a number of statues, temples, and shrines in this part of the forum, but by far the bulk of his intention is focused on the statuary. Excavations reveal that there were at least five structures on the western terrace, apart from the fountain of Poseidon,[87] yet in his description of the terrace Pausanias mentions only two temples explicitly, along with an establishment for all the gods that he refers to as a "shrine" (ἱερόν). In contrast, he mentions a total of nine statues of divinities. No doubt some of these statues were open-air statues, as the three statues of Zeus explicitly are, but we have examined at least one case where Pausanias mentions a statue without mentioning the temple it is housed in: the statue of Aphrodite by Hermogenes of Kythera, which probably stood in Temple F. It is probable that the same is true for the statue of Apollo Klarios, a likely home for which is Temple G. We have also noted that one of the two Hermes statues mentioned by Pausanias is housed in a temple that Pausanias mentions only as an afterthought: "There are statues of Hermes, both of bronze and upright, but for one of them a temple has also been built."

---

[86] 2.2.6.
[87] That is, Temples F, G, K, D and the Babbius Monument. Then again, the number is four if Millis is correct that Temple D was built subsequent to Pausanias' visit (Millis 2004).

The marked tendency to ignore temples and focus on what they contain is a curious one, since temples fall under the category of "sacred things" (*hiera*) that Pausanias is normally interested in. A possible explanation lies in the fact that these temples, to the extent that they can be reconstructed from the scanty remains, seem to be prostyle podium temples, an architectural form that, to modern eyes at least, is distinctively Roman.[88] As always when dealing with questions of "Romanization" in an era when architecture throughout the empire embodies an inextricable synergy of traditions, we cannot assume that Pausanias or any of his contemporaries would have immediately labeled these temples as "Roman."[89] Nevertheless, the differences between these temples and the more traditional sort of Greek temple would probably not have been lost on a careful observer like Pausanias.[90]

A similar response to something that is more unequivocally Roman may be reflected in Pausanias' treatment of the colossal Temple E (see Figure 5.4), a temple that stood on high ground to the west of the forum and was surely a prominent sight both from the forum and from other places in the city. As we have seen, if Pausanias refers to this conspicuous temple at all, he refers to it as "the temple of Octavia, the sister of Augustus, who ruled the Romans after Caesar, the founder of present-day Corinth" (2.3.1). Most scholars agree that Pausanias is mistaken here: Octavia is not known to have been the recipient of major cult honors anywhere in the Greek east, and there is certainly no known reason why the Corinthians would honor her with their most opulent new temple. Opinions as to the real purpose of Temple E have been less unanimous. Perhaps the most popular theory is that it was built to house some aspect of the cult of the Roman emperors,[91] but in recent years forceful arguments have been made that it served as the Capitolium of Roman Corinth, a colonial counterpart to the temple on the Capitoline hill in Rome housing the triad of tutelary Roman deities,

---

[88] As noted by Williams 1987: 26–27.

[89] Although the prominent Latin dedication inscription which existed at least on Temple F (and perhaps others) may have been an additional nudge in that direction.

[90] See Arafat 1996: 45–58, on Pausanias' sensitivity to visual cues as indicators of age.

[91] See: Roux 1958: 112–116; Williams 1989; Williams and Zervos 1990. This theory is based partly on Pausanias' reference (with Pausanias perhaps mistaking a female portrait representing the imperial family as a portrait of Octavia) and partly on the basis of coinage showing a hexastyle temple dedicated to the *Gens Iulia* (the Julian Family). See Imhoof-Blumer and Gardner 1887: 22, Plate E; and Amandry 1988: 59–66 for the coinage in question. More recently, Mary Walbank has suggested that Temple E was built as the Capitolium for the Roman colony: Walbank 1989: cf. 1996: 204–206; 1997: 122. Though he vehemently disagrees with some aspects of Walbank's interpretation, Torelli 2001: 157–167 endorses the identification of Temple E as the Capitolium; however, he does not believe that Pausanias' reference to the temple of Octavia pertains to Temple E, but to a temple of the *Gens Iulia* located somewhere in unexcavated territory to the east of the forum (an idea he had already advanced in Musti and Torelli 1986: *ad loc.*).

Jupiter, Juno, and Minerva.[92] Regardless of the actual identity of Temple E, what is important for present purposes is that Pausanias somehow came to understand, rightly or wrongly, that it was constructed for the worship of a deified member of the Roman imperial family. As we shall see in Chapter 8, Pausanias' attitude to the so-called "Imperial Cult" was at best ambiguous, and his notion that Temple E was devoted not to the worship of an emperor but to the worship of the sister of an emperor may be sufficient explanation for his decision to dismiss this most magnificent of Corinthian temples with the barest of mentions.

In his treatment of the temples lying to the west of the forum, we see Pausanias removing from the landscape features, including sacred features, that somehow, either in their newness or their Romanness or both, fail to conform to the image of the city he wants to portray. In contrast to this strategy, however, we also see Pausanias emphasizing things that are new and indubitably Roman in other parts of his description, as shown in the following statements from his description of sights on the Lechaion road (2.3.5):

λουτρὰ δὲ ἔστι μὲν πολλαχοῦ Κορινθίοις καὶ ἄλλα, τὰ μὲν ἀπὸ τοῦ κοινοῦ, τὸ δὲ βασιλέως Ἀδριανοῦ κατασκευάσαντος . . . κρῆναι δὲ πολλαὶ μὲν ἀνὰ τὴν πόλιν πεποίηνται πᾶσαν ἅτε ἀφθόνου ῥέοντος σφισιν ὕδατος καὶ ὃ δὴ βασιλεὺς Ἀδριανὸς ἐσήγαγεν ἐκ Στυμφήλου

The Corinthians have baths in many places, some of them built at public expense, one built by the emperor Hadrian . . . Many fountains have been built throughout the whole city, since they have plenty of flowing water in addition to what the emperor Hadrian brought in from Stymphalos.

[92] Walbank 1989 (cf. Walbank 1996: 204–206; 1997: 122); Torelli 2001: 157–167, reviving (in part) the theory of Sarah Freeman (Stillwell, Scranton, and Freeman 1941: 232–6) in the original publication of the temple. Both Torelli 2001: 164–167 and Osanna 2001: 193–194 resurrect Freeman's suggestion that Pausanias is making reference to Temple E later on when he mentions the shrine (ἱερόν) of "Zeus Kapetolios" (i.e. Jupiter Capitolinus) "beyond" (ὑπέρ) the theater (2.4.5). Walbank 1989: 367 sees the topographical difficulties of that interpretation (see p. 162 above on the location of this shrine) but opines (correctly in my view) that the identification of Temple E as the Capitolium does not depend on that reference. Most recently, Romano 2003: 283–4 has argued, on the basis of his analysis of the evidence for colonial city planning, that the precinct of Temple E was not part of the original plan of the colony, something that might be seen as weighing against the notion of Temple E as the Capitolium. The temple was lavishly rebuilt in the second century CE, and its colonnaded precinct expanded significantly. In a period when Corinth was losing some of its identity as a Roman colony and striving to integrate itself into the philhellenic cosmopolis of the eastern empire, this is perhaps something that the Corinthians would do more readily for an edifice of the imperial cult than they would for the Capitoline triad.

Baths and aqueducts, at least of the sort Pausanias refers to here,[93] are types of structures in which the Romans excelled. While it is possible that after several centuries of Roman domination the Greeks of the eastern empire had ceased to see such things as intrusions of a foreign architectural tradition, Pausanias unabashedly attributes these particular waterworks to the emperor himself. Hence, we are presented with an apparent inconsistency: although Pausanias seems to de-emphasize Roman additions to the Corinthian landscape in the case of the temples to the west of the forum, here he seems to go out of his way to celebrate such additions. This may have something to do with Pausanias' desire to portray Corinth, in spite of its newness, as a vital and functioning community. As we saw in our discussion of Pausanias' statement about Panopeus, certain aspects of physical infrastructure, including waterworks, are part of what Pausanias normally expects from a thriving *polis* (10.4.1). While Corinth's lack of antiquarian riches and of genuine connections to the city's storied pre-Roman history may disappoint Pausanias, a vital, prosperous Corinth can still be emblematic of the abiding vigor of Greece as a whole. In this context, what appear to us to be "Roman" elements in the urban landscape can serve as crucial infrastructure for a city that is a cornerstone of a Greece that continues to function even though its best days may be past. It would be hazardous to remove such references from their context and use them to argue that Pausanias had a positive attitude in general toward Roman additions to the Greek landscape.[94]

Why these two contrasting motives, to deny the present and to assert the present, should come to the fore in different parts of Pausanias' account may have something to do with one further aspect of the strategies that shape his account. We saw in Chapter 4 that Pausanias varies the types and amounts of information he provides from one territory to the next in order to create a rough equivalence in the length of the ten books. A similar effort can be seen in his account of Corinth. On each of the three routes Pausanias traces out of the forum, the number of discrete monuments Pausanias mentions is approximately the same. If one were to judge solely by the number of objects mentioned on the routes, one might surmise that they were roughly the same length, but as we have seen, this is far from the case: the Lechaion road route proceeds only a short way beyond the forum; the Sikyon road route follows a meandering path all the way to the city wall, and the

---

[93] For an overview of the bath complexes that have been excavated in Corinth, see: Biers 2003; for the aqueduct mentioned here by Pausanias, see: Biers 1978; Lolos 1997.

[94] As does, for instance, Arafat 1996: 184.

Table 5.1. *Sights mentioned on routes from the Corinthian forum*

I. Lechaion road (2.3.2–2.3.5):	II. Sikyon road (2.3.6–2.4.5)	III. Acrocorinth road (2.4.6–2.4.7)
• Propylaia	• Temple of Apollo	• First shrine of Isis
• Bronze Herakles	• Fountain of Glauke	• Second shrine of Isis
• Spring of Peirene	• Odeion	• First shrine of Serapis
• Peribolos of Apollo	• Tomb of Medea's	• Second shrine of Serapis
• Bronze Hermes	children	• Altars of Helios
• Poseidon group	• Temple of Athena	• Shrine of Necessity and
• Baths of Eurykles	Chalinitis	Force
• Poseidon statue	• Theater	• Temple and throne of the
• Artemis statue	• Herakles by Daidalos	Mother of the Gods
• Bellerophon fountain	• Shrine of Zeus	• Temple of Moirai
	Kapetolios	• Temple of Demeter and
	• Gymnasium	Kore (one or two temples?)
	• Spring of Lerna	• Shrine of Hera Bounaia
	• Temple of Zeus	
	• Temple of Asklepios	

Acrocorinth route, the longest of all, extends as far as the citadel itself. As we have also seen, Pausanias gives few clues as to absolute distance and direction on any of these routes, leaving the reader to imagine what he or she will about where these monuments stand in the broader urban landscape. While there is no reason to believe that Pausanias is actively misrepresenting the monuments that lay along these routes, he is undoubtedly exercising his prerogative as author to select and arrange the information he will share with his audience. The disparity between the actual length of the routes in question and the impression Pausanias' account gives of them shows that Pausanias has goals in mind other than imparting an accurate sense of the spatial dimensions of Corinthian topography. Just as Pausanias complements the description of monuments with a greater or lesser amount of history, mythology, geography, science, and tales of wonder to balance the content of each of the books, in the same way he achieves some measure of balance and symmetry between the three Corinthian routes. To the extent that such balance and symmetry can be seen as characteristic of the Hellenic tradition, we can see this as yet another strategy in Pausanias' attempt to recover Corinth for Hellenism. From this perspective, one might suggest an additional motive for Pausanias' foregrounding of the latter contributions of Eurykles and Hadrian to Corinth's water resources: dilating on this topic allows Pausanias to give more heft to his description of sights on the Lechaion road, the shortest of the three routes in terms of physical space.

Yet even when it comes to balancing these three routes against one another, Pausanias is not as mechanical and predictable as he might be. While he enumerates a similar number of sights along each of the three routes, the amount of text devoted to each route is not, in fact, similar. This is chiefly because of the large amount of myth-historical material that Pausanias adds to the second route, the route toward Sikyon. It is on this route that Pausanias engages in the lengthy excursuses on the legendary kings of Corinth and the story of Athena and Pegasos. The *logos* about Corinth's early history is the sort of thing that in later books (and even later in Book 2) Pausanias will produce at the very beginning of his treatment of a city by way of introduction. In the case of Corinth, however, the historical information Pausanias offers at the beginning of his account is confined largely to Corinth's fate at the hands of the Romans, and it is only while discussing the sights on the road to Sikyon that he delves more deeply into the city's past. Perhaps Pausanias felt that the destruction and latter-day refounding of Corinth was important enough to stand on its own, without distracting information about earlier events. Then again, it may also be the case that Pausanias, at this point in the composition of the *Periegesis*, had not settled upon the method of surveying a city's history thoroughly before plunging into the topographical description.[95] At Athens, he follows a very similar procedure to what we see at Corinth, offering no historical introduction to the city and producing a brief account of Athens' legendary kings only when he encounters monuments that pertain to them within the city itself.[96]

In any case, a question that remains to be considered is why Pausanias chooses the particular point he does to insert his *logos* on the Corinthian kings: on the route to Sikyon, in connection with the tomb of Medea's children and the shrine of Athena Chalinitis located on this route. As is the case at Athens, it may simply be that Pausanias waited until his itinerary encountered a monument that provided a means of introducing the topic. But it may be more than coincidence that the *logos* about the kings comes in combination with the story of Medea and her children. As was mentioned above, it is in the context of this story that Pausanias comments wistfully on the failure of the present-day Corinthians to maintain the ancient rituals. Perhaps it was in considering the monuments in this part of the city that the discrepancy between the old Corinth and the new

[95] See Chapter 8 on the development of Pausanias' treatment of local history.   [96] 1.2.6; 1.5.2–4.

Corinth was foremost in Pausanias' mind. A desire to capture that discrepancy and communicate it to the reader in the language of monuments
and legends may have induced Pausanias to expand his second route with
logoi regardless of the effect it had on the symmetry of his account. That
the demands of symmetry could yield to other authorial priorities is even
better illustrated in the case of the story of Bellerophon and Pegasos. This
myth, one of the most famous myths connected with a Corinthian hero,
is introduced when Pausanias mentions the old wooden statue of Athena
that he finds in the shrine of Athena Chalinitis on the road to Sikyon.
Given Athena's role in the taming of Pegasos, mention of the story in connection with this shrine is wholly appropriate. But in order to adduce the
story at this point, Pausanias passes up a perfectly good opportunity to
introduce the topic of Bellerophon earlier, when he mentions, along the
Lechaion road, a fountain surmounted by a sculptural representation of
Bellerophon and Pegasos, with water gushing from the horse's hoof (2.3.5).
Had he inserted the Bellerophon *logos* at this point, it would have served the
purposes of symmetry, making the Lechaion road account closer in length
to that of the Sikyon road, but for some reason Pausanias forgoes that
opportunity.

I believe that what we see in Pausanias' choice of where to put the
Bellerophon story is what might be called a "rhetoric of smallness," which
functions throughout Pausanias' account of Corinth. It is not the large
lavish marble statue of Bellerophon that Pausanias honors with the telling
of Bellerophon's story; it is the simple, sacred, archaic wooden statue of
the goddess. Similar archaic *xoana*, the ones of Dionysos, attract Pausanias'
attention like a magnet at the very beginning of his description of sights in
Corinth. He bypasses the rich appointments of the modern city, the gleam-
ing marble-plated stoas and basilicas. He dismisses with scarcely more than
a few words the magnificent Temple E and even the massive (and archaic)
"Temple of Apollo," and picks out instead the small temples, even, in some
cases, omitting mention of the temples themselves and narrowing in on the
statuary housed within them. To an audience familiar with the speeches
of Favorinus and other accounts of this famous city – to an audience,
many of whom had probably visited Corinth themselves – how incongruous Pausanias' account must have seemed. To such an audience, Pausanias
seems to be saying that the true Corinth lies today in that which is least
conspicuous to the visitor.

CONCLUSIONS

In sum, Pausanias' composition of his account of Corinth seems guided by a number of motives that occasionally seem to contradict each other, but considered as a whole these different motives can be seen as the responses of a consistent cognitive predisposition. We also see that while Pausanias reports quite accurately on what there is to see at Corinth, various rhetorical and literary purposes are fulfilled in the selection and arrangement of the information he provides, and the pursuit of those purposes takes precedence over whatever desire Pausanias might have to present a comprehensive or practical guide to the city. We can tell this much about Pausanias' description of Corinth because of the uncommonly good access we have at Corinth to archaeological data pertaining to the period of Pausanias' visit(s). Because of its unique history among Greek cities, Corinth may be a special case, but until similar archaeological data can be obtained for other cities Pausanias describes in detail, it would be hazardous to assume that Pausanias does not enact similar choices in selection and arrangement and does not exercise a similar "rhetoric of smallness" in the case of other sites. When archaeologists uncover a temple as large as Temple E in a site described by Pausanias, it may be a bit hasty to assume that it has to be a temple that Pausanias mentions.

CHAPTER 6

The landscape of language

We have examined the structure of Pausanias' *Periegesis* on both a large scale and a small scale. Remaining to be considered are some of the features of Pausanias' account that make his work among the most unparalleled in the corpus of surviving Greek literature. Some of the more interesting and unique aspects of Pausanias' writings reside in the realm of language and literary style. To begin our study of this facet of the *Periegesis*, let us return once more to the beginning of the work. As we saw in Chapter 1, instead of identifying himself, announcing his purpose, addressing his audience, flattering his friends and patrons, Pausanias plunges directly into the business of topographical description (1.1.1):

Τῆς ἠπείρου τῆς Ἑλληνικῆς κατὰ νήσους τὰς Κυκλάδας καὶ πέλαγος τὸ Αἰγαῖον ἄκρα Σούνιον πρόκειται γῆς τῆς Ἀττικῆς.

Of the Greek mainland, in the direction of the Cyclades islands and the Aegean sea, Sounion promontory lies before the land of Attica.

Some have suggested that the abruptness of this beginning indicates that something is missing, that a prologue or introductory section has been lost.[1] Barring the discovery of new manuscript evidence, there is no way to prove whether or not such a loss has occurred. But before we conclude that it has, we should perhaps ask ourselves what the implications are if this is in fact the opening that Pausanias intended for his work. I believe a coherent case can be made that the present opening of the *Periegesis* is Pausanias' original opening, and that far from being a pedestrian and unimaginative beginning, this first sentence introduces the *Periegesis* and broadcasts the author's intentions in a manner that is subtly assertive. What is striking about these words is not so much their meaning but the order in which they come. As Carl Robert pointed out, the geographical topic of the work as a whole, the Greek mainland, stands in chiastic opposition to the subject

---

[1] Most recently, Bowie 2001: 27–28; cf. Gurlitt 1890: 2–3; Pritchett 1999: 162–167.

of this first book, the land of Attica, each of them balancing the sentence on either end.[2] But the subtleties of this opening do not stop there. In ancient Greek, there are basically three ways to say "the Aegean Sea," that is, three ways to deploy the article, attribute and noun. One can say (translating painfully literally) "the Aegean Sea" (τὸ Αἰγαῖον πέλαγος), "the Sea the Aegean" (τὸ πέλαγος τὸ Αἰγαῖον), or "Sea the Aegean" (πέλαγος τὸ Αἰγαῖον). Of these three arrangements, the third is the rarest, and it is this that Pausanias employs not once but three times in the first sentence of his work (νήσους τὰς Κυκλάδας . . . πέλαγος τὸ Αἰγαῖον . . . γῆς τῆς Ἀττικῆς: "Islands the Cyclades . . . Sea the Aegean . . . Land the Attic").[3] Ove Strid, the last author to tackle the problem of Pausanias' style in any depth, recognizes this mannerism, which frequently recurs throughout the *Periegesis*, as a deliberate echo of Herodotos, a distinctive turn of phrase that Pausanias adopts from Herodotos and reiterates "to the point of madness."[4] In a pattern we will see repeated with other phenomena, Pausanias employs this figure more frequently than his model and in a greater variety of contexts. It is hard to believe that Pausanias was not conscious of his use of this pattern, or that he did not go about it with a particular effect in mind. It follows that his use of this mode of expression three times in the opening sentence is a deliberate attempt on his part to make a claim for the sort of work that is to follow.

But what sort of claim? One's initial impulse might be to imagine that Pausanias is advertising his work as being in the style of Herodotos. To a certain extent, this is probably true: Herodotean echoes and affinities have long been recognized in the *Periegesis* on every level.[5] But, as we shall see, what is even more important to realize is that for every measure of Herodotos Pausanias includes in the stylistic recipe of his *Periegesis*, he includes at least two measures of something that is definitely not Herodotos. Writing in an age that saw its share of Herodotean mimicry, Pausanias will not allow himself or his work to be so easily categorized. Without getting too enmired in particulars at this point, we can say that Pausanias displays

---

[2] Robert 1909: 264–5; see also Meyer 1954: 550–551; Musti and Beschi 1982; Chamoux 1996: 48.

[3] Kühner–Gerth 1890–1904 II.1.613–614 §463.3A; Schmid 1887–1897: 2.46–47; Cooper 1998: 1.428–9; Devine and Stephens 2000: 235–241, 254–8. Phrases involving proper names for geographical features do behave somewhat differently from those involving common nouns (cf. Cooper 1998: 1.419–425), but Pausanias' manner of expression is still unusual. Ἀττικῆς τῆς γῆς, or Κυκλάδας τὰς νήσους would be less remarkable. Omission of the first article from phrases of the type ὁ ἀνήρ ὁ ἀγαθός is generally more common after prepositions, which might domesticate to some extent the first two examples in this sentence: κατὰ νήσους τὰς Κυκλάδας καὶ πέλαγος τὸ Αἰγαῖον, but not the third (γῆς τῆς Ἀττικῆς).

[4] Strid 1976: 78–80; cf. Hitzig and Blümner 1896–1910: 2.182–3; Engeli 1907: 45–6.

[5] See n. 45 below.

in the opening sentence of the *Periegesis* stylistic characteristics which will appear throughout the course of the work: his prose is not commonplace, colloquial or vernacular, nor does it conform to the dominant stylistic trends of the day. Instead, Pausanias' prose style bears all the hallmarks of being a highly original creation that could rely for support on neither the momentum of everyday speech nor on the learned habits inculcated by the classicizing curriculum that was likely at the foundation of his education. Regardless of whether we deem the result to be pleasing, it was, without question, a painstaking and, as far as we know, unique effort.

Style has been a persistent sticking-point in the study of Pausanias. While many idiosyncrasies of Pausanias' style have long been recognized, there have been few efforts to analyze these features in detail and fewer still to examine the role of Pausanias' stylistic choices as part of the dialog he engages in with his peers, his predecessors, and his readership. For those disposed to see Pausanias as the dependable dullard, the author's style has always been something of an embarrassment, since its laboriously crafted artifice implies the effort of an author who was less spontaneous and more ambitious than is compatible with the image of Pausanias as a plodding, unpretentious information-gatherer. Typically, this embarrassment has been countered by two simultaneous strategies: 1) positing a dichotomy between the surface phenomena of style and the content of the *Periegesis* and construing the former as meaningless ornamental accretions that Pausanias quaintly and ill-advisedly allows to grow over his otherwise guileless reportage; 2) characterizing Pausanias' stylistic experiments as utter failures, as though they were nothing more than further evidence of the author's comforting mental mediocrity. The reader will recall from Chapter 1 Frazer's trenchant quip, "Pausanias cannot be blamed for trying to write well; the pity is that with all his pains he did not write better."[6] Such statements are not hard to find in the scholarship on Pausanias, and are by no means confined to nineteenth-century scholarship. If we examine the evidence offered for negative judgments like these, however, we find little of a detailed nature. Indeed, it is hard to imagine what sort of objective evidence could be offered for such criticisms, since the notion of "writing well" is inherently a subjective concept. Most scholars (this one included) regard good writing as something that one knows when one sees, but any attempt to specify or regularize the standards of good writing beyond the superficialities of good grammar and spelling founder on the ultimately chaotic complexity of factors that go into making a particular

[6] Frazer 1898: 1.lxx.

bit of writing seem worthy to a particular reader. My aim here is not to deny
any validity to such judgments, merely to emphasize their contingency and
to call to mind the obvious fact that the impression a modern reader gets in
reading Pausanias is likely to be different in an incalculable number of ways
from the impression that Pausanias' contemporaries derived from the same
text. One of the chief complaints about Pausanias' style is what seems to
most modern readers to be the dry and mechanical monotony of some of
the topographical sections, but as David Konstan has recently pointed out,
given the catalog-like nature of much of the other literature of the period
(for instance, Aelian's *Varia historia* and Athenaios' *Deipnosophistai*), we
have no grounds for assuming that ancient readers would have found that
aspect of the work nearly as off-putting as modern readers do.[7] To judge
from the surviving literature, meticulous detail could, in the right hands,
be a selling-point for readers of this period.

At the beginning of his magisterial 2,000-page study of the phenomenon
of Atticism in Greek literature (a topic we will soon be discussing in some
detail), Wilhelm Schmid had some wise and extraordinarily impassioned
things to say about the difficulties inherent in his project. *Mutatis mutandis*
the same words could be written in regard to the evaluation of any aspect
of ancient Greek literary style, particularly of the Roman period:

But who would have the audacity, in a situation where so many psychological,
historical, individual influences combine; in so boundless a field of study as the
abundantly expansive Greek language provides to begin with; in a period of development for which a valid assessment must be based on the most thorough knowledge of the entirety of older Greek literature for the purpose of uncovering every
trail of imitation; and no less a knowledge of the contemporary vernacular language in order to achieve the capacity to recognize every deviation from Attic
purity; and finally in the face of the insufficiency of the lexica and grammars
for this period of the language and the terrible condition of most of the literary
texts that are brought into consideration here – who, in light of these difficulties,
would have the audacity to promise a complete and exhaustive treatment of the
subject?[8]

---

[7] Konstan 2001a: 58–60. Cf. Arafat 2000: 191.
[8] Schmid 1887–1897: 1.vii. Schmid's original German: "Aber wer möchte sich getrauen da, wo so
viele allgemein psychologische, historische, individuelle Einflüsse zusammenwirken, in einem so
unendlichen Beobachtungsfeld, wie es gerade die üppig entfaltete griechische Sprache darbietet, in
einer Epoche der Entwicklung, für deren genaue Beurteilung die eingehendste Kenntnis der gesamten
älteren griechischen Litteratur erforderlich wäre, um alle Wege der Nachahmung aufzufinden, und
nicht minder die Kenntnis der gleichzeitigen Volkssprache, um alle Abirrungen von der atticistischen
Reinheit sich zum Bewusstsein zu bringen, endlich bei der Unzulänglichkeit der Lexika und Gram-
matiken für diese Sprachperiode und der üblen Verfassung der meisten hier in Frage kommenden
Schriftstellertexte – wer möchte sich in Anbetracht dieser Schwierigkeiten getrauen, für vollständige
Erschöpfung des Gegenstands zu bürgen?"

At the time Schmid was writing this (1887), it was possible to hold the positivistic belief that the definitive treatment he envisioned could eventually be produced, assuming that enough researchers could work on the problem for a sufficient length of time. Though awed by the enormity of the task, Schmid could comfort himself in the thought that all he had to do was lay down a solid foundation that future scholars could use to construct an edifice of ever more precise understanding. Nowadays, a literary critic attuned to the indeterminacy of texts and the historical contingency of our understanding of them would question both the motives for undertaking such a task and the possibility of succeeding at it. This would be true in the case of any body of literature in any language but is particularly true for the literature of Pausanias' time. The "most thorough knowledge of the entirety of older Greek literature" that Schmid lists as one of the prerequisites for understanding style in this period is simply not possible, not because of any deficiency in the abilities of modern researchers but because the vast bulk of Greek literature that went before Pausanias and that was known to Pausanias is now missing. The assumption that what we have left is representative of the whole in any useful manner is one that is self-serving, self-perpetuating, and ultimately (for reasons we will soon examine) unlikely. The same is true to an even greater extent for another one of Schmid's desiderata: the "knowledge of the contemporary vernacular language." For this, we have access to a small number of texts and a somewhat larger, but still limited, corpus of papyri, graffiti and other found writings. These sources provide us with a general picture of the developments in popular speech, and allow us some insight, for instance, into the great gap that had opened up in Pausanias' day between popular speech and the language of even the most unambitious literary work.[9] We also gain from these sources some detailed information about the languages and dialects used in everyday interactions in the Greek communities of certain places, chiefly Egypt, where the bulk of papyri are found. Unfortunately, one thing that these valuable finds show us is that there was considerable variation (as one might expect) in the vernacular speech from one area to another. For the region from which Pausanias came, little information on contemporary everyday language exists; hence, we have little on which to base a firm judgment as to how much the vernacular language that Pausanias grew up hearing provided a basis which his style developed from and rebelled against.[10] Finally, as little

---

[9] Palmer 1980: 174–198; Browning 1983: 19–42. On the methodological problems of assessing language registers in this period, see Frösén 1974.

[10] For a discussion of local dialects in Anatolia in the Roman period, see Brixhe 1987. See also: Browning 1983: 23; Gignac 1981: 57–60; Frézouls 1991. Inscriptions from the region of Magnesia on Sipylos are published in Ihnken 1978.

as we have to work with in these two areas, we have even less grounds for imagining ourselves capable of acquiring a full understanding of the "many psychological, historical, individual influences" that animated Pausanias' choices and conditioned the interpretation of those choices in the minds of readers of his own era.

If those were not reasons enough for caution, we must also confront the fact that modern tastes and modern standards for the appreciation of ancient literature are to a certain extent dependent upon the tastes and standards of the ancients themselves, and particularly those of the ancients who espoused literary doctrines that were dominant in the periods in which Pausanias' text was first published and later transmitted. Schoolteachers and grammarians taught certain standards of style; certain authors were held up as models to emulate; the texts of those authors were studied, copied, purchased, and housed in libraries for safe keeping. Literature that conformed to the pre-ferred canons, or at least did not deviate from them too radically, had a much better chance of surviving the centuries than literature of a different sort. Our image of what literature was, and what differentiates good liter-ature from bad literature, is inevitably conditioned by that ancient process of selection. More often than not, the literature that did not meet the stan-dards of ancient times does not survive in modern times, and is no longer available for us to study and to arrive at independent assessments about. Much of what we know of non-conforming literature, moreover, comes from clearly biased descriptions and unflattering selections of excerpts by the "guardians of language,"[11] the grammarians and other intellectuals of late antiquity who considered the defense of proper style and language tan-tamount to guarding the borders of the empire against the barbarians. As we will soon see when we discuss Pausanias' relationship to the styles of rhetoric known collectively to the ancients as Asianism, when a modern scholar such as Schmid or Norden attempts to discuss the types of literature that lost out in this process, he can do little but repeat and restate the neg-ative judgments against it by ancient scholars. In literary history, as in any kind of history, the winners largely control the way things are remembered.

All of this does not mean that nothing can be said about style in general, or about Pausanias' style in particular, but it does place limits on the kinds of statements we can make and the assuredness with which we can make them. In particular, assessments about whether Pausanias was a bad or good author, intelligent or unintelligent, pleasant to read or painful to read, tell us as much about the person making the assessment as they do about Pausanias.

[11] Kaster 1988.

What we can do is make observations about how Pausanias compares to other authors on certain criteria which in themselves are objective (though the selection of which criteria to examine is admittedly not) and draw inferences, however tentative and hypothetical, about the significance of the similarities and differences. What we can also do, and what I will try to do in this chapter, is point out ways in which the choices Pausanias makes on the level of language and style are congruent with other choices that he makes in the broader structural elements of his work. I propose that the study of Pausanias' style is not an investigation into mere epiphenomena, but instead is an investigation into an organic part of what makes the *Periegesis* the unique work that it is. The same mind that chose to say γῆς τῆς Ἀττικῆς rather than τῆς Ἀττικῆς γῆς also chose the content and devised the structure of the *Periegesis* as a whole.

PAUSANIAS AND ATTICISM

Mention of Attica provides a gateway to our next topic, Pausanias' relationship with Atticism. As was mentioned in Chapter 2, Atticism was a central aspect of the doctrines that ruled the day among the elite literary figures writing in Greek in Pausanias' time. Schoolmasters promoted the works of classical authors as ideals to strive toward in the writing of prose and in the composing of speeches, primarily (though not excusively) Attic authors such as Xenophon and Demosthenes, and this sort of education inevitably had a profound effect on the shape that literary expression took and on the matter of which texts got published widely and preserved.[12] This was a process that had been going on some time before Pausanias began to write. The Atticizing trend is first attested among Roman authors of the late republic, who attempted to replicate the virtues of classical Greek oratory in Latin, but the concept was soon adopted by authors in Greek, most notably Dionysios of Halikarnassos and Caecilius of Kale Akte, and expanded to encompass an ambitious doctrine of purism in Greek language and vocabulary.[13] In the first and second centuries CE, the archaizing

[12] Reynolds and Wilson 1991: 44–48; Russell 1983: 1–21; Kaster 1988: 15–31; Morgan 1998: 152–189; Cribiore 2001a: 220–244; Atherton 1998: 217–222. On the pervasive effect of the system of education on literature and on social relations, see Anderson 1993: 47–68; Gleason 1995: xx–xxvi; Schmitz 1997: 39–66, 136–159; Swain 1996: 89–100; Connolly 2001; Kaster 2001; Webb 2001; Whitmarsh 2001: 90–130. For an interesting example of the effects on adult literary expression of a particular school text, see Cribiore 2001b. On the nature and consequences of canon formation in this period, cf. Worthington 1994; Rutherford 1998: 37–53.

[13] Cf. Cicero *Brutus* 284–288; *Orator* 27–29; Blass 1865: 169–221; Schmid 1887–1897: 1.1–26; Kennedy 1972: 97–98, 240–241, 365–7; Dihle 1977; Gelzer 1979: 13–37; Swain 1996: 39–40; Palmer 1980: 174–198; Dihle 1994: 53–59.

tendency of Atticism began to be pushed to new limits, and authors made a deliberate effort to purify the language of all that was not classically Athenian.[14] This movement is most easily illustrated in the realms of vocabulary and orthography: dictionaries were written for the express purpose of helping their users distinguish between Attic and non-Attic vocabulary,[15] and obsolete Attic-dialect forms were consciously sought out and put into use as easily identifiable emblems of Attic sophistication.

Pausanias lived through the period that saw the apogee of this passion for Attic correctness. His contemporary, the orator Aelius Aristeides, is known as the most punctilious of all surviving authors of the period in his avoidance of anything non-Attic.[16] It is through a comparison with Aristeides that we can begin to get some sense of where Pausanias stood in relation to the Atticizing movement in general. In the realm of orthography, for instance, the use of the uniquely Attic double-t (-ττ-) in place of the double-s (-σσ-) found in other dialects and in the literary *koine* of the Hellenistic and early Roman periods impressed even some of the ancients as a mannerism that could be ridiculous if taken too far. In Attic, the word for "sea" is *thalatta* (θάλαττα), in *koine*, and in most other dialects, it is *thalassa* (θάλασσα); in Attic, a word for "inferior" is *hêttôn* (ἥττων), in other dialects *hêssôn* (ἥσσων), and so on.[17] If we focus for the moment on this element of Atticism, Pausanias uses the word *thalassa* and its derivatives 281 times,[18] as against a single occurrence of the Attic *thalatta* (7.18.1).[19] For Aristeides, the numbers are almost exactly opposite: he uses *thalatta* and derivatives 372 times in comparison to 3 occurrences of *thalassa*, all in direct quotations of other authors.[20] Pausanias uses forms of *hêssôn* 22 times and the Attic equivalent *hêttôn* only once (7.8.7). Aristeides, in contrast, uses forms of *hêttôn* 121 times, and does not use *hêssôn* at all. We see a similar contrast when it comes to other elements that help to make up the panoply of distinctions between what was Attic and what was non-Attic. For instance, *gignomai* (γίγνομαι) was a common verb in classical Greek meaning "become." Over the years, it came to be replaced in the

[14] Schmid 1887–1897: 1.192–215; Kennedy 1963: 330–336; Anderson 1993: 86–100; Swain 1996: 43–64; Schmitz 1997: 67–96.
[15] Surviving examples include the *Lexicon of the Ten Attic Orators* of Valerius Harpokration and the *Onomasticon* of Julius Pollux.
[16] Cf. Schmid 1887–1897: 2.309–313; Boulanger 1923: 395–435. Behr 1994 gives a useful critique of recent work on Aristeides.
[17] Schmid 1887–1897: 4.579; Deferrari 1916: 1–4; Swain 1996: 48–49. Cf. Dover 1997: 83–95.
[18] Figures here and in the tables below derived from the *Thesaurus Linguae Graecae*; those for Pausanias have been cross-checked whenever possible against the numbers in Pirenne-Delforge and Prunelle 1997.
[19] Pirenne-Delforge and Purnelle 1997: 1.473 list this reference under θάλασσα rather than θάλαττα, because the edition that they follow, Rocha-Pereira, reads θάλασσα, see below, note 22.
[20] Aristeides *Egyptian Oration* 36.112; *On the Passing Remark* 28.45 and 48.

literary *koine* (and probably in popular speech) by the consonantally simplified *ginomai* (γίνομαι). Aristeides prefers the archaizing *gignomai* over
ginomai by a ratio of 478 to 1. In stark contrast, Pausanias uses nothing
but *ginomai* in a total of 199 instances of the verb. Another interesting
orthographic issue worth examining is the treatment of the Greek word
for "temple," a word that Pausanias employs frequently in the course of
his descriptions of cities and shrines. The *koine* form for the word, *naos*
(ναός), stands in contrast to the Attic form *neôs* (νεώς).[21] Pausanias uses
the non-Attic version of the word almost exclusively: 447 to 2. Aristeides,
though he refers to temples much less frequently in general, prefers the
Attic form by a ratio of 59 to 9. Arguments based on dialectical and
orthographic differences like this are always inherently risky, since such
distinctions between forms are particularly susceptible to being blurred
in the process of manuscript transmission. A copyist may consciously or
unconsciously convert unusual dialect forms to their more familiar equiv-
alents. A more sophisticated copyist, if he recognizes that the author of
the text he is reading is an Atticist, may introduce Attic forms where
they did not exist in the original.[22] Nevertheless, given a large enough
range of texts and authors, general tendencies can be plausibly identified.

The comparison between Pausanias and Aristeides gives us the Attic/non-
Attic distinction in its starkest terms, but there is the danger of getting too
oversimplified a picture from looking at just these two. Other writers of the
period were less punctilious about their Atticism than Aristeides, and a considerable literature even developed criticizing the artificiality of Atticism and
ridiculing its excesses. The satirist Lucian, whose estimated dates approximate those of Pausanias, wrote a number of humorous pieces on the subject
of Atticism, including *Trial of the Consonants*, a mock court case in which
the letter Sigma sues the letter Tau for usurping its rightful place in words
like *thalassa*. In another work, *Lexiphanes* ("Mr. Word-flaunter"), Lucian
applies the term ὑπεραττικός (hyper-Attic), apparently a word of his own

---

[21] Schmid 1887–1897: 2.18, 4.582.
[22] Deferrari 1916: 80–82; West 1973: 18–19; Reynolds and Wilson 1991: 47–48; Bompaire 1994: 67;
Dover 1997: 86. An interesting case in point is the solitary instance (cited above) of Pausanias' use
of the Attic form *thalatta* rather than *thalassa* in 7.18.1. Aside from the latest Teubner edition by Rocha-
Pereira, all of the twentieth-century critical editions of the text (Spiro, Papachatzes, Casevitz, Moggi)
read *thalattan* (θάλατταν). The 1896 edition of Hitzig, however (Hitzig and Blümner 1896–1910),
reports that two manuscripts read Θεσσαλίαν ("Thessaly," which is obviously nothing Pausanias
ever would have written), but that all the others, save one, read *thalassan* (θάλασσαν). The more
recent editors have adopted the *thalattan* of the one manuscript apparently as the *lectio difficilior* (the
principle of text criticism that holds that the reading that is more difficult to explain as a copying
error is the one that is more likely to be correct): it is easy to see why a copyist of the Middle Ages
would change *thalatta* to *thalassa* (the form he was familiar with from his own dialect of Greek), but
less easy to explain why the change would be made in the other direction. Rocha-Pereira adopts the
reading θάλασσαν without any explanation for the choice in her *apparatus criticus*.

coining, to describe the title character's inept attempts at aping ancient Athenian diction.[23] Another writer of the second century, Athenaios, takes a jab at overambitious Atticism by having a particularly zealous practitioner as one of the characters in his *Deipnosophistai* (*Dinner-Party Intellectuals*). Ulpian of Tyre, as described by Athenaios, is so devoted to Attic correctness that whenever he was offered a certain type of food, such as a sow's paunch or a wild boar, he would not taste it until he ascertained whether the word used to name it was attested (*keitai*) or unattested (*ou keitai*) in the vocabulary of the Attic masters. For this excessive linguistic scrupulousness, he earned the nickname "Attested-unattested" (*Keitoukeitos*).[24] In considering such comic treatments, it is important to keep in mind that comedy of this sort depends to a certain extent on the genuine importance and prevalence of the phenomenon being lampooned. Like the ridicule of the Victorian class system in the operettas of W. S. Gilbert, the humor of Lucian and Athenaios would be pointless if Atticism were not a powerful force in some circles.

Other authors leveled more serious attacks at Atticism. Some medical writers (lambasted by contemporary Attic purists as *amatheis iatroi* – "uneducated physicians")[25] refrained from radical Atticism, both out of deference to a strong non-Athenian strain in the tradition of medical writing (Hippocrates, for instance, wrote in the Ionic dialect) and out of a desire for clarity in terminology.[26] Galen, private physician to the emperors Marcus Aurelius and Commodus and the greatest medical writer of the day, kept up a spirited war of words (and war about words) with the Atticizers and other people – both outside and inside his profession – whom he saw as enemies of plain and clear language.[27] This effort included, ironically, a 48-volume lexicon explaining Attic words for medical terms (to clarify the usage of such terms in other medical writers).[28] "I have used terms in the

---

[23] Lucian *Lexiphanes* 25; cf. Bompaire 1958: 630–66; Weissenberger 1996: 68–107; Camerotto 1998: 197–8; for other Lucianic criticisms of Atticism, see also *Demonax* 26; *How to Write History* 21; *Instructor of Orators* 16–17; *A Mistake in Greeting, passim*, along with Swain 1996: 47.
[24] Athenaeus 1.1; cf. *Suda s.v.* 'Keitoukeitos' (Kappa 1482 Adler).
[25] At least by one particularly strict Attic purist (who was also a contemporary of Galen), the proscriptive grammarian Phrynichos *Ecl. s.v.* διεφθορός (cf. *s.v.* ἀνεῖναι). Elsewhere, Phrynichos distinguishes what "the physicians" say and what "we" say (e.g. *s.v.* κατασχάσαι; cf. ἀφήμερος, πυρετός, λέκιθος, ἐξάπηχυ). Phrynichos' rival Pollux regularly refers to what "the physicians" say as if they spoke a separate language (e.g. 2.50, 2.70, 2.71, 2.141 etc.).
[26] Swain 1996: 56–62.
[27] Edlow 1977: 3–8, 32–39; Swain 1996: 56–62, 357–379.
[28] Not preserved; referred to at *Ord.Lib.Prop.* 19.60–61 (references to Galen's works refer to volume and page of Kühn's edition where possible and follow the abbreviations listed in Hankinson 1991: 238–247 and Hankinson 1998: 282–288). Surviving are numerous distinctions in other works by Galen betweeen what "we" say and what the Atticists say (cf. Phrynichos' diametrically opposed formulation in n. 25 above). Examples: *Alim.Fac.* 6.490 (on the word for "frying pan"); 6.51

way that people nowadays use them," he says in one tract, "since I think it is better to explain things clearly than to Atticize in the ancient manner."[29] As Simon Swain points out, the extent to which Galen felt he had to defend himself and his writing against the strictures of radical Atticism is a powerful indication of how strong a hold Atticism had on the discourse of the imperial elite.[30] Even if the topic was nothing more lofty than the nutritional benefits of vegetables, Galen feared that lesser writers than he might feel the urge to Atticize in order to exude an air of sophistication and culture: "Whether you want to start the second syllable of 'asparagus' with a Phi or with a Pi (like most people) is not going to be debated here, for this is written not for those who are eager to Atticize in their speech but for those who are eager to be healthy."[31] Another author who writes explicit criticisms of radical Atticism is the skeptic philosopher (and physician) Sextus Empiricus. For Sextus, as for Galen, Atticism and other prescriptive purisms were fruitless impediments to the clarity of everyday speech:[32]

. . . δυοῖν ὄντων τῶν ἑλληνισμῶν . . . ἄχρηστον δὲ τὸν πρῶτον διὰ τὰς λεχθησομένας. ὥσπερ γὰρ ἐν πόλει νομίσματός τινος προχωροῦντος κατὰ τὸ ἐγχώριον ὁ μὲν τούτῳ στοιχῶν δύναται καὶ τὰς ἐν ἐκείνῃ τῇ πόλει διεξαγωγὰς ἀπαραποδίστως ποιεῖσθαι, ὁ δὲ τοῦτο μὲν μὴ παραδεχόμενος ἄλλο δέ τι καινὸν χαράσσων ἑαυτῷ καὶ τούτῳ νομιστεύεσθαι θέλων μάταιος καθέστηκεν. . . .

Of the two kinds of Hellenism [contrived and colloquial] . . . we say that the former is detrimental for the following reasons: just as in a city when a certain type of coin is circulating according to local custom, the one who pays with that kind of coin is able to perform his transactions in that city without hindrance. But the one who does not accept that and strikes some new and different type for himself and tries to put it into circulation ends up looking like a fool.

In reality, there were as many different attitudes toward Atticism as there were authors. Yet even if we add other authors to the comparison, including avowed enemies of Atticism like Galen and Sextus Empiricus, Pausanias still

---

("the word 'vetch' [*bikios*] is quite customary for us and is never called anything else; but among the Atticists I suppose it is called *arakos* or *lathyros*"); *UP* 3.92 (on the word for "elbow." Here, the distinction is between the Hippocratics and the Atticists). In *Bon.Mal.Suc.* 6.780–81, he complains that "more recent physicians" use an "artificial" (σύνθετος) word for "dates" (i.e. the fruit of the palm tree) in an attempt to project Attic sophistication, even though the word in question, according to Galen, is not attested in the ancient authors. See also the passages cited by Swain 1996: 56–62. Some sense of what Galen's Attic lexicon might have been like is provided by a surviving lexicon by an anonymous author dubbed the "Anti-Atticist" by modern scholars. The text is preserved, along with other lexicographical texts, in the manuscript known as the *Lexica Segueriana* (cf. Schmid 1887–1897: 1.208–9). This author delights in finding attestations in classical Attic authors for words which contemporary Atticizers forbade.

[29] *Alim.Fac.* 6.579.   [30] Swain 1996: 56–63.   [31] *Alim.Fac.* 6.641.
[32] Sextus Empiricus *AM* 1.177; cf. Dalimier 1991; Karadimas 1996. Swain 1996: 62–63.

stands out. The following tables show comparative numbers for obvious Attic features in several authors of the Roman period. Aside from Pausanias and Aristeides, the tables include Sextus Empiricus and Galen along with Strabo, Plutarch, and Arrian. Schmid labeled two of these authors, Plutarch and Galen, as *Halbatticisten* (half-Atticists),[33] though the description would probably be just as appropriate for any of the others, aside from Aristeides. Strabo, Plutarch, and Arrian have the further advantage that at least some of their writings deal with topics more similar to Pausanias' own, namely geography and history. If generic considerations have anything to do with Pausanias' avoidance of Attic forms, comparison with these authors might elucidate that factor. In the following tables, each author is ranked (in admittedly oversimplified terms) from "most Attic" to "least Attic," as measured by the relative frequency of their use of the Attic forms in question. In addition to the forms discussed above, I include a table that presents the usage-figures for the words *hêtta/hêssa* (ἧττα/ἧσσα) and *hêttômai/hêssômai* (ἡττῶμαι/ἡσσῶμαι) a noun and a verb meaning "defeat" and "be defeated" respectively. It will be instructive to compare the figures for these words to those of *hêttôn/hêssôn*, from which both words derive.

Tables 6.1–5. *Frequency of Attic and non-Attic features in various authors*

	thalatta	*thalassa*
Aristeides (most Attic)	372	3[34]
Strabo	769	24
Lucian[35]	54	41
Galen	110	90
Plutarch	396	376
Sextus Empiricus	5	9
Arrian	12	168[36]
Pausanias (least Attic)	1	281

Table 6.1

[33] Schmid 1887–1897: I.vii.

[34] All three of these citations come in direct quotes of other authors.

[35] For Lucian, non-Attic forms appearing in *On the Syrian Goddess* and *Astrology* have not been included in the figures, but Attic forms appearing in those works have. Forms of both sorts from the *Trial of the Consonants* have been excluded. The figures for the θάλασσα/θάλαττα split illustrate some of the difficulties of including a role-playing author like Lucian in such a study; of the fifty-four occurrences of θάλαττα, twenty come from a single work, the *True Stories*. Likewise, of the forty-one occurrences of θάλασσα, twenty-three come from the *Dialogues of the Sea Gods*.

[36] This figure does not include fifty-nine occurrences from the *Indica*, a work deliberately written in Ionic dialect.

	hêttôn	*hêssôn*
Aristeides (most Attic)[37]	121	0
Strabo	75	1
Plutarch	332	6
Lucian	26	1
Galen	1,330	174
Sextus Empiricus	54	14
Pausanias (least Attic)	1	22

Table 6.2

	hêtta/hêttômai	*hêssa/hêssômai*
Lucian (most Attic)[38]	16	0
Strabo	11	0
Aristeides	99	1
Plutarch	257	3
Arrian	21	3
Galen	28	8
Pausanias (least Attic)	10	3

Table 6.3

	gignomai[39]	*ginomai*
Aristeides (most Attic)	478	1
Lucian	242	80
Arrian	178	79
Galen	4,290	6,370
Plutarch	372	801
Sextus Empiricus	55	693
Strabo	3	143
Pausanias (least Attic)	0	199

Table 6.4

---

[37] Arrian has been excluded from this list due to the low number of occurrences of these words. He uses forms of ἥττων five times and ἥσσων not at all.
[38] Sextus Empiricus has been excluded from this list. His corpus has only one occurrence of the noun ἥττα (*AM* 1.295).
[39] These figures include only forms built on the present stem of the verb γιγν-/γιν-. Other forms of the verb do not have the -γν- consonant sequence that is simplified in the non-Attic form.

	neôs	*naos*[40]
Aristeides	59	9
Arrian	9	2
Lucian	24	10
Strabo	30	13
Plutarch	43	64
Pausanias (least Attic)	2	441

Table 6.5

Unsurprisingly, these tables show Aristeides to be at or near the top of the list for all these examples of Attic diction. What is more unexpected is to find Pausanias at the bottom of every single category. In each case, he is less likely than any of the other authors to use the Attic form in question. The difference is most stark in the case of words that were probably part of everyday vocabulary, such as *gignomai/ginomai* or *thalatta/thalassa*. With such words, it is arguable that the Attic form would be likely to strike the writer as foreign and unusual, and Pausanias' avoidance of the Attic forms of these words is all but complete. Other words, such as *hêttôn/hêssôn*, seem chiefly to be known to writers of the Roman period in their Attic form. In this instance, no author – aside from Pausanias – prefers the non-Attic form. Pausanias' avoidance of the Attic form is nearly as emphatic as his avoidance of *thalatta* and *gignomai*. In the case of *hêtta/hêttômai*, however, not even Pausanias can resist the tendency to express this word in its Attic manifestation. Still, he uses the non-Attic equivalent more than any author.

What does all this say about Pausanias' stylistic preferences? Other authors who appear regularly near the bottom of these lists, such as Plutarch and Arrian, obviously make no concerted effort to Atticize consistently, but still they end up using a higher proportion of Attic forms than does Pausanias. Even Lucian, Galen, and Sextus Empiricus, who actively campaign against the excesses of Attic fanaticism, allow more Attic forms into their writing than Pausanias. The mixture of Attic and non-Attic in most of the writers under consideration is enough to suggest by itself that for educated people of the time it was difficult not to Atticize. So thoroughly steeped were they in the language of the classical Attic masters that

[40] Sextus Empiricus does not appear in this table, since there are no occurrences of either form in his writings. Galen has also been excluded: his gigantic corpus contains only four instances of this word, all in the Attic form νεώς.

employment of distinctly Attic forms became, in the case of some words at least, part of their natural, unaffected mode of expression. If we ask why Pausanias seems to have been relatively immune to this trend, two possible answers present themselves: 1) he was less thoroughly educated than the other authors, or educated differently from them; 2) he intentionally avoided Atticizing. The fact that Pausanias was not *completely* immune from the trend militates against answer (1). As we have seen, Pausanias does occasionally employ an Attic form alongside the non-Attic forms that he clearly prefers. In the opposition of ἧττα and ἡττῶμαι to ἧσσα and ἡσσῶμαι, Pausanias actually prefers, in this case alone, the Attic form of the word. He does so to a lesser degree than the other authors, but still the contrast with his avoidance of other Attic forms is striking. Another interesting phenomenon to note is that the vast majority of cases where Pausanias employs the Attic -ττ- occur in the course of lengthy historical excursuses,[41] a phenomenon that suggests that Pausanias was allowing himself to be influenced by the language of his historical sources. Again, this suggests that the appearance of these forms was familiar enough to him that their occurrences in his sources, or indeed in his own writing, would not immediately strike him as a solecism that needed to be corrected. Pausanias knew what the Attic forms were and could use them properly, but made what must

---

[41] "Lengthy" for present purposes being defined as encompassing at least one section of the text. In Book 1, two examples occur in Pausanias' narrative of the history of Hellenistic kings (1.9.1–13.9): 1.13.1 (ἡττήθη, twice), and one in his account of the exploits of the Athenian admiral Tolmides: 1.27.5 (ἡττᾶτο). In Book 3, there is one example in the lengthy account of Spartan history (3.1.1–10.8): 3.5.4 (ἧττα). There are four in the lengthy narration of the Messenian wars in Book 4 (4.1.1–30.1): 4.7.11 (ἀηττήτοις), 4.8.10 (ἡττωμένοις), 4.11.4 (κρείττους), 4.25.5 (ἡλαττώθησαν). Two are embedded in the introduction on Achaean history in Book 7 (7.6.1–17.7): 7.8.2 (προστάττειν), 7.8.7 (ἧττον). In Book 9, there is one example in the course of Pausanias' myth-history of Orchomenos (9.34.6–37.8): 9.37.6 (ἐλάττονα). In Book 10, there are two examples, one in Pausanias' general history of Phokis (10.1.3–3.4): 10.1.7 (ἡττᾶσθαι), and one in the course of his account of the invasion of the Gauls (10.19.5–23.14): 10.23.2 (ἐξέπληττον). There is also an example in the tenth book in a direct quotation of a hexameter oracle ascribed to Musaios: 10.9.11 (ἧττης). Of the five examples remaining, it is interesting to note that three of them occur soon after one of these historical sections: after the Spartan history at 3.11.6 (ἡττηθείς); after the Messenian history at 4.31.2 (ἔλαττον), and after the Achaean history at 7.18.1 (θάλατταν, on which see, however, note 22 above). Perhaps in these instances Pausanias is under the influence of a sort of dialectal momentum. The same thing may be occurring in one further example that occurs in the course of the account of Orchomenian history. I did not include this in my list above because it comes in the midst of a statement that seems to be in Pausanias' own voice. This is when he says that "the Greeks are terrific at ascribing more wonder to foreign things than domestic ones, inasmuch as men famous for their writings have seen fit to describe the pyramids in Egypt in utmost detail, while they have not made the slightest mention of the Treasury of Minyas or the walls of Tiryns, which are worthy of no less (ἐλάττονος) wonder" (9.36.5). There is only one further example, 1.36.2 (ἡττωμένου), which is not obviously susceptible to any of the explanations offered here, except that it does occur in a brief reference to historical events.

have been a conscious and mostly successful effort to keep his text free of them. This effort to resist the dominant Atticizing trends of the day, then, must be counted as one of the intentional aspects of the style in which Pausanias composes his *Periegesis*. This stylistic choice serves as part of a broader strategy of striving for stylistic differentiation, other elements of which we will now go on to investigate.

THE CENTRIPETAL HERODOTOS

If Pausanias did not model his prose on that of the classical Attic masters, then what were the inspirations for his style? Recent scholarship has emphasized the role of *mimesis* in Greek literature of the Roman period. In their training, budding authors and orators were encouraged not only to take on the roles of historical figures and imagine themselves present at pivotal historical events, but they were also taught to study the styles of classical masters and to learn to incorporate those styles into their writing.[42] By invoking the stylistic image of the privileged literary figures of the past, an author of this period demonstrated his mastery of the education that was thought to separate a civilized man from his inferiors. In addition, the embodiment of recognized stylistic paradigms enabled the author to communicate intricately encoded messages to his readership about the literary tradition his work functioned within and the social role he expected his work to play.[43] Mature works of the period include *tours de force* in which the author displays his ability to mimic the style of a single ancient role model (some of which we will consider below), but more often the use to which writers put the rich repertoire of classical styles was considerably more complex, consisting not of a slavish imitation of a single model but a creative and polyvocal interaction with a variety of literary heritages.[44] By combining different styles, and by exploiting the spaces between recognized patterns to create an authorial voice that was distinctive but still clearly implicated in the style of others, authors took full advantage of the communicative potential of emblematic ways of writing to create a multifaceted, multi-layered intertext with a wide range of time-honored predecessors. This is what we will find to be the case with Pausanias. Pausanias' text is redolent of reminiscences of other authors, yet it would

---

[42] Bompaire 1958: 15–181; Reardon 1971: 7–10; Morgan 1998: 251–255; Whitmarsh 2001: 46–89.

[43] For a contemporary expression of the value of *mimesis* see [Longinus] *On the Sublime* 13–14, where authors striving for sublimity are encouraged to engage in τῶν ἔμπροσθεν μεγάλων συγγραφέων καὶ ποιητῶν μίμησίς τε καὶ ζήλωσις (imitation and emulation of previous great writers and poets).

[44] See Camerotto 1998: 75–136; Rutherford 1998: 96–100; Heath 1999: 46–48; Whitmarsh 2001: 41–89.

be a mistake to say that his style veers more closely to one than to the other. Instead, it occupies a middle ground between them all, a distinct but richly allusive space that Pausanias stakes out as his own.

A good place to begin a consideration of Pausanias' relation with his predecessors is with Herodotos, since the affinities that Pausanias culti-vated with the Father of History are one of the few elements of Pausanias' style that have been universally recognized.[45] The notion that Pausanias had Herodotos' *Histories* at the forefront of his mind throughout the com-position of his work can be supported by a number of observations: if it were not for the fact that Pausanias' treatment of Olympia is split into two books (Books 5 and 6), the *Periegesis* would have the same number of books (9) as the *Histories*. Like Pausanias, Herodotos incorporates accounts of his travels in his writings, and reports on places he discusses in his work as an eyewitness. In the historical sections of the *Periegesis*, Pausanias, like Herodotos, frequently reports varying versions of events and sometimes expressly refrains from deciding which one is correct. Like Herodotos, Pausanias portrays a traditional moral and religious outlook, one that sees the hand of divinity in historical events and which sees human fortune as fragile and vacillating. Pausanias follows Herodotos in having an eye for unusual customs and for natural curiosities: his description of things like the faunal holocaust of the sacrifice for Artemis Laphria in Patrai (7.18.11–13) or his occasional observations regarding elephants (5.12.1–3), singing fish (8.21.2), tritons, manticores, tigers, rhinoceroses, Paeonian bulls, elk, and flying snakes (9.20.4–21.6) compare well to Herodotos' interest in odd barbarian customs and the *mirabilia* that he reports from the edges of the earth. In general terms, there is little in the *Periegesis* that one could not imagine coming from the pen of Herodotos, were it possible for Herodotos to have undertaken a topographical and historical account of Greece in the Roman era. Conversely, there are few topics in the *Histories* that one could not imagine Pausanias having handled, if he had taken upon himself the task of an ethnographically inclusive account of the Persian wars. When it comes to the presentation of an authorial *persona*, Pausanias' pursuit of a Herodotean model is unmistakable.

In terms of language and more broad considerations of how the two texts are written, there are still more parallels. As was mentioned in Chapter 2, there are precedents in Herodotos for Pausanias' characteristic linking of

---

[45] Pfundnter 1866: *passim*; Wernecke 1884: *passim*; Gurlitt, 1890: 15–20; Frazer 1898: 1.lxix; Engeli 1907: 109–110; Christ–Schmid–Stählin 1924: 2.760; Segre 1927; Regenbogen 1956: 1072–1073; Heer 1979: 97–99; Habicht 1998: 97 and n. 7, 133, 154; Musti 1984: 7–18, and 1996: 33–34; Meadows 1995: 94–96; Arafat 1996: 23; Ameling 1996: 147–149; Moggi 1996: 83–87. Bowie 2001: 26–27.

logoi and *theôrêmata*. Pausanias also replicates Herodotos' fondness for lengthy digressions: when the presence of Sardinian offerings at Delphi motivates Pausanias to dilate extensively on the history of Sardinia (10.17.1–13), or when Pausanias launches into a detailed discussion of Ethiopia, Libya, and the Atlantic Ocean, occasioned solely by his discovery of "Ethiopian" faces carved on the vessel held by the statue of the goddess Nemesis at Rhamnous (1.33.3–6),[46] one cannot help but think of the way Herodotos frequently engages in similar digressions that are – on the surface, at least – obliquely pertinent to the matter at hand.[47] One major historical excursus in Pausanias' account, his narration of the Gallic invasion of Greece in the third century BCE (10.19.4–23.4),[48] seems patterned fundamentally on Herodotos' account of the second Persian invasion of Greece: when Herodotos' Persians and Pausanias' Gauls arrive, the Greeks in both cases mount a doomed but valiant defense at the pass of Thermopylai. In both Herodotos and Pausanias, the defense is broken when the invaders discover a mountain path (the same path in both cases, guarded both times by a contingent of Phocians[49]) by which the pass can be circumvented. After breaching the pass at Thermopylai, the Persians and the Gauls both descend upon the Oracle of Apollo at Delphi, where they are assailed by violent signs and portents sent by the angry god. It could be that the two invasions were in fact similar in many respects, but that does not decrease the likelihood that Pausanias looked to Herodotos for a model both when he chose to narrate this particular event in detail and when he set about deciding how to do so.[50]

One of the most important ways in which Pausanias draws on Herodotos is in the adaptation of entire sentences and phrases that recall prominent statements made by the earlier writer. For instance, a programmatic statement near the beginning of Herodotos' *Histories* announces the scope of the historian's work: προβήσομαι ἐς τὸ πρόσω τοῦ λόγου, ὁμοίως μικρὰ καὶ μεγάλα ἄστεα ἀνθρώπων ἐπεξιών. Τὰ γὰρ τὸ πάλαι μεγάλα ἦν,

---

[46] An occasion for one of Pausanias' few direct references to Herodotos (1.33.5), and, interestingly enough, it is a somewhat erroneous reference. Pausanias says that Herodotos, in referring to the people of northern Africa, calls them the Nasamonean Atlantes. In fact, the Nasamoneans and the Atlantes are two different people in Herodotos' text (Hdt. 4.182–184; cf. Frazer 1898: 1.459; Musti and Beschi 1982: 394–5). Is this perhaps an example of an "error of familiarity"?

[47] I refer to such passages as "digressions" only to signify that they lack much relevance that is immediately obvious in their contexts. I do not deny that either Herodotos or Pausanias may have had deeper or less obvious motives for including them.

[48] Recounted more briefly also at 1.3.5–4.6; cf. Hdt. 7.175–233; 8.35–39.

[49] Paus. 9.22.8–11 ~ Hdt. 7.213–218.

[50] For a detailed comparison of the two accounts, see Nachtergael 1975: 145–164; see also: Bearzot 1992: 103–105; Ameling 1996: 145–158.

τὰ πολλὰ αὐτῶν σμικρὰ γέγονε· τὰ δὲ ἐπ᾽ ἐμέο ἦν μεγάλα, πρότερον ἦν σμικρά ("I shall proceed further in my account, pursuing in like fashion both small and great cities of men. For those that were great long ago, many of them have become small, and those that were great in my own time were small previously"; Herodotos 1.5). Pausanias coopts this sentence to create what many have taken to be his own declaration of the intended scope of his work, a statement we have already discussed in Chapter 3: δεῖ δέ με ἀφικέσθαι τοῦ λόγου πρόσω, πάντα ὁμοίως ἐπεξιόντα τὰ Ἑλληνικά ("I must go further in my account, pursuing in like fashion all things Greek") (1.26.4). Herodotos' τὸ πρόσω τοῦ λόγου ("further in my account") is matched by Pausanias' τοῦ λόγου πρόσω, and Herodotos' words for "pursuing in like fashion" (ὁμοίως . . . ἐπεξιόντα) are copied verbatim by Pausanias. The latter half of the same statement by Herodotos, where he speaks of great cities becoming small and small cities becoming great, is in all likelihood inspiration for another important passage in the *Periegesis* (8.33.1):

εἰ δὲ ἡ Μεγάλη πόλις προθυμίᾳ τε τῇ πάσῃ συνοικισθεῖσα ὑπὸ Ἀρκάδων καὶ ἐπὶ μεγίσταις τῶν Ἑλλήνων ἐλπίσιν ἐς αὐτὴν κόσμον τὸν ἅπαντα καὶ εὐδαιμονίαν τὴν ἀρχαίαν ἀφῄρηται καὶ τὰ πολλά ἐστιν αὐτῆς ἐρείπια ἐφ᾽ ἡμῶν, θαῦμα οὐδὲν ἐποιησάμην, εἰδὼς τὸ δαιμόνιον νεώτερα ἀεί τινα ἐθέλον ἐργάζεσθαι, καὶ ὁμοίως τὰ πάντα τά τε ἐχυρὰ καὶ τὰ ἀσθενῆ καὶ τὰ γινόμενά τε καὶ ὁπόσα ἀπόλλυνται μεταβάλλουσαν τὴν τύχην, καὶ ὅπως ἂν αὐτῇ παριστῆται μετὰ ἰσχυρᾶς ἀνάγκης ἄγουσαν.

But if Megalopolis, founded with all enthusiasm by the Arcadians, and to the great hopes of the Greeks toward her, is bereft of all adornment and her ancient good fortune and is, generally, in ruins in our times, I was not at all surprised, knowing that the divinity always tends to make things different and that Tyche [Fortune] brings change to all things alike, both the strong and the weak and the waxing and the things that wane, and leads them along with forceful compulsion, in whichever way occurs to her.

Pausanias goes on to expand on Herodotos' concise reference to the fates of great cities and small cities with a long catalogue of cities whose fortunes had changed from good to bad or vice versa between ancient days and Pausanias' own (8.33.2–4). In introducing the role of divinity in such changes of fortune (something not present in Herodotos' statement), Pausanias seems to draw on a second famous passage from Herodotos, where Solon is advising Croesus that his current good fortune may not last (1.32):[51]

---

[51] Cf. Hdt. 3.40, 7.46.

Ὦ Κροῖσε, ἐπιστάμενόν με τὸ θεῖον πᾶν ἐὸν φθονερόν τε καὶ ταραχῶδες ἐπειρωτᾷς ἀνθρωπηίων πρηγμάτων πέρι.

O Croesus, when you ask me about human affairs you are asking one who understands that the divinity is a completely grudging and disruptive force.

Completing this cycle of allusions, Pausanias also draws from passages like Solon's advice to Croesus the idea that the divine forces can be jealous or hostile, an idea which he applies to the fate of Demosthenes and Homer (2.33.3) and to the failure of Agesilaos' Asian campaign (3.9.7).[52] But for Herodotos and for Pausanias, the gods can also serve as forces for order by punishing injustice. Of the Cyrenean queen Pheretime, who took bloody revenge on the city of Barka for the death of her son and subsequently died with a horrible infestation of worms, Herodotos says (4.205): ὡς ἄρα ἀνθρώποισι αἱ λίην ἰσχυραὶ τιμωρίαι πρὸς θεῶν ἐπίφθονοι γίνονται ("thus indeed excessively strong vengeance on the part of human beings is hateful in the eyes of the gods"). Pausanias borrows these words, performs minor alterations on them, and applies them to the case of the mythical Theban figure Antiope, who was driven mad by Dionysos after she took brutal vengeance on the wife of Lykos (9.17.6): ἐπίφθονοι δὲ ἀεί πως παρὰ θεῶν αἱ ὑπερβολαὶ τῶν τιμωριῶν εἰσι ("excesses of vengeance are in some way always hateful in the eyes of the gods"). Mention was made above of the fact that Pausanias' critical treatment of his sources could be compared to that of Herodotos. Sometimes Pausanias' debt in this area goes beyond a similarity of approach to an actual similarity in words; for instance, Pausanias says at one point, ἐμοὶ μὲν οὖν λέγειν μὲν τὰ ὑπὸ Ἑλλήνων λεγόμενα ἀνάγκη, πείθεσθαι δὲ πᾶσιν οὐκέτι ἀνάγκη ("it is necessary for me to say the things that are said by the Greeks, but it is not at all necessary for me to believe them all"; 6.3.8), closely echoing another declaration of Herodotos: Ἐγὼ δὲ ὀφείλω λέγειν τὰ λεγόμενα, πείθεσθαί γε μὲν οὐ παντάπασιν ὀφείλω ("I am obliged to say the things that are said, but I am not obliged to believe them at all"; Herodotos 7.152).[53]

Numerous other similarites between the two authors, from the level of the overall structure of their works down to their choice of individual words, could be pointed out, and have been cataloged by previous scholars so thoroughly that to multiply the examples here would be otiose.[54] In addition to similarities of thought and expression, there are also obvious affiinities in the figures of speech the two authors like to employ, and even

---

[52] Cf. Pfundtner 1866: 11–12.   [53] Cf. Pfundtner 1866: 9–10.
[54] Esp. Pfundtner 1866; Wernicke 1884. In addition to ones cited below, the reader will find other striking examples at Paus. 1.5.4 ~ Hdt. 9.16; Paus. 1.25.3 ~ Hdt. 5.97.

in the way they use certain individual words. Some of these similarities we will discuss shortly, but to confine ourselves for the moment to the sort of imitation that the examples given above demonstrate, we can note that Pausanias is hardly subtle about his expropriation of Herodotean material. The passages of Herodotos that he coopts are often famous ones, from crucial and memorable parts of the *Histories*. In the course of the *Periegesis*, it becomes clear that Pausanias expected his audience to be familiar with the histories of Herodotos. He refrains from giving details about the reform of the Athenian tribes by Cleisthenes on the grounds that Herodotos has already covered it;[55] evidently for the same reasons he refuses to narrate in detail the battle of Plataia;[56] and he declines to judge whether the mythical story of Io is more correctly told by Herodotos or by "the Greeks" without feeling the need to explain what Herodotos' version was;[57] and in general he refrains from narrating in detail any of the stories for which Herodotos was famous. The familiarity with Herodotos' text that Pausanias assumes in his readers suggests that he also expected his audience to recognize his verbal and stylistic nods to the Halicarnassian.

At the same time, however, we mustn't be too quick to categorize Pausanias' style as Herodotean *tout court*. Other works of the period, works that Pausanias arguably could have read and been influenced by, come much closer to replicating Herodotos' style. Although the chronology is not completely clear, it seems likely that the bulk of Pausanias' writing postdated the publishing of two important Herodotean imitations, Arrian's *Indica* (an account of India based partly on the exploratory journey of Alexander the Great's admiral Nearchos down the Indus river) and an essay ascribed to Lucian known as *On the Syrian Goddess*.[58] The most vivid and pervasive of the Herodotisms in these texts is the fact that they are written in Herodotos'

---

[55] Paus. 1.5.2. [56] Paus. 3.17.7
[57] Paus. 2.16.2 (a clear reference to the version of the myth of Io Herodotos ascribes to Persian sources [Hdt. 1.1]). The overall handling of this story is another nod to Herodotos on Pausanias' part; Herodotos also points out the contrast between the version he narrates (the one he ascribes to Persians, that is) and the traditional story of Io as told by "the Greeks" (1.1).
[58] Work on this chapter was substantially complete when I gained access to the new, richly annotated edition of the Lucianic essay by Jane Lightfoot (Lightfoot 2003). This will be the standard reference to consult on this work for the foreseeable future. There are no solid grounds for dating *On the Syrian Goddess*, though if it is by Lucian (see note 60), Lucian's career overlapped with Pausanias' to a considerable extent both chronologically and geographically (cf. Baldwin 1973: 7–20; Jones 1986: 8–23; Lightfoot 2003: 207–8), and the period of the 160s, when Lucian is known to have been interested in historiographical issues, as evinced by *How to Write History* and perhaps *True Stories* (both of which will be discussed below), would be at least as good a guess as any other. Lightfoot, on the basis of thematic parallels, finds it plausible that Lucian might have seen at least the first two books or so of the *Periegesis* before writing *DDS*. On Polański's intriguing suggestion that the *DDS* may be from the fourth century CE or later (Polański 1998: 98–9) see Lightfoot 2003: 202–204. Arrian's *Indica* was probably written soon after the *Anabasis*, since Arrian announces his

Ionic dialect, a strain of Greek that fell out of fashion as a medium of literary expression soon after the text of Herodotos was disseminated.[59] While
the authenticity of *On the Syrian Goddess* has been challenged (as is the case
with many works in the Lucianic corpus), most scholars now seem inclined
to accept it as genuine.[60] But the question of authenticity (except where it
bears on the chronological relationship with Pausanias' work) makes little
difference for the arguments that will be made here. Perhaps significantly,
the topic of *On the Syrian Goddess* bears a certain resemblance to the sort
of thing that Pausanias concerns himself with.[61] It comprises a description of the shrine and the rites that honor a local goddess in the narrator's
own homeland.[62] The first few sentences illustrate some of the Herodotean
elements of the work:

intent to write the *Indica* in the course of the *Anabasis* (5.4.3). Some date the *Anabasis* to the 120s
(e.g. Bosworth 1980–1995: 1.9–11); others, however (e.g. Tonnet 1988: 1.60–101), would place it later.
Tonnet offers a specific range: between 137 and 165, and would put the *Indica* later within the same
range. Either way, it would predate the writing of most of the *Periegesis*. See Sisti 2001: lv–lviii for a
good overview of the debate (Sisti himself leans tentatively toward an early date).

59 We know of other works of this period and later periods written in an artificial Ionic dialect. Aretaios
of Cappadocia wrote medical works in Ionic dialect in imitation of Hippokrates. A writer of the
Hadrianic period, Kephalion (or Kephalon), apparently wrote a work of history in Ionic in nine
books (like Herodotos) and gave to each of these books the name of one of the nine Muses, as had
come to happen with Herodotos' work (*Suda, s.v.* Kappa 1449; critique in Photius, *Library* 68.34a).
Later, we hear of Dionysios of Miletos (*Suda* Delta 1180: *Persika* in Ionic dialect); a Roman historian
Cordatus (*Suda* Kappa 1905: Roman history [written in Ionic Greek] in fifteen books covering from
the foundation of Rome to the reign of Alexander Caesar); and in the Byzantine period the history
of Constantine the Just by Praxagora. Unfortunately, no more than references to any of these works
survive, so their language and style is not available for comparison to the surviving texts that will be
discussed here. Cf. Allinson 1886; Lightfoot 2003: 91–97, 139–142.

60 For a thorough overview of the problem, see Lightfoot 2003: 184–208. Lightfoot acknowledges
that certainty is impossible, but regards the case against Lucianic authorship as unconvincing and
adduces new and, to my mind, convincing arguments in favor of the work's authenticity. See also
Bompaire 1958: 646–653; Anderson 1976: 68–72; Hall 1981: 374–81; Jones 1986: 41; Branham 1989:
152–2; Swain 1996: 304–5; Elsner 2001a: 124–5. Among recent dissenters, Baslez (1994) doubts the
authenticity on the basis of what she sees as inaccuracies regarding Semitic cult practices that a true
native of Syria like Lucian, and a true devotee of the cult (as the author claims to be) would not have
committed. Perhaps Baslez's most potent argument is that the author misunderstands the practice of
dedicating a lock of hair to the deity. The author presents this as something that he did himself
(*On the Syrian Goddess* 60) as a rite of passage into manhood. According to Baslez, this ceremony
is actually performed by priests as a symbol of their dedication to the god. (Baslez 1994: 175–6).
This and Baslez's other arguments are a rather a thin foundation for arguing against authenticity,
however, particularly for an author as fond of role-playing and misdirection as Lucian (see below on
the possible satiric and comic elements in the account). See also Polański 1998 for another contrarian
view.

61 See Lightfoot 2003: 218, for a number of more exact thematic parallels between the two.

62 The narrator describes himself as an "Assyrian" (1); cf. Lightfoot 2003: 182–183, 204–207, who points
out that the author calling himself "Assyrian" does not settle the question of his ethnic or cultural
relationship to the shrine and cult at Hierapolis. As was discussed in Chapter 1, parallel problems
exist when considering the relationship of the Greek-speaking "Lydian" Pausanias to the mainland
of Greece that he makes the subject of his *Periegesis*.

Ἔστιν ἐν Συρίῃ πόλις οὐ πολλὸν ἀπὸ τοῦ Εὐφρήτεω ποταμοῦ, καλέεται δὲ Ἱρή, καὶ ἔστιν ἱρὴ τῆς Ἥρης τῆς Ἀσσυρίης. δοκέει δέ μοι τόδε τὸ οὔνομα οὐχ ἅμα τῇ πόλει οἰκεομένη ἐγένετο, ἀλλὰ τὸ μὲν ἀρχαῖον ἄλλο ἦν, μετὰ δὲ σφίσι τῶν ἱρῶν μεγάλων γιγνομένων ἐς τόδε ἡ ἐπωνυμίη ἀπίκετο. περὶ ταύτης ὦν τῆς πόλιος ἔρχομαι ἐρέων ὁκόσα ἐν αὐτῇ ἐστιν·

There is in Syria a city not far from the Euphrates river. It is called Holy, and it is holy to the Assyrian Hera.[63] In my opinion this name did not arise at the same time as the city was established. Instead, the ancient name was different, but after the Great Holy Rites began among them the appellation came to this. Concerning this city, then, I will proceed to describe whatever is in it.

If we were to rewrite this using the forms of the standard literary language of the day (something closer to the dialect Lucian uses in his other writings), the differences are easy to spot even for a reader who knows no Greek, including the use of Alpha (α) in place of Eta (η) in certain circumstances, the contraction of adjacent vowels, differences in declensional endings, etc.:[64]

Ἔστιν ἐν Συρίᾳ πόλις οὐ πολὺ ἀπὸ τοῦ Εὐφράτου ποταμοῦ, καλεῖται δὲ Ἱερά, καὶ ἔστιν ἱερά τῆς Ἥρας τῆς Ἀσσυρίας. δοκεῖ δέ μοι, τόδε τὸ ὄνομα οὐχ ἅμα τῇ πόλει οἰκουμένη ἐγένετο, ἀλλὰ τὸ μὲν ἀρχαῖον ἄλλο ἦν, μετὰ δὲ σφίσι τῶν ἱερῶν μεγάλων γιγνομένων ἐς τόδε ἡ ἐπωνυμία ἀφίκετο. περὶ ταύτης οὖν τῆς πόλεως ἔρχομαι ἐρῶν ὁπόσα ἐν αὐτῇ ἐστιν·

Lucian's resurrection of Herodotos' Ionic is not perfect:[65] in the example given, for instance, he uses the Attic form of the participle γιγνομένων (becoming) where Herodotos would have written γινομένων, and elsewhere for the infinitive of the verb "to be" he consistently uses ἔμμεναι,[66] which is not an Ionic form at all but an artifact of the archaic Aeolic dialect probably most familiar to the work's original readers from the dialectically eclectic language of Homer (Herodotos uses εἶναι[67]). But in other respects, the language and style are clearly modeled on that of Herodotos. Like Pausanias, the author employs certain Herodotean turns of phrase, such as (in the passage given) ἔρχομαι ἐρέων ("I will proceed to say"),[68] presents

[63] I.e. Atargatis.
[64] Of course, merely changing the word forms, as I do in the example below, does not remove all the Ionic or Herodotean elements from this passage. The purpose of this "translation" of mine is only to highlight some of the distinctive Ionic forms that the author employs.
[65] For a thorough study of the relation between the Ionic of Herodotos and that of On the Syrian Goddess see Lightfoot 2003: 91–142.
[66] On the Syrian Goddess 4, 9, 16, 21, 34, 36, etc.
[67] With the exception of one occurrence of ἔμμεναι in Herodotos' verbatim quotation of a Delphic oracle (1.85). On γίγνομαι and ἔμμεναι, see: Allinson 1886: 214–217; Lightfoot 2003: 108–109, 120.
[68] Other examples of Herodotean catch-phrases: πρῶτοι τῶν ἡμεῖς ἴδμεν ("the first of the ones we know"): On the Syrian Goddess 2; cf. Hdt. 1.6, 3.122, 4.42, 5.119, 6.112, 8.105, 9.64, etc. Pausanias

conflicting accounts and explanations in Herodotean fashion,[69] and frequently asserts, as did Herodotos, on his own authority as an eyewitness.[70] While the *Indica* is unique among Arrian's known works in its Ionisms, Lucian seems to have considered fluency in Ionic an integral element of his authorial virtuosity. In other works, Lucian has characters from the past (including, in a passage we will consider later, Herodotos himself) speak Ionic in dialogue,[71] and another essay in the Lucianic corpus, *Astrology*, is also in Herodotean Ionic, though the authenticity of this work is even more strenuously disputed than that of *On the Syrian Goddess*.[72]

Pausanias' imitation of Herodotos does not go nearly as far. While some features of his literary dialect (such as the use of forms like *thalassa* instead of *thalatta*) are common with Herodotos' Ionic, he employs no forms that are *distinctly* Ionic. Yet the implications of his imitation of Herodotos, such as it is, need to be investigated alongside the practices and attitudes of other authors of the period. Authors of the Second Sophistic often praised Herodotos for the fluidity and clarity of his prose.[73] Though Herodotos did not write in Attic dialect and though his style was quite different from the privileged Attic masters, the seemingly effortless transparency of his

frequently employs an equivalent phrase πρῶτος . . . τῶν ἴσμεν (1.16.2, 4.17.2, 6.11.4, 8.7.6, 9.35.4, etc.); *On the Syrian Goddess* 15: ῎Αττη γένος μέν Λυδὸς ἦν ("Attis was Lydian by birth") echoing Hdt. 1.6: Κροῖσος ἦν Λυδὸς μὲν γένος ("Croesus was Lydian by birth"); *On the Syrian Goddess* 11: τοὺς ἐγὼ πάντας ἐρέω, δέκομαι μὲν οὐδαμά (I will tell all [of these stories] but by no means do I accept them): cf. Hdt. 7.152 (see above for Pausanias' variation of the same phrase at 6.3.8). One last Herodotean formula shared both by *On the Syrian Goddess* and Pausanias is embodied in the following phrase (27): Κομβάβου μέν μοι τοσάδε εἰρήσθω (about Kombabos let that much be said by me). This formula, with minor variations, is frequently used by both Herodotos and Pausanias to bring an end to the discussion of one topic and make way for a transition to the next (e.g. Hdt. 1.92, 2.34, 4.36, 4.127, 6.55; cf. Paus. 1.16.2, 4.17.2, 4.30.6, 6.11.4, 8.7.6, 9.35.4, 9.36.4). For further examples, see Lightfoot 2003: 142–174. The extended foundation myth presented at *On the Syrian Goddess* 19–22 involving Queen Stratonike and the noble youth Kombabos bears some similarity in its premise to Herodotos' tale of Gyges and the wife of Kandaules (1.8–13); cf. Anderson 1976: 78–81; Saïd 1994: 152–3; Elsner 2001a: 145; Lightfoot 2003: 399–400.

[69] E.g. 8, 14, 11–16, 28.

[70] These assertions are far more prevalent in the first third of the work (1, 3, 6, 7, 9, 10, 13, 14; but also 36, 40, 60), a phenomenon that will be discussed in the next chapter. Cf. Hdt. 2.12, 2.29.

[71] *Lives for Sale* 3, 14. *On the Hall* 20 (where Herodotos appears as a character); cf. Swain 1996: 305; Anderson 1976: 68–69 also notes an imitation (more thematic than linguistic or stylistic) of Herodotos in Lucian's *Charon* 13.

[72] Cf. Bompaire 1958: 653–4; Hall 1981: 381–7; Jones 1986: 170. Lightfoot 2003: 141–2, 191–196 makes a strong case for the authenticity of both the *Astrology* and *On the Syrian Goddess* largely on the basis of similarities in their pseudo-Ionism.

[73] Dionysios of Halikarnassos *On Thucydides* 23; *On Composition* 12, 19; *Letter to Gnaeus Pompeius* 3; Cicero *Orator* 29: "sine ullis salebris qualis sedatus amnis fluit" (without any jolts [Herodotos] flows like a peaceful stream); Quintilian 10.1.73; Hermogenes *On Forms* 2, p. 408 Rabe; from a different perspective, the author of *On the Sublime* praises Herodotos' success at achieving sublimity through various means: [Longinus] 22.1, 2, 26; 28.3; 31.2; 38.4 (yet Herodotos is not always sublime: cf. 43.1). Cf. Schmid 1887–1897: 1.80; Woodman 1988: 45–47; Momigliano 1958: 134–5.

writing shared common ground with the ἀφέλεια ('unaffectedness') that
Atticists strove to achieve in certain types of literary expression.[74] When
it came to matters of content, however, Herodotos was far from universally admired. Authors of the period criticized Herodotos for his historical inaccuracies and bias (most famously, perhaps, Plutarch in his essay
On the Malice of Herodotos), for the outlandishness and fictitiousness of
many of his tales of marvels in far-off lands, and for pursuing the goals
of pleasure and entertainment in his history-writing at the expense of the
truth.[75] The business of defining oneself against Herodotos, asserting one's
own strengths in opposition to his weaknesses, was a task faced even by his
earliest successors in the field of historiography. Probably within Herodotos'
own lifetime Thucydides characterized his own work in a way which most
readers, from ancient times onward, have understood as an implicit criticism aimed primarily at Herodotos:[76]

καὶ ἐς μὲν ἀκρόασιν ἴσως τὸ μὴ μυθῶδες αὐτῶν ἀτερπέστερον φανεῖται· ὅσοι
δὲ βουλήσονται τῶν τε γενομένων τὸ σαφὲς σκοπεῖν καὶ τῶν μελλόντων ποτὲ
αὖθις κατὰ τὸ ἀνθρώπινον τοιούτων καὶ παραπλησίων ἔσεσθαι, ὠφέλιμα
κρίνειν αὐτὰ ἀρκούντως ἕξει.

And perhaps the fact that [my work] is not myth-like will seem somewhat unpleas-
ant in the hearing of it, but whoever wants to consider clearly past events, which
future events will at some point replicate or resemble, human nature being what
it is, it will turn out to be sufficiently useful.

---

[74] Schmid 1887–1897: 1.80; 4.577.
[75] Cf. Christ–Schmid–Stählin 1920–1924: 1.2.669; Momigliano 1958: 132–135; Hartog 1988: 295–297;
Georgiadou and Larmour 1994: 1463–1470; Dorati 2000: 37–52. Negative reactions to Herodotos
begin to appear within his own lifetime or soon afterwards. See the discussion of Thucydides below.
Also the fourth-century historian Ktesias of Knidos claimed to have spent several years as a physician
in the royal court of Persia, and criticized Herodotos directly in his treatment of oriental matters
(e.g. Diodoros 2.15.2 = *FGrH* 688F1b) and the Hellenistic Egyptian chronographer Manetho wrote
a work *Against Herodotos* (*FGrH* 609T7, F13). Examples of criticism of Herodotos in the Roman
period, in addition to the ones discussed below, include: Diodoros 1.69.6; Favorinus [Dion] 37.7;
Josephus *Against Apion* 1.16–17; Aelius Aristeides 36.41–63, esp. 41, 48, 57; Galen, *Anat.Admin.* 2.393,
and essays by otherwise obscure individuals who are probably to be dated to the first or second
centuries CE, Aelius Harpokration (*RE s.v.* 'Harpokration' [3]; cf. *Suda* Alpha 4013 [Adler]) and
Valerius Pollio (*RE s.v.* 'Valerius' [293]; cf. *Suda* Pi 2166 [Adler]). Latin authors also expressed similar
misgivings about Herodotos, e.g.: Cicero *De divinatione* 2.116; *De legibus* 1.1.5.
[76] Thucydides 1.22.4. This is not the place to delve into the issue of what precisely Thucydides meant
by τὸ μὴ μυθῶδες (which is what I translate here as "the fact that [my work] is not myth-like"),
much less the other controversial phrases he employs (such as ἐς ἀκρόασιν ["in the hearing"] and
κατὰ τὸ ἀνθρώπινον ["human nature being what it is"]). On these questions, see the discussion and
references in Gomme 1956: 1.148–9; Hornblower 1996: 1.60–62, and on τὸ μὴ μυθῶδες specifically
see: Woodman 1988: 23–24; Hartog 1988: 304–5; Flory 1990. Gomme (ibid.) cautions prudently
against assuming that Herodotos was Thucydides' only target in this statement, but that does
not alter the fact that it was understood as applying to Herodotos by later writers in antiquity.
Cf. Momigliano 1958: 130–132.

The Thucydidean image of Herodotos' work as something "myth-like" (μυθῶδες) and as entertainment void of substance is reprised many times in the Roman period. Typical is the limited and backhanded praise of Dion of Prusa (18.10):

Ἡροδότῳ μὲν οὖν, εἴ ποτε εὐφροσύνης σοι <δεῖ>, μετὰ πολλῆς ἡσυχίας ἐντεύξῃ. τὸ γὰρ ἀνειμένον καὶ τὸ γλυκὺ τῆς ἀπαγγελίας ὑπόνοιαν παρέξει μυθῶδες μᾶλλον ἢ ἱστορικὸν τὸ σύγγραμμα εἶναι.

If you ever have need of cheering-up, it is with much tranquility that you will read Herodotos. For the relaxedness and the sweetness of his diction will give you the impression that his writing is myth-like (μυθῶδες), rather than historical.

Lucian himself wrote an essay entitled *How to Write History*, which lambastes the practices of contemporary historians and suggests proper models and methods for historians to follow. The premise of the essay is that the recent war between the Romans and the Parthians[77] had generated an unbearable spate of bad history from second-rate and *ad hoc* historians, some of whom, apparently, looked to Herodotos as a model. In one section, Lucian holds up for ridicule an unnamed chronicler of the recent war and quotes sentences from the beginning of his work that clearly show the aping of Herodotos, including Ionic dialect forms (ἐρέων instead of ἐρῶν; ἔδεε versus ἔδει):[78]

Καὶ μὴν οὐδ᾽ ἐκείνου ὅσιον ἀμνημονῆσαι, ὃς τοιάνδε ἀρχὴν ἤρξατο· "Ἔρχομαι ἐρέων περὶ Ῥωμαίων καὶ Περσέων," καὶ μικρὸν ὕστερον· "Ἔδεε γὰρ Πέρσῃσι γενέσθαι κακῶς."

Moreover it would not even be proper to mention the one who began with such a beginning: "I will go on to speak about the Romans and the Persians," and a little later: "It was necessary for things to turn out badly for the Persians."

Both of the quotations Lucian produces are transparently Herodotean phrases.[79] Interestingly, the first of them, "I will go on to speak" (ἔρχομαι ἐρέων) is also used by Lucian (if it is indeed Lucian) in the beginning of *On the Syrian Goddess*, as we have seen in the quote above. Elsewhere in

---

[77] It is this war, which lasted from 162 to 165 CE, that allows us to date Lucian's essay with a precision that is uncommon for works in his corpus. Jones 1986: 60–61; Strobel 1994: 1315–16. See also: Avenarius 1956; Hohmeyer 1965.

[78] *De Hist. Consc.* 18. Whether this author and the other unnamed authors Lucian criticizes in this work actually existed or not is a matter of some debate in modern scholarship: see, for instance: Baldwin 1973: 80–95; Jones 1986: 60–67; Strobel 1994: 1334–1355, who offers a convenient review of previous scholarship on the issue.

[79] Cf., respectively, Hdt. 1.5, 2.40, 2.99, 3.80, 7.49, and 2.161, 4.79, 9.109 (cf. also 1.8: χρῆν γὰρ Κανδαύλῃ γενέσθαι κακῶς).

How to Write History, Lucian criticizes historians who exhibit other characteristics that could be seen as Herodotean: some historians, he says, give the important events they are ostensibly narrating short shrift in favor of lengthy excursuses on insignificant details or entertaining side issues (19–20, 27–28), a tendency which he attributes to incompetence: "on account of weakness on the subject of significant matters or ignorance of what needs to be said they turn to such *ecphraseis*..." (20).[80] Though Herodotos is not named in this section, the description calls to mind the digressive tendency in Herodotos that is also shared by Pausanias. Some of Lucian's comments in this section, in fact, sound uncomfortably close to being criticisms that one might level (and that have been leveled in modern times) at Pausanias, to the extent that one wonders whether Lucian might have seen the first book of Pausanias' *Periegesis* (which we know was at least written, if not published, by the time Lucian was writing this work): "[a certain bad historian] narrates all the cities and all the mountains and all the plains and the rivers, in pursuit of the utmost clarity and forcefulness, or so he thinks" (19); "it is as if someone would fail to notice, or to praise, or to explain to those who haven't seen it the overall beauty of the [statue of] Zeus in Olympia ... and marvel instead at the craftsmanship and the fine polish on his footstool and the symmetry of the base, describing these things with the most exquisite care" (27).[81] Lucian goes on to criticize another author, who makes claims of Herodotean autopsy for the events of the eastern war without having set foot out of his native Corinth, ascribing to that author a famous Herodotean phrase "ears are less trustworthy than eyes" (29),[82] a phrase which here, and elsewhere, Lucian expropriates for parodic effect from its original erotic context in Herodotos, where King Kandaules is trying to persuade his reluctant lieutenant Gyges to spy on his wife nude in order to be convinced of her surpassing beauty.[83] Later in the essay, finally, Lucian compares Herodotos unfavorably with Thucydides,

[80] ὑπὸ... ἀσθενείας τῆς ἐν τοῖς χρησίμοις ἢ ἀγνοίας τῶν λεκτέων ἐπὶ τὰς τοιαύτας... ἐκφράσεις τρέπονται; cf. 27: ὑπὸ δὲ ἰδιωτείας καὶ ἀπειροκαλίας καὶ ἀγνοίας τῶν λεκτέων ἢ σιωπητέων τὰ μικρότατα πάνυ λιπαρῶς καὶ φιλοπόνως ἑρμηνεύουσιν ἐμβραδύνοντες (on account of unprofessionalism, lack of taste, and ignorance of what needs to be said and what needs to be passed over in silence, they waste time explaining the smallest matters very relentlessly and laboriously).
[81] ὥσπερ ἂν εἴ τις τοῦ Διὸς τοῦ ἐν Ὀλυμπίᾳ τὸ μὲν ὅλον κάλλος... μὴ βλέποι μηδὲ ἐπαινοίη μηδὲ τοῖς οὐκ εἰδόσιν ἐξηγοῖτο, τοῦ ὑποποδίου δὲ τό τε εὐθυεργὲς καὶ τὸ εὔξεστον θαυμάζοι καὶ τῆς κρηπῖδος τὸ εὔρυθμον, καὶ ταῦτα πάνυ μετὰ πολλῆς φροντίδος διεξιών.
[82] ὦτα ὀφθαλμῶν ἀπιστότερα.
[83] Hdt. 1.8, where the original phrase is ὦτα γὰρ τυγχάνει ἀνθρώποισι ἐόντα ἀπιστότερα ὀφθαλμῶν (people's ears happen to be less trustworthy than eyes). Lucian repeats this phrase more exactly when he brings on Herodotos as a speaking character (in Ionic dialect) in *On the Hall* 20. On this latter passage, see Goldhill 2001: 164–5.

echoing, as did Dion in the passage quoted above, Thucydides' claim that his history avoids the "mythic quality" (μυθῶδες) of other writers (implicitly, Herodotos).[84]

Lucian's most famous and influential work, his *True Stories*, is a two-volume fantasy doggedly satirizing previous works that pass off ridiculous tales of exotic wonders as accurate eyewitness accounts. One plausible suggestion is that the *True Stories* was intended as an extended illustration of the sort of bad history writing that Lucian derides in *How to Write History*.[85] Although Lucian names other writers as perpetrators of such works, including Ktesias and Iamboulos, and names not Herodotos but Homer (particularly the farrago of fantastic experiences that Homer puts into the mouth of Odysseus in the *Odyssey*) as the *fons et caput* of this genre,[86] the spectre of Herodotos is not far beneath the surface at any point in the account. When Lucian's narrator visits the Island of the Damned, he finds the shade of Herodotos occupying a very unenviable position, one that he comically contrasts with his own expected fate in the afterlife:[87]

προσετίθεσαν δὲ οἱ περιηγηταὶ καὶ τοὺς ἑκάστων βίους καὶ τὰς ἁμαρτίας ἐφ᾽αἷς κολάζονται· καὶ μεγίστας ἁπασῶν τιμωρίας ὑπέμενον οἱ ψευσάμενοί τι παρὰ τὸν βίον καὶ οἱ μὴ τὰ ἀληθῆ συγγεγραφότες, ἐν οἷς καὶ Κτησίας ὁ Κνίδιος ἦν καὶ Ἡρόδοτος καὶ ἄλλοι πολλοί. τούτους οὖν ὁρῶν ἐγὼ χρηστὰς εἶχον εἰς τοὖπιὸν τὰς ἐλπίδας· οὐδὲν γὰρ ἐμαυτῷ ψεῦδος εἰπόντι συνηπιστάμην.

The guides (*periêgêtai*) added information about the lives of each and the sins for which they were being tortured. Undergoing the greatest punishments of all were those who had lied about something in the course of their lives and those who had written things that were not true. Among these was Ktesias of Knidos and Herodotos and many others. When I saw them it gave me good hopes for the future, since I was confident in my own mind that I had uttered nothing false.

The humor of the last sentence lies in the fact that Lucian had warned the readers at the beginning of the *True Stories* that in spite of the title there was not a word of truth in the work.[88] Even though the adventures that the narrator experiences in the *True Stories* include a tale of a trip to

---

[84] *De Hist. Consc.* 42.   [85] Georgiadou and Larmour 1994: 1478–1506.

[86] *True Stories* 1.3. Another source of inspiration for Lucian was probably the lost work *Unbelievable Things Beyond Thoule* by Antonius Diogenes; summarized by Photius 166.109a–112a, who also comments on the debt Lucian and other authors owe to this work. Unlike the works and authors Lucian actually names, however, there is no reason to suspect that Diogenes intended his work to be seen as anything but a parodic fantasy; cf. Morgan 1985; Romm 1992: 204–214.

[87] Lucian *True Stories* 2.31; cf. Camerotto 1998: 139–140. Herodotos is also referred to explicitly as the source for the phenomenon of a particular land giving off a distinctive odor at *True Stories* 2.5 (cf. Hdt. 3.113).

[88] *True Stories* 1.4.

the moon (1.9–26), a sojourn inside the belly of a sea monster (1.30–2.2), visits to a Cheese Island, a Cork Island, the Island of the Blessed, and encounters with creatures such as horse-vultures, vine-women and cloud-centaurs, there were apparently some readers for whom this disavowal of seriousness was necessary. As was mentioned briefly in Chapter 1, an earlier writer of the Roman period, Diodoros Siculus, had included in his universal history (without the slightest expression of skepticism) a passage from a fantasy account ascribed to Iamboulos of a journey to an island in the Indian Ocean, home of a utopian society of people who purposely split their tongues down the middle and thus could carry on two conversations simultaneously.[89]

Partly because of such works as the *True Stories* and *How to Write History*, many scholars, even ones who believe that *On the Syrian Goddess* is by Lucian, suspect that it is satirical in intent: an extended parody of dubious Herodotean ethnographies describing exotic places and customs, or else, if not parody, at least a tongue-in-cheek performance in which the author's attitude toward the model he is imitating is something other than reverent.[90] Not only the Ionic dialect and Herodotean catch-phrases, but the overall naïveté, credulity and religiosity that the author projects seem difficult to read as a serious expression on the part of Lucian, who presents in most of his other works a jaundiced, (small-c) cynical, and skeptical attitude toward most matters, especially religion. The author of *On the Syrian Goddess* speaks with no obvious irony of the θείη ναυτιλίη (divine navigation) that faultlessly guides a ship from Egypt directly to the Phoenician city of Byblos every year for a celebration of Adonis (*On the Syrian Goddess* 7), and describes without suspicion of priestly chicanery how an oracular statue at Hierapolis indicates the will of the god by rocking backwards and forwards – the author even recounts an occasion he witnessed personally when the statue lifted itself above the priests who were carrying it and hovered over their heads![91] Could this really be a serious expression from the pen of the author who had exposed so savagely the religious confidence games and parlor tricks of Alexander of Abonouteichos?[92]

---

[89] Diodoros 2.55.1–59.9. On Iamboulos, cf. Romm 1992: 212–213; Hartog 2001: 101.
[90] Bompaire 1958: 649–53; Anderson 1976: 72–78; Branham 1989: 152–3; Saïd 1994: 149–153; Elsner 2001a; Lightfoot 2003: 185–200 (these three latest authors do not see the presence of comic elements as being incompatible with the notion that parts of the work are sincere reflections of the author's religious and ethnic identity; see below).
[91] *On the Syrian Goddess* 37.
[92] Lucian *Alexander, or the False Prophet*. Another revealing example from *On the Syrian Goddess* comes when the author discusses the phenomenon wherein the "Adonis" river in Syria turns red at the time of the Adonis festival (8). The author reports the supernatural explanation offered by the locals

As we shall see shortly, the answer to that question is not a simple one, but even the less ambiguous examples of the criticism and ridicule of Herodotos and Herodotean writing in this period, both from Lucian and from other writers, raise interesting questions about Pausanias. Would an author who wished his work to be taken seriously tread so obviously and deliberately in Herodotos' footsteps? As Elsner succinctly puts it, "to affirm a literary ancestry in Herodotus was, in this period, to profess an ambiguous if not downright controversial genre for a book."[93] Yet within the writings of the time, alongside the criticism and the parody, there seems to be room for invoking an image of Herodotos that is more respectable. In *How to Write History*, it is not Herodotos himself whom Lucian criticizes primarily but his modern imitators, and as such Lucian's tactics in this essay are consistent with his stance in other works, where he parodies those who take the business of *mimesis* to slavish extremes.[94] Lucian directs his scorn in this essay not only at perpetrators of Herodotisms; he also lampoons history writing that involves ham-handed imitation of other models, including Homer (14), Thucydides (15, 19), Xenophon (23), medical writers (16), and philosophers (17). To some extent, there is no denying that for Lucian criticism of Herodotos' latter-day emulators shades into criticism of Herodotos himself. But neither Lucian's misgivings about Herodotean methods nor the abuse to which he felt that the Herodotean model was applied in his own time prevents him from ranking Herodotos alongside Thucydides as one of the very best history writers (οἱ ἄριστοι τῶν συγγραφέων).[95] Nor does it prevent him from saying the following words about Herodotos at the beginning of one of his short works known as *prolaliai* ("preludes" to longer recitations or declamations):[96]

Ἡροδότου εἴθε μὲν καὶ τὰ ἄλλα μιμήσασθαι δυνατὸν ἦν. οὐ πάντα φημὶ ὅσα προσῆν αὐτῷ (μεῖζον γὰρ εὐχῆς τοῦτό γε) ἀλλὰ κἂν ἓν ἐκ τῶν ἁπάντων οἷον ἢ κάλλος τῶν λόγων ἢ ἁρμονίαν αὐτῶν ἢ τὸ οἰκεῖον τῇ Ἰωνίᾳ καὶ προσφυὲς ἢ τῆς γνώμης τὸ περιττὸν ἢ ὅσα μυρία καλὰ ἐκεῖνος ἅμα πάντα συλλαβὼν ἔχει πέρα τῆς εἰς μίμησιν ἐλπίδος. ἃ δὲ ἐποίησεν ἐπὶ τοῖς συγγράμμασιν καὶ

(that it is caused by the blood of Adonis) as well as a third party's naturalistic explanation. While the author agrees with the naturalistic explanation, he still claims that it is a θείη . . . συντυχίη (divine coincidence) that the phenomenon occurs at the time of the Adonis festival. It is worth noting in passing that the presentation of competing accounts and the rationalism that stops well short of skepticism on display here are pitch-perfect imitations of Herodotos. Cf. Nesselrath 2001: 153–166; Lightfoot 2003: 169–70, 327–8.

93 Elsner 2001a: 128.
94 Camerotto 1998: 191–196; Lightfoot 2003: 185.   95 *De Hist. Consc.* 54.
96 Lucian *Herodotos, or Aetion* 1. On the possibility of this being a *prolalia* for *On the Syrian Goddess* itself, see Lightfoot 2003: 207–8.

ὡς πολλοῦ ἄξιος τοῖς Ἕλλησιν ἅπασιν ἐν βραχεῖ κατέστη, καὶ ἐγὼ καὶ σὺ καὶ
ἄλλος ἂν μιμησαίμεθα.

If only I were able to emulate Herodotos in other respects, I don't mean all of
his qualities (that would be more than I could hope for) but even just one out
of all, such as the beauty of his words, or their harmony, or the suitability and
fidelity to the spirit of Ionia, or the excellence of his intellect or any of the myriad
other qualities he has all in one package that surpass one's prospect of emulation.
But what he accomplished on the basis of his writings, and how very valuable he
showed himself to be, in short, to all the Greeks: if only I or you or anyone else
could imitate him.

It is arguable that much of the criticism of Herodotos in this period is in
part an indirect acknowledgment of the unavoidability of Herodotos as a
model. For certain topics and certain approaches to historical themes (which
topics and approaches is an issue we will discuss presently), Herodotos
was the dominant prototype. For a period steeped in the literary ethic of
mimesis, to engage in certain types of writing was to engage, willingly or
unwillingly, with Herodotos as a predecessor, and putting on the strait-
jacket of stylistic archaism naturally involves a certain amount of resistance
and recalcitrance. An intrinsic part of the classical ethos that authors of
the period strove toward involved a relationship with one's predecessors
that was somewhat agonistic. When Aristeides finds fault with Herodotos
in his own Herodotean account of Egypt, he is following the pattern laid
down by Herodotos himself when he criticized the eyewitness reports from
Egypt by *his* predecessor Hekataios.[97] In coping with the authority of
Herodotos and claiming an authority of one's own that could stand on
the same stage with his, one could follow the strategies Herodotos himself
followed (challenging one's predecessors on points of fact) or one could
follow, as do Dion, Lucian, Galen, and others, the strategy established
in Herodotos' own lifetime by Thucydides, by challenging his aims and
approaches.

Yet the relationship of writers of the Roman period to Herodotos is not
even as simple as that. Other motives can be seen at work in the various responses to Herodotos that survive. Plutarch's essay *On the Malice of
Herodotos* is so savage in its attack on Herodotos that some earlier scholars
had a hard time believing that the normally even-tempered Plutarch could
have written it.[98] One of the things clearly inspiring Plutarch's vehemence

---

[97] Hdt. 2.143, etc.
[98] Nowadays, Plutarchean authorship seems universally accepted. References in *RE* 41: 872 (K. Ziegler
1951); cf. also all the other modern scholarship on this essay in subsequent notes, none of the authors
of which expresses serious doubt about Plutarch's authorship.

is a motive that is also important in Pausanias and *On the Syrian Goddess*, namely a sort of local chauvinism and epichoric exceptionalism. Herodotos' narrative of the Persian wars leaves a rather unflattering image of the role of the Boiotians in that epoch-making conflict, an image that Plutarch, a Boiotian from Chaironeia, feels constrained to counter. In the introduction of his work, he cites as a main reason for his assault on Herodotos his belief that Herodotos directs his malicious historiographical practices "especially against the Boiotians and the Corinthians"[99] (845F). *On the Malice of Herodotos* may, in fact, be the only surviving example of a long-standing local tradition of blame literature that sought to extricate the Boiotians from the shame of having supported the Persian side. Plutarch himself cites the work of one prececessor in this area, Aristophanes of Boiotia, and there may have been others.[100] Some scholars have also argued that Plutarch's essay shows signs of being a rhetorical *tour de force*, an example of a type of rhetoric with ancestry at least as old as Gorgias' *Defense of Helen*, in which the orator adopts a controversial position and uses every weapon in his eristic arsenal to persuade the reader.[101] The roots of such exercises were planted deep in the rhetorical training of the Roman era. Budding orators were encouraged to flex their rhetorical muscles by composing laudations (*enkômia*) and vituperations (*psogoi*) of subjects that were frequently unlikely targets of praise or blame. The existing pedagogical *progymnasmata* (preparatory exercises) of the fourth-century orator Libanios include some interesting examples, including *enkômia* praising the virtues of the ox (9.8)[102] and of Thersites, a character from the *Iliad*, whom Homer strives to portray as repulsively as possible (9.4).[103] His *psogoi*, correspondingly, often hold up for censure characters who were normally thought of as admirable, such as Achilles (9.1) and Hektor (9.2).[104] These exercises are full of the sort of one-sided, abusive and tendentious rhetoric that once caused scholars to doubt Plutarchean authorship of *On the Malice of Herodotos*. Libanios'

---

[99] Cf. Swain 1996: 86.
[100] Testimonia and fragments of Aristophanes can be found at *FGrH* 379. Plutarch cites him at 864D and 867A. On the anti-Herodotean rhetorical tradition, see: Momigliano 1958: 131–135; Ramón Palerm 2000: 388–9.
[101] Cf. Russell 1972: 60–61; Mossman 1988: 88 (who somewhat oversimplifies Russell's position on this issue); Seavey 1991; Martin 1997: 721; Ramón Palerm 2000.
[102] A sample: ἄνευ δὲ βοὸς οὐκ ἂν ἀρόσαι, μὴ ἀρῶν δὲ οὐκ ἂν σπείραι, μὴ σπείρων δὲ οὐκ ἂν ἀμήσαιτο· οὕτω τὸ τῶν βοῶν γένος συνέχει τὸν βίον ἀνθρώποις (9.8.6): "Without the ox, it is not possible to plow, and with no plowing there is no planting, and with no planting there is no harvest. Thus the race of oxen makes human life possible."
[103] Cf. *Iliad* 2.212–221. A translation of Libanios' *enkômion* of Thersites by Malcolm Heath is accessible at http://www.leeds.ac.uk/classics/resources/rhetoric/prog-lib.htm.
[104] Schouler 1984: 1.108–117; Webb 2001: 301–303.

vituperation of the classical Athenian orator Aischines, for instance, begins this way (9.4):

καὶ θαυμαστὸν οὐδὲν εἰ γεγονὼς ἐκ δουλοῦ πατρὸς καὶ τούτου πονηροῦ καὶ πόρνης μητρὸς καὶ τραφεὶς ὡς εἰκὸς τὸν ἐκ τοιούτων φύντα μηδὲν γενναῖον μηδὲ καλὸν μήτε ἐπετήδευσε μήτε εἶπε μήτε ἔπραξε.

. . . and it's no wonder if, having been born from a father who was a slave and a rascal as well and from a whore for a mother, and having been raised as you might expect one to be raised who sprang from such roots, he neither practiced nor said nor did anything noble or fine.

Elsewhere, Libanios generally speaks approvingly of Herodotos, but among the copious epistles that he published there is one letter in which he refers to a speech in which "I [sc. Libanios] fight against Herodotos" (in the same sentence he also mentions another speech in which he "fights" against Aristeides).[105] As one modern student of Libanios points out, deeming Herodotos worthy of such a treatment could, to the literary figures of the Roman period, be one of the most sincere forms of doing homage to a revered predecessor.[106] Libanios' oration against Herodotos is not extant, but we can probably get some idea of what it was like by reading Plutarch's essay.

To point out the polemical features and the rhetorical pedigree of *On the Malice of Herodotos* is not to suggest that Plutarch's criticism of Herodotos is just a pretense; many studies have demonstrated that whatever we might think of the historiographical principles that Plutarch delineates in this essay, they are principles that Plutarch himself adheres to with reasonable consistency in his own forays into the field of history.[107] In works such as the *Parallel Lives*, Plutarch evinces an ethical approach to his subjects that (to borrow the words of C. P. Jones) "preferred lenience to severity, patriotism to impartiality, optimism to pessimism."[108] The presence of polemical rhetoric in the essay does not decrease the likelihood that Plutarch's criticism of Herodotos was sincere;[109] what it does do, however, is imply that there was another side to the issue. That Plutarch expects his argument to be controversial is indicated by the very beginning of the essay when he tells his addressee: "Many, Alexander, have been deceived in matters of fact by

---

[105] *Epistle* 315 (Foerster): ἐγὼ δὲ δύο λόγους, ὧν ἐν μὲν τῷ πρὸς Ἡρόδοτον, ἐν δὲ τῷ πρὸς Ἀριστείδην μάχομαι, πέπομφα ("I have sent two speeches, of which in one I fight against Herodotos, in the other against Aristeides").
[106] Schouler 1984: 2.520–1.
[107] Russell 1972: 60; Wardman 1974: 189–196; Hershbell 1993: 154–157; Swain 1996: 86; Duff 1999: 58–9; Pelling 2002: 150–152.
[108] Jones 1972: 88.   [109] See especially: Hohmeyer 1967; Hershbell 1993; Marincola 1994.

the style of Herodotos, since it is simple, bereft of toil, and freely flowing; even more have suffered the same in regard to his character" (854E–F). Though Plutarch may be exaggerating (once again, for rhetorical effect) the number of people who allowed themselves to be "deceived" by Herodotos so uncritically, this statement, and the confrontational nature of the entire essay, suggest that Herodotos was not already universally despised, and there is no reason to assume that Plutarch's rhetoric would have persuaded anyone who did not despise Herodotos to begin with. A century or so before Plutarch, Dionysios of Halikarnassos, in his work *On Imitation*, offers an assessment of Herodotos that in many respects is the mirror image of Plutarch's argument. He encourages students of rhetoric to prefer Herodotos over Thucydides as an object of emulation in historical writing: Herodotos was wiser in his choice of subject, a glorious triumph for the Greeks instead of an ignominious internecine war, and it is Thucydides, rather than Herodotos, who writes grudgingly (φθονερῶς) of the Greeks and with particular malice toward the Athenians.[110] Dionysios, to be sure, has his own local pride at stake in this argument (Herodotos also was from Halikarnassos), but it is hardly unlikely that at least some people of later generations would have been closer to his opinion of Herodotos than to Plutarch's. We have seen above how Lucian, in his *Herodotos*, claims (how seriously we can never be sure with Lucian) that Herodotos not only offers a pleasing style but also something of great value "to all the Greeks" in his *Histories*. Even Plutarch seems to feel that there is some usefulness to Herodotos' text; he uses Herodotos as a source a number of times both in the *Lives* (though perhaps not as often as someone who did not share his historiographical misgivings would have) and in other essays. Outside of *On the Malice of Herodotos* the occasions in which he directly disagrees with Herodotos are relatively rare.[111]

---

[110] Dionysios' essay *On Imitation* is not extant. His comments on Herodotos and Thucydides are preserved in an excerpt he includes in his *Letter to Pompey* 3.

[111] Cf. *Themistocles* 7, 17, 21 (on which, see Frost 1980: 55 n. 51); *Aristeides* 16; *On the Decline of Oracles* 436C; *On Fraternal Love* 479B; *On the Domination of One Man in a Republic* 826E; *Whether Virtue can be Taught* 440A; *Table Talk* 729A. These are all passages where Plutarch names Herodotos. See *Solon* 27 for an anonymous reference (cf. Mossman 1988: 92–93). Plutarch is also fond of Herodotean proverbs and maxims: for instance, *On the Decline of Oracles* 417C, *On Exile* 607C, *Table Talk* 636E, and *One Cannot Live Happily Following Epicurus* 1086C (~ Hdt. 2.171). See also the praise of Herodotos' (and Xenophon's) style in *One Cannot Live Happily Following Epicurus* at 1039B. Plutarch's complex relationship with Herodotos is perhaps best illustrated by two occasions on which he paraphrases Herodotos' famous phrase, "When a woman takes off her tunic she also takes off her sense of propriety" (Hdt. 1.8). In *On the Proper Method of Listening* 37D, Plutarch agrees with the sentiment; in *Instructions for Marriage* 139C, he disagrees. See Hershbell 1993: 146–151 for more detailed discussion of Plutarch's references to Herodotos.

Arguably, then, *On the Malice of Herodotos* shows Plutarch using a number of different voices: genuine historiographical scruples and genuine local pride are expressed by means of transparently rhetorical posturing. What from our perspective may seem to be a contradictory multiplicity of stances in Plutarch's essay can be used as a key to a better appraisal of some of the other works we have been discussing. In the case of *On the Syrian Goddess*, the debate over whether the author's Herodotisms were intended as parodic or sincere tends to overlook the fact that with any author of this period, particularly with an author such as Lucian who made a living on irony, role-playing, and satire that often included the author himself as one of its targets, the issue of parody vs. sincerity need not be an either/or question.[112] Lucian's (?) choice of the Ionic dialect may have, and probably did, send multiple messages to the reader: most obviously, he announces that the work he is writing is part of a generic tradition – in this case, descriptive ethnography – that has Herodotos as its most prominent forefather; he may be signaling that in his work he is adopting some of the methods of Herodotos: placing a premium on *autopsiê* (seeing-for-one's-self) and the transparent weighing of alternative accounts (both of which methods are foregrounded in *On the Syrian Goddess*); he may be attempting to undergird his account with something of the attitude of Herodotos, particularly the attitude that Herodotos displays in his ethnography of Egypt (a part of Herodotos' work that the later author unmistakably connects to his Syrian ethnography [*On the Syrian Goddess* 2]), where he evinces a reverence for the immense age of Egyptian culture and grants the Egyptians primacy in some areas, particularly in religion, over the Greeks.[113] As Elsner has pointed out, the author's account of Syrian religion is thoroughly Hellenizing in its naming of the gods (the "Syrian Goddess" in question is always called Hera, never Atargatis) and in its preference for foundational myths that are congruent with Greek traditions; but at the same time the author also asserts the superiority of certain aspects of what he purports to be Syrian religious beliefs and practices over those of the Greeks.[114] This complex combination of chauvinism and cultural humility parallels almost exactly that of Herodotos on the subject of Egyptian religion. Yet in addition to all

---

[112] Something recognized already by Jones 1986: 42; cf. Saïd 1994; Camerotto 1998: 120–129; Elsner 2001a; Lightfoot 2003: 185–200.

[113] Cf., especially, Hdt. 2.49. One of Plutarch's complaints against Herodotos is that he has too little respect for Greek religion, e.g. *On the Malice of Herodotus* 857E; cf. Hartog 1988: 299.

[114] Elsner 2001a: 136–149; cf. Baslez 1994: 172–3. On the difficulty of saying anything useful about what is Syrian and not Syrian in this text, while being assailed on the one side by the complexities of ethnicity in the Antonine age and on the other side by the indeterminacies of literary stance-taking, see Lightfoot 2003: 172–184.

these signals transmitted by the Herodotean patina of the work, the author of *On the Syrian Goddess* may also, and simultaneously, be mixing in a sly and tacit warning to readers who were aware of the ways that Herodotos could be criticized that neither the authority of this author, nor of his narrator, should be accepted completely at face value, any more than the authority of Herodotos or any other historian should be accepted uncritically. Such auto-undercutting of the authorial stance would be perfectly characteristic of Lucian's ludic persona. A similar self-mocking complexity resides in another aspect of Lucian's writing that we have already discussed: there is no reason to suppose that Lucian's criticism of the excesses of Atticism is anything but sincere; yet Lucian's own writings (as the tables above illustrate) are among the most punctiliously Atticizing documents that survive from the era.[115] The irony of this would, I suspect, not have been lost on Lucian. When Elsner says of the tone of *On the Syrian Goddess* that it is "poised with a breathtaking deftness on the very edge of irony and sincerity"[116] he is perhaps being overly precise in what our knowledge of the text's intention and reception warrants us to conclude,[117] but his words succinctly reflect the multivalent appearance of this tantalizing work. What we can say without overreaching ourselves is that whatever satiric elements are present in *On the Syrian Goddess*, and even in other works of the period, their existence does not preclude a serious intention to the text or to any element of it, including the imitation of Herodotos.[118]

However we judge the import of the Herodotean imitation in *On the Syrian Goddess*, it is not necessarily the case that all Herodotean imitations of the period were read the same way. The reception of any of the texts we have been considering would depend not only on style and content of the text itself and on the network of associations that the references in the text played into but on the identity of the author and the reputation the author had among his audience. If ancient readers knew (as we don't) that the author of *On the Syrian Goddess* was Lucian, and if they were familiar with

---

[115] Cf. Schmid 1887–1897: 1.216–432; see also: Deferrari 1916; Bompaire 1958: 633–636 and Bompaire 1994; Whitmarsh 2001: 127–128.

[116] Elsner 2001a: 144.

[117] When Elsner (2001a: 124) says, in opposition to the reading of the text as burlesque, "Who are we to judge the sacred rituals of the ancient East; let alone the tone of their retelling by a voice which many have read as deeply sincere?" the point of his question is well taken, but he elides an important corollary question: who are we to judge the sacred rituals of the ancient East, let alone the tone of their retelling by a voice which many have read as deeply insincere? In the absence of any ancient reactions to the work, both interpretations are modern ones, hence deprived of much essential context.

[118] I am glad to find that a similar conclusion is reached, by a different route, by Lightfoot 2003: 196–199.

Lucian's work and had perhaps even read the *True Stories* and *How to Write History* (which we can't be sure was chronologically possible), then their understanding of much in the text, including the Herodotean elements, would differ from the reaction they would have if they did not have that context. The same is of course true, *a fortiori*, of modern interpreters.

No one has, to my knowledge, suggested that Arrian's *Indica* is intended as parody or burlesque or criticism of Herodotos. Arrian (as far as we know) did not write the sort of richly ironic and polyvocal texts that Lucian did, and the *Indica* was written as a coda to the *Anabasis*, Arrian's relatively straight-faced history of the campaigns of Alexander in Asia.[119] What then, would the implications of Arrian's choice of the Ionic dialect be? Once again, we can only speculate, but it seems plausible to suggest that while some of the motives may have been similar to those of the author of *On the Syrian Goddess*, others would have been understood quite differently. Like *On the Syrian Goddess*, and like several parts of Herodotos' history, the *Indica* is a work of exotic oriental ethnography, and it is by no means unlikely that Arrian was trying, by imitation, to do homage to the master of such works. Unlike Herodotos' account and that of (?) Lucian, however, Arrian does not claim that this work is based on his own eyewitness experience, and therein may lie another key to Arrian's relationship with Herodotos. By choosing a dialect distinctly different from his own, or at least distinctly different from that of the *Anabasis*, Arrian may be signaling to his readers a disjunction between the *Indica* and his other works, both in terms of his own personal identity and in terms of his authorial stance. As we shall see, Arrian wrote other works of an ethnographic or geographic nature that were based on his own personal experience, and while he was not an eyewitness to the historical events he describes in the *Anabasis*, or personally familiar with much of the terrain that Alexander's campaigns covered, the bulk of the *Anabasis* was concerned not with geography and ethnography but with military affairs and the internal functioning of Alexander's retinue, issues that Arrian, as a man of extensive military and political experience, felt uniquely qualified among writers of the period to interpret. The deliberate choice of an alien dialect for the *Indica* may have stemmed in part from Arrian's desire to communicate to a public familiar with his earlier works that he was stepping beyond the normal limits of his authority.[120]

---

[119] The *Indica* was based on the accounts of Megasthenes (*FGrH* 715) and Nearchos (*FGrH* 133); cf. Roos 1927; Stadter 1980: 115–132. For comparison between the Herodotism of the *Indica* and that of *On the Syrian Goddess*, see Lightfoot 2003: 94–95, 140.

[120] Cf. Lightfoot 2003: 94–95.

To return to Pausanias, I would argue that Herodotean imitations in the period of the Second Sophistic could mean different things in the hands of different writers. We are more at a loss on this issue in the case of Pausanias than we are with Arrian or Lucian because no other work by Pausanias survives against which the authorial stance of the *Periegesis* can be interpreted. But the least we can say is that there is room in the authorial and receptional framework of the period for enacting a *mimesis* of Herodotos that is neither satiric nor inherently self-defeating. Moreover, while Pausanias is hardly a humorist like Lucian, the possibility that some of his references to Herodotos were delivered with a wry smile is not to be excluded. Something distinctly bathetic lurks around many of Pausanias' Herodotisms. For instance, when Pausanias borrows Herodotos' words πρόσω τοῦ λόγου, ὁμοίως . . . ἐπεξιών ("[I will proceed] further in my account . . . . treating in like fashion"),[121] there is a discrepancy in the contexts of the words between the two authors: for Herodotos, the declaration forms part of an important programmatic statement that he issues at the end of the quasi-mythical introduction concerning kidnapped women and before he launches into the genuinely "historical" part of his work with the story of Croesus. When Pausanias borrows these words, he employs them for what seems, on the surface at least, a considerably more mundane purpose: bringing an end to a minor historical digression in the midst of his account of the Athenian acropolis and effecting a transition back to the description of monuments. Pausanias engages in playful allusion to the same crucial part of Herodotos' text in another passage. For Herodotos, Croesus was a Lydian (Κροῖσος ἦν Λυδὸς μὲν γένος), who was the first that he personally knew of (τὸν δὲ οἶδα αὐτὸς πρῶτον) to initiate hostile acts against the Greeks.[122] Pausanias, in discussing whether any inhabitants of Achaea participated in the Greek rebellion against the Macedonians at Lamia (323 BCE), says that he personally knows of a Lydian man (οἶδα δὲ καὶ ἄνδρα αὐτὸς Λυδόν) who came as a private individual to help the Greeks.[123] As a native of Lydia himself, Pausanias may well have appreciated the way this latter-day compatriot's actions toward the Greeks (trying to help them win freedom rather than trying to take away their freedom) went some way toward redeeming the Lydians from the legacy of Croesus, and he would have particularly enjoyed the irony in the fact that the later Lydian's name, Adrastos, was the same as the hapless suppliant who brought misfortune to Croesus by killing his son unintentionally.[124] For most writers of the period, the business of *mimesis*

---

[121] Pausanias 1.26.4 ~ Hdt. 1.5   [122] Hdt. 1.5.   [123] Paus. 7.6.6.   [124] Hdt. 1.34–45.

had a certain level of built-in irony; the author of a mimetic text was engaging in a perfomance, an exercise in role-playing of which he himself was
completely conscious and of which he expected his audience to be conscious
as well. There is no reason to suppose that Pausanias was any different in
this respect.

   The issue of Pausanias' underappreciated capacity for irony and humor
(even humor directed at himself) is something we will encounter further
in the final chapter, but Pausanias' choice of Herodotos as a model also has
more serious implications for our understanding of the way he positions
himself in relation to the literary culture of his time. In line with his avoidance of radical Atticism, Pausanias' choice reflects an indifference, if not an
antipathy, toward powerful literary prejudices that favored Attic masters as
objects of emulation. Adopting Herodotean Ionic would have been a less
challenging choice. By imitating a model wholesale, the author willingly
abandons much of his own voice and leaves the decisions on issues of style
and self-presentation to his model rather than presenting to an audience
the revealing choices that one makes in a more original and individual
enactment of mimesis. Pausanias' nuanced Herodotism demonstrates the
possibility of a serious, complex mimetic creativity that takes something
different from Atticism as its foundation.[125] His embracing of Herodotos
also undoubtedly reflects the generic affinities that he viewed his work as
partaking in. We have already had occasion to encounter, for instance,
Domenico Musti's insight that Pausanias' *Periegesis* can be seen as a "cen-
tripetal" ethnography that counters Herodotos' "centrifugal" momentum
in the ethnographic parts of his work: Herodotos brings the edges of the
known world to those who live (in Greek terms) at its center. Pausanias
brings the geographical center of Greek historical identity to a Greek population whose demographic center had migrated further east and whose
political center had migrated further west.[126] The *Periegesis* does not take
the issue of Herodotean imitation as far as either the *Indica* or *On the Syrian
Goddess*. Pausanias is not trying to replicate Herodotos in his work; he is
trying to recall Herodotos. Although his debt to the Halikarnassian is the
easiest to recognize for modern scholars, the nature of that debt must be
understood in the context of the other literary heritages that Pausanias'
style embodies. It is to an inquiry of those other objects of *mimesis* that we
must now turn.

[125] Cf. Lightfoot 2003: 201.   [126] Musti 1984.

THE TOPOGRAPHY OF LANGUAGE

As exemplified by the opening sentence of the *Periegesis*, the most striking characteristic of Pausanias' style lies not in exotic dialect forms but in word order and sentence structure. While his vocabulary is relatively straightforward and utilitarian, and his grammar (in the sense of his use of the tenses and moods of his verbs and the cases of nouns) is unremarkable, one cannot read very far into the text of Pausanias in Greek without being struck by the peculiar ways that his words are strung together. Ove Strid identified a number of rhetorical figures and non-standard word orders that Pausanias employs frequently, including various types of hyperbaton (the separation of words that normally occur together in a sentence, such as a noun and an attributive adjective modifying it). Numerous examples of these oddities of word order appear on almost every page of Pausanias' text. In Book 7, for instance, in a digression discussing the phenomena that accompany earthquakes, Pausanias includes the following sentence (7.24.8):

τὰ δὲ καὶ ἀστέρων ὤφθη σχήματα οὔτε ἐγνωσμένα ὑπὸ τῶν πρότερον καὶ μεγάλην τοῖς ὁρῶσιν ἐμποιοῦντα ἔκπληξιν

And also the configurations of stars were seen in forms that were known to no one before and they created great astonishment in those who saw them.

In the phrase translated here as "the configurations," the word meaning "the" (τὰ) and the word meaning "configurations" (σχήματα) are separated elaborately from one another in the Greek not only by the words meaning "and also" (δὲ καί) and the dependent genitive "of the stars" (ἀστέρων) – types of words which can come between a noun and its article even in the most quotidian Greek – but also by the verb of which the noun is the subject, "were seen" (ὤφθη). As in the case of most of the stylistic peculiarities we will be considering, to translate this literally, "the . . . were seen . . . shapes," configurations would exaggerate the oddness of the impression the passage would have made on a reader fluent in Greek; but word order of this sort was definitely an unusual means of expressing oneself in prose (deviation from expected word order in general is far more common in poetry).[127] For good measure, Pausanias engages in a more common type of hyperbaton in the second part of the sentence, inserting between the words for "great astonishment" (μεγάλην . . . ἔκπληξιν) the words for "those who see them" and "create," yielding a run of words that would literally say ". . . great (for those who see them) (creating) astonishment." Pausanias' description of

---

[127] Strid 1976: 60–61 (esp. §8a).

three statues of Zeus in the agora of Corinth illustrates a similar stylistic quirk: τὸ μὲν ἐπίκλησιν οὐκ εἶχε, τὸν δὲ αὐτῶν Χθόνιον καὶ τὸν τρίτον καλοῦσιν Ὕψιστον ("one did not have an epithet, but one of them [they call] Chthonios and the third they call Hypsistos"). In this construction, a verb that governs objects in two conjoined clauses occurs only in the second clause.[128] In English, this would be barely intelligible: ". . . one of them Chthonios and the third they call Hypsistos." Constructions of this sort are quite rare in Greek prose of any period; it is a phenomenon known largely from poetry.[129]

Not all characteristic features that Pausanias employs involve non-standard word order. In various guises, pleonasm, the use of more words to express a concept than are strictly necessary, is also a strong trend. Pausanias is fond, for instance, of *epanalepsis*, the semantically unnecessary reiteration of a noun by use of pronouns, as in the following example from Pausanias' description of a ritual in Hermione (2.35.7): τέσσαρες δὲ ἔνδον ὑπολειπόμεναι γρᾶες, **αὗται** τὴν βοῦν εἰσιν αἱ κατεργαζόμεναι ("the four old women left behind inside, **these** are the ones who put the cow to death").[130] Strictly speaking, the word "these" is not necessary; eliminate it and the sentence is perfectly legible. Examples of *anakyklesis*, the reiteration of a verb using a participial form of the same verb, also abound; for instance, from the description of Troizen (2.30.6): Ἀθηνᾶν καὶ Ποσειδῶνα ἀμφισβητῆσαι λέγουσι περὶ τῆς χώρας, ἀμφισβητήσαντας δὲ ἔχειν ἐν κοινῷ ("They say that Athena and Poseidon *quarreled* over the land, and *having quarreled* hold it in common").[131] A more efficient (though not necessarily better) way to say the same thing would have been Ἀθηνᾶν καὶ Ποσειδῶνα λέγουσι περὶ τῆς χώρας ἀμφισβητήσαντας ἔχειν ἐν κοινῷ ("They say that Athena and Poseidon, having quarreled over the land, hold it in common"). Yet another type of expression that tends toward redundancy is *pseudoanaphora*, the repetition of a verb, or a participial form of the verb, at the beginning of a clause that explains and expands on the meaning of a previous clause in which the verb appears.[132] In describing the tomb of Amphion and Zethos at Thebes, for instance, Pausanias makes the following observation: ὑφαιρεῖσθαι δὲ ἐθέλουσιν ἀπ' αὐτοῦ τῆς γῆς οἱ Τιθορέαν ἐν τῇ Φωκίδι ἔχοντες, ἐθέλουσι δέ, ἐπειδὰν τὸν ἐν τῷ οὐρανῷ ταῦρον ὁ ἥλιος διεξίῃ (The inhabitants of Tithorea in Phokis *like* to steal some earth

[128] Strid 1976: 56–60, following Kiefner 1964, uses the term *Versparung* for this construction.
[129] Strid 1976: 56; cf. Kiefner 1964.
[130] Strid 1976: 15–21; cf. Grundmann 1885: 226; Hitzig and Blümner 1896–1910: 1.122.
[131] Hitzig and Blümner 1896–1910: 1.293–4; Strid 1976: 22–23.
[132] Engeli 1907: 46–48; Strid 1976: 23–24.

from it, and *they like* [to do that] when the sun is passing through the bull in the heavens). Obviously, a shorter (though again, not necessarily better) sentence could be obtained simply by omitting the second appearance of the verb.

Unnecessary repetition, or pleonasm in general, is more characteristic of colloquial or casual speech than written expression.¹³³ Another element of Pausanias' stylistic repertoire that imparts something of the same feel is *appositio partitiva*, or σχῆμα καθ' ὅλον καὶ μέρος (construction by whole and by part).¹³⁴ In this figure, a series of nouns, or a single noun comprising a plurality, is resolved into its constituent parts using a pair of parallel clauses (marked by the Greek particles μέν and δέ) in apposition. For instance, a list of statues at the shrine of Apollo at Amyklai runs as follows (3.18.8): Ἀρίστανδρος δὲ Πάριος καὶ Πολύκλειτος Ἀργεῖος ὁ μὲν γυναῖκα ἐποίησεν ἔχουσαν λύραν . . . Πολύκλειτος δὲ Ἀφροδίτην παρὰ Ἀμυκλαίῳ καλουμένην ("Aristandros of Paros and Polykleitos of Argos – the one made a woman holding a lyre . . . and Polykleitos [made] an Aphrodite called 'beside the Amyklaian'"). As in this case, such sentences often involve *anakolouthon* (a disruption of the grammatical sequence): the initial subjects of the sentence, Aristandros and Polykleitos, are left hanging without a verb they can both serve as subject for. Sentences of this sort give the appearance of having been composed in stride, with the structure of the sentence not being thought out completely until the author is in the midst of it. Many of the examples of *appositio partitiva*, however, are complicated by what seems to be a deliberate striving for variation that belies the impression of unrefined prose which the construction as a whole conveys. For instance, Pausanias frequently changes the grammatical case or construction from one of the appositional elements to the next.¹³⁵ Here is an example from his enumeration of statues in Olympia (6.13.11): Ἀγαθίνῳ τε τῷ Θρασυβούλου καὶ Τηλεμάχῳ, Τηλεμάχῳ μὲν ἐπὶ ἵππων νίκη γέγονεν ἡ εἰκών, Ἀγαθῖνον δὲ ἀνέθεσαν Ἀχαιοὶ Πελληνεῖς ("For Agathinos the son of Thrasyboulos and for Telemachos – for Telemachos the image was made for his victory in the horse race, but Achaeans of Pellene erected [the statue of] Agathinos"). In expanding the initial phrase "for Agathinos . . . and for Telemachos," which consists of two nouns in the dative case, the first of the following clauses presents us with Telemachos again in the dative case (Τηλεμάχῳ μέν . . .), while in the second Pausanias has moved Agathinos into the accusative case and made him the direct object of the verb of the

¹³³ Cf. Dover 1997: 146.
¹³⁴ Strid 1976: 24–37; cf. Grundmann 1885: 225; Robert 1909: 214–215.
¹³⁵ Strid 1976: 25–28; cf. Engeli 1907: 144–158 for this and similar phenomena.

clause ('Αγαθῖνον δέ . . .). Accompanying this grammatical variation is also a variation in the type of information added about each element of the pair. For Telemachos, Pausanias tells us why his statue was erected, while in the case of Agathinos, Pausanias tells us who erected his statue. Variation in general has long been recognized as a definitive principle that Pausanias aspires to, and scholars have noted what seems to be a striving for variety in every aspect of the work, including the structure and content of the various books, the vocabulary he chooses, and, as here, grammatical constructions.[136] The standard explanation for this tendency on the level of vocabulary and sentence structure is that Pausanias hoped to counteract the inherent monotony of his descriptions of series of similar monuments by mixing up the wording.[137] But this is not the whole explanation. Pausanias uses these figures as frequently when he is narrating historical events as he does when he is describing monuments sequentially. These features are part of a uniform style that Pausanias maintains with remarkable consistency in every section of his work.

Strid's study catalogues a number of other stylistic effects, including anaphora (the repetition of a word at the beginning of sequential independent clauses), chiasmus (the arrangement of parallel expressions in *ab:ba* format), asyndeton (the omission of conjunctions where they would normally be expected), and litotes (understatement: saying "not small," for instance, when one means "very big"). There is no need to replicate Strid's efforts here *in toto*; the last of Pausanias' stylistic peculiarities we will consider is his fondness for parenthetical expressions, particularly explanatory parentheses introduced by the particle γάρ ("for," or "because").[138] For example, in describing the building on the Athenian acropolis known as the Erechtheion, Pausanias makes the following statement (1.26.5): γραφαὶ δὲ ἐπὶ τῶν τοίχων τοῦ γένους εἰσι τοῦ Βουταδῶν καὶ – διπλοῦν γάρ ἐστι τὸ οἴκημα – ὕδωρ ἐστὶν ἔνδον θαλάσσιον ἐν φρέατι ("there are paintings on the walls of the family of the Boutadai and – for the building is double – there is sea water inside in a well"). This particular case is one of the rare examples where Pausanias' unusual sentence structure causes real problems in interpretation: archaeologists who study the Erechtheion still argue about what Pausanias means when he calls it a "double building" and what relation the building's "doubleness" is supposed to have to the paintings of the Boutadai and the well of sea water. In passing, it is worth pointing out that this sentence also illustrates Pausanias' penchant

---

[136] See especially Engeli 1907.
[137] E.g. Strid 1976: 62–63.   [138] Strid 1976: 37–42; cf. Grundmann 1885: 223–225.

for non-standard word order: in the initial clause, the verb εἰσί ("there are") is inserted idiosyncratically between a noun phrase and a phrase in the genitive case that depends on it: γραφαὶ . . . τοῦ γένους εἰσι τοῦ Βουταδῶν ("paintings . . . of the family [there are] of the Boutadai"). In some passages, Pausanias' experiments with word order and sentence structure occur together in great profusion.

In considering the field of Pausanias' stylistic techniques, Strid came to the significant conclusion that all of them had precedents in previous authors that Pausanias possibly, or probably, looked to as models. Unsurprisingly, a number of them are also found frequently in Herodotos. Some of the figures, particularly pleonastic ones such as *epanalepsis, pseudoanaphora* and *anakyklesis*, seem designed to capture some of the colloquial, easily flowing essence of Herodotos' style.[139] Other features, however, including *anakolouthon*, intrusive parentheses, and rare types of hyperbaton, seem to embody a contrasting desire to make the reader work hard to comprehend the author's meaning. This aspect of Pausanias' style was captured well (though with characteristic condescension) by Frazer:[140]

There is a sense of strain and effort about [his style]. The sentences are devoid of rhythm and harmony. They do not march, but hobble and shamble and shuffle along. At the end of one of them the reader is not let down easily by a graceful cadence, a dying fall; he is tripped up suddenly and left sprawling, till he can pull himself together, take breath, and grapple with the next. It is a loose, clumsy, ill-jointed, ill-compacted, rickety, ramshackle style, without ease or grace or elegance of any sort. . . . a style that has less of the unruffled flow, the limpid clearness, the exquisite grace, the sweet simplicity of the Herodotean prose it might be hard to discover. The sound of one is like the chiming of a silver bell; that of the other like the creaking of a corn-crake.

In the contrast he describes between Herodotos and Pausanias, Frazer, who seems to assume unjustifiably that Pausanias would have written like Herodotos if he could, puts his finger on something that is obvious to anyone who reads the works of the two authors side by side. Despite the profound *mimesis* of Herodotos, which includes, naturally, the mimicking of some stylistic quirks, the overall impression that Pausanias' style imparts is nothing like that of Herodotos. Pausanias was aiming at something other than, or in addition to, a Herodotean stylistic model. The

---

[139] Strid 1976: 22, 23, 40, 45, 54, 69, 78–80, 99.

[140] Frazer 1898: i.lxix; cf. Christ–Schmid–Stählin 1920–1924: 2.760: "sein massloses eitles Jagen nach Abwechslung des Ausdrucks, nach Abweichung von der gebrauchlichsten direkten Bezeichnungsweise" ([Pausanias'] egregious, pointless hunt for variation of expression, for deviation from the most common direct manner of expression); Schmid 1887–1897: 2.284: "besonders verschroben ist . . . die Wortstellung bei Pausanias" (the order of words in Pausanias is . . . especially perverse).

question becomes, then, what other stylistic models Pausanias might have used in constructing his own manner of writing. Corroborating with citations and statistics the impression of many previous authors, Strid suggested that after Herodotos, Pausanias looked to Thucydides as a source of stylistic imitation, specifically in the areas of *anakolouthon*, anaphora, chiasmus, litotes, parentheses, and certain types of hyperbaton.[141]

Even in antiquity, Thucydides was known for his deliberately difficult prose style. It is surely more than coincidence that the words Frazer uses to describe Pausanias bear a striking resemblance to words that ancient authors apply to the style of Thucydides.[142] For instance, the author of the treatise known as *On Style* describes the effect of reading Thucydides in the following way: καὶ ὁ Θουκυδίδης δὲ πανταχοῦ σχεδὸν φεύγει τὸ λεῖον καὶ ὁμαλὲς τῆς συνθέσεως, καὶ ἀεὶ μᾶλλόν τι προσκρούοντι ἔοικεν, ὥσπερ οἱ τὰς τραχείας ὁδοὺς πορευόμενοι (Thucydides nearly continuously avoids smoothness and evenness in composition, and instead always resembles someone stubbing his toe, as those who travel on rough roads do);[143] Dionysios of Halikarnassos describes him as "twisting up and down, rasping and drilling each individual part of his diction";[144] and the author of *On the Sublime* says similarly, ἔτι μᾶλλον ὁ Θουκυδίδης καὶ τῇ φύσει πάντως ἡνωμένα καὶ ἀδιανέμητα ὅμως ταῖς ὑπερβάσεσιν ἀπ' ἀλλήλων ἄγειν δεινότατος (and even more [sc. than Herodotos] is Thucydides very clever at dragging things apart, no matter how intrinsically united and indivisible they are, with his *hyperbata*).[145] Hyperbata seem to be one of the chief stylistic quirks associated with Thucydides in the ancient authors.[146] The authors of *On Style* and *On the Sublime* see this technique in a positive light, as something that helps increase the tension and pathos

---

[141] Strid 1976: 30–33, 50, 62, 72, 75–77, 81, 96, 99; cf. Pfundtner 1866: 2–3; Fischbach 1893: 164–5.

[142] Cf. Ros 1938: 49–85; such ancient descriptions are, of course, echoed in more recent descriptions of Thucydides' style, though without the contempt that is sometimes directed at Pausanias: e.g. Christ 1898: 343: "auch wenn man sich in den Thukydideischen Stil gut hingelesen hat, wird man oft einen Satz zwei- un drei-Mal lesen müssen, bis man alles, was der Autor in die Worte hineinlegen wollte, vollständig erfasst" (even when one has become well acquainted with Thucydidean style one will often have to read a sentence two or three times before one can completely grasp everything that the author intended to invest in his words); cf. also: Schmid–Stählin 1929–1948: 5.194–5; Dover 1973: 9–13; Goldhill 2002: 31–37. Woodman 1988: 46–47 argues that the difficulty of Thucydides' style has enhanced his reputation as a serious historian (in contrast to Herodotos, for instance).

[143] [Demetrius] *On Style* 48.

[144] *On Thucydides* 24: στρέφων ἄνω καὶ κάτω καὶ καθ' ἓν ἕκαστον τῶν τῆς φράσεως μορίων ῥινῶν καὶ τορεύων; cf. also Cicero *Orator* 30: "ipsae illae contiones ita multas habent obscuras abditasque sententias vix ut intellegantur" (those very speeches [in Thucydides] have so many obscure and hidden ideas that they can barely be understood); Quintilian 10.1.73: "densus et brevis et semper instans sibi" (dense and elliptical and always putting pressure on himself).

[145] [Longinus] *On the Sublime* 22.

[146] Cf. also Dion. Hal. *On Thucydides* 24, *Epistle to Ammaeus* 15–17; Marcellinus *Vita* 51, 56.

of Thucydides' narrative at appropriate times. Other ancient critics are less complimentary; the rhetorician Theon advises his students: "Be careful not to use hyperbata [in narrative] like the ones you will find in abundance in Thucydides."[147] Hermogenes states that Thucydides "wishes to be lofty and grave ... but overshoots the mark in ... his innovations in composition."[148] We have no equivalent ancient reactions to Pausanias' stylistic peculiarites, but the similarity that we find in the criticisms of modern authors like Frazer (who were weaned on the standards for Greek prose style espoused by authors such as Hermogenes and Theon) points to an actual similarity between the two authors.

Yet throwing Thucydides into the mimetic mixture that Pausanias produces will not answer all our questions about his style. Thucydidean influence had been argued for Pausanias by authors prior to Strid, but most of the parallels that were pointed out reside on the level of content rather than language,[149] and even so, the frequency of plausible and distinctive Thucydidean reflections in Pausanias is far dwarfed by the author's reminiscences of Herodotos. In the most recent published comment on this issue, Ewen Bowie admits (admirably) that his ranking of Thucydides as one of Pausanias' chief models, second to Herodotos, is based on the "impressions" he has formed while reading the text, and that those impressions are "necessarily subjective."[150] In the realm of content, one recent study has argued that there is no incontrovertible evidence that Pausanias was particularly familiar with Thucydides' work.[151] When it comes to style, even for the "Thucydidean" features that Strid catalogues, a number of them are attested in authors other than Thucydides (including Herodotos).

In gauging the influence of any author on Pausanias, there is a fundamental limitation to Strid's stylistic analysis: while he catalogs comprehensively, on the basis of careful scrutiny of sample passages throughout the *Periegesis*, the frequency of particular stylistic features in Pausanias,

---

[147] Theon *Progymnasmata* 4.   [148] Hermogenes *On Forms* 2, p. 409–410 (Rabe).
[149] Especially, Fischbach 1893.   [150] Bowie 2001: 25–26; cf. Bowie 1996: 212–213.
[151] Eide 1992. As an example, Eide points out that Pausanias uses Philistos, rather than Thucydides, as a source for his references to the Sicilian Expedition. The implication is that had Pausanias known Thucydides well he would have naturally chosen Thucydides as the source to follow. We need not accept this conclusion to agree that such an argument, while it could never be made for Herodotos, is not completely implausible for Thucydides. Meadows 1995: 98–99, points out that Pausanias' account of Spartan history is particularly thin for the period of the Peloponnesian war, suggesting that even if Pausanias knew Thucydides' text, he was not as intimately familiar with it as he was with Herodotos, or was sufficiently uninspired by it to consult it carefully when compiling his history of Sparta. Pausanias cites Thucydides once as a source (6.19.4) and occasionally presents historical accounts that could be drawn from Thucydides but could also have come from an alternative or intermediary source (e.g. 3.7.11; 8.52.3).

he provides no comparable figures, for the authors whom he suggests as Pausanias' stylistic models. In the absence of such figures, Strid's analysis fails to grapple with one of the most striking facts about Pausanias' style: while the figures that he uses may have multiple precedents in earlier authors, and may also occur in other authors of the Roman period, the sheer number of stylistic peculiarities that Pausanias introduces into his text far surpasses that employed by any of the authors that Strid takes into consideration. While for any given feature another author may equal or surpass Pausanias in frequency,[152] in the total number of all these features put together Pausanias has no rival. To explain this aspect of Pausanias' style, the unprecedented proliferation of notable idiosyncracies, we must look elsewhere for inspiration.

When we get to this level in the analysis of *mimesis*, we are confronted with severe epistemological difficulties. While we can be sure that Pausanias read Herodotos and could expect his audience to understand his Herodotean references as Herodotean, in cases where the *mimesis* is not as explicit we have no grounds for such certainty. There may be authors whose writings no longer exist whom Pausanias looked to for stylistic inspiration, and even in the cases of authors whose works do exist, like Thucydides, we cannot be sure whether Pausanias was responding to that author's text directly or was instead inspired by a third author's imitation of the same source. Even with these provisos, however, I think there is at least one other author worth suggesting as a stylistic model for Pausanias. As a partial explanation for the profusion of literary figures in Pausanias' style, I would resurrect an old idea that is currently very much out of favor: that Pausanias' style shows some influence of an earlier native of his home town of Magnesia on Sipylos, the third-century BCE orator and historian Hegesias, notorious to his detractors as the father of the style of rhetoric known to them as Asianism.[153]

---

[152] See, for instance, Strid 1976: 62.

[153] On "Asianism," see: Schmid 1887–1897: 1.3–5; Wilamowitz 1900; Norden 1915: 1.126–152; Kennedy 1963: 302–303; 1972: 98–100; Gelzer 1979: 37–41; Dihle 1994: 53–57; Swain 1996: 22–23. "Asianism" is a problematic term since it originates as a label among authors (e.g. Cicero *Brutus* 51, 325; *Orator* 24–29, 230–231; Dion. Hal. *On the Ancient Orators* 2; Theon *Progymn.* 2., and Strabo in the quote produced below) who define their own stylistic preferences in opposition to "Asianism" or, in the case of Cicero, find themselves accused of Asianism by younger "Attic" orators. Cicero, who was educated in rhetoric in Asia and in Rhodes (*Brutus* 315–316; cf. *Orator* 25) and who describes his own Roman mentor Hortensius Hortalus as an Asianist (*Brutus* 325), lived long enough to see "Asianism" become a pejorative term in the face of the burgeoning trend toward Atticism. By the time he writes *Brutus* in 46 BCE, he considers a restrained sort of "Asianism" suitable for young men, but not for mature orators (*Brutus* 325). Use of the term here should not be taken to imply the existence of a formal school of "Asianist" rhetoric, nor of an intrinsic connection between this style of rhetoric and the continent of Asia. Cf. Kennedy 1972: 97–100; Narducci 2002: 408–412; Vasaly 2002: 82–87.

A SIPYLENE SCHOOL?

In a very brief essay first published in 1824, the venerable philologist Augustus Boeckh suggested that Pausanias may have patterned his style on Hegesias.[154] If this theory is correct, if Pausanias was a follower of Hegesias, Pausanias would stand virtually alone among surviving Greek authors of his era. Long before the time of Pausanias, the complex of styles known as Asianism, which its opponents characterized as being excessively florid, mannered, and impertinently dramatic, had been thoroughly eclipsed by the more austere and restrained Attic style.[155] The victors in this intellectual conflict were not gracious: most authors who concerned themselves with style, from the time of Dionysios of Halikarnassos (first century BCE) onward, spoke of Hegesias and Asianism with palpable scorn. Even the geographer Strabo, upon mentioning Magnesia, the homeland of Hegesias,[156] sees fit to use the opportunity to cast aspersions on the style of rhetoric practiced by Hegesias (14.1.41 C648): Ἡγησίας ὁ ῥήτωρ, ὃς ἦρξε μάλιστα τοῦ Ἀσιανοῦ λεγομένου στύλου, παραφθείρας τὸ καθεστηκὸς ἔθος τὸ Ἀττικόν ("Hegesias the orator, who is especially responsible for starting the style called Asianic by corrupting the established Attic manner"). "By Zeus and all the other gods," Dionysios railed, wondering whether Hegesias wrote the way he did out of ignorance or deliberate perversity, "I am inclined to believe the latter: even ignorance manages to succeed sometimes; not to succeed at all takes premeditation."[157] If Pausanias could be characterized as a follower of Hegesias, it would be very significant to our understanding of how he envisioned his own role in the literary culture; he would once again be setting himself in opposition to the dominant trends of Atticism in his day and doing so in perhaps the most emphatic way possible. Given the general opprobrium attached to Hegesias and his rhetorical style among respected authors of the day, allying oneself with Hegesian Asianism would be tantamount to declaring oneself not only non-Atticizing but anti-Atticizing. Boeckh's hypothesis, although it attracted the approbation of scholars as perceptive as Gurlitt and Frazer in the nineteenth and early twentieth

---

[154] "Prooemium semestris hiberni a. MDCCCXXIV (De Pausaniae stilo Asiano)" = Boeckh 1874: 4.208–212.

[155] Schmid 1887–1897: 1.4–6; Norden 1915: 1.131–147. Swain 1996: 21–25.

[156] This statement comes in Strabo's discussion of Magnesia on Meander. Strabo was apparently confused about which Magnesia Hegesias hailed from.

[157] Dion. Hal. *On Composition* 18; other criticisms of Hegesias can be found in: Cicero *Brutus* 286–7, *Orator* 226, 230; Dion. Hal. *On Composition* 4, 18; Theon *Progymnasmata* 71.

centuries,[158] has found considerably less favor in recent decades.[159] The reasons scholars have advanced for the rejection of the Hegesias hypothesis are good ones, and there are certainly weaknesses in Boeckh's demonstration of his thesis, but I believe a version of this hypothesis can be salvaged, and along with it a unique place for Pausanias in the history of Greek literature.

Any scholar trying to make valid statements about the style of Hegesias must begin by acknowledging the fact that very little of Hegesias' writings survives. Dionysios of Halikarnassos preserves one lengthy quotation from his history of Alexander (*De Comp. Verb.* 18); Strabo quotes a couple of sentences concerning the sights of Athens (9.1.16); and some twenty other fragments of a sentence or two in length are preserved, chiefly in the writings of Dionysios and of Agatharchides of Knidos.[160] Nearly all these citations are polemical in nature, chosen by the authors who quote Hegesias to illustrate what they see as his worst habits as an author. Taking these passages as truly reflective of Hegesias' style is therefore more problematic than if what we had was a more random collection of fragments. The conspicuous idiosyncrasies that emerge from these fragments include lurid catachresis (misuse or tasteless expansion of the meaning of a word), as when we are told that "Dionysos spat no small amount into the water of the Thebans, for it is sweet . . .";[161] a penchant for paronomasia (punning or word play): "terrible that unsown should be the land that bore the Sown Ones";[162] anaphora ("I see the Akropolis . . . I see Eleusis");[163] and hyperbaton, most frequently involving the scattering of parts of a noun phrase on either side of the verb: ἡ Θηβαίων ἐκκέκοπται πόλις ("the city of the Thebans [ἡ Θηβαίων . . . πόλις] has been rooted out [ἐκκέκοπται]").[164] That this is a maliciously un-representative sample of Hegesias' style is suggested by the fact that relatively few examples of these obvious mannerisms are present in the longest fragment, the passage from the Alexander history quoted by Dionysios (F 5). As with most of the other surviving citations of Hegesias' words, Dionysios quotes this passage, a description of the torture and death of the

---

[158] Gurlitt 1890: 16–20; Frazer 1898: 1.lxix–lxx; cf. Meyer 1954: 50–53.
[159] Christ–Schmid–Stählin 1920–1924: 2.760; Strid 1976; Bowie 2001: 26–7.
[160] The fragments of Hegesias are collected at *FGrH* 142. I have left out of consideration fragments where it is not clear that Hegesias is being quoted directly, or where his words have been translated into Latin (e.g. F 1–4; 23, 27–29).
[161] *FGrH* 142 F 20; cf. also F16–17. Cf. Norden 1915: 1.137–138; Dover 1997: 119–130.
[162] FGrH 142 F14, again in reference to Thebes, with wordplay between the words ἄσπορον (unsown) and Σπαρτούς (The Spartoi, or Sown Ones, the autochthonous heroes of Thebes). Cf. also F 7, 13, 25. See Norden 1915: 1.136–7 (citing Quintilian 12.10.16) for a description of these and other quirks as characteristic of Asianism.
[163] *FGrH* 142 F 24.   [164] *FGrH* 142 F 12, cf. F 18, F 24.

leader of the resistance to Alexander at Gaza, in order to illustrate Hegesias' incompetence, but here Dionysios' main objection is not to Hegesias' perverted word order and tasteless figures of speech but to the monotony of Hegesias' prose rhythm, a characteristic that was particularly associated with Asianism by its opponents.[165] Hegesias seems to strive deliberately to end nearly every one of his sentences with a similar clausula (rhythmical cadence): of the fourteen sentences in the passage,[166] nine of them end with the rhythm of cretic + trochaeus (-u-l-x) and three others with cretic + ditrochaeus (-u-l-u-x). These are two of the most common *clausulae* in Greek (and Latin) prose rhythm, but the frequency with which Hegesias deploys them offends Dionysios' Atticist sensibilities, which dictate a less contrived and less monotonous rhythm. The same clausulae can be found in many of the other fragments of Hegesias.[167]

In addition to all these genuine fragments of Hegesias, we must consider one additional passage; not a passage by Hegesias himself but a parody of Hegesian diction written (once again) by Dionysios of Halikarnassos. Near the beginning of his work *On the Composition of Words* (*De Comp. Verb.* 4) Dionysios attempts to illustrate the importance of word order (σύνθεσις) by rewriting a famous sentence from the beginning of Herodotos' *Histories* (1.5), changing nothing but the order of the words and converting the forms of Herodotos' Ionic dialect into more familiar Attic forms. Here is Dionysios' initial version of Herodotos' sentence. The words that figure significantly in Dionysios' parodic recasting of the sentence are highlighted in bold type:

Κροῖσος ἦν Λυδὸς μὲν γένος, παῖς δ' Ἀλυάττου, τύραννος δ' ἐθνῶν τῶν ἐντὸς Ἅλυος ποταμοῦ· ὃς ῥέων ἀπὸ μεσημβρίας μεταξὺ Σύρων τε καὶ Παφλαγόνων ἐξίησι πρὸς βορέαν ἄνεμον εἰς τὸν Εὔξεινον καλούμενον πόντον.

Croesus was Lydian by race and the son of Alyattes, and he was tyrant of the nations this side of the Halys river, which flows from the south, between the Syrians and the Paphlagonians, and empties in the direction of the north wind into the sea that is called Euxine [the Black Sea].

In line with the typical view of Herodotos in the Roman period, Dionysios characterizes the historian's style in this sentence as "enticing" (ὑπαγωγικόν) and "historical" (ἱστορικόν), the latter term apparently in

---

[165] Dion. Hal. *On Composition* 18; Cicero *Orator* 27, 168–173, 231; Theon *Progymnasmata* 71.
[166] Following the punctuation of Jacoby in *FGrH*.
[167] Cretic + trochaeus: F 6, 7, 12, 15, 17, 18, 20, 24, 25; cretic + ditrochaeus: F 8, 12, 24. On prose rhythm in general, and in "Asianist" writing in particular, cf. Blass 1865: 27–35; Schmid 1887–1897: 1.3–5; Wilamowitz 1900: 33–37; Norden 1915: 1.135–7; De Groot 1921: 62–68.

reference to the narrative fluidity of Herodotos' language. Next, Dionysios rewrites the sentence with a different word order. This version of the sentence (not reproduced here) he describes as "direct" (ὀρθόν) and "challenging" (ἐναγώνιον), comparing the style to that of Thucydides. Finally, he rewrites the sentence a third time, again changing little but the word order:

Ἀλυάττου μὲν υἱὸς ἦν Κροῖσος, γένος δὲ Λυδός, τῶν δ᾽ ἐντὸς Ἅλυος ποταμοῦ τύραννος ἐθνῶν· ὃς ἀπὸ μεσημβρίας ῥέων Σύρων τε καὶ Παφλαγόνων μεταξὺ πρὸς βορέαν ἐξίησιν ἄνεμον ἐς τὸν καλούμενον πόντον Εὔξεινον.

This version is the one that Dionysios compares to the style of Hegesias. It is worth noting that Dionysios does not specifically claim that Hegesias writes this way, but he does call the style, more vaguely, "Hegesian" ('Ηγησιακόν), and he goes on to enumerate its degeneracies; it is "dandified" (μικρόκομψον), "ignoble" (ἀγεννές), and "soft" (μαλθακόν – with implications of effeminacy). What sorts of alterations in word order bring about this transformation from the admirable style of Herodotos to the despised style of Hegesias? Of the numerous changes in the passage, two are of particular interest. Herodotos' first sentence is almost a textbook example of straightforward Greek prose. The topic of the sentence, Croesus, is put first, and two important facts about Croesus are introduced in a successive phrases using μέν and δέ, the pair of particles that classical Greek authors used, sometimes with obsessional frequency, to mark off an antithesis between parallel but contrasting elements of a sentence.[168] The "Hegesian" sentence confounds this expected scheme by placing not Croesus but Alyattes, Croesus' father, in the topic position and by having him stand immediately before the μέν, where typically the element of the phrase that serves as the point of contrast with the δὲ phrase stands.[169] Herodotos, more expectedly, places the contrasting elements, Λυδός ("Lydian" – Croesus' ethnic identity) and υἱός ("son" – Croesus' familial identity) before the μέν and the δέ respectively; and proceeding a little farther in Herodotos' original we find a second δέ preceded by a third contrasting element, τύραννος ("tyrant" – Croesus' professional identity). In the Hegesian version, moreover, Dionysios has inverted the order of the phrases describing Croesus; where Herodotos moves from the general ("Lydian by race") to the specific ("son of Alyattes") to the still more specific ("tyrant"), the Hegesian version proceeds in the opposite direction. There are few unbendable rules of word order in

---

[168] Cf. Denniston 1950: 371–374.   [169] Cf. Dover 1960: 49–50.

Greek, and no rules about what must come before the μέν and the δέ. Examples of the same sort of phrasing used in Dionysios' Hegesian parody could be found in other authors whom Dionysios admires, including Herodotos,[170] and the word order of the Hegesian version would hardly be likely to impede understanding. But by contrast with Herodotos' simple diction in this phrase, Dionysios manages to make what he terms "Hegesian" style seem contrived and perversely overwrought.

The second noteworthy characteristic of Dionysios' Hegesian parody is a type of hyperbaton, of which Dionysios gives us two examples in this brief passage. When Herodotos says quite straitghtforwardly that the Halys river "empties in the direction of the north wind," the words that he uses for "in the direction of the north wind" form a prepositional phrase: πρὸς βορέαν ἄνεμον. Normally in Greek, as in English, a prepositional phrase stands as an integral unit within the sentence that is not interrupted by other substantial parts of the sentence. In the Hegesian parody, however, Dionysios deposits the main verb into the middle of the prepositional phrase: πρὸς βορέαν ἐξίησιν ἄνεμον (literally, "in the direction of the north – empties – wind").[171] With the less rigid word order of Greek, this artifice would not be nearly as jarring and incomprehensible as it is in the literal English translation, but it would certainly be recognizable as an artifice. Similarly, when Herodotos says, τύραννος δ' ἐθνῶν τῶν ἐντὸς Ἅλυος ποταμοῦ (tyrant of the nations this side of the Halys river) he is using a common word order for combining a noun (τύραννος: "tyrant") with a genitive phrase depending on it (ἐθνῶν τῶν . . .: "of the nations . . ."). The Hegesian parody places the noun *within* the genitive phrase: τῶν δ' ἐντὸς Ἅλυος ποταμοῦ τύραννος ἐθνῶν (literally "of the this-side-of-the-Halys-river – tyrant – nations"), which is once again an example of the placing of a substantial part of the sentence in the midst of a unit within the sentence that is normally free from such intrusions.[172] In this instance, where he is illustrating the importance of word order, Dionysios focuses solely on what he perceives as Hegesias' crimes against proper word order. Since the content and the vocabulary are strictly Herodotean, there is no opportunity here to demonstrate Hegesias' supposed fondness for gaudy word play.

The fact that the long Alexander fragment includes fewer examples of the oddities of Dionysios' pastiche may have something to do with genre. In writing his account of Alexander, a historiographical effort, Hegesias may have striven for a plainer style than he did in his oratory and his other

---

[170] Cf. Dik 1995: 47–51; Dover 1960: 66–68.
[171] Cf. Devine and Stephens 2000: 12, 211–232.	[172] Cf. Devine and Stephens 2000: 10–11.

writings: as we have seen, the excerpt of the Alexander history that Dionysios gives us also displays fewer of the other stylistic quirks that stand out prominently in the other fragments.[173] The discrepancy between the Alexander-history fragment and Dionysios' Hegesian rewriting of Herodotos also reveals the latter for what it is: a parody, a deliberate exaggeration that takes what one must assume to be a typical feature of Hegesias' style and propagates it to the point of absurdity. Dionysios is not objecting to variations of word order in principle, any more than he objects in principle to metrical clausulae in his discussion of the passage from Hegesias' Alexander history. As is the case with Pausanias' idiosyncrasies, all the hyperbata and other ornaments that the Hegesias parody displays, taken individually, can be attested in classical authors. What Dionysios objects to in his own parody of the Hegesian style is the frequency and the pointlessness with which such figures occur. One of the criticisms Atticist writers leveled against the "Asianists" was that the liberties they took with word order served superficial purposes, either to create a particular metrical effect or simply for the sake of variation or to parade the author's freedom from convention. Altered word order was one tactic that authors could employ legitimately to produce sublimity (δεινότης); subverting the expected order of words could produce "the most genuine impression of intense pathos"[174] and focus emphasis on a crucial element of the sentence.[175] In Dionysios' parody, there seems to be no such motivation for the convolutions of word order.

The importance of this passage is that it forms the centerpiece, and indeed the only Hegesian passage discussed in detail, in Boeckh's argument for a Hegesian influence on Pausanias. The style of Dionysios' parody of Hegesias is what Boeckh found most similar to the idiosyncrasies he recognized in the later Sipylene. From a present-day perspective, Boeckh's argument seems remarkably sketchy. In addition to focusing on the Dionysian parody of Hegesias rather than on Hegesias himself, Boeckh discusses only one passage from Pausanias in detail, the opening sentence of the work.[176] As was the case for Dionysios in this passage, the most distinctive feature of Hegesian Asianism for Boeckh is the "unnatural" word order, and his comparison

---

[173] Cf. Blass 1865: 25–26; some of the fragments deal with topics that might have been treated in the Alexander history (e.g. F 7, 8, 9, 11, 12, 14, 15–17), such as the destruction of Thebes and Olynthus, but that does not necessarily mean (*pace* Jacoby) that they were taken from the Alexander history.

[174] [Longinus] *On the Sublime* 22 χαρακτὴρ ἐναγωνίου πάθους ἀληθέστατος.

[175] Dionysius *On Composition* 12, 19; Alexander *On Figures* 2.24; Theon *Progymnasmata* 4; Cicero *Orator* 230–231; Quintilian 8.2.14; 8.6.62–65, etc. Cf. Schmid 1887–1897: 2.284.

[176] Boeckh also comments in general that Pausanias' narration of the Messenian wars in Book 4 seems to him particularly Hegesianic, without offering any specific examples from that book or further specifying what features of it were evidence of Hegesias' influence.

between Hegesias and Pausanias rests almost completely on this basis. In Boeckh's words (which, it will be noted, are distinctly similar to the later words of Frazer quoted above):[177]

... When one whose ears are accustomed to Attic rhythms recites Pausanias aloud, he will find not even one period that rolls off the tongue properly; so broken, truncated, backwards and disturbed everything is; words that you would think need to be put before other words are put after them; those that need to be put after are placed ahead. In sum, the collocation of words is really such that the author seems to be playing games with the readers so as not to be properly understood.

The last sentence of Boeckh's description of Pausanias' style is particularly interesting because it comes close to being objectively untrue. While unusual word orders of various types are characteristic of Pausanias' prose style, they do not, in general, form a barrier to understanding. Anyone who has read a significant amount of Greek can verify that Pausanias' Greek is not terribly difficult to understand: the convolutions in his word order and his occasionally jerky syntax are countered by the simplicity of his vocabulary and the straightforwardness of what he is trying to express. This statement on Boeckh's part gives us a glimpse of an important phenomenon that was mentioned earlier: the extent to which standards of Attic style dominated the appreciation of ancient Greek prose not only in the second century but even in the nineteenth. This is something that Boeckh himself came close to admitting when he prefaced his criticism of Pausanias with the words "for those whose ears are accustomed to Attic rhythms." In Boeckh's view, anything departing from Attic austerity and simplicity is, by definition, not only degenerate but unintelligible.

The rejection of Boeckh's arguments by modern scholars, however, rests not on their sketchiness or their bias, but on the lack of positive evidence for them once we proceed beyond the level of superficialities. Many apparent characteristics of Hegesias' style are not recognizable as part of Pausanias' literary repertoire, including the wordplay and the florid, figure-filled language. Other characteristics that the ancients associated with Asianism that are not as easily illustrated in the preserved fragments of Hegesias are also not found in Pausanias. These include short, choppy periods instead of the lengthy, intricately constructed periods associated with virtuosity in

---

[177] Boeckh 1874: 209. This is a translation of Boeckh's Latin, which runs as follows: "iam vero cuius aures Atticis numeris assueverint, dum Pausaniam viva voce recitat, ne unam quidem periodum apte cadentem deprenhenderit: ita omnia fracta, concisa, inversa, perturbata sunt; quae praeponenda ceteris verbis fuisse arbitreris, ea postposita, quae postponenda, ea occupata sunt; denique verborum collocatio prorsus ea est, ut auctor legentes quasi deludere videatur, ne recte intelligi possit."

the Atticist paradigm,[178] and a rigorous avoidance of hiatus (allowing vowels to occur adjacent to one another at the boundaries between words).[179] Pausanias' periods are of respectable length and complexity, and he shows no particular aversion to hiatus. Hegesias' penchant for rhythmical prose, however, is a potential point of comparison that cannot be dismissed quite as quickly. As we have already mentioned, radical Atticism avoided repetitious metrical clausulae at the ends of sentences and clauses.[180] Pausanias does strive to create clausulae in his text, a fact which is often not given as much credit as it should. Frequently in the course of the *Periegesis*, for instance, Pausanias describes something or other as "worth seeing" (θέας ἄξιον). Scholars have expended much effort in trying to analyze what makes something "worth seeing" in Pausanias' opinion, and monuments have even been identified and dated on the basis of whether or not Pausanias referred to them as "worth seeing." The fact tends to be overlooked that at least one of Pausanias' motivations for using this phrase is metrical: in cases where θέας ἄξιον comes at the end of a sentence or colon and is preceded by a heavy syllable, conditions that occur quite frequently, it forms the end of a dicretic clausula (-u-l-ux). On the whole, however, Pausanias does not even begin to approach the penchant for metrical effects that Hegesias displays in the preserved fragments. In another one of the few stylistic studies of Pausanias published within the last fifty years, Hana Szelest compared Pausanias' prosody with that of several other authors, both of the Roman period and other eras, and found that Pausanias does favor the two clausulae represented most frequently in the extended fragment from Hegesias' Alexander history, the dicretic (-u-l-ux) and the cretic + trochaeus (-u-l-x). But while Hegesias ends over 70 percent of the sentences in that fragment with one of these cadences (nine cretic + trochaeus and three dicretic, out of fourteen sentences), Pausanias only avails himself of the opportunity a little over 27 percent of the time (19.7 percent cretic + trochaeus, 7.9 percent dicretic).[181] In this regard, Szelest finds that Pausanias differs little from a number of other authors of the period, including Lucian, Philo, and Chariton. In fact, the rate at which Pausanias deploys these clausulae resembles that of the classical Athenian authors Demosthenes and Thucydides, as well as Herodotos.[182] Even in the area of meter, therefore, we have no basis for describing Pausanias as Hegesian. The contrast between Pausanias and Hegesias on this point is particularly significant since, according to ancient and modern critics alike, one of the goals motivating unusual

---

[178] Norden 1915: 1.134; cf. Cicero *Or.* 226.   [179] Norden 1915: 1.145; cf. Strid 1976: 65–66.
[180] See above, notes 165 and 167.   [181] Szelest 1953: 10–15 and Table I.
[182] Szelest 1953: Table IIa; see also the table for classical authors in De Groot 1921: 105.

word orders in Asianist rhetoric was the desire to create metrical clausulae at the ends of periods.[183] This would not seem to be motivation for Pausanias' liberties in word order.

The absence of many Hegesian characteristics in Pausanias, combined with the presence of many Pausanian idiosyncrasies in authors other than Hegesias, led Strid to conclude that there was no evidence for Hegesian influence on Pausanias.[184] Yet the insight of so astute a scholar as Boeckh ought not to be dismissed so easily. The observation upon which he built his theory of Hegesian influence is incontrovertible: no other patch of prose in the corpus of Greek literature comes closer to Pausanias' fondness for non-standard word order than Dionysios' parodic variation on Herodotos *à la* Hegesias, and this is a fact that needs explaining. As was the case with Herodotos, it is not necessary for Pausanias to have replicated *every* aspect of Hegesias' style for us to suggest that Hegesias was among Pausanias' stylistic models. All that needs to be shown is that Pausanias and Hegesias share common traits that cannot be more plausibly explained by influence from another source. I suggest that Pausanias' fondness for gymnastic word order fits this criterion. As was stated above, Dionysios' parody, which yields the best evidence for this aspect of Hegesias' style, is obviously an exaggeration, but for a parody to have any point at all it must in some respect resemble the truth. It can hardly be doubted that at least in Dionysios' mind there was a connection between Hegesian style and the sort of liberties with word order that we find also in Pausanias.[185] Strid attempts to deny the significance of this by arguing that it is contortions of word order *for the sake of rhythm* that was a hallmark of Hegesian style, not contortions of word order alone, as we find in Pausanias.[186] This observation is valid as far as it goes, but it overlooks the fact that regardless of Hegesias' purposes, the deviations from standard word order that he produced could take on a life of their own as a recognizable stylistic trait. While Dionysios' parody does, as one would expect of an adept parody, reproduce Hegesianic rhythmicality,[187] it is for the purpose of illustrating corrupt word order, *not* rhythmicality, that Dionysios concocts his parody, and one of the Hegesianic transformations of Herodotos' original word order, the phrase πρὸς βορέαν ἐξίησιν ἄνεμον

---

[183] Norden 1915: 1.135–137; Christ–Schmid–Stählin 1920–1924: 2.760, n. 9; cf. *Orat.* 27 and 231, and Theon *Progymn.* 71.

[184] Strid 1976: 64, 99–103.

[185] Theon *Progymn.* 2 also ranks perversions of word order (along with meter) as hallmarks of Hegesias' objectionable style.

[186] Strid 1976: 64 and n. 44.

[187] The endings of the four clauses marked by major punctuation in Jacoby's text are as follows: -u- -x (cretic + trochaeus); -u-u (ditrochaeus); -u-u-- (cretic + bacchaic); -u- -x (cretic + trochaeus).

(toward the north – empties – wind) occurs in the middle of its sentence and produces no clausula. We have already seen, moreover, that sensitivity to the power of word order is a concern for literary theorists of the day, quite apart from the issue of meter.[188]

There is also a certain circumstantial logic that supports the notion of Hegesias' influence on Pausanias. Given Hegesias' notorious reputation, it is hardly likely that Pausanias grew up in ignorance of him, particularly if, as seems probable, Pausanias and the father of Asianism shared the same home town. Hence, even if Pausanias somehow chose independently to pursue a style rich in hyperbata and other figures, it is unlikely that he would not see the parallel between his style and that of Hegesias. The suggestion, therefore, that Pausanias was influenced by the model of his countryman in his fondness for unusal word order is hardly implausible. This is not, of course, to say that Pausanias was an Asianist, or that he tried to replicate Hegesias' style the way that Lucian or Arrian wrote works in Ionic dialect in imitation of Herodotos. As in the case of Herodotos, Pausanias does not ape Hegesias: he has nothing to do with Hegesias' passion for rhythm, or with his use of paronomasia and catachresis. His allusion to Hegesias is selective, and forms a part of a complex web of mimetic allusions to other recognizable styles, including those of Herodotos. If the hypothesis of Hegesian influence has any validity, the next question to ask is why Pausanias would deliberately choose Hegesias as a model. By recalling the style of a writer who was so roundly despised, would Pausanias not have risked bringing the same opprobrium down on his own work? One possible answer would be that Pausanias, reared in the backwoods of Mr. Sipylos and perhaps unexposed to the best of educations, might not have realized the impression such a stylistic choice would be likely to make on a more sophisticated (and sophistic) readership. An alternative explanation is available, however, one that parallels the argument made above about Pausanias' relation to the ambiguous image of Herodotos and brings us back full circle to the question of modern constructions of ancient prose style. Our modern view of the relative quality of "Asianic" style is dependent on the surviving opinions of ancient scholars which are, as we have seen, unanimously hostile. The description of Asianic rhetoric found in the pages of fundamental works on ancient prose style, such as those of Schmid and Norden, are little more than paraphrases of the opinions of Dionysios, Theon, Longinus (or whoever it was who wrote *On the Sublime*), Cicero, and others who

[188] See above, nn. 174 and 175.

were all strongly inimical to that style.[189] Our opinion of Asianic rhetoric
is unavoidably dependent on these second-hand appraisals for a very simple reason: no extended example of prose that we can confidently identify
as Asianic survives, apart from the fragments of Hegesias and others collected for polemical purposes by the very same anti-Asianic authorites. Two
longer texts are often cited in discussions of Asianic rhetoric: the fragments
of a descriptive travel narrative by Herakleides Kritikos (a work that will
be discussed further in Chapter 7), and the lengthy, bombastic dedication
inscription erected at Nemrud Dagh by king Antiochos of Commagene.[190]
But the only reason for describing these texts as Asianic is that they embody
some of the characteristics that the surviving hostile tradition marks out
as emblematic of Asianic rhetoric (and, in the case of the latter text, that
it came from Asia). The use of these texts as examples of Asianic prose is
therefore based on argumentation that is largely circular, and the effect,
especially in the case of the Antiochos inscription, is simply to reinforce the
prejudices of our ancient sources without corroborating them in any valid
way. In light of this, we have no basis for assuming that a writer such as
Pausanias would have felt that an allusion to Hegesianic style would have
put him automatically beyond the pale of acceptable prose writing. There
is some evidence that writing and rhetoric embodying some of the features
pejoratively described as "Asianic" had a longer life in the area of Pausanias'
homeland than elsewhere. Philostratos describes for us a contemporary
of Pausanias, the sophist Onomarchos of Andros: πρόσοικος δὲ ὢν τῆς
Ἀσίας τῆς Ἰωνικῆς ἰδέας οἷον ὀφθαλμίας ἔσπασε ("living in the vicinity
of Asia he contracted the Ionian style like a case of pinkeye").[191] A sample
of Onomarchos' prose that Philostratos preserves for us exhibits some features that could easily be described as Hegesian: paronomasia, asyndeton,
hyperbaton, and repetitive clausulae. Given the dominant anti-"Asianist"

---

[189] cf. Walker 2000: 45–70, and see n. 153 above. A good example are the words of Norden (1915: 132):
"So Asianic rhetoric was in fact a product of the land and was interpreted as such. Weakness and
hollow pathos are the distinguishing characteristics of both the Hellenistic Asians and their oratory."
(So ist auch die Asianische Beredsamkeit ein Produkt des landes tatsächlich gewesen und als solches
aufgefasst. Weichlichkeit und hohles Pathos sind die Charactereigenschaften wie der hellenistischen
Asiaten so ihrer Beredsamkeit). A likely inspiration for this comes from Cicero *Brutus* 51: nam ut
semel e Piraeo eloquentia evecta est omnis peragravit insulas atque ita peregrinata tota Asia est,
ut se externis oblineret moribus omnemque illam salubritatem Atticae dictionis et quasi sanitatem
perderet ac loqui paene dedisceret ("for once oratory was exported from Piraeus and wandered
through the islands, it spent such a long sojourn in Asia [Minor] that it polluted itself with foreign
ways and lost all of that renowned wholesomeness of Attic diction and, so to speak, its healthiness,
and almost forgot how to speak"). The softness and effeminacy of Asiatic Greeks was a vigorous
stereotype as early as the time of Herodotos (cf. Hall 1989: 102–113; Spawforth 2001: 380–384; also
Cicero *Orator* 25).
[190] Norden 1915: 140–146 (where the complete text of the inscription is reproduced).
[191] Philostratos *Lives of the Sophists* 599.

literary culture of the day, and the effects that that culture inevitably had on the selection and survival of texts, the fact that no more of Onomarchos' writings (or of similar writings by other authors) survives does not warrant the conclusion that an author of the day could not walk a Hegesian stylistic path and expect a favorable reception at least in some circles.

In any case, as we have seen, Pausanias' *mimesis* of Hegesias (if such it is) is highly selective. It could be that Pausanias believed he could do homage to Hegesias without risking the disturbing effect that a reproduction of Hegesias' style *in toto* might have produced. His motivation for doing so could be, on the one hand, the same non-Atticizing tendency we see in the other aspects of his style that we have considered in this chapter. By including Hegesias as a recognizable object of emulation in the formulation of his style, Pausanias would have been choosing a model as distinct as possible from the reigning Atticism of the day. At the same time, we might see in Pausanias' recollection of Hegesias an expression of the same sort of local pride and a thirst for local identity as we noted in Plutarch's attack on Herodotos. Of all the many factors and choices that went into creating Pausanias' style, this one would be perhaps the most expressive of his personal identity as a native of Magnesia on Sipylos.

CONCLUSIONS

As we consider the problems of Pausanias' style, the prudent words of Schmid cited near the beginning of this chapter must be kept in mind. In the absence of authorial declarations of intent, of other works by Pausanias, of similar works by authors of the period, and of references to Pausanias in the literature of his contemporaries, the aims and the effects of Pausanias' choices must remain, for us, in the realm of the hypothetical. But we can note in the construction of Pausanias' style some of the same tendencies we have seen in other facets of his work, and thereby arrive at some suggestions about Pausanias' motives that at least have the benefit of internal consistency. Living at the high point of an age where the present was enmeshed with the past, Pausanias was faced with a problem: how does one represent the past without allowing the past to be defined and expropriated by the present? In Pausanias' day, there was nothing more modern than taking on a past-time persona: using obsolete Attic forms, for example, or writing a Herodotean ethnographic work in Ionic dialect. These imitations of the past become divorced from the past by the fact that they are the cutting-edge of the present. To elude that trap, Pausanias strikes out to create something distinctively novel, and hence something that, for its very newness, is capable of approaching the old more closely.

In the place of Atticism, Pausanias chooses non-Atticism; in the place of classicizing ἀφέλεια, Pausanias creates a text of deliberate difficulty; in the place of following the ancient authorities on the subject of Greece's past, Pausanias chooses to *become* the authority by seeing the past for himself and standing where ancient people stood. Pausanias' archaism is not the old archaism; it is a new archaism.

We have seen that in his construction of the physical and cultural landscapes of Greece, Pausanias seems to position himself on a thin baulk between the old and the new, between the Roman and the Greek, between the common knowledge about Hellenic cultural heritage and his own autoptic experience of it. This balancing act is replicated in his complex relationship to the literary culture, both past and contemporary. His text clearly follows a Herodotean model, but for some reason or mixture of reasons, possibly including the conflicted reputation of Herodotos among the *cognoscenti* of the time, he seems to be at pains not to ally himself too closely with Herodotos. In this direction, we may begin to approach the motivation for those elements of his style that seem "Thucydidean," or at any rate non-Herodotean. It is possible that in adopting these less fluid aspects of his individual voice, Pausanias had as his goal a deliberate disjunction between his own style and that of Herodotos, thus demonstrating his independence from the latter at the same time that he was doing him homage. To quote one last time the jaundiced yet perceptive words of Frazer, "a style that has less of the unruffled flow, the limpid clearness, the exquisite grace, the sweet simplicity of the Herodotean prose it might be hard to discover." In Pausanias' time, the one thing that Herodotos earned almost universal praise for was the very qualities that Frazer enumerates here: the unruffled flow, the sweet simplicity. While imitating much else in Herodotos, this is one element of imitation that Pausanias avoids, and in doing so we may see once again his attempt to distance himself not only from Herodotos but also from the common opinions of the literary elite. Frazer, of course, marks this characteristic of Pausanias' work down to incompetence, but it is fully congruent with other aspects of Pausanias' stylistic preferences and must, therefore, be seen as a conscious choice. If we ask why Pausanias would do this, why he would deliberately avoid exhibiting the one trait of Herodotos that everyone seemed to admire, we might find one answer by looking again at Plutarch's anti-Herodotean essay. The first charge that Plutarch hurls at Herodotos in *On the Malice of Herodotos* converts Herodotos' transcendent virtuosity into a fault: his language is so beautiful, so compelling, that it blinds readers to his historiographical bad faith.[192] A desire to gain distance

---

[192] Plutarch *On the Malice of Herodotos* 854e.

from the paradigm that Herodotos established, with all its dubious associations, is also one possible motive behind Thucydides' idiosyncratic style.[193] Even if Pausanias did not consciously look to Thucydides as a model, it is possible that they both independently arrived at similar solutions to the same problem.

While political readings of the stylistic choices an author makes may not be as fashionable as they were in previous decades, the writings of the authors cited above leave little doubt that there were important social and political implications inherent in the extent to which one practiced Atticism in one's writings. In a work that serves as a snapshot of the process of canon formation in the Roman period, one of the early Greek proponents of Atticism, Dionysios of Halikarnassos, gives explicit credit to the new political order instituted by Rome for the renaissance of Attic standards in Greek literature:[194]

ἐν γὰρ δὴ τοῖς πρὸ ἡμῶν χρόνοις ἡ μὲν ἀρχαία καὶ φιλόσοφος ῥητορικὴ προπηλακιζομένη καὶ δεινὰς ὕβρεις ὑπομένουσα κατελύετο . . . ἑτέρα δέ τις ἐπὶ τὴν ἐκείνης παρελθοῦσα τάξιν . . .

In the times preceding ours the ancient and philosophical rhetorical art, deformed and suffering grievous violations, was disintegrating; and another craft came forward to take its place . . .

In regard to this "other craft" that Dionysios speaks of, he concurs with earlier Roman authors in giving it a geographical focus in the continent of Asia. He is speaking of nothing other than the "Asianist" rhetoric represented by the likes of Hegesias:

ἐν πάσῃ πόλει καὶ οὐδεμιᾶς ἧττον ἐν ταῖς εὐπαιδεύτοις (τουτὶ γὰρ ἁπάντων τῶν κακῶν ἔσχατον) ἡ μὲν Ἀττικὴ μοῦσα καὶ ἀρχαία καὶ αὐτόχθων ἄτιμον εἰλήφει σχῆμα, τῶν ἑαυτῆς ἐκπεσοῦσα ἀγαθῶν, ἡ δὲ ἔκ τινων βαράθρων τῆς Ἀσίας ἐχθὲς καὶ πρώην ἀφικομένη, Μυσὴ ἢ Φρυγία τις ἢ Καρικόν τι κακόν, [ἢ βάρβαρον] Ἑλληνίδας ἠξίου διοικεῖν πόλεις ἀπελάσασα τῶν κοινῶν τὴν ἑτέραν, ἡ ἀμαθὴς τὴν φιλόσοφον καὶ ἡ μαινομένη τὴν σώφρονα. . . .

In every city, and no less so in the highly cultured ones (a fact that is the pinnacle of all disgraces) the Attic, ancient, and indigenous Muse took on a dishonorable form, falling short of its natural excellence, and one from some barbarian land of Asia, arriving just yesterday or the day before, a Mysian one, or a Phrygian one, or some monstrosity from Caria, took upon herself the stewardship of the Greek cities and banished the former from the commonwealth. The ignorant banished the philosophical, the frenzied the prudent.

---

[193] Dion. Hal. *De Thuc.* 24, 51.
[194] Dionysios *On the Ancient Orators* 1–3 (abridged). On Dionysios and Rome, see: Hidber 1996; Martin 1998.

Passing over the irony in the fact that Dionysios himself was a native of Halikarnassos in Caria, we will continue on to the next stage of Dionysios' account of the progress of rhetoric. In Dionysios' own time, he says, things are looking up, as the Atticizing movement (of which he himself is one of the chief spokesmen) takes hold:

ἀλλὰ γὰρ οὐ μόνον Ἀνδρῶν δικαίων χρόνος σωτὴρ ἄριστος· κατὰ Πίνδαρον, ἀλλὰ καὶ τεχνῶν νὴ Δία καὶ ἐπιτηδευμάτων γε καὶ παντὸς ἄλλου σπουδαίου χρήματος. ἔδειξε δὲ ὁ καθ᾽ ἡμᾶς χρόνος, . . . καὶ ἀπέδωκε τῇ μὲν ἀρχαίᾳ καὶ σώφρονι ῥητορικῇ τὴν δικαίαν τιμήν . . .

But "time" is not only, as Pindar says, "the supreme savior of just men," but also of the arts by Zeus, and of customs and of every other important thing. The time we live in has demonstrated that . . . and it has given to the ancient and prudent art of rhetoric its just honor.

Vindication is almost complete, except for a few backwaters in the homeland of the degenerate pretender to the seat of the rhetorical muse:

καὶ ταχεῖαν τὴν μεταβολὴν καὶ μεγάλην τὴν ἐπίδοσιν αὐτῶν παρεσκεύασε γενέσθαι. ἔξω γὰρ ὀλίγων τινῶν Ἀσιανῶν πόλεων, αἷς δι᾽ ἀμαθίαν βραδεῖά ἐστιν ἡ τῶν καλῶν μάθησις, αἱ λοιπαὶ πέπαυνται τοὺς φορτικοὺς καὶ ψυχροὺς καὶ ἀναισθήτους ἀγαπῶσαι λόγους . . .

And the change that it brought about was quick, and the benefit great. For outside of a few Asian cities in which ignorance makes the learning of fine things sluggish, the rest have stopped favoring vulgar and frigid and tasteless speeches.

Finally, the credit for this improved state of affairs goes not to the Greeks themselves but to the new political masters of the Greek world and to the place where, paradoxically, the concept of Atticism seems to have been born:

αἰτία δ᾽ οἶμαι καὶ ἀρχὴ τῆς τοσαύτης μεταβολῆς ἐγένετο ἡ πάντων κρατοῦσα Ῥώμη πρὸς ἑαυτὴν ἀναγκάζουσα τὰς ὅλας πόλεις ἀποβλέπειν καὶ ταύτης δὲ αὐτῆς οἱ δυναστεύοντες κατ᾽ ἀρετὴν καὶ ἀπὸ τοῦ κρατίστου τὰ κοινὰ διοικοῦντες, εὐπαίδευτοι πάνυ καὶ γενναῖοι τὰς κρίσεις γενόμενοι, ὑφ᾽ ὧν κοσμούμενον τό τε φρόνιμον τῆς πόλεως μέρος ἔτι μᾶλλον ἐπιδέδωκεν καὶ τὸ ἀνόητον ἠνάγκασται νοῦν ἔχειν

I think the reason and the incentive for this change was all-powerful Rome, since she compelled all the cities to look to her, and her rulers managed the affairs of the commonwealth with virtue and from a position of great strength. They acquired a high level of culture and had a noble sense of judgment. Under their guidance the sensible part of the city gained an even greater advantage and compelled the witless to acquire wits.

In the words of one of its greatest exponents, then, Atticism, one of the cardinal manifestations of the privileging of the classical heritage of Hellenism, arose not from Greece itself but from Rome. While Atticism served many social, literary, and political purposes, in Dionysios' view it is one more example of the way Rome appropriated Greek culture and then deployed it in domesticated form, consciously or unconsciously, as part of a strategy of empire. Atticism was in effect a Roman movement. Pausanias' resistance to Atticism must therefore be counted as one aspect of his response to the realities of Roman rule.

Behind the discussion I have offered here is an assumption that proves consistent with the available evidence but which remains, nevertheless, an assumption: that Pausanias' stylistic choices were deliberate ones and not the result of ignorance of the reigning standards of style. Those who prefer to think of Pausanias as the dependable dullard might be tempted to see in him a concrete example of Dionysios' statement that some cities in Asia remained unaffected by the renaissance of good Attic taste "due to ignorance," but the available evidence militates against that notion. In discussing the cultural milieu in which Pausanias operated, it must be remembered that Pausanias' native land was not at the end of the world; it was not, for instance, nearly as distant from the centers of imperial culture as Lucian's home in Samosata. Magnesia itself (as far as we know) seems to have offered little in the way of cultural distinction aside from monuments to Tantalos and Niobe and the dubious heritage of Hegesias, but it lay less than a day's journey from the city of Smyrna on the Ionian coast. Smyrna was one of the leading cultural capitals of the Greek East in Pausanias' day, and was a particular focus for the thriving sophistic "movement" of the time. Niketes, the first-century orator whom Philostratos defines as the earliest practitioner of sophistic in the Roman period, was a native of Smyrna and lived there as one of its most influential citizens.[195] Other leading cultural figures of the period, including Polemon of Laodicea,[196] the hyper-Atticist Aelius Aristeides,[197] and Niketes' pupil and successor Scopelian lived in Smyrna, taught there, or visited there frequently.[198] Smyrna, according to Philostratos, "sacrificed, more than any other city, to the Muses of the sophists."[199] If Ionia was the lyre of the sophistic Muse, he says elsewhere,

---

[195] Philostratos *Lives of the Sophists* 511.   [196] *Lives of the Sophists* 490.

[197] Who resided as a valetudinarian at the Asklepieion of Smyrna and is given credit by Philostratos for the rebuilding of the city after a devastating earthquake (in 166 CE): *Lives of the Sophists* 166.

[198] On Scopelian: *Lives of the Sophists* 516–518. Other sophists who had some connection to Smyrna include Euodianos (*Lives of the Sophists* 596), Hermokrates of Phokis (*Lives of the Sophists* 608) and Herakleides of Lycia (*Lives of the Sophists* 613).

[199] *Lives of the Sophists* 613.

then Smyrna was like the bridge of that lyre.[200] Pausanias clearly visited Smyrna, and regardless of what we think of his intelligence, he was obviously a well-read man and also well traveled. The list of places he claims to have visited includes most of the greatest cultural centers of the time, including Pergamon, Athens of course, Alexandria, and Rome itself.[201] It is hardly likely that he was unaware of the fashionable literary movements of his day; at the very least (in my opinion), the burden of proof should be on those who would say that he was. Pausanias does not belong to the literary mainstream, but he was not oblivious of it. The multi-layered *mimesis* he enacts of Herodotos and others is fully congruent in its general nature with similar mimetic strategies in the writings of other authors of the period. That the specific choices he made in this process were different from those that most other authors of surviving texts made must be understood as a deliberate reaction to the culture around him rather than a product of ignorance or disengagement. Pausanias' style is not the bumbling of a half-educated literary incompetent; it is too consistent, too purposeful, for that. However off-putting a modern reader might find the overall effect, one must admit that he pursues this style with dogged consistency from beginning to end. It is a style that recalls without reproducing a number of predecessors from the hallowed past. But while Pausanias' style engages in dialogue with those predecessors, it is simultaneously a dialogue with his contemporaries, who respond to the same ancient models positively or negatively in their own works. The *Periegesis* partakes of the rich language of communication through allusion that operates beyond the plane of the semantic in the backward-gazing literature of the Roman period.

Pausanias' stylistic choices, including his reaction to Atticism as well as his use of Herodotos and (possibly) Thucydides and Hegesias as models, naturally have implications for the sort of work he thought he was writing, and the question of genre will occupy us in the succeeding chapter. Before leaving the topic of style and language, however, one other possible source of stylistic inspiration needs to be mentioned. From the pages of Strid's careful analysis, it emerges that Pausanias was not alone in his lifetime among authors who borrowed modes of expression from Herodotos in the creation of their own distinct style: many of the Herodotean turns of phrase that Strid identifies are also found in the non-Ionic works of Pausanias' older contemporary, Arrian,[202] and as we have seen above, Arrian, like Pausanias

---

[200] *Lives of the Sophists* 516.
[201] On Pausanias' travels, see Frazer 1898: 1.xx–xxi.
[202] Strid 1976, e.g. 22, and 22, n. 30, 26, 44, 45, 54; cf. Bosworth 1980–1995: 1.34–36.

Figure 6.1. Some of the ruins of Pergamon, one of the centers of imperial culture close to Pausanias' home.

though to a lesser degree, avoided radical Atticisms.²⁰³ Although Pausanias makes no overt reference to Arrian in his work, it is hardly far-fetched to suppose that Pausanias was aware of him. Arrian was a prominent political figure in Roman Anatolia; he served in important posts in his home city of Nikomedia in northwestern Anatolia, was suffect consul in Rome and proconsul of Cappadocia (northeastern Anatolia) during the reign of Hadrian. In his later years, he spent time in Athens, and in the year 145/6 CE was honored by the Athenian people with the title of Archon.²⁰⁴ There is no way to be certain that he was there at the same time Pausanias was but it is hardly unlikely. People with Arrian's name, Flavius Arrianus, perhaps relatives of Arrian or Arrian himself, appear in Athenian inscriptions dated as late as 165 CE,²⁰⁵ not long after the probable date of Book 1 of the *Periegesis*. Pausanias was almost certainly aware of Arrian's work and may have learned from it some important lessons on building a style that did homage to ancient predecessors without being imitative of them.²⁰⁶ The affinities between the two authors constitute one more piece of evidence for Pausanias' active engagement with the literary culture of his day. Part of our discussion in Chapter 7 will reveal other ways in which Arrian's influence may have made itself felt in Pausanias' text.

²⁰³ Cf. Tonnet 1988: 1.353–421.
²⁰⁴ Bosworth 1980–1995: 1.1–6; Stadter 1980: 1–17; Tonnet 1988: 1.1–59; Bosworth 1993: 226–233.
²⁰⁵ *IG* II² 205.5, 1773, 1776; Bosworth 1980–1995: 1.5.
²⁰⁶ Similarities of style between Pausanias and Arrian were also noted by: Grundmann 1885: 199–200; Gurlitt 1890: 20 and 75, n. 32; Norden 1915: 1.394; Reardon 1971: 221; Musti 1984: 15; Ameling 1996: 121, 133.

CHAPTER 7

Sui generis

In recent decades, generic criticism (that is, study of the nature and history of literary genres) has been an important motif in the scholarship of ancient Greek and Latin literature. The vital social functions of ancient literature, the traditional and partially (or largely) oral nature of its form and its content, and probably a number of other factors that we cannot identify or enumerate all combine to make genre a crucial consideration to take into account when assessing the choices that an ancient Greek or Roman author makes. The current common wisdom is that the act of writing in a certain field, the act of composing a poem or a certain type of prose work, implicated the ancient author (with varying degrees of ineluctability) in a number of canons of style, language, content, and self-presentation. Those canons were more pervasive and normative than what modern authors typically face, and they tended to determine aspects of the literary effort that in modern times are considered completely within the author's prerogative to decide upon. The choral odes of tragedy and comedy are written in Doric dialect rather than Attic, even though all surviving examples are written by Athenian authors. Thucydides uses some non-Attic word-forms in his history writing, apparently because preceding prose works were written in Ionic dialect. Serious uncertainty exists over whether first-person statements by early poets like Sappho or Pindar reflect the poet's personal thoughts and feelings, or whether they embody the *persona* that their genre demands of the first-person position in the context of the relationship between poet, performer, and audience.

Consideration of the profound influence of generic conventions in ancient literature has naturally made the assignment of the *Periegesis* to a recognized generic category a concern to students of Pausanias. Results, however, have been equivocal, and with good reason. Not only are we bereft of any but the most indirect and allusive help in this area from the author himself, but there is also some reason for thinking that the effort is somewhat misguided for an author of Pausanias' time. The period of the Second

Sophistic was a time of great innovation in the area of genre: just as the *mimesis* of a classical style typically involved the sophisticated amalgamation of various literary influences, Pausanias' contemporaries seem to have taken pains to avoid the constraints of writing within a single genre. New forms, reminiscent of and inspired by old forms but unmistakably different from them, were regularly put before the literary public in this period; one thinks of Plutarch's ethical biographies, Lucian's serio-comic dialogues and satirical essays, the deliberately unstructured gallimaufry of facts and anecdotes of Aelian's *Poikilê Historia* ("Varied History").[1] All these works partake of certain recognizable generic conventions of the classical period, but all of them also expand the limits of those genres or combine them with others. Athenaios' *Deipnosophistai* ("Dinner-Party Intellectuals"), for instance, plays off the classical archetype represented primarily by Plato's *Symposium*, wherein a social gathering serves as the frame for a discussion of philosophical issues, but it explodes the limits of that genre to include an enormously varied amount of information, much of it hardly philosophical.[2] These examples suggest that manipulation of generic traditions was one of the marks of an educated author, and I will argue below that Pausanias embodies this outlook as well as any other author of the period. As with the finer points of Pausanias' style, where we saw Pausanias fashioning a unique manner of expression from the stylistic spolia of numerous predecessors, in the form and content of his work Pausanias creates a new genre of his own, one that is built on reminiscences of other genres but nevertheless is unhindered by the strictest of their requirements.

ANCIENT *BLUE GUIDE*?

On the subject of the genre of the *Periegesis*, there is one topic that unfortunately cannot be avoided. Until recently a good portion of modern scholarship has acquiesced in calling the *Periegesis* a "travel guide," the ancient counterpart, that is, to a modern Baedeker or *Blue Guide*. Quite frequently, this characterization goes hand in hand with the Dependable Dullard hypothesis. We have already seen how Frazer influentially invokes the travel-guide thesis to explain why so much of Pausanias' text consists – allegedly – of monotonous concatenations of "this place is so many furlongs from that . . ."[3] In the same spirit, Frazer's predecessor Wilhelm

---

[1] On genre innovation in this period, see Whitmarsh 2001: 71–87.
[2] This is not to say that Athenaios did not have predecessors in his experimentation with the limits of this genre. Cf. Romeri 2000: 266–271.
[3] Frazer 1898: I.xxii.

Gurlitt makes a distinction between two different sorts of modern guide: one being a superficial ready reference for tourists to read as they stand in front of monuments, and another being a more scholarly and authoritative work designed for reading "in the drawing room" (*in der Stube*). He then proceeds to equate Pausanias with the former type, and opines: "we are obviously in the unfortunate position of having to use this 'tourist-guide' as a chief source for our knowledge of ancient art history."[4]

While the travel-guide hypothesis still surfaces from time to time, objections to it go back to the early days of modern scholarship on Pausanias, and are even more prevalent now among the new wave of Pausanias studies, the authors of which have a natural interest in portraying the *Periegesis* as something more sophisticated than a "mere" travel guide.[5] The problem, however, is not that the hypothesis is wrong – it may well be right in some sense; the problem instead is that both supporters and opponents tend to assume what is implied by the word "mere" in the previous sentence: that a "travel guide" is by its very nature something sub-literary and not worth the trouble to examine in literary or cultural terms. Some of the objections lodged against the travel-guide hypothesis are indeed trivial: that the *Periegesis* in its original ten-scroll format would be unwieldy for an ancient traveler to lug around to the sights; that the format of the scroll itself would inhibit the ability to read selectively and to find one's place quickly, things which the indexes and page numbers of modern travel guides facilitate; that the work has no information on lodging, almost none on food, relatively little on sources of drinking water and road conditions, and only slightly more about the character of the people whose lands the traveler will be crossing. The first two issues are answered sufficiently by the observation that no travel guide, not even a modern one, needs to be read on-site to be useful, and that people's memories were purposely exercised and developed in the educational system of Pausanias' day.[6] The amount of information retained by an ancient traveler who had read Pausanias before departing on his trip, or during a siesta in the course of a touring day, would

---

4 Gurlitt 1890: 10 ("wir freilich sind in der peinlichen Lage, daß wir diesen 'Fremdenführer' als die eine Hauptquelle für unsere Kenntnis antiker Kunstgeschichte verwenden müssen . . .").

5 Recent works that maintain the travel-guide hypothesis include: Habicht 1998: 21–23; Arafat 1996: 33. Early objections include those of: Robert 1909: 6–7; Kalkmann 1886: 7–8; Regenbogen 1956: 1011. Veyne 1988: 3, restated the objections for the more recent Pausanias revival, followed soon afterwards by Elsner 1992.

6 An ancient method of memory training encouraged pupils to imagine themselves walking through a familiar physical space such as a town or a house, and to associate parts of the text to be remembered with landmarks in the imagined space (cf. *Rhetorica ad Herennium* 3.16–24; Cicero *De Oratore* 2.86–88 [355–360]; Quintilian 12.2.11–26). On the possible connection between this method and Pausanias' methodology, see Elsner 2001b: 19–20.

probably be considerably more than that retained by an average modern consumer of travel guides. Moreover, travelers of the educated class tended to tour with pack-animals that could sustain the burden of the ten scrolls (along with much else), and their train tended to include servants who could be called upon to scan through the scrolls to find the proper place. The third objection, the absence of practical advice for the traveler in the *Periegesis*, loses force when one considers that even modern guides with specific focuses, such as the historically minded *Blue Guide* series, will, like Pausanias, present relatively little information either on contemporary society or on food and lodging. Proof that the *Periegesis* could be used as a travel guide is provided by the fact that it still is used as a travel guide by some visitors to mainland Greece, especially those who are interested (as were many of Pausanias' contemporaries) in the distant past.[7] Nor is there much reason to doubt that Pausanias imagined that his work would be useful to travelers who visited Greece in his time. The main evidence for this is not, as Frazer suggests, the punctilious concern for locating each landmark in relation to each other (a concern which, as we have seen, is substantially a construction of Pausanias' modern readers) but a phenomenon we will soon be discussing: the numerous second-person references that Pausanias includes in his topographical positioning ("you will see . . ."; "you will cross . . ."). To a certain extent, these references can be seen as fulfilling literary purposes: serving the cause of *enargeia* by encouraging the reader to imagine himself on the scene; providing a bit of variety to contrast with the author's normal use of impersonal references ("for one proceeding . . ."; "for those who cross. . ."). Once again, a comparison between Pausanias and his favorite model is enlightening: Herodotos uses second-person forms in describing some places where he is hardly likely to have expected many of his readers to be going. For instance, four days upriver from Elephantine, the southernmost Egyptian city, Herodotos tells his readers: "You will come to a flat plain in which the Nile flows around an island."[8] Thus, we need not see Pausanias' references to the second person as presuming the on-site presence of his readers, yet in contrast to Herodotos, Pausanias employed second-person forms in places that people of his time did actually visit,

---

[7] Although modern publishers seem to feel that the text needs to be tinkered with to make it usable: modern efforts to accommodate the text of Pausanias to the needs of actual travelers include translations of the *Periegesis* which have either been abridged (Meyer 1954) or rearranged and abridged (Levi 1971). On the use of Pausanias by modern travelers, see: Wagstaff 2001; Henderson 2001; Beard 2001; Sutton 2001.

[8] Hdt. 2.29 (καὶ ἔπειτα ἀπίξεαι ἐς πεδίον λεῖον, ἐν τῷ νῆσον περιρρέει ὁ Νεῖλος). This passage is commented on by Longinus[?], *On the Sublime* 26, who praises the way Herodotos "turn[s] hearing into vision" by this method.

so it would be perverse to suggest that he never imagined that his readers would follow his footsteps in their own travels.

So the *Periegesis* might well be described as a "travel guide," but little study has been devoted to understanding what a "travel guide" would be in Pausanias' culture, and how recognizing the *Periegesis* as a "travel guide" would affect our understanding of it. Into the discussion of this topic a number of expectations tend to be transported from modern representatives of the "travel guide" genre, expectations which, as we have seen, are ill-advised in the case of Pausanias. For instance, modern travel guides tend to be completely utilitarian and aspire to no literary goals beyond precision and succinctness; their geographical scope tends to be predetermined by political geography (tour guides of "China," "India," "California," for instance); one can assume that a modern author of a travel guide is always trying to give the reader clear directions from one site to another, even if he or she does not always succeed in doing so. Some of these assumptions are clearly invalid in the case of Pausanias, and there is no warrant for assuming the others. Most particularly, the assumption that a "travel guide" should be primarily utilitarian, that the author should subordinate whatever literary ambitions he may have to the goals of perspicacity and completeness, is particularly inappropriate for Pausanias. As we have seen, a traveler following Pausanias' text faithfully would find himself going from Corinth to Phleious by way of Sikyon, from Argos to Asine by way of Troizen, from Sparta to Olympia by way of Messene, and from Mantineia to Tegea by way of Megalopolis. In each of these cases, the route described by Pausanias is far from being the most direct and most convenient one. Clearly, in laying out these routes, Pausanias had goals in mind other than helping the reader find his way.

As we have seen, the period in which Pausanias lived was a time when travel and tourism were popular, yet neither in this period nor any other in antiquity do we have much evidence for people using "travel guides" in the course of their travels. One explanation for this lack lies in the differences between ancient and modern travel as a social process. Greek-speaking travelers visiting the Greek motherland, whether they were ethnically Greek themselves or simply well-educated members of the imperial elite, would naturally be encountering a language and a culture that was already substantially familiar to them. Many upper-class travelers, including perhaps Pausanias himself, were probably furnished with letters of introduction, or could rely on ties of friendship to prominent locals, who would provide them with food and shelter. These same hosts would be responsible for seeing to it that their guests were furnished with sufficient directions and guidance for any sightseeing that they wanted to do. An instructive example of this type of well-connected tourism, from a period near-contemporary to that of Pausanias, is presented in Plutarch's *De Pythiae Oraculis*, where a foreign visitor to Delphi is accompanied by a retinue of local friends and acquaintances as he makes a tour of the shrine and then proceeds to the outlying sites of Lykoreia and the Corycian cave.[9]

Plutarch's essay also presents us with a vivid picture of the activities of professional or official guides (whom Plutarch calls "periegetes" [περιηγηταί]) at Delphi, who provide the visitor with a wealth of information about the offerings in the sanctuary. Such guides operated at other sites as well, and Pausanias himself encounters them not only at such major attractions as Delphi and Olympia, but even at less famous sites like Sikyon (2.9.7), Megara (1.41.2),[10] and Patrai (7.6.5). Many modern scholars have tended to view these ancient guides with suspicion and disrespect: Gurlitt calls them a "plague,"[11] and Frazer's characterization of them is even more deprecatory:[12]

We know from other ancient writers that in antiquity, *as at the present day* [emphasis added], towns of any note were infested by persons of this class who lay in wait for and pounced on the stranger as their natural prey, wrangled over his body, and having secured their victim led him about from place to place pointing out the chief sites to him and pouring into his ear a stream of anecdotes and explanations, indifferent to his anguish and deaf to his entreaties to stop, until having exhausted their learning and his patience they pocketed their fee and took their leave.

Frazer cites a number of ancient texts to support this description (including Cicero *In Verrem* 4.59, [Lucian] *Amores* 8, and the dialogue of Plutarch), none of which is nearly so bilious, and most of which are not a bit critical of the tour guides. One gets the sense that Frazer may be responding more to the swarms of persistent ciceroni that European travelers encountered at foreign sites in his day than to anything he has read in the ancient sources.[13] Pausanias himself is far less critical of the local guides he encounters. He does make a point of accusing them of error on some occasions,[14] but in an even greater number of passages he merely reports what they say without criticism or comment, and it seems likely that they served as the source for a fair amount of the information that he includes in his account.[15]

[9] *De Pythiae Oraculis* 394F and *passim.*
[10] A site Pausanias himself describes as being extraordinarily unprosperous (1.36.3).
[11] Gurlitt 1890: 10 (*Plage*).   [12] Frazer 1898: 1.lxxvi.   [13] See also Casson 1974: 263–267.
[14] E.g. 1.35.8; 2.23.6; 5.18.6–7. See also 5.21.9, where he presents an alternative to what the guides say without saying which version he believes to be right.
[15] See, for instance, 1.41.2; 2.9.7; 4.33.6; 5.10.7; 5.20.4 (where we even learn the name of one of Pausanias' guides at Olympia, Aristarchos); 7.6.5.

Nor does Plutarch seem to have a generally negative view of these guides; Plutarch has one of the characters of his dialogue complain about their long-windedness (395A), but he does not impugn their usefulness or accuracy. As C. P. Jones has recently pointed out, there is good evidence that "periegetes" or "exegetes" were members of the educated local elite. Inscriptional evidence even attests to *exêgêtês* ("expounder," in Jones' translation) or *periêgêtês* as the title of an official position held by men of distinction at certain cities and sanctuaries.[16]

The utilitarian information in modern travel guides is an index of the fact that modern travelers are to a much greater extent cut off – linguistically, culturally, and socially – from the peoples in whose lands they travel. Between their hosts and their local guides, a traveler of Pausanias' ilk could gain more detailed and reliable information about directions, resting places, food, roads, and brigands than they ever could from any written source. Relieved of the responsibility of leading the traveler step by step, then, Pausanias is free to do other things with the format of his "travel guide," and the previous chapters have attempted to show that he eagerly availed himself of that opportunity. In short, there is no problem with labeling the *Periegesis* as a "travel guide," as long as one agrees that that is the beginning rather than the end of one's assessment of Pausanias' aims and methods and the generic affinities of his work. Even as a travel guide, the *Periegesis* must be approached on its own terms, without modernizing generic preconceptions about what a "travel guide" should be. Although modern tour guides can be executed with great skill and even artistry, the authors of such works approach their tasks with many of the decisions made for them that Pausanias had to make for himself.

A PERIEGETICAL GENRE?

If the attempt to define Pausanias as a "travel guide" frequently leads to invalid *a priori* assumptions as to the nature of the work, the same can

---

[16] Jones 2001: 36–39, who cites numerous examples from Olympia (*IvO* 59–141; the term *periêgêtês* is used in 77.9; 83.2; 110.17; 120.10); and from elsewhere (following Bischoff 1938: 725–6): *IG* IV.723 (Hermione) and *IG* XII.2.484.23–29 (Mytilene), both attesting to the high status of the individuals so entitled. (cf. also *IG* III.1335 [=*IG* II².7447]) This is not to say that the only duty of these office holders would have been to conduct tours for visitors, but that may have been one of their duties in some places (cf. for instance the *periêgêtai* at Delphi in Plutarch's account). As Jones points out, Strabo (17.1.29) finds *exêgêtai* at Heliopolis in Egypt. Strabo's reference, οἱ ἱεροποιοὶ . . . καὶ ἐξηγηταὶ τοῖς ξένοις τῶν περὶ τὰ ἱερά (the rite-performers and the expounders of matters concerning the sacred things for foreigners), is ambiguous in two respects: are the rite-performers and expounders two different sets of people, and are the "sacred things" (ἱερά) physical things like shrines (that can be shown to a visitor), or are they rituals (that need to be explained to a visitor)?

be said, ultimately, for the attempt to define the nature of the *Periegesis* by its title. Other works (only a handful of them survive in more than fragments, however) bear the title *periegesis* and, like Pausanias' text, consist in significant measure of the description of sites and monuments. This has given rise in modern scholarship to the notion of a "periegetical genre," of which Pausanias' text is the supreme surviving example.[17] One of the early proponents of this notion, Giorgio Pasquali, proposed that the origin of this genre lay in the tradition of early Ionian geography and ethnography as represented in the first instance by Herodotos and Hekataios of Miletos (a predecessor of Herodotos, who wrote one of the earliest known attempts in Greek to describe the known world).[18] This would help explain the presence of the numerous Herodotisms in Pausanias, or rather it would if a similar degree of Herodotean *mimesis* were demonstrable in the texts of other *periegeseis*.[19] Pasquali's theory here suffers from a weakness that we will see repeated in other attempts to define the nature of a putative genre of *periegesis*: since most of the works entitled *Periegesis*, aside from Pausanias', exist in nothing but brief and second-hand citations and paraphrases, it is only by reading the features of Pausanias back into the fragments of the other authors that we can make more than the most superficial hypotheses about the nature of this genre. Using the features of this "genre" to draw any conclusions about Pausanias is therefore a textbook case of circular argumentation. This is something that was recognized early on by Gurlitt but not always heeded by later scholars:[20]

It does almost no good when someone forms, from the scanty fragments of periegetical literature which has come down to us, a more or less definitive impression of the content, form, and aim of periegetical works in general and then uses this as a yardstick with which to measure the single complete extant work [sc. Pausanias'] of this literary genre.

Treating Pausanias' text as an example of a periegetical genre has other methodological difficulties facing it: one arises from the fact that Pausanias himself never used the term *Periegesis* to refer to his own work. When he does (rarely) refer to the entirety of his work, it is with the relatively

---

[17] E.g. Preller 1838: 155–199; Pasquali 1913; Elsner 2001b: 4–8; Bowie 2001: 25–27; Lightfoot, 2003: 161–174. Cohen 2001: 94–98 seems to mean the same thing when she speaks of "the ancient genre of travel literature."

[18] The *Periodos Gês* ("Circuit of the Earth").   [19] Cf. Lightfoot 2003: 136.

[20] Gurlitt 1890: 5 (Es kann zu nichts helfen wenn man sich aus den spärlichen Bruchstücke der periegetischen Literatur, welche auf uns gekommen sind, eine mehr oder weniger zutreffende Vorstellung von Inhalt, Form und Zweck periegetischer Werke in allgemeinen bildet und diese dann als Maßstab verwendet, an welchen das einzige vollständig erhaltene Werk dieser Literaturgattung zu messen sei).

uninformative terms *logos* (account) or *syngraphê* (write-up).[21] More frequently, he is accustomed to refer only to individual sections, as when he refers to Book 9 as τὰ Βοιώτιά μοι τοῦ λόγου ("the Boiotian [portions] of my account") or to a passage in Book 1 as being ἐν τῇ Ἀτθίδι συγγραφῇ ("in the Attic write-up"). The title *Periegesis*, however, appears on all the manuscripts except one,[22] and it also appears to be the title by which Stephanus of Byzantium, the sixth-century CE lexicographer who is the first to cite Pausanias explicitly, knew the work. This latter fact alone is a strong (but hardly conclusive) bit of evidence that *Periegesis* was Pausanias' own title for the work as a whole.

Even so, there remains the problem of what Pausanias would have meant by entitling his work *Periegesis*. From an etymological perspective, the noun *periegesis* is derived from the verb *periêgeomai*, meaning literally "lead around." One might venture to conclude from this that a physical "leading" around or "guiding" was part of the author's intent for the work, an idea that fits well with the notion of the *Periegesis* as a "tour guide." But long before Pausanias, the word *periêgêsis* and other derivatives of the verb *hêgeomai* (literally, "lead") had adopted less literal meanings in the semantic vicinity of "explicate" and "explain," and could be applied to any sort of description, whether accompanied by physical movement or not.[23] Correspondingly, as a title for a work of literature, *Periegesis* is applied to just about any text that consists largely of the description of regions, localities, or monuments. To understand just how different a work entitled *Periegesis* could be from Pausanias' work, one need only take a look at the astonishingly influential "*Periegesis* of the Inhabited World" (Οἰκουμένης Περιήγησις) of a certain Dionysios, apparently a near-contemporary of Pausanias, whose 1,187 hexameter verses encompassed the entire known world, or at least the world known to Eratosthenes, who seems to be the latest source consulted by the author.[24] As Ernst Bischoff, the author of a fundamental article on *periegetai* points out, this Dionysios achieved such renown that he became known simply as "the Periegete" (ὁ περιηγητής) in late sources, just as Strabo was simply "the Geographer" (ὁ γεωγράφος), and Homer simply "the Poet" (ὁ ποιητής).[25] In his extensive commentary on the poem,

---

[21] συγγραφή is a more specific term than λόγος: it is applied most often to works of prose, particularly history and narrative (cf. LSJ *s.v.* συγγραφή II.1)

[22] One manuscript (Madrid 4564) calls the work Ἱστορία (*Histories*), but given the unitary nature of the manuscript tradition, this can probably be safely disregarded (see Diller 1957: 178). On the basis of this, and also on the basis of 1.26.4, Trendelenburg (1911) proposed that the original title was *Hellenika* ("Greek Things" or, commonly, "Greek History").

[23] E.g. Plato's *Laws* 770B.   [24] Müller 1861: 2.xv–xxv; 103–137.

[25] Bischoff 1938: 726–727; cf. scholia to Lycophron 1206 and Aristophanes *Wealth* 586.

Eustathios provides additional insight into the broad application of the term:[26]

Εἴληχε [Διονύσιος] δὲ τὴν περιηγητοῦ κλῆσιν, παρὰ τὸ περιηγεῖσθαι, ὅπερ τὴν κατὰ λεπτὸν δηλοῦν ἀφήγησιν βούλεται· καθὸ καὶ τῶν τινες ῥητόρων ὁ μέν. περιήγησαί μοι, φησὶ, τὰ ἐν ᾅδου, ὃ ἔστιν, ἔκθου πρὸς λεπτὸν ἀφηγούμενος· ὁ δὲ περιήγησιν ὕβρεως τὴν ὁμοίαν λέγει ἀφήγησιν. Τὸ δὲ περιηγεῖσθαι καὶ περιοδεύειν λέγεται, ὡς ὅτε τις περιοδεῦσαι λέγει τὴν Πελοπόννησον, τὸ δὲ αὐτὸ ἔστιν εἰπεῖν καὶ καταγράφεσθαι καὶ μετρεῖσθαι. Οὕτω γάρ που αὐτὸς ὁ Διονύσιος θάλασσάν τινα ἐρεῖ καταγράψασθαι καὶ ἀναμετρήσασθαι.

[Dionysios] has been given the title of "Periegete", which comes from περι-ηγεῖσθαι, which signifies explanation [ἀφήγησις] in detail, as in the case of some of the orators; one of them[27] says: "περιήγησαί μοι τὰ ἐν ᾅδου," which means: "Set it out for me in detail as you explain." Another orator speaks of a *periegesis* of hybris, which signifies the same sort of explanation. But *periegeisthai* also means a similar thing as "to make a circuit of" [*perihodeusai*], as when someone says, "make a circuit of the Peloponnesos." It is also the same as saying "to describe and to measure." Thus, Dionysios himself says that he has "described" and "measured" a certain sea.

Under such a capacious definition, a written *periegesis* could be anything from an actual travel guide to a general description, and consequently little can be concluded about the nature and intention of works entitled *periegesis* (including that of Pausanias) on the basis of the title alone. The term *periegesis* may be no more indicative of a certain style, language, format, method, or purpose than calling a work a *philosophy* or a *history*.

Some fragmentary *periegeseis*, however, seem more closely akin to Pausanias, in that they are in prose and include (among other things) descriptions of sites and artworks. Bischoff categorized these as "antiquarian Periegesis"[28] and it is among such authors, if anywhere, that one must search for a generic tradition of "periegesis" that Pausanias adheres or reacts to. Bischoff catalogued over sixty authors who were 1) referred to as "periegetes" in ancient sources; 2) credited with works entitled *Periegesis*, or 3) wrote works with titles that seem to be compatible with an antiquarian or perieget-ical theme.[29] In Bischoff's own estimation, enough information survives about only a few of these authors for us to use them in a reconstruction of the features of "antiquarian Periegesis."[30] What seem to be three of the earliest attested possessors of the title of "periegete" are also among the ones cited most frequently in comparisons with Pausanias: Diodoros "the Periegete"

---

[26] Text from Müller 1861: 2.211.   [27] Lucian, *Dialogues of the Dead* 6.1.   [28] Bischoff 1938: 728.
[29] Bischoff 1938: 728–742.   [30] Bischoff 1938: 742.

(fourth century BCE),[31] Heliodoros of Athens (of perhaps the second century BCE),[32] and Polemon of Ilion (around 200 BCE).[33] Fragments and citations of these authors are more plentiful than those of most other "periegetes," so our notion of what their works were like has at least some evidentiary basis. From these fragments, we can see some basic traits in their literary efforts that immediately make them more comparable to Pausanias than to other "periegetes," such as the poetic periegete Dionysios: Diodoros wrote at least three prose volumes *On Monuments* (the monuments in question all, apparently, in Athens); Heliodoros wrote *On the Acropolis of Athens*, and among Polemon's copious and variegated output are works with titles like *On the Acropolis at Athens, On the Paintings in the Propylaia* [sc. of the acropolis at Athens], *On the Paintings in the Painted Stoa in Sikyon*, and a *Periegesis of Ilion*. Although none of these works aspires to cover a similar geographical scope to that of Pausanias' *Periegesis*, each of them deals with a topic that Pausanias either did cover or could easily have covered. Both Polemon and Diodoros were touted, in fact, as possible victims of Pausanias' plagiarism in the days of *Quellenkritik*, and even now some scholars believe that Diodoros served as a source with which Pausanias supplemented his autopsy in his description of some parts of Athens.[34]

In dealing with these authors, we are faced with difficulties similar to those we encountered with the fragments of Hegesias in the previous chapter. The bulk of the information about what their works contain comes not in direct quotations of their actual words but in paraphrases and in simple attributions of isolated facts; for instance: "Some say that Theophrastos studied with [Plato], just as Polemon says Demosthenes did."[35] The information attributed to Polemon here could come from any sort of work. In the process of citing and excerpting, content is often, if not usually, divorced from context, rendering the latter difficult or even impossible to recover. When the late antique lexicon-writers Harpokration and Stephanos of Byzantium cite Diodoros' work *On the Demes*, the citations always contain the same sorts of information: the names of the demes (the "villages" or

---

[31] *FGrH* 372, with comments of Jacoby at *FGrH* 3B 138–144. Cf. also Bischoff 1938: 728.
[32] *FGrH* 373, with comments of Jacoby at *FGrH* 3B 144–147. Cf. also Bischoff 1938: 728; Pasquali 1913: 165–176 (who, in addition to the fragments in which Heliodoros is explicitly cited, would also ascribe to him most of the information on monuments found in the pseudo-Plutarchean *Lives of the Ten Orators*. Neither Jacoby nor Bischoff follow Pasquali's lead in this respect. Heliodoros is cited only once in that work [849C]).
[33] Preller 1838 (esp. 6–11 on Polemon's date [for which cf. *Suda*, Pi 1888]); Müller 1868–1883 3.108–148; Bischoff 1938: 728–32; Pasquali 1913: 176–184. Mette 1978: 40–41. A Polemon of Ilion with a father of the same name as is reported for the father of the periegete is mentioned on an inscription from Delphi (*IG* VIII.281) dated to 177–176 BCE. This could be our Polemon but may also be a relative.
[34] Most recently: Knoepfler 1996; Jacoby 1944.   [35] Polemon F 9 = Diog. Laert. 3.46.

administrative districts of Attica); the form of the ethnic adjective appropriate to each deme; the name of the "tribe" (a broader affiliation in the Athenian political system) to which each deme belonged.[36] The citations are limited to this information because that is the information that the lexicographers (or their sources) were interested in. We cannot assume that Diodoros included nothing besides this information in his work. Had he given extensive descriptions of the location of each deme-center, their sanctuaries, their religious festivals, and the economic ways and means of their population, the citations that are preserved in these sources would be no different.

Nevertheless, within the fragments of these authors we can find at least a tentative standpoint from which to assess their relationship with Pausanias. More fragments of Polemon's work (over a hundred) survive than the other two, so we will begin with him: in his works with "periegetical" titles, such as those mentioned above, and even in some of his works that seem like they should be non-periegetical, such as his *Epistles* and his *Responses* ('Αντιγραφαί) to the historians Timaios and Neanthes, Polemon evinces an interest in a number of Pausanian topics: offerings at shrines (Fragments 1, 27);[37] the biography and history of individuals (3a, 4, 8, 9, 25); myth and myth-history (10–13, 24, 31, 32); the lives and careers of artists (2, 17, 41, 66); and religious customs (3a, 6, 8, 12, 39, 40, 49, 61, 72, 74, 83, 90).[38] All of these are topics that figure prominently in the *logoi* that Pausanias appends to monuments. One assumes, with some likelihood of being correct, that much of the same sorts of information in Polemon's topographical works was attached to monuments, and that the quoters or paraphrasers to whom we owe the references to Polemon did not see any reason to mention the monuments with which the citations were associated in their original context. Some fragments do show such a context for Polemon's *logoi*; for instance, the "Kimonian monuments," which were situated outside the Melitidai gates at Athens, provide the occasion (and the evidence) for Polemon to assert that Thucydides and Herodotos were related to Kimon's family, since their graves are found in that group of monuments.[39] Like Pausanias, Polemon also shows interest in contests

---

[36] Diodoros, Fragments 1–31 Jacoby.
[37] Numbers for the fragments of Polemon are those of Preller 1838, followed by Müller 1868–1883, with some additions.
[38] Cf. Rutherford 2001: 47–49 on the religious interests of Polemon in comparison to other "periegetes."
[39] Polemon F 4 (cf. Diodoros F 37). Pausanias does not mention the "Kimonian Monuments" as such, but in the context of a statue he sees on the acropolis of a man named Oinobios, who sponsored a decree for the recall of Thucydides to Athens (and who is probably to be connected with a general named Oinobios in an Attic inscription, *IG* I² 108.38), Pausanias mentions that the grave of Thucydides was outside the Melitidai gate (1.23.9). The source of the Polemon fragment (Marcellinus

(athletic and/or musical) and victors (21, 22, 26, 27, 47), and quotes (or at least mentions) inscriptions on monuments (22, 79–80),[40] as does Pausanias on numerous occasions.[41] Athenaios reports that Polemon had the nickname *Stêlokopas* ("Wearer-out-of-plaques"), presumably for his tireless interrogation of the inscriptions on monuments.[42]

Wilamowitz's idea that Pausanias plagiarized Polemon has long been discarded, and I have no intention of reviving it here; yet Wilamowitz was no fool: the fragments of Polemon do furnish a basis for the hypothesis that both Polemon and Pausanias are operating in a common literary tradition and striving toward similar generic ends. A look at the less copious fragments of the other two writers confirms this: Diodoros also speaks of monuments (Fragment 35), history (37), and religious customs (38). Heliodoros handles architecture (1), history/biography (5), and, in one of the only verbatim quotations of Heliodoros' writings preserved, he delivers a sentence that could have come from the pages of Pausanias himself, describing the statue of Athena Nike in Athens with a terse enumeration of iconographical attributes: "The Athena Nike is a wingless wooden image holding in her right hand a pomegranate and in her left hand a helmet."[43] None of the references to artworks in the fragments of any of these authors betrays any sort of subjective or emotional reaction to the artwork; their interest seems to be purely antiquarian and iconographical, rather than aesthetic. The same is true, in large measure, of Pausanias.[44]

Many of these similarities might be seen as arising inevitably from the task of describing monuments, which at least theoretically an author might conceive the idea of doing without reference to any literary predecessors. But there is at least one curious feature found both in Pausanias and in the fragments of these authors that cannot be so explained. The fragments of Polemon in particular show an interest (magnified, no doubt, by the salacious tastes of the writers who cite him)[45] in erotic matters, particularly for tales involving courtesans, flute girls, and other women of the sex and

---

Life of Thucydides 16) ascribes it to Polemon's work *On the Acropolis*. The fact that in the course of their discussions of the Athenian acropolis, both Pausanias and Polemon found some reason to mention the grave of Thucydides in a completely different part of the city is a building block for Wilamowitz's theory of large-scale copying of Polemon on the part of Pausanias (Wilamowitz 1877: 344–353). Cf. Frazer 1898: 2.287–288; Musti and Beschi 1982: 347–348.

[40] See also Mette 1978: 40; fragments 79 and 80 are ascribed to a work that seems to have been entirely devoted to, or organized around, inscriptions.

[41] On Pausanias' use of inscriptions, see Habicht 1984 and 1998: 64–94; Tzifopoulos 1991.

[42] Athenaios 6.234d; cf. Preller 1838: 12–14; Müller 1868–1883: 3.110; Pasquali 1913: 177.

[43] Heliodoros F 2. [44] Kreilinger 1997: 475–77; Snodgrass 2001: 127–8.

[45] Chiefly Athenaios, who, for the thirteenth book of his *Deipnosophistai*, seems to have combed through the corpus of periegetical literature carefully to uncover as many tales of courtesans and other outlaw women as possible.

entertainment professions (3a–b, 14–16, 18, 27, 28, 44a–b).[46] In one fragment, Diodoros evinces an interest in the same topics (36). Perhaps such references, by injecting an element of the burlesque, were attempts to enliven
what could otherwise be a dry catalog of monuments, a reason that is often
advanced for the striving for *variatio* in Pausanias. A similar motive may
lie behind references to odd machinery (such as Polemon's description of
a wind-chime in Dodona)[47] and to neo-legends about famous individuals (such as the story Heliodoros tells about Antiochos Epiphanes pouring
wine into the fountain at Antioch, just as Midas is said to have done when
he wanted to capture Silenos).[48] When it comes to women of ambiguous
propriety, Pausanias does not maintain a consistent interest over the course
of the *Periegesis*, but he does include two examples in prominent places
early on: right outside the Propylaia of the Athenian acropolis, Pausanias
refers to a statue of a lioness, which he identifies as a monument to Leaina
(the name means "Lioness"), a courtesan of the tyrant-slayer Aristogeiton
(1.23.2); in the grove called Kraneion near the walls of Corinth, Pausanias
comments on the memorial he finds there to Laïs, another famous courtesan. Polemon (44a–b) also mentions Laïs, but places her tomb in Thessaly
rather than Corinth. Pausanias is aware that the Thessalians also claim Laïs'
tomb, but he refrains from choosing sides explicitly in the dispute.[49]

Pausanias thus seems to have close ties to a family of writers stretching
back at least to the late classical or early Hellenistic period, for whom the

---

[46] Pasquali 1913: 179–180. See Schneider 1999 for an interesting study of one of these references in
Polemon (F 3a–b): Polemon in his work *On the Acropolis* is said to have cited an Athenian decree
forbidding the name of one of the panhellenic athletic festivals to be given to a slave, a freedwoman,
a prostitute, or a flute girl. This may be in reference to a painting in the Pinakotheke, mentioned
by Pausanias (1.22.7) and others, in which Alcibiades is shown reclining in the arms of a female
personification of Nemea in order to symbolize the victories at Nemea his horse teams had won.
Either Polemon or someone Polemon was responding to seems to have interpreted this portrayal of
"Nemea" as being a flute girl of that name.

[47] Polemon F 30.   [48] Heliodoros F 8.

[49] Polemon F 44a–b (= Athenaios 13.588c–d; 589a–b); this comes as part of a long discourse by
Athenaios on this courtesan. At the end of the second of these, following what appears to be
Polemon's explanation and citation of a tomb inscription from Laïs' grave in Thessaly, there comes
the following statement: αὐτοσχεδιάζουσιν οὖν οἱ λέγοντες αὐτὴν ἐν Κορίνθῳ τεθάφθαι πρὸς
τῷ Κρανείῳ ("those who say that she is buried in Corinth near the Kraneion are making it up").
Athenaios assigns the quotations from Polemon to his work *In Response to Timaios*. On that basis,
Preller 1838 (followed by Müller 1868–1883: 3.128) understands this statement as part of the quote
from Polemon and assumes the historian Timaios to be the source of the notion that Laïs was buried
in Corinth. It is perhaps just as likely, however, that this statement is a comment added by Athenaios
at the end of his quotation of Polemon, and that it is a response not to Timaios but to the Corinthian
claim reported by Pausanias. There may be some significance in the fact that the two monuments
Pausanias mentions are both situated in proximity to fortification walls, both take the shape of a
lioness and both stand in proximity to a sanctuary of Aphrodite, but no satisfying explanation has
been suggested to my knowledge. Cf Frazer 1898: 2.273–274.

term "antiquarian periegesis" is hardly inappropriate. As common characteristics of this genre, we can suggest the following: an interest in monuments and stories relating to them (Pausanias' *logoi* and *theôrêmata*); an
interest in things associated with monuments (inscriptions, artists, etc.); an
interest in religion and mythology; the tendency to deal with monuments in
specific localities; a tendency to deal with artworks on an objective and
informational level without expressing a subjective aesthetic response to it;
an appetite for unusual and recherché (or even risqué) stories. Beyond this,
however, one must be careful not to exaggerate the correspondence between
Pausanias and these earlier writers. We noted above Gurlitt's cautious advice
against using these fragmentary authors as a "yardstick" with which to measure Pausanias. Bischoff, after quoting Gurlitt on this point, recommended
turning the yardstick around and using it in the opposite direction, and
subsequent scholars have tended to follow his recommendation:[50]

In fact, only the opposite approach is feasible; one must gain an impression of
attitudes and characteristic expressions from one's reading of Pausanias in order to
be able even to begin to discern from the fragments whether a work really belongs
to that [genre of] antiquarian periegesis.

Instead of using the fragments to elucidate Pausanias, therefore, Bischoff
suggests that Pausanias should be used to elucidate the fragments. There
are no doubt cases where this approach may be useful, but when it comes
to determining the extent to which Pausanias, Diodoros, Heliodoros,
Polemon, and the other attested periegetes are adhering to the same set
of generic conventions, Bischoff's approach is no more sound than the one
that Gurlitt cautions against. In both cases, one must assume to begin with
what one is trying to demonstrate: that the authors in question do indeed
share the same generic conventions. A sounder approach is to take as characteristic of this genre only those features that are attested in more than
one author of the genre. When we find something attested only in one
author, we should at least consider the possibility that it is an innovation
introduced by that author, rather than a common generic feature that by
sheer bad luck has failed to be preserved in the surviving writings of the
other practitioners.

In one respect, Pausanias has long been given credit for one such innovation over his periegetical predecessors: Polemon, Heliodoros, Diodoros,

---

[50] Bischoff 1938: 727 ("Es ist sogar nur der umgekehrte Weg gangbar: man muß aus der Lektüre des
Pausanias sich Gesichtspunkte und charackteristische Wendungen einprägen, um überhaupt erst
aus den Fragmenten über die etwaige Zugehörigkeit eines Werkes zu jener antiquarischen Periegese
entscheiden zu können").

and the others seem to have preferred intensive treatments of smaller geographical areas than Pausanias: in contrast to Pausanias' ten books on the entirety of Greece, Polemon devoted four books, and Diodoros at least three, to the Athenian acropolis alone. But the difference between Pausanias and his predecessors (as they appear from their fragments) is not just one of scale but of method. One of the supposed characteristics of the genre of *periegesis* is a systematic topographical ordering: the listing of series of monuments in spatial sequence along routes or itineraries that the reader could follow (even if he or she did not actually do so).[51] This, as we have seen, is at the root of Pausanias' method of describing places, but it is surprisingly difficult to document in the fragments of any of the other periegetes. In another classic case of *petitio principii*, Giorgio Pasquali noted the absence of evidence for such ordering in the fragments of Heliodoros, yet concluded nevertheless that it must have been present in Heliodoros' original work:[52] ". . . why otherwise would we have the title of periegete so strongly attested for Heliodoros?" One could only ask that question by assuming to begin with, on the basis of Pausanias or on the basis of the equivocal semantics of the word (or both), that a "periegete" must arrange his work in topographical fashion.

The fragments of the earlier periegetes overwhelmingly suggest that their works were arranged on different principles. As Pasquali does for Heliodoros, Bischoff notes that the chief method of organization observable in Polemon's fragments is topical, not spatial.[53] Relatively few fragments of Polemon (or of any of the fragmentary periegetes) refer to more than one monument to begin with, but where they do the monuments are more frequently linked by theme than by spatial proximity. A typical example is the following from Polemon:[54]

---

[51] Cf. Bischoff 1938: 728: "As indispensable for the concept of the 'antiquarian periegesis' one can at least be certain of the fact that it leads one around like a tour guide; that is, it at least maintains the fiction that the reader is taking in information on routes that he either is making or could make" (Als unerlässlich für den Begriff der 'antiquarischen Periegese' kann man wohl überhaupt nur festhalten, daß sie herumführt wie der Fremdenführer, d.h. zum mindesten die Fiktion festhält, daß der Leser das Wissen auf Wegen, die er macht oder machen könnte, aufnimmt).

[52] Pasquali 1913: 169 ("Aber ein topographischer Leitfaden muß sich doch durch die ganze Schrift gezogen haben: warum sonst der Name Perieget, der für Heliodor vortrefflich bezeugt ist?").

[53] Bischoff 1938: 731–2.

[54] One of the few extended verbatim fragments ascribed to Polemon (fr. 20) may also be pertinent in this regard. In this fragment, Polemon discusses dedications found in three buildings at Olympia; the "temple" of the Metapontians (Polemon uses the word ναός ["temple"] for what Pausanias calls a θησαυρός [treasury] [Paus. 6.19.11]); the "temple" of the Byzantians; and the temple of Hera. The lists of artifacts in each building is detailed, terse, and completely lacking in any sense of order or location. For instance: "temple of the Byzantians: in which [there is] a cypress Triton holding a silver cup, a silver siren, two silver *carchesia*, a silver kylix, a golden oinochoe, two drinking horns." There

As Polemon the periegete says in his *On the Dedications in Sparta*, there is a statue of the renowned courtesan Kottina, who he also says dedicated a bronze bull, writing as follows: "And the small statue of Kottina the courtesan, after whom a certain building is named even now on account of her prominence; it is very near to Kolone, where the Dionysos shrine is; it is conspicuous and familiar to many of those in the city. There is an offering made by her above the [sanctuary] of [Athena] Chalkioikos, a certain bronze bullock, and the aforementioned small statue."

ὡς φησι Πολέμων ὁ περιηγητὴς ἐν τῷ Περὶ τῶν ἐν Λακεδαίμονι ἀναθη-
μάτων, εἰκών ἐστι τῆς διαβοήτου ἑταίρας Κοττίνας, ἥν φησι καὶ βοῦν ἀναθεῖ-
ναι χαλκῆν, γράφων οὕτως "Καὶ τὸ Κοττίνας δὲ τῆς ἑταίρας εἰκόνιον, ἧς
διὰ τὴν ἐπιφάνειαν οἴκημά τι λέγεται καὶ νῦν, ἐγγυτάτω τῆς Κολώνης,
ἵνα τὸ Διονύσιόν ἐστιν, ἐπιφανὲς καὶ πολλοῖς ἐγνωσμένον τῶν ἐν τῇ πόλει.
Ἀνάθημα δ' αὐτῆς ἐστιν ὑπὲρ τὸ τῆς Χαλκιοίκου, βοΐδιόν τι χαλκοῦν, καὶ τὸ
προειρημένον εἰκόνιον."

A couple of things that must be kept in mind with this and all fragments that purport to reproduce the cited authority's actual words are: 1) that frequently when an author seems to be quoting his authority directly (even to the extent of saying things like γράφων οὕτως .. "writing as follows"), he is often paraphrasing, and 2) there were no quotation marks in the original text, so frequently it is difficult to tell where the quote ends and the quoting author's comments begin. Nevertheless, reading the sentence as printed above, with Preller's punctuation, we can see that the three items that are the focus of Polemon's description – the statue of Kottina, the building named after her, and the bull she dedicated near the sanctuary of Athena, are not described as being in proximity to one another. Indeed, to judge by Pausanias' account of the city of Sparta they are not in fact in proximity to one another. Pausanias mentions none of Kottina's monuments but he locates the sanctuary of Athena Chalkioikos on the acropolis (3.17.1–18.1), while the Dionysos shrine is elsewhere in the city, on the hill that both authors call Kolone (3.13.7).[55] Spatial relationships are referred to in the Polemon passage, but instead of following a continuous topographical route between what might be called "peer monuments," each of Kottina's monuments is located separately in relation to a more prominent landmark. This is a pattern we find repeated a number of times amongst the

is some doubt whether this fragment displays the actual wording of Polemon – even Athenaios, who has preserved the fragment for us, is unsure of the author, and it may be an epitome or a summary of what Polemon actually said. It is significant, however, that the three buildings named are given in no particular topographical order, either explicitly or implicitly, and this seems hardly likely to be a characteristic introduced by an epitomizer.

55 Perhaps the hill neighboring the acropolis hill to the south-east. cf. Stibbe 1989.

periegetical fragments. One of the more significant fragments of Diodoros is the following:[56]

Diodoros the periegete in his *On the Monuments* has said, more out of supposition than knowledge, that near the harbor of Peiraieus something like an elbow projects from the headland by Alkimos, and when one passes this, on the inward side where the sea is calm, there is a foundation of considerable size and the altar-like structure around it is the grave of Themistokles.

Διόδωρος δ' ὁ περιηγητὴς ἐν τοῖς Περὶ τῶν μνημάτων εἴρηκεν, ὡς ὑπονοῶν μᾶλλον ἢ γινώσκων, ὅτι περὶ τὸν λιμένα τοῦ Πειραιῶς ἀπὸ τοῦ κατὰ τὸν Ἄλκιμον ἀκρωτηρίου πρόκειταί τις οἷον ἀγκὼν, καὶ κάμψαντι τοῦτον ἐντὸς ᾗ τὸ ὑπεύδιον τῆς θαλάττης κρηπίς ἐστιν εὐμεγέθης καὶ τὸ περὶ αὐτὴν βωμοειδὲς τάφος τοῦ Θεμιστοκλέους.

Again, the spatial specifications given in this passage do not constitute a continuous topographical itinerary in the manner of Pausanias, but serve instead to locate a single monument, the grave of Themistokles.[57] If more of Diodoros' account were presented here, we might learn that the grave of Themistokles served as the starting-point for a continuous itinerary, but in light of the way the author locates the grave in relation to broader features of the landscape, the *only* role it could play in such a sequence would be at the beginning. Monuments are introduced this way in the fragments of the other authors with a frequency that cannot be explained as mere happenstance. This was the *usual* way that monuments were introduced and located in pre-Pausanian *periegeseis*. To move beyond the three fragmentary periegetes we have been focusing on, one of the most intriguing fragments of a periegetical account is the so-called *Hawara Periegesis*, a text found on a mangled scrap of papyrus from Hawara in Egypt which was first recognized by Ulrich Wilcken in the 1890s as a description of the harbors and walls of Athens.[58] Rather than reproduce the lacunose text here, I will list in order the landmarks and monuments that seem securely present in the fragment:

1. a harbor (probably, by process of elimination, the largest harbor at Peiraieus, called Kantharos)
   - ship sheds or docks around it

[56] Diodoros F 35 (= Plutarch *Themistokles* 32).

[57] Cf. Polemon F 75: Καὶ Πολέμων δὲ ἐν τῷ Περὶ τοῦ Μορύχου ἐν Συρακούσαις φησὶν ἐπ' ἄκρᾳ τῇ Νήσῳ πρὸς τῷ τῆς Ὀλυμπίας ἱερῷ, ἐκτὸς τοῦ τείχους, ἐσχάραν τινὰ εἶναι (And Polemon in his *On the Morychos in Syracuse* says that on the tip of the island near the shrine of the Olympian outside of the walls there is a certain ash-altar).

[58] Wilcken 1910; Jacoby *FGrH* 369, with comments in 3B.132–136. There is little internal or external evidence to date the text. Wilcken (1910: 220–224) suggests tentatively the third century BCE, or at any rate after Alexander the Great (d. 323 BCE) and before the sack of Athens by Sulla (86 BCE).

2. Zea harbor
   – ship sheds
   – on the south side: a sundial
3. Mounychia
   – famous (περιβόητον) shrine of Artemis Mounychia
4. The Phaleron wall (referred to with a past-tense verb, indicating that it no longer existed).
5. The long walls between Peiraieus and Athens
6. The city of Athens itself, with reference to its mythical foundation by Theseus.

As with the other fragmentary *periegeseis*, the author of this fragment notes spatial relationships mentioned between various landmarks and monuments, and although it is not explicit in the text there is a general topographical logic to the account: it moves first from west to east, from the Kantharos harbor, to Zea, to Mounychia, and then up to the city itself. But, as Wilcken noted, between Kantharos and Zea, two harbors situated on either side of the Peiraieus peninsula, lies the urban area of Peiraieus itself, with many monuments and shrines (as Pausanias, among others, attests). Of this, the author of the papyrus says nothing. Therefore, the fundamental organization of this account is primarily topical, treating first 'harbors' and then 'walls', rather than spatial.[59]

One further comparandum that deserves mention in this context is a fragmentary work which is often ranked among *periegeseis* even though it shares few characteristics of the "antiquarian periegesis" we have been discussing.[60] Three relatively large fragments of a travel-based work by Herakleides Kritikos are preserved in a manuscript with other geographical texts. Among earlier scholarship, this text is ascribed to an anonymous author called pseudo-Dikaiarchos, due to the clearly erroneous crediting of the work to Dikaiarchos of Messene in the manuscript.[61] The fragments, probably datable to the third century BCE, are diverse: Fragment 1 contains a lively and vivid description of a number of Greek cities, including Athens, the cities of Boiotia, and Chalkis in Euboia; Fragment 2 deals with the mountains and natural resources of the land around Mount Pelion in Thessaly; Fragment 3 contains a disputatious essay on the geographical limits of Hellas. Of these fragments, Fragment 2 goes into far more detail on the natural world than Pausanias ever does, and in contrast to Herakleides' Fragment 3, Pausanias, while he is not shy about stating his own opinion and disputing those of others, rarely allows a controversy to occupy him

---

[59] Wilcken 1910: 216–217.   [60] Bischoff 1938: 798–799.   [61] Müller 1861 97–110; Pfister 1951.

for more than a sentence or two. By far the fragment most comparable to Pausanias is the first one. In his description of Greek cities, Herakleides follows a topographical thread from city to city, describing in detail (far more consistently than does Pausanias) the distance and the quality of the road between each pair of cities. For instance (fr. 1.26):

Ἐξ Ἀνθηδόνος εἰς Χαλκίδα στάδια ὁ μέχρι τοῦ Σαλγανέως ὁδὸς παρὰ τὸν αἰγιαλὸν λεία τε πᾶσα καὶ μαλακή· τῇ μὲν καθήκουσα εἰς θάλατταν, τῇ δὲ ὄρος οὐχ ὑψηλὸν μὲν ἔχουσα, λάσιον δὲ καὶ ὕδασι πηγαίοις κατάρρυτον.

From Anthedon to Chalkis [is] 60 stadia; up to Salganeus the road [is] along the shore, all smooth and gentle; on the one side it runs along the sea and on the other it borders a mountain that is not tall but is forested and thoroughly washed by water from springs.

But once within a city, he shows no interest in arranging his descriptions in spatial sequence. When he does mention buildings or sites in a city, his organization is topical rather than spatial (1.1):

1.1. γυμνάσια τρία, Ἀκαδημία, Λύκειον, Κυνόσαργες, πάντα κατάδενδρά τε καὶ τοῖς ἐδάφεσι ποώδη, χόρτοι παντοθαλεῖς φιλοσόφων παντοδαπήν, ψυχῆς ἀπάται καὶ ἀναπαύσεις . . .

[There are] three gymnasia [in Athens]: the Academy, Lyceum, and Kynosarges, all tree-covered and grassy underfoot, gardens blooming with all sorts of philosophers, deceits, and resting-places for the soul . . .

We also see in this excerpt Herakleides' sardonic humor and fondness for wordplay, things that he exhibits much more frequently than Pausanias. Unlike Pausanias, Herakleides also invariably comments on the national character of the people in the cities he visits. For instance, about the people of Tanagra he says:

1.9. πάντες γεωργοὶ, οὐκ ἐργάται· δικαιοσύνην, πίστιν, ξενίαν ἀγαθοὶ διαφυλάξαι·

They are all farmers, not workmen; good at observing justice, trustworthiness, and hospitality.

Other differences between Herakleides and Pausanias have been well noted by Frazer and others.[62] Here, we might just briefly mention that he seems to lack any interest in monuments (only in Athens does he mention some of the city's famous architecture) or in religion. On the basis of Fragment 1 in isolation, Herakleides might be seen as the sort of "travel guide" that would be of use to the average upper-class traveler in either

---

[62] Frazer 1898: 1.xliii–xlviii (who offers a translation of the first fragment into English).

his own time or Pausanias': within the cities, he avoids giving information
about tourist attractions that one could learn about from one's hosts or
from local guides. He does, however, give information about getting from
one city to the next, and about certain characteristics of the inhabitants
of the various cities that local guides might not be frank about. In any
event, he is an important author to consider in the context of this study
for two reasons: first of all, he is a reminder of how diverse ancient works
involving the description of places can be from one another; some of the
"periegetes" whose remains are more fragmentary than Polemo may be
closer to Herakleides than to Pausanias; secondly, he shows how a writer
who is careful to arrange certain parts of his account in topographical order
can still follow a principle of organization that is topical.

Of course, Pausanias frequently engages in topical arrangement as well.
His account of the harbors and walls of Athens, in fact, bears certain similarities to that of the Hawara periegete (1.1.2–5), and one of the things I have
tried to argue in previous chapters is that Pausanias engages in such arrangement more often than is generally recognized. But the fact remains that
there is no solid evidence in any of the fragments of any of the periegetical
authors that they engaged in the sort of topographical itinerary-tracing that
is the most recognizable hallmark of Pausanias' method.[63] I suggest that this
method, as applied to the typical subject-matter of "antiquarian periegesis,"
is an invention of Pausanias himself. The implications for Pausanias' aims,
if this is true, are an interesting subject of speculation. The topical method
of the other periegetes has the effect of abstracting the monuments from
the landscape. What is important about the monuments, they seem to be
saying, is not where they stand but what they stand for, namely the *logoi* to
which they give access. Pausanias' method is more experiential, both creating an (idealized) representation of the author's own experiences on site
and enabling the reader to imagine him or herself experiencing the same
thing. This bespeaks a greater sense of the value of the experience and also
a greater sense of the importance of the land itself and the way monuments

---

[63] Perhaps the closest thing to an exception to this statement comes in a fragment of a periegetical
account that occurs in the lexicon of Harpokration, and which Harpokration ascribes to "either
Menekles or Kallikrates" (*FGrH* 370 F2 = Harpokration *s.v.* Ἑρμαῖ): "ἀπὸ γὰρ τῆς Ποικίλης καὶ
τῆς τοῦ βασιλέως στοᾶς εἰσὶν οἱ Ἑρμαῖ καλούμενοι" ("[for one proceeding] from the Poikile [stoa]
and the Royal stoa are the so-called Hermai"). This could be the beginning, or even conceivably the
middle, of a Pausanian topographical sequence, but it could also be a case like the others where the
two stoas are used as famous landmarks to situate the less prominent area (or street) called the Hermai
(a place where numerous pillar-statues of Hermes [called 'Herms'] were erected). The other fragments
of this author (whichever name is correct, if either) also occur in Harpokration, *s.v.* Ἑκατόμπεδον
and Κεραμεικός. Polemon F 39 mentions a series of three monuments in close proximity to one
another in Syracuse, but these monuments are also topically linked to one another.

within the landscape relate not only to other monuments of the same sort but also to different kinds of monuments in their vicinity.

I would argue that another area in which Pausanias distinguishes himself from his predecessors is in his Herodotean imitation. As we have seen, one of the things commonly said about the periegetical genre is that it is a descendant of the traditional "old-Ionian" geography and ethnography as embodied by Herodotos and Hekataios. Once again, however, one wonders if this is a conclusion that would have ever been reached if Pausanias, with all his overt Herodotisms, never existed, or if it weren't assumed from the beginning that Pausanias' predilections could be read into the existing fragments of the other authors. Apart from the general similarity that the periegetes combine *logoi* and *theôrêmata* as do Herodotos and Hekataios (though in far different proportions), one will look long and hard among the fragments of the periegetes for the sort of obvious signs of this generic heritage that occur on every page of the *Periegesis*. Certainly, there are none of the deliberate impersonations of Herodotean phrases or stylistic mannerisms; in terms of language, there are no distinctive Ionisms and no concerted effort to avoid distinctive Atticisms. Some fragments of Polemon use the Attic form for temple (νεώς),[64] while others use the non-Attic ναός.[65] Arguments based on dialect forms in fragmentary authors are particularly risky, since one usually cannot tell how extensively the quoting author may have altered such forms in the process of quoting. In the Hawara papyrus, however, where we can be more sure of having the author's own words, we find the Attic form for "forty," τετ]ταράκοντα (vs. non-Attic τεσσεράκοντα). I would propose that it was Pausanias himself who conceived the notion of packaging periegetical material in the framework of an obvious *mimesis* of Herodotos. However much a debt was owed to Herodotos and Hekataios by writers like Heliodoros and Polemon, it took someone of the hyperactively language-and-style-conscious period in which Pausanias lived to make those inherent ties manifest on the level of language.

Of course, Pausanias' imitation of Herodotos may have other motivations as well. One conspicuous absence in the *logoi* of the fragmentary periegetes is the sort of material that was normally the province of canonical historiography, namely military and political history. In its place, one finds biographical anecdotes, titillating stories of courtesans and flute girls, controversies over such issues as who invented wrestling,[66] and so on.

---

[64] E.g. F 73, 75; other Atticisms: κηρύττει (F 86) rather than κηρύσσει.
[65] E.g. F 20; other non-Atticisms: γινομένων (F 83); θάλασσαν (F 75 alongside νεώ!).
[66] Polemon F 55.

Pausanias, on the other hand, while he includes much of this kind of
material as well, weaves lengthy historical accounts into his *Periegesis* from
nearly the beginning. There is no evidence that any of the other fragmentary *periegeseis* contained anything like Pausanias' history of the Messenian
wars (4.4.1–27.11) or the Gallic Incursion (10.19.5–23.14), or even any of
the shorter historical excursuses that pepper Pausanias' account. It could
be that in pursuing a new combination of periegetical antiquarianism with
autoptic ethnography and the stuff of standard history, Pausanias felt more
closely akin to Herodotos than any of his periegetical predecessors do.
Although the image of Herodotos referred to in contemporary literature of
Pausanias' day was more the ethnographer of far-off lands and the cataloger
of foreign (and sometimes unbelievable) marvels, his *Histories* consisted of
a combination of those sorts of topics with the history of the Persian wars
themselves, and Pausanias seem to have striven for a more Herodotean formula not only in the amount of *logoi* and *theôrêmata* in his account but
also in the types of *logoi* that he pursues.

GENERIC VARIATIO

Yet once again, even if Pausanias stuck more closely to Herodotos than
other writers, Herodotean *mimesis* is not a sufficient explanation for every
feature of his account. Pausanias' habit of tracing itineraries from monument to monument and from site to site is certainly not Herodotean,
and if this facet of his work is not common to the genre of "antiquarian
periegesis" it is legitimate to ask from where the idea for it might have
come to Pausanias. One possible source would be geographical works,
the only completely surviving one of which is by Strabo, an earlier writer
of the Roman period, who, like Pausanias, was a Greek-speaking native
of Anatolia. There is no concrete evidence that Pausanias used Strabo as
a source, or was even aware of him, but the methodical and sequential
way that Strabo's geography, or works like it, covered the earth may have
inspired Pausanias as he sought to expand the normal territorial scope of
a periegetical work. Strabo covers the circuit of the Mediterranean, listing
sites along the coast, often with precise figures for distances, and describing
the hinterlands of each ethnic division of the known world before moving
on to the next one. Strabo also delves, as ancient geography frequently
did, into the history and mythological traditions of the various places he
described. As Katherine Clarke has recently argued, geography was considered by some of its practitioners, including Strabo, as a counterpart of
history, or, perhaps more accurately, as history arranged spatially rather than

chronologically,[67] an attitude which Pausanias in many respects seems to share. There are, of course, numerous differences between the types of writings that Strabo and Pausanias engage in. Strabo, although he is interested in history, has little interest in monuments; his geographical scope is much broader than Pausanias', with an attendant diminution of detail; while he is widely traveled, he makes no pretense of autopsy for all of the places he encompasses in his account; and – most importantly for present purposes – while his descriptions of coastal sites tend to be linear and sequential, his descriptions of the inland territories are usually synoptic: he delineates the extent of the land in broad terms and he is less concerned with specifying the positions of individual sites. With Pausanias, the opposite priorities tend to prevail. He often neglects the coastline or treats it cursorily (even erroneously, as we saw in Chapter 4), while linking inland sites together with detailed itineraries. Further inspiration for inland itineraries may have come from works like those of Herakleides Kritikos, who gives consistent information on roads and distances between cities. Yet, at least in the fragments we possess, Herakleides does not concern himself with intra-urban itineraries, and Herakleides' account is so unusual among the preserved literature that we really know too little to say whether it might have made an impact on Pausanias.

One final potential source of inspiration worth mentioning is the varied body of Greek works that come down to us under the titles of *Periplous* ("Coastal Voyage"), *Stadiasmos* ("Distance Reckoning"), or some other similarly unassuming appellation.[68] Such works generally project or even profess the aim of being merely utilitarian or informational, but many have what seem to be more lofty literary ambitions (some are even written in verse).[69] Despite such ambitions, many *Periploi* and *Stadiasmoi* consist in large part of simple lists of sites and distances. Here, for instance, is a typical passage, from the late, anonymous text entitled *Periplous* [or *Stadiasmos*] *tês megalês thalassês* (*Coastal Voyage* [or *Distance Reckoning*] *around the Great* [i.e. *Mediterranean*] *Sea*):[70]

---

[67] Clarke 1999.
[68] Such as the *Anaplous Bosporou* (*Voyage up the Bosporos*) written by Dionysios of Byzantium. Also worth mentioning here may be the *Itineraria*, which listed distances for overland routes, but the earliest ones which survive (such as the *Antonine Itinerary*) are written in Latin (as befits their use for official business on the imperial road system) and are late (third century CE, though apparently based on earlier models), and consist largely of simple lists of place names and distances as unadorned with additional information and commentary as the sparest *periplous*. See Janni 1998.
[69] See: Janni 1984: 23–25; Dilke 1985: 130–144.   [70] Müller 1861: 1.427–514.

Ἀπὸ Ἀλεξανδρείας εἰς χερσόνησον – λιμήν ἐστι – στάδιοι β'.
Ἀπὸ χερσονήσου εἰς Δυσμὰς – λιμήν ἐστι ἀγωγῆς χιλίων οὐ μείζονος –
στάδιοι ζ.
Ἀπὸ Δυσμῶν εἰς Πλινθίνην – σάλος ἐστίν ὁ τόπος ἀλίμενος – στάδιοι φ'.
Ἀπὸ Πλινθίνης ἐπὶ Ταπόσιριν – πόλις ἐστὶν ἀλίμενος· ἱερὸν τοῦ Ὀσίριδος –
στάδιοι ζ.

From Alexandria to Chersonesos – there is a harbor – 2 *stadioi*.
From Chersonesos to Dusmai – there is a harbor for loads of 1,000 and no more –
7 *stadioi*.
From Dusmai to Plinthine – it is an open stretch; the place is harborless – 90
stadioi.
From Plinthine to Taposiris – there is a city without a harbor; a shrine of Osiris –
7 *stadioi*.

This is more spare and utilitarian than anything found in Pausanias; its listing of distances is more regular and mechanical, and the types of information more limited and predictable. Yet the systematic listing of sites in such works, each one in relation to the one previous, is the closest parallel in the preserved Greek literature to the sort of itinerary-building that Pausanias engages in. If we must search for a source of Pausanias' method outside of his own native imagination, works like this are perhaps where we will find it.

BACK TO THE BEGINNING

Mention of *periploi* brings us back to the beginning of the *Periegesis* for yet another attempt to gage the author's initial presentation of his work. In its abruptness, its terseness, and its seaborne perspective (which Pausanias will soon decisively abandon, however) the opening of the *Periegesis* bears a certain resemblance to the parts of some *periploi*, including the *Periplous of the Great Sea* quoted above; yet even the author of that *Periplous* sees fit to furnish his catalog of sailing information (apparently itself an excerpt from a larger work) with an introduction, one in which he addresses the work's dedicatee (a person he calls "most honored brother"), outlines the scope of his work, and explains its purpose ("so that you may read and become acquainted with these things also": ὅπως καὶ τούτων ἀναγνοὺς ἔμπειρος ἔσῃ). Even for the most unassuming of geographical accounts, it is not unusual for the author to assist his reader and his own reputation by providing a prolog or introductory statement. For works of the scope and depth of Pausanias', prologs are almost obligatory. The surviving geographies of Strabo and Ptolemy, for instance, offer lengthy introductions in which the authors define their area of inquiry and situate themselves in relation to their predecessors.[71]

Such examples are reason enough to find the lack of a prolog curious, but they do not constitute proof that an original prolog to the *Periegesis* has gone missing. We must therefore remain open to other possible explanations. Another text that provides an interesting comparandum that can be dated nearer in time to Pausanias (first century CE) is the anonymous work known as *Periplous tes Erythras Thalasses* (*Coastal Voyage around the Red Sea*), which begins thus:[72]

Τῶν ἀποδεδειγμένων ὅρμων τῆς Ἐρυθρᾶς θαλάσσης καὶ τῶν περὶ αὐτὴν ἐμπορίων πρῶτός ἐστι λιμὴν τῆς Αἰγύπτου Μυὸς ὅρμος. Μετὰ δὲ αὐτὸν εἰσπλεόντων ἀπὸ χιλίων ὀκτακοσίων σταδίων ἐν δεξιᾷ ἡ Βερνίκη.

Of the designated anchorages in the Red Sea and of the trading settlements around it, the first harbor in Egypt is the anchorage Muos. After it, for those sailing on for a distance of 1,800 *stadia*, Berenike lies on the right.

Like the *Periegesis*, the text begins in the middle of things, and also, like the *Periegesis*, expresses movement from one place to the next by means of impersonal participles. The two texts are not completely comparable, of course: while the *Periplous* of the Red Sea is a brief text and relatively uniform in its catalog-like contents, the same cannot be said for the *Periegesis*. Nevertheless, the parallel between the opening of this text and that of the *Periegesis* is striking.

There is one other comparandum, even closer in time to Pausanias, which has features that suggest an even more interesting literary affinity. The author in this case is not someone nameless or obscure, but one of the most prominent of Pausanias' elder contemporaries, Arrian. The text in question is Arrian's *Periplous Euxeinou Pontou* (*Coastal Voyage around the Euxine [Black] Sea*), written during Arrian's appointment as legate to the province of Cappadocia in the early 130s CE. It begins as follows (1.1–2):

Αὐτοκράτορι Καίσαρι Τραϊανῷ Ἀδριανῷ Σεβαστῷ Ἀρριανὸς χαίρειν. Εἰς Τραπεζοῦντα ἥκομεν, πόλιν Ἑλληνίδα, ὡς λέγει ὁ Ξενοφῶν ἐκεῖνος, ἐπὶ θαλάττῃ ᾠκισμένην, Σινωπέων ἄποικον, καὶ τὴν μὲν θάλασσαν τὴν τοῦ Εὐξείνου ἄσμενοι κατείδομεν ὅθενπερ καὶ Ξενοφῶν καὶ σύ. καὶ οἱ βωμοὶ ἀνεστᾶσιν ἤδη, λίθου μέντοι γε τοῦ τραχέος, καὶ τὰ γράμματα διὰ τοῦτο οὐκ εὔδηλα κεχάρακται, τὸ δὲ Ἑλληνικὸν ἐπίγραμμα καὶ ἡμαρτημένως γέγραπται, οἷα δὴ ὑπὸ βαρβάρων γραφέν.

[71] See Clarke 1999: 49–54.   [72] Müller 1861: 1.257–305; Casson 1989: 6–7.

To Emperor Caesar Traianus Hadrianus Augustus[73] Arrian sends greetings.
We arrived at Trapezous, a Greek city, as the renowned Xenophon says, founded
on the sea, a colony of the Sinopeans; and we were delighted to look down on
the waters of the Euxine from the same place as did Xenophon and also you. The
altars were standing already, but in rough-hewn stone, and on account of this the
inscribed letters were not easy to read. The Greek inscription was even written
incorrectly, as one might expect of something written by barbarians.

As we read on, we discover, rather than read, that the altars Arrian
cryptically refers to are part of the apparatus relating to the imperial
cult at Trapezous, a topic upon which Arrian spends some time advising and informing the emperor before beginning his account of his and his
entourage's voyage along the coast.

Again, there are obvious differences between Arrian's *Periplous* and the
Periegesis. The former is an epistolary report, an account written consistently
in the first person and addressed to a specific recipient, the emperor, who is
apostrophized continually as "you." Actions of the traveler and the things
that he sees are reported in the past tense as things that occurred on a
particular journey in the past, as opposed to Pausanias' eternalizing use
of the present tense in most cases. As a dispatch from an officer of the
empire to his commander-in-chief, Arrian's work deals, especially in the
first part (1–16), with topics that Pausanias never touches upon, such as
the arranging of imperial dedications (1–2) and strategic assessments of
military emplacements (e.g. 12). Finally, the itinerary followed by Arrian's
Periplous remains seaborne, rather than turning overland, and in contrast to
Pausanias' notorious silence on the physical realities of traveling – whether
by land or by sea – Arrian provides information on winds and sailing
conditions, and even describes for the emperor's edification and delectation
a harrowing encounter with a storm at sea (5).

Despite these differences, there is one point of similarity that is of potential import for the interpretation of the beginning of the *Periegesis*. One
could argue that the openings of both the *Periplous* and the *Periegesis* (as it
stands) operate on a rhetoric of deliberate understatement. Since Arrian's
text is unchallenged and the social context to which it belongs more obvious, we will begin there with an examination of how this rhetoric operates:
beyond the salutation, Arrian wastes no words on introducing his topic,
or explaining what it was that brought him to the shores of the Black Sea,
or what he hoped his addressee (or the more general reader) sought to get
out of the reading of the text. He begins directly with the account of his

---

[73] Sc. Hadrian. For text and translation of the *Periplous*, see Silberman 1995. Cf. also: Silberman 1993;
Braund 1994: 178–187.

journeys: "We arrived at Trapezous . . ." It is clear that Arrian wants his epistolary report to be understood as genuine; one that he, in his role as imperial official, addresses directly to the emperor who has dispatched him. The way Arrian launches immediately into his report helps maintain this pose: in this context, references to the nature of his command, the purpose of his journey, or the purpose for which he writes about his journey would be out of place, since they are things that the addressee of the work, the emperor, would already know. It matters little for present purposes whether the *Periplous* actually *was* a genuine letter that Arrian wrote to Hadrian.[74] Arrian's intent would be largely the same, regardless of whether he composed it originally for publication or arranged the publication of a text that was originally intended for the emperor's eyes alone. Either way, the unceremonious opening is either created or retained as a deliberate attempt to convey to an audience different from the addressee a sense of immediacy, guilelessness, objectivity, and the authority of an eyewitness. All these characteristics support Arrian's purposes, which, on the one hand, include an accurate description of Black Sea sites that the reader would accept as authoritative, but, on the other hand, also include a desire on the part of the author to establish, or at any rate signal, his status in broader realms. The main topic of Arrian's *Periplous*, alongside Black Sea geography, is Arrian himself – his relationship with Hadrian is advertised in the very first sentences, and the deliberate simplicity and lack of ornament one finds in the opening is part of how Arrian characterizes that relationship: it is as though we are listening in on a conversation between the emperor and a trusted advisor, in which the latter would not think, and would have no need, to mask or distort the truth.[75] This very relationship, and the sense the text gives of listening in on a private communication between men of power, is doubtlessly part of what Arrian hoped would make the text of interest to his readers.

Also in the first sentence, Arrian heralds connections of a different sort, to his personal model Xenophon. As we have seen, Arrian was a person who, in genuine second-century fashion, modeled his own public identity on a figure from the classical past. Like the classical Athenian author Xenophon, Arrian prided himself on being a man of action as well as letters (he had a distinguished military and political career in service of the empire), one who, like Xenophon, balanced the practicality and hard-headedness of his military and political writings with accounts of the serene lessons learned

---

[74] See Silberman 1993 and Silberman 1995: xvi–xvii; Bosworth 1993: 242–253.
[75] Bosworth 1993: 249.

at the feet of a well known sage-like figure (for Xenophon: Socrates; for Arrian: Epictetus).[76] Arrian's writings as a historian and as an authority on tactics are patterned explicitly after Xenophon's *œuvre*, and Arrian even borrowed the title of his best-known work, the *Anabasis of Alexander*, from Xenophon's *Anabasis* [*Upland March*] *of Cyrus*, in which the author recounts his own adventures as a mercenary in Asia. Arrian even referred to himself as a second Xenophon, and may have gone so far as to add the surname Xenophon officially to the Roman *nomen* (Flavius) and the Greek *cognomen* (Arrianos) that he already possessed.[77]

In the homeward march of his mercenary army that Xenophon describes in his *Anabasis*, the Greeks reach the sea, and Greek territory, at Trapezous (4.8.22). It is this turning-point in the story of Xenophon and his merce- naries that Arrian alludes to at the beginning of the *Periplous*, when he says, "We came to Trapezous, a Greek city, as the renowned Xenophon says, founded upon the sea as a colony of Sinopeans." This first sentence of the *Periplous* not only invokes Xenophon's name but echoes his very words from the *Anabasis*: ἦλθον ἐπὶ θάλατταν εἰς Τραπεζοῦντα πόλιν Ἑλληνίδα οἰκουμένην ἐν τῷ Εὐξείνῳ Πόντῳ, Σινωπέων ἀποικίαν (4.8.22). ("they came to Trapezous on the sea, a Greek city settled on the Euxine Sea, a colony of Sinopeans"). Arrian's next words in the *Periplous*, καὶ τὴν μὲν θάλασσαν τὴν τοῦ Εὐξείνου ἄσμενοι κατείδομεν ὅθενπερ καὶ Ξενοφῶν καὶ σύ ("with pleasure we looked down at the water of the Euxine Sea from the same place as did Xenophon and you as well"), further echo the langauge of Xenophon at the best-known point in the *Anabasis*, when Xenophon's men first glimpse the sea and begin shouting the word "*Thalatta!*" ("Sea!"): ἐπεὶ δὲ οἱ πρῶτοι ἐγένοντο ἐπὶ τοῦ ὄρους καὶ κατεῖδον τὴν θάλατταν, κραυγὴ πολλὴ ἐγένετο (4.7.22) ("when the first men reached the top of the mountain and looked down at the sea, a great shout arose"). Through- out the rest of the *periplous*, Arrian alludes to Xenophon on a number of occasions (2.3; 11.1; 12.5; 13.6; 25.1).

Without making a single overt statement of introduction, then, Arrian establishes his *bona fides* by alluding to his relationship to Hadrian, his status as Xenophon's second-century successor, and his authority as an experienced eyewitness. The understated form of his beginning enhances, rather than diminishes, this effect since it treats the author's qualifications in these areas as something that can go without saying for Hadrian and (*a fortiori*) the reader. Pausanias is certainly not trying to accomplish the

[76] Bosworth 1980–1995: 1.1–6; Stadter 1980: 1–13; 32–49; Tonnet 1988: 9–59; Bosworth 1993: 226–233.
[77] The *praenomen* that Arrian possessed as a Roman citizen is uncertain. Aulus or Lucius are possibilities. See Tonnet 1988: 1.18.

exact same thing that Arrian does in his opening. The *Periegesis* has no addressee, imperial or otherwise, and Pausanias give us no explicit guidance as to the literary model he wishes us to measure his work against, as does Arrian. But the use of understatement can be seen as a way that Pausanias establishes an attitude of authority for the reader. It is as if he were to say: "Here is an account of Greece; the author is so well suited to the task of presenting you with this account that he need not spend time demonstrating his qualifications." Pausanias' avoidance of the sorts of self-defining, self-promoting things one would expect in his day from the author of a long, involved work many years in the making would probably strike the reader as communication by omission. In a time when one of the functions of literature was to signal the position of the author and his addressees in the social firmament of *pepaideumenoi* ("the educated," or "the cultured") – a thing that Arrian does in the *Periplous* with his comfortable, familiar manner of addressing, in Greek, the philhellenic emperor – Pausanias' silence serves as a means by which he can establish for himself a unique position.

As was intimated in the previous chapter, the fact that this self-presentation through silence occurs in both Arrian and Pausanias may be more than just coincidence. Arrian's *Periplous* was a product of the 130s, thus within Pausanias' lifetime yet before (apparently) he began composing the *Periegesis*. Since Arrian was one of the most celebrated authors of the day, a political and military notable in addition to being an inhabitant of high literary and intellectual circles, and since his *Periplous* dealt with a part of the world that was near to Pausanias' homeland, it is no great leap to suggest that Pausanias was probably familiar with the *Periplous* and that it could have influenced the way Pausanias chose to cast his own account.

A curious coincidence may provide some small corroboration of the connection between the beginning of Arrian's *Periplous* and the beginning of the *Periegesis*. An anonymous *periplous* of the Black Sea, by a Byzantine writer of uncertain date, begins with what is perhaps the most similar beginning to that of Pausanias' *Periegesis* in all the preserved literature (1):[78]

Κατὰ τὸν Θρᾴκιον Βόσπορον καὶ τὸ στόμα τοῦ Εὐξείνου Πόντου ἐν τοῖς δεξιοῖς τῆς Ἀσίας μέρεσιν, ἅπερ ἐστὶ τοῦ Βιθυνῶν ἔθνους, κεῖται χωρίον Ἱερὸν καλούμενον, ἐν ᾧ νεώς ἐστι Διὸς Οὐρίου προσαγορευόμενος. Τοῦτο δὲ τὸ χωρίον ἀφετήριόν ἐστι τῶν εἰς τὸν Πόντον πλεόντων. Εἰσπλεύσαντι δὲ εἰς τὸν Πόντον, δεξιὰν τὴν Ἀσίαν ἔχοντι καὶ περιπλέοντι τὸ λειπόμενον μέρος τοῦ Βιθυνῶν ἔθνους, τὸ πρὸς τῷ Πόντῳ κείμενον, ὁ περίπλους οὕτως ἔχει.

---

[78] For text, Müller *GGM*; for introduction to the author, see *GGM* 2.lxiv–lxv.

In the direction of the Thracian Bosporos and the mouth of the Euxine Sea, in the right-hand parts of Asia which belong to the Bithynian nation, lies a place called Hieron. In it is a temple said to be of Zeus Ourios. This place is the starting-point for those sailing to Pontos. For one sailing to Pontos, keeping Asia on the right and sailing along the remaining parts of the nation of the Bithynians, which are located next to Pontos, this is how the coastal voyage goes . . .

A quick list of prominent similarities between this passage and the opening of the *Periegesis:* the initial orientation of the reader in reference to several landmarks (cf. in Pausanias, κατὰ νήσους τὰς Κυκλάδας καὶ πέλαγος τὸ Αἰγαῖον); the use of the preposition κατὰ (translated here as "in the direction of") for that purpose; the use of impersonal focalizing participles to transfer the reader from one point to the next (πλεόντων: "of those sailing"; εἰσπλεύσαντι . . . ἔχοντι . . . περιπλέοντι: "for one sailing toward . . . keeping . . . making a coastal voyage . . ."); the mention of a temple as the first man-made landmark. So close is the similarity that one might entertain the supposition that this late author was modeling his opening on Pausanias, were it not for two things: first, our Byzantine text is not a completely original creation but instead a pastiche of earlier texts, including large patches of the *Periplous* of Arrian – and the passage with which this pastiche begins is taken wholesale from the *middle* of a late antique epitome of a first-century BCE *periplous* by Menippos of Pergamon.[79] Secondly, the model toward which the Byzantine compilation was constructed seems to be clear, since the single manuscript that records the work's beginning ascribes the text to Arrian. It might be possible to see this as the result of an error on the part of some later editor, were it not for the fact that in addition to the name of Arrian someone has also added a version of the epistolary salutation to Hadrian that prefaced Arrian's *Periplous:* Τραιανῷ Ἀδριανῷ Σεβαστῷ Ἀρριανός. (Arrian [sends greetings] to Traianus Hadrianus Augustus). Thus, it seems that our compiler attempted to refashion the *Periplous* of Arrian and "improve" it with the addition of material from other sources. In doing so, he saw nothing inconsistent with Arrian's epistolary tone in replacing the text's original beginning with something sounding strikingly like Pausanias.

CONCLUSIONS

This inquiry into Pausanias' generic affinities may seem to have come up with mostly negative results: the *Periegesis* is not a travel guide; it is

[79] Müller *GGM* 2.lxiv

not a geography; it is not a work like that of Herakleides Kritikos; it is not a full-blown imitation of Herodotean historiography, nor of Arrianic epistolography; it is not a *periplous*, and it is not, finally, a *periegesis*. Yet rather than adhere to one of these possibilities out of a desperate need to define the *Periegesis* as *something* we can recognize and pigeonhole, we should realize that when we look at the *Periegesis* from this perspective what we are seeing is basically the same thing we saw when we considered more small-scale issues of language and style in Chapter 6. Pausanias eschews the simple route of writing in an established tradition, and combines recognizable aspects of a number of traditions to create his own genre. The rules and the expectations of that new genre are ones that Pausanias is free to juggle into his own configuration. Once again, as with the stylistic elements that we examined in the previous chapter, the name of Pausanias' elder contemporary Arrian comes up as a possible conduit for literary ideas that Pausanias takes advantage of. The *Periegesis* is nothing like anything Arrian is known to have written, but in his own literary efforts, Arrian may have shown Pausanias the contemporary possibilities of a dynamic *mimesis* of Herodotos, the writing of serious history, the combining of *periplous-*style spatial organization with historical accounts and, in his writings on Alexander and the period following Alexander's death, the pertinence of Hellenistic history to Greeks of his time, a theme which we will examine Pausanias' own development of in the next chapter.

CHAPTER 8

A periegete's progress

From some perspectives, the elephant that is the *Periegesis* seems to have a uniform appearance. Up to this point, we have been examining the numerous methods Pausanias employs in the arrangement and expression of his material, and while variation is a primary concern to the author – different places call for a different mixture of *logoi* and *theôrêmata*, a more topographical or more topical method of describing sites, a greater or lesser complexity in the network of itineraries, etc. – over the course of the work, the panoply of topographical and narrative methods Pausanias can employ at any given point varies little. There are no fundamental ways that Pausanias approaches cities, shrines, temples, artworks, myths, gods, and historical events in the tenth book that he hasn't already used as early as the first book. Moreover, the laboriously crafted and idiosyncratic prose style in which Pausanias casts his account varies little from book to book.

Such consistency might give the impression that the *Periegesis* is a creature brought to life by its creator in one uninterrupted impulse over a short period of time, but we know that is not the case. We know that Pausanias was at work on the *Periegesis* for over a decade, perhaps over two or even three. We can also surmise that the travel and study involved in the creation of the work introduced the author to a number of potentially mind-changing or even life-changing discoveries and experiences over and above what a person would normally encounter in a similar span of time. In the previous chapters, I endeavored to show that the infrastructure of the *Periegesis* was something that its author thought out very carefully and always strove to keep under control, but the purposeful consistency of the work must itself be counted as part of Pausanias' self-presentation. At the same time that he is constructing his literary representation of Greek landscapes, Pausanias is constructing an image of himself that is as monolithic and unwavering as the marble statues he describes, or even more so. "From the beginning," he tells us in one well-noted passage (3.11.1), "my account has preferred to pick out those things that are most noteworthy . . . from the multitude of things not worth relating. Since that was a good decision there is no way I will go back on it."[1] Though this passage refers specifically to the author's selectivity, the sentiment it embodies could just as easily be applied to the entire array of techniques with which Pausanias goes about the business of narrating and describing. The numerous cross-references between different parts of the text, which begin in Book 1 (1.24.5 referring to Book 9) and continue at a steady pace, are one index of this effort. In the first chapter, we pointed out Mario Moggi's observation that Pausanias provides such cross-references far more frequently than any other author.[2] This habit not only attests to the fact that the work was well planned but also that the author wanted his work to *appear* well planned. Many of the monuments themselves, especially the extremely ancient ones that Pausanias was most taken with, were disintegrating even in his time. As if to counteract the impermanency of the remaining material embodiments of Hellenism, Pausanias offers himself and his *Periegesis* as a "monument more permanent than bronze."

Pausanias' monument-like self-presentation is something that modern commentators have tended to buy into too readily. Just as Pausanias' portrait of Greece is molded by his cognitive predispositions, our image of Pausanias is to some extent influenced by our expectation that he is consistent, an expectation that the author does his best to foster. Studies of Pausanias (including this one, for the most part) tend to be synoptic. If one wants to investigate Pausanias' treatment of Greek heroes, for instance, one scans the text for references to them, writes each reference on a notecard, puts together all the notecards referring to the same hero, and then collates the results to arrive at an understanding of Pausanias' view (singular) on the subject. For certain types of studies, such an approach is unavoidable, but by its very nature it falls short of providing a complete picture. It fails to take into account the context that helps to give meaning to each particular passage, and part of that context must be understood diachronically, because the Pausanias who was writing about Athens in the 150s or early 160s is not the same Pausanias who was writing about Delphi in the 170s or 180s. Beneath the image of monolithic permanence that Pausanias constructs for himself, there are occasionally glimpses of a person whose outlook evolves over time. This chapter will be devoted to uncovering some of the traces of that evolution, and while we can never hope to come to any firm conclusions about what motivated Pausanias' attitudes and his changes in attitude, the topics we will focus on here are ones for which it is possible to suggest,

---

[1] ἐμοὶ γὰρ ἐξ ἀρχῆς ἠθέλησεν ὁ λόγος ἀπὸ πολλῶν καὶ οὐκ ἀξίων ἀφηγήσεως . . . ἀποκρῖναι τὰ ἀξιολογώτατα.
[2] Moggi 1993: 402–403.

however tentatively, that Pausanias' experiences as he traveled in Greece and learned more about the topography of Greece's present and its past exerted some effect.

Certain aspects of Pausanias' authorial and attitudinal development over the course of the composition of the *Periegesis* have long been recognized. There is, for instance, the apparent change in Pausanias' methods between Book 1 and subsequent books. There is also the well-commented-upon "conversion" in his religious views that he professes in Book 8. There is much that remains to be said on both these topics from a diachronic perspective, but this chapter will begin by focusing primarily on one area where Pausanias' views tend to be treated as monolithic, namely his attitude toward Greek history.

PAUSANIAS THE HISTORIAN: BETWEEN CHAIRONEIA AND ROME

In my discussion of the problem of genre, I agreed with the many before me who have suggested that Pausanias viewed his work as something akin to history-writing. As fundamental as the idea of being a historian seems to have been to Pausanias, however, I will argue here that his attitudes toward history and his concept of his role as a recorder of history are areas in which we can see a definite change over the course of the ten books. The obvious place to start in examining this issue is Book 1; not only is this book the first to be written, but Book 1 is the place where the reader first meets Pausanias in all his guises, and the impression thus formed can affect the way the reader understands Pausanias' perspective in the rest of the work. Somewhat surprisingly, given the common opinion that Pausanias was preoccupied with the period of Greek history that preceded the Macedonian conquest, the first historical event mentioned in Book 1 relates not to an event of that early period but to the so-called Chremonidean war of the third century BCE. In accordance with the terms of an alliance with Athens and other Greek states against the ruler of Macedon (Antigonos Gonatas), another king of Macedonian descent, Ptolemy II of Egypt, sent a naval force to Attica under the command of a man named Patroklos. It was this Patroklos – the third-century BCE Patroklos, not the famous character from the *Iliad*, nor a local hero, nor a figure from any of Athens' renowned conflicts of the classical period – who gave his name to an island that Pausanias sees not far from the promontory of Laurion and makes note of in the very first section of his *Periegesis* (1.1.1).

This reference to an episode from the post-classical period presages a theme that famously occupies a good deal of the first half of Book 1:

Hellenistic history – more specifically, the history of the third century BCE and a few decades to either side of it in the fourth and second centuries. Pausanias devotes several substantial excursuses in the first book to rulers of this period: Ptolemy I and II, kings of Egypt, together with the Pergamene king Attalos I (1.6.1–8.1); Ptolemy VI Philometor (1.9.1–3); Lysimachos, king of Thrace (1.9.5–10.5); Pyrrhos of Epeiros (1.11.1–13.9) and Seleukos I, king of Syria and Mesopotamia (1.16.1–3). Book 1 also contains other passages relating to post-classical history: Pausanias' first historical excursus of any appreciable length is on the invasion of the Gauls in 279 BCE (1.4.1–6).[3] Later, he writes about the sack of Athens by Sulla during the Mithridatic war in 86 BCE (1.20.4–7) and about the Lamian war (a rebellion against Macedon that occurred among Greek cities after the death of Alexander the Great) and the subsequent anti-Macedonian activities of the Athenian leader Olympiodoros (1.25.2–26.3). Pausanias certainly does not ignore post-classical history in the other books: there are important digressions on the careers of the Hellenistic leaders Aratos in Book 2 and Philopoimen in Book 8;[4] there is Pausanias' account of the Roman conflicts with the Achaean League in Book 7, and his more expansive retelling of the Gallic invasion in Book 10. Moreover, none of Pausanias' lengthier excursions on the history of a particular area or people (e.g. Sparta in Book 3, Messenia in Book 4) excludes post-classical events entirely. But in Book 1, particularly the first half, the forays into Hellenistic history come in far greater profusion than they do elsewhere. Within these accounts, Pausanias' narratives of the Greco-Macedonian monarchs who dominated the eastern Mediterranean in the wake of Alexander the Great (each narrative appended to the mention of a statue of the monarch that Pausanias sees in the Athenian Agora) form something of a unified group, and it is these that we will examine first.

Pausanias' digressions on the Hellenistic kings have hardly been ignored in modern scholarship.[5] Often, these excursuses provide unique testimony found in no other author's writings, so the questions of Pausanias' accuracy and the possible sources that he relied on (he names none, aside from Hieronymos of Kardia, whom he expressly doesn't follow in all respects) are naturally of great interest. Few attempts have been made, however, to examine these accounts as expressions of Pausanias' own historical outlook and to explain how they contribute to (or detract from) his overall goals in

---

[3] The same invasion which (as was mentioned in Chapter 6) will be narrated at greater length (and with copious echoes of Herodotos) in Book 10 (10.19.5–23.11).

[4] Aratos: 2.8.2–9.5; Philopoimen: 8.49.1–53.6.

[5] Major studies include: Segre 1927; Regenbogen 1956: 1068–1069; Bearzot 1992; Ameling 1996.

writing the *Periegesis*. A recent and welcome exception is an article by Walter Ameling, who advances the thesis that Pausanias dwells on the Hellenistic period because it provides a crucial link between the classical days of Greek autonomy that Pausanias so admired and the Roman domination that was part of his everyday reality.[6] There is a lot to be said for this thesis, but I would argue that it is a hypothesis that works better for Pausanias' later excursions into Hellenistic history than it does for the ones in Book 1 and other early books. The amount of Hellenistic history in Book 1 is one of the things that distinguish it from later books, but what is important in my view, and what represents a significant change in outlook for Pausanias, is not so much the Hellenistic content of these histories but the way they interact with the topographical matrix that Pausanias places them in.

The question of why Pausanias spends so much time on the Hellenistic period in Book 1 is one that he uncharacteristically gives us some help with in his own words. The occasion for Pausanias' first royal digressions comes when he describes the monument of the Eponymous Heroes in the Athenian Agora (1.5.2).[7] This monument supported statues of the (mostly legendary) heroes who gave their names to the "tribes" (φυλαί) into which the Athenian populace was divided for political purposes. In addition to the ten original heroes, certain latter-day benefactors of the city had had the honor at various times of having new tribes named after them and having their statues erected on the monument. Pausanias reports that in his day there were three of these more recent additions to the monument: Ptolemy,[8] Attalos, and the Roman emperor Hadrian. Before launching into his digression about the two Hellenistic kings, Pausanias says that (in contrast to Hadrian) there was general ignorance about Ptolemy and Attalos in his own time (1.6.1):

The things pertaining to Attalos and Ptolemy were older in time so that common knowledge [φήμη][9] about them no longer remains, and those who associated with the kings in order to write histories of their deeds were forgotten about even sooner. For this reason it occurred to me to explicate their affairs as well . . .[10]

---

[6] Ameling 1996.   [7] On this monument, see Thompson and Wycherley 1972: 38–45.
[8] Actually Ptolemy III, though Pausanias later reveals (1.6.8) that he thinks it is Ptolemy II. On the identification of the proper Ptolemy, see Frazer 1898: 2.80.
[9] Usually in Pausanias φήμη refers to a rumor or popular opinion of questionable veracity (e.g. 1.26.6; 2.16.5; 3.1.2; 5.7.3, etc.). On two occasions in the first book (here and at 1.3.3) and nowhere else, it seems to refer to a more valid form of popular knowledge, the lack or deficiency of which is regrettable, and which Pausanias' efforts are designed to supplement.
[10] τὰ δὲ ἐς Ἄτταλον καὶ Πτολεμαῖον ἡλικίᾳ τε ἦν ἀρχαιότερα, ὡς μὴ μένειν ἔτι τὴν φήμην αὐτῶν, καὶ οἱ συγγενόμενοι τοῖς βασιλεῦσιν ἐπὶ συγγραφῇ τῶν ἔργων καὶ πρότερον ἔτι ἠμελήθησαν· τούτων ἕνεκά μοι καὶ τὰ τῶνδε ἐπῆλθε δηλῶσαι . . .

Figure 8.1. The remains of the monument for the Eponymous Heroes in the
Athenian agora.

The ample scholarship that this statement has attracted has generally
focused on whether Pausanias is correct when he asserts that little was
known about these kings in his day.[11] A related question is whether the
reason Pausanias offers here for his digression is sincere or whether he has
some unspoken motive for which this explanation is a convenient screen.[12]
These are issues we will be better able to address after looking in more
detail at the accounts themselves. A closer look reveals these digressions to
be something quite other than random eructations of historical trivia; they
show the hallmarks of being well thought-out and of interrelating with
one another in a manner that communicates a consistent historico-ethical
ideology.

In choosing the Ptolemies and Attalos as the first Hellenistic kings to
digress upon, Pausanias is dealing with figures that his account has already
alluded to without naming. His first historical reference is, as we have
seen, to the fleet sent to Attica under the command of Patroklos during
the Chremonidean war. Ptolemy II, as Pausanias informs us toward the
end of this later digression, is the one who sent that fleet (1.7.3). Similarly,

[11] Segre 1927: 222–223; Regenbogen 1956: 1068–1070; Hornblower 1981: 72; Bearzot 1992: 11–12;
Chamoux 1996: 65; Ameling 1996: 134; Bowie 1996: 211–213; Arafat 1996: 170–171.
[12] See esp. Bowie 1996: 211–213; Arafat 1996: 170–171.

his brief excursus on the Gallic invasion of the previous decade (1.4.1–6) concludes with a reference to the role of the Pergamenes in bringing a final end to the Gallic threat by driving them into central Anatolia (1.4.6). Pausanias does not mention his name here, but it was in fact Attalos I who performed this feat, as Pausanias points out later in his digression on Attalos (1.8.1). It could be that these brief references early in the book are meant as intentional foreshadowing of the more detailed treatments to come. The final Pergamene victory over the Gauls came several decades after 279, when the incursion into Greece described in 1.4.1–6 occurred. Pausanias elides the time difference, perhaps with a view toward preparing the reader for hearing more about Attalos in the later digression.

This earlier reference to Pergamene matters also gives some slight help in redressing an imbalance that occurs in the later digression on the Ptolemies and Attalos: though Pausanias seems to promise a commensurate treatment of both kings, the bulk of the excursus deals with the Ptolemies; Attalos and the Pergamene dynasty only appear in the last section of the excursus (1.8.1). Pausanias' account of the Ptolemies begins with the founder of the dynasty, Ptolemy son of Lagos. He traces Ptolemy's rise to power, the consolidation of his hold on the throne of Egypt, his battles with other successor kings, chiefly Perdikkas and Antigonos, his many wives (Pausanias mischievously suggests that polygyny was a trait Ptolemy inherited from the man rumored to be his real father, Philip II), and his passing of the kingship down to his son Ptolemy II, whom Pausanias (erroneously) believes to be the member of the dynasty whom the Athenians honored with eponymy. Of Ptolemy II, Pausanias informs us that he married his sister, killed two of his brothers, faced the rebellion of his half-brother Magas, and waged war against Magas and Antiochos. By the end of the second Ptolemy, the reader may well be wondering what this all has to do with Athens, so perhaps to answer that implicit question (1.7.3) Pausanias informs us that it was Ptolemy II who sent the fleet that he had mentioned before to aid the Athenians against the Macedonians (under Patroklos in the Chremonidean war: 1.1.1).

Even for the best of historians, the period of the successors to Alexander is a confusing one, with a host of homonymous Ptolemies, Anitochoses, Antigonoses, and important events that occur concurrently in various places. Pausanias does not overcome all these obstacles, and for all the length of this digression there is a certain sketchiness that belies Pausanias' claim to be reviving the memory of forgotten historical figures: the reader is not expected to know who Ptolemy was, but can apparently be counted on to know: 1) who Perdikkas was (1.6.3); 2) why the exiling of Seleukos by Antigonos is important (1.6.4); and 3) what war it was that Antigonos had fought against Eumenes (1.6.7). In terms of content, we find Pausanias focusing on the royal lineage – that is, how the kingship is passed down from generation to generation – and on palace intrigue, including incest and parricide, crimes that are the traditional constituents of tragedy. These themes will continue in Pausanias' other discussions of Hellenistic royalty. In the brief appendix on Attalos I (1.8.1), Pausanias states little more than that the royal succession passed from Philhetairos to Eumenes I to Attalos I to Eumenes II, and that the first Attalos' greatest achievement was his driving the Gauls inland from the Anatolian seaboard. This, of course, is the Pergamene achievement he had mentioned in his earlier digression, and Pausanias promises still more information on Attalos in a future digression (παρενθήκη) devoted to Lysimachos. Apparently, Pausanias has made a decision to handle the Attalids piecemeal.

Not long after finishing with his digression on the Ptolemies, Pausanias comes to another landmark in the Athenian Agora, the giant Odeion (concert-hall) that had been constructed in the Augustan period over the formerly open space of the Agora's center. In front of this Odeion stand statues, among which at least three Hellenistic kings of Egypt are represented. Two of these kings, Ptolemies I and II, Pausanias has already discussed, so on this occasion he only notes that the statue of Ptolemy II is accompanied by one of his sister (and wife) Arsinoe (1.8.6). But there is another Ptolemy here as well, Ptolemy [VI] Philometor. Pausanias persists in his attentions to the Egyptian dynasty with a relatively brief digression on Philometor (1.9.1–3). Again, Pausanias focuses on Alexandrian intrigue and familial dysfunctionality, commenting on what he sees as sarcasm inherent in this Ptolemy's epithet (*Philometor* = 'Mother-lover') and briefly relating the wars he waged and the indignities he suffered as a result of the enmity of his mother and the younger brother whose claim to the throne his mother supported. Pausanias ends this digression by bringing us back to the statue in the agora: "The Athenians, having been treated well by him in many ways that are not worth explaining, set up a bronze statue of him and of Berenike, who was the only one of his children who was legitimate" (1.9.3).

Nearby are statues of Philip II and Alexander, whose biographies provided "too much to be side-jobs [πάρεργα] in another account" (1.9.4). Though he demurs from telling their history, he draws a contrast between these two and the Egyptian epigoni he had digressed upon earlier: the Athenians honored the Egyptians out of "a real sense of respect and since they were their benefactors." But the recognition they gave to Philip and Alexander was more a result of "flattery (κολακεία) directed toward them by the masses." For similar ignoble motives, according to Pausanias, the Athenians also set up (presumably in the same place in the agora) a statue of another one of the Hellenistic successor-kings, Lysimachos. This is the launching point for yet another Hellenistic digression, one that rivals in length the digression on the Ptolemies and Attalos (1.9.5–10.5). Pausanias tells us how Lysimachos gained control of the Thracian part of the Macedonian Empire after Alexander's death, and catalogs his wars against the Thracians and other barbarians, against Antigonos and his successors, and against Pyrrhos of Epeiros. Despite his uncomplimentary estimation of the Athenians' motives for honoring him, Pausanias' account of Lysimachos' career is generally favorable: for instance, he criticizes one of his sources, Hieronymos of Kardia, for suggesting that Lysimachos had defiled Epeirote graves in the course of his war against Pyrrhos. The tone changes a bit when sites in Anatolia near to Pausanias' home enter into the story: Lysimachos founds the present-day city of Ephesos, populating it with settlers from Lebedos and Kolophon, cities which he had destroyed in the course of his war on Antigonos. Poets wrote dirges over the fate of Kolophon (or didn't write dirges, as in the case of Hermesianax of Kolophon, whose failure to bequeath a lament over Kolophon to posterity leads Pausanias to conclude that he must have been dead by this time). After bringing Lysimachos to the height of his career, Pausanias issues the gnomic statement: "Many calamities happen to people on account of Eros" (1.10.3), before offering as a case-in-point Lysimachos' marriage to Arsinoe (the daughter of Ptolemy I and sister to his son's wife) and the end of Lysimachos' reign as a result of the palace intrigues that ensue. At the end of the digression, Pausanias makes good on his earlier promise (1.8.1) of more information about the Attalid dynasty of Pergamon. He describes how the founder of the dynasty, Philhetairos, alarmed by the shaky condition of Lysimachos' reign, seized Pergamon and offered his loyalty to Seleukos.

With that, Pausanias is done with Lysimachos but not with Hellenistic history. The Athenians also have a statue (also in front of the Odeion, one presumes, although Pausanias does not specify) of Pyrrhos, king of Epeiros. Having mentioned Pyrrhos in the course of his discussion of Lysimachos, he now undertakes to narrate that king's history more fully. This becomes Pausanias' longest historical digression so far (1.11.1–13.9), the longest, in fact, until we get to the history of the Spartan kings in Book 3, and among the longest in the entire work to focus on the career of a single individual.[13] Before delving into this lengthy excursus in greater detail, it would

---

[13] Its only rivals are the biographies of Philopoimen (8.49.1–52.6) and Epaminondas (9.13.1–15.6), and the difference in length between the Pyrrhos digression and these two is very slight. The Pyrrhos digression is approximately twice as long as the digression on Aratos in Book 2 (2.8.1–9.5).

be good first to summarize some of the conspicuous common features
of the Hellenistic histories we have examined so far: in terms of content,
Pausanias tends to focus on wars between kings, and on crimes and intrigues
within the various palaces. A certain penchant for variation is also evident:
rather than tell the story of Attalos in one setting, as with the other kings,
Pausanias appends small bits of his Pergamene *logos* to other narratives. In
this and other respects, we also see Pausanias making an effort to maintain ties between these various excursuses, though the cross-referencing
and interrelation between them may also reflect the narrow scope of
Pausanias' historical research. Though Pausanias apparently makes some
effort to engage in serious research, including the consultation of third-
century sources such as Hieronymos,[14] he ends up committing a somewhat
troubling number of certain or probable inaccuracies: such as mistaking
Ptolemy II for Ptolemy III, and attributing Ptolemy Philometor's epithet to
sarcasm (Ptolemy and his mother were initially appointed to rule jointly).
Apparently (though this is less certain), the desecration of Epeirote graves
that he blames Hieronymos for attributing to Lysimachos (1.9.7) was in
fact a misunderstanding on his part of a reference to the desecration of
Macedonian graves by Pyrrhos.[15] There is also a certain vagueness with
regard to chronology (as in the case of Attalos' relation to the Gallic invasion
of 279) and with historical facts that from our perspective seem crucial if not
indispensable to an understanding of the period and personalities in question. Some of these same qualities will be evident in his work on Pyrrhos.

   Pausanias' "life" of Pyrrhos begins in grand fashion with the tracing of
the Epeirote's lineage back to his heroic namesake, Achilles' son Pyrrhos.
One of Pyrrhos' three sons, Pergamos, goes to Teuthrania[16] and founds
Pergamon (a continuation of the Pergamene motif in Pausanias' Hellenistic histories), while another son, Pielos, stays in Epeiros and becomes the
ancestor of the dynasty that produces the latter-day Pyrrhos. After describing the accession of Pyrrhos as a result of the chaotic interactions between
the royal houses of Epeiros and Macedon – the chaos centering around
Olympias, the mother of Alexander the Great and first cousin to Pyrrhos'

---

[14] Segre 1927: 217 (followed by Hornblower [1981]: 247) argues that Pausanias probably did not consult
Hieronymos directly, but the evidence he cites is rather weak.
[15] Plutarch *Pyrrhos* 26; cf. Jacoby *FGrH* IID.546–547; Hornblower 1981: 247.
[16] Here and earlier in the first mention of the Pergamenes (1.4.5), Pausanias uses the term "Teuthrania"
as the older name for the territory in which Pergamon was located. Some (e.g. Frazer 2.73) have
alleged that this is an error, since Teuthrania is attested in Strabo and other sources as a separate
settlement near to Pergamon (cf. Xenophon *Hell.* 3.1.6; Strabo 12.3.22; 12.8.2; Steph. Byz. 98). It
is possible, however, that Pausanias, a native of a neighboring district who had certainly visited
Pergamon, is reflecting local traditions that may differ from written ones.

father – Pausanias recounts Pyrrhos' consolidation of his reign through a strategic alliance with Ptolemy I of Egypt. Thereupon Pausanias begins to narrate the audacious military campaigns for which Pyrrhos was famous in his adult career. In a sentence pregnant with foreboding, Pausanias states: "When Pyrrhos became king, the first of the Greeks he attacked were the Corcyreans" (1.11.6).[17] Trenchant as it is, this statement is at odds with Plutarch, who states in his *Life of Pyrrhos* that Pyrrhos received the island of Corcyra (modern Corfu) without a fight as part of a marriage agreement with Agathokles, the tyrant of Syracuse.[18] While some have tried to reconcile the two authors' statements by supposing some later rebellion by the Corcyreans that Pyrrhos later had to put down, even this is incompatible with Pausanias' subsequent assertions, which characterize Pyrrhos' action as a strategically motivated aggression without provocation on the part of the Corcyreans: "For he saw the island lying in front of his own territory and did not want it to be a base of action for others against him."

Subsequently, Pausanias refers to the conflicts Pyrrhos had with Demetrios and Lysimachos (1.11.6), conflicts which he had already alluded to in previous digressions, and then makes a transition to the next stage of Pyrrhos' career with the words: "We know of no Greek earlier than Pyrrhos who waged war on the Romans." There are reminiscences of both Herodotos and Thucydides in this part of Pausanias' account. His identification of Pyrrhos as "the first we know" is reminiscent of similar expressions of priority in Herodotos, as are other passages in Pausanias that were mentioned already in Chapter 6.[19] This passage regarding Pyrrhos echoes more specifically the most famous and significant example in Herodotos' text, where Herodotos identifies Croesus as being the "first [Asian dynast] I myself know" to begin hostilities with the Greeks (Hdt. 1.5). The parallel is emphasized a few lines later when Pausanias repeats the same basic idea in more specific terms: "Pyrrhos is the first from that part of Greece that is across the Ionian sea to cross over to face the Romans." This specification is necessary since, as becomes clear from the sequel in Pausanias' own accounts, other Greeks had been fighting the Romans before Pyrrhos' arrival – the Greeks of Tarentum were in fact the ones who invited Pyrrhos to make this fateful crossing to aid them in their war against the Romans. Herodotos likewise, after making the sweeping statement cited above identifying Croesus as the first to begin hostilities between east and west, later

---

[17] Could Pausanias possibly have had in mind Tacitus *Annales* 1.6 (speaking of the beginning of the reign of Tiberius): "primum facinus novi principatus fuit Postumi Agrippae caedes" ("the first crime of the new principate was the murder of Postumus Agrippa")?

[18] Plutarch *Pyrrhos* 9.   [19] Chapter 6, pp. 190–194.

restates that idea with a bit more nuance: Croesus was "the first of whom we know who subjected some of the Greeks to the payment of tribute and made alliances with others."[20] Arguably, this restatement by Herodotos serves to distinguish Croesus from his predecessors in the Lydian kingship who (as Herodotos' own account makes clear) had already engaged in aggression against the Greeks of the Anatolian coast. We have already examined Pausanias' references to Pyrrhos here as being significant for determining Pausanias' notion of who was "Greek" and where "Greece" was.[21] Pyrrhos stands in an ambiguous position in this regard: when he wages war on the Corcyreans at the beginning of his reign, he is an outsider attacking "Hellenes," but when he crosses the Ionian Sea to confront the Romans, he becomes a "Hellene" himself (1.11.6).[22]

The Thucydidean element of this passage comes in the very next sentence: Pausanias defends his assertion of Pyrrhos' priority with the following extraordinary statement (1.11.7):

For no further battle is said to have occurred for Diomedes and the Argives with him against Aeneas, and while the Athenians hoped (among many other things) to conquer Italy, the setback in Syracuse hindered them from taking the measure of the Romans; and Alexander the son of Neoptolemos,[23] being of the same generation as Pyrrhos and older by birth, died among the Leukanians before facing the Romans in battle.[24]

This is reminiscent of the way Thucydides, in the *Archaeology* at the beginning of his history of the Peloponnesian war, defends the importance of that war by cataloging previous conflicts and showing how they come up short in comparison (Thuc. 1.1–23). Pausanias' allusive reference to the legendary figures of Aeneas and Diomedes (Diomedes, a Greek Trojan-war hero, is said to have migrated to Italy after the war, like the Trojan hero Aeneas) also gives his Pyrrhos history a mythical flavor, as did his initial reference to the heroic origins of Pyrrhos' family. A little bit later in his account, Pausanias says that Pyrrhos called to mind the fall of Troy and considered it a good omen for his own prospects since he was a descendant of Achilles fighting against the descendants of the Trojan Aeneas (1.12.1). Moreover, the reference to supposed Athenian designs on Italy from the

[20] Hdt. 1.6.   [21] Above, p. 60   [22] See above, Chapter 6.
[23] One of Pyrrhos' predecessors on the Epeirote throne.
[24] Διομήδει μὲν γὰρ καὶ Ἀργείων τοῖς σὺν αὐτῷ οὐδεμίαν ἔτι γενέσθαι πρὸς Αἰνείαν λέγεται μάχην· Ἀθηναίοις δὲ ἄλλα τε πολλὰ ἐλπίσασι καὶ Ἰταλίαν πᾶσαν καταστρέψασθαι τὸ ἐν Συρακούσαις πταῖσμα ἐμποδὼν ἐγένετο μὴ καὶ Ῥωμαίων λαβεῖν πεῖραν· Ἀλέξανδρος δὲ ὁ Νεοπτολέμου, γένους τε ὢν Πύρρῳ τοῦ αὐτοῦ καὶ ἡλικίᾳ πρεσβύτερος, ἀποθανὼν ἐν Λευκανοῖς ἔφθη πρὶν ἐς χεῖρας ἐλθεῖν Ῥωμαίοις.

period of the Peloponnesian war, and to their defeat at Syracuse, associates the scope of Pyrrhos' ambitions with the legendary hubris of Alkibiades, who, in Thucydides' narrative, leads the Athenians into a reckless and catastrophic entanglement in the west out of his own thirst for glory. Just as the Athenians were lured into the Sicilian expedition by their Sicilian allies' descriptions of the riches that awaited them if they gain mastery of the island, the Greeks of Tarentum lure Pyrrhos into invading by tales of the prosperity of Italy (1.12.1).[25] Herodotos may, once again, be an additional source of inspiration in this passage as well. The reference to three potential conflicts in very different periods of the past reflects one way that Herodotos aggrandizes the expedition of Xerxes against Greece in 480 BCE by comparing it to a number of massive military movements in the past, including the Trojan war.[26]

Pausanias speaks of the wonder he felt upon reading of Pyrrhos' daring (τόλμα) and his ability to foresee (πρόνοια) strategic exigencies (1.12.3), but neither these qualities nor the epic proportions of Pyrrhos' ambitions shield him from defeat. While in Italy, he allows himself to be drawn into a separate conflict with the Carthaginians over the city of Syracuse, and ends up losing both to them and to the Romans in quick succession (1.13.1). To escape from Italy with his army intact, he resorts to a campaign of disinformation; he leads the Romans to believe (falsely) that reinforcements from allied Hellenistic dynasts are on their way (1.13.1), and this ruse deters the Romans long enough for Pyrrhos to make his escape. Curiously, in all this Pausanias avoids stating clearly that Pyrrhos actually defeated the Romans in two major battles (at Heraclea in 280 and at Ausculum in 279) and was threatening to take Rome when he turned aside to Sicily. Pausanias states that on his arrival in Italy Pyrrhos took the Romans by surprise and thereby "threw them into confusion" (ἐτάραξεν),[27] and that the elephants that he unleashed against the Romans (when? where? Pausanias doesn't say) succeeded in frightening them (δεῖμα ἔλαβε Ῥωμαίους),[28] but nowhere does he express the Romans' defeat as unambiguously as when he talks of Pyrrhos' own defeats later in the same campaign: Pyrrhos "was bested" (ἡττήθη) by the Carthaginians and subsequently "stumbled mightily" (προσέπταισε μεγάλως) against the Romans (1.13.1). While he is clear about the fact that Pyrrhos was defeated, once again Pausanias is a bit vague about when and where. He states that on returning from his campaign in Sicily he was defeated by the Romans at Tarentum (which

---

[25] In Plutarch's account (*Pyrrhos* 13.5–6 and 14.3), Pyrrhos is already aware of Italy's riches and needs no instruction by envoys.

[26] Herodotos 7.20.1   [27] 1.13.2.   [28] 1.12.3.

to Pausanias seems to be the only specific location in Italy associated with this campaign), whereas Plutarch (with greater verisimilitude) places his defeat at Beneventum.[29] Another curious element in the tale of Pyrrhos' downfall, one with further epic intimations, comes in Pausanias' discussion of Pyrrhos' losing battle against the Carthaginians at Syracuse (1.12.5): "Full of himself," Pausanias says of Pyrrhos (φρονήσας δὲ ἐφ' αὑτῷ), he dared to engage the Carthaginians (who were highly experienced in naval warfare) in a sea battle, employing as sailors his Epeirotes, "who, even after the sack of Troy, were, most of them, ignorant of the sea and did not yet know how to use salt." Pausanias' source for the state of the Epeirote naval and culinary expertise in the third century BCE is none other than Homer, whom he goes on to quote directly: "These men [the Epeirotes] do not know the sea, nor do they eat food mixed with salt."[30]

Soon after returning to Greece, Pyrrhos declares war on Antigonos (II) Gonatas, who at that time was lord of Macedonia. The initial victories that Pyrrhos achieved in this war were attested to by verse inscriptions on spoils that Pyrrhos dedicated in shrines in Thessaly and in Dodona (in Epeiros). Pausanias quotes these inscriptions verbatim, without specifying whether he saw them himself or read about them in a written source (1.13.2–3). As dedication inscriptions are wont to do, they refer to the dedicator's heritage as a descendant of Achilles and allude to the theme of humbled pride (in this case, that of the Macedonians), thereby reinforcing themes that Pausanias himself had developed in his narration of Pyrrhos' career. And as one might expect from the narrative trajectory of those earlier passages, humiliation soon catches up with Pyrrhos himself. Instead of following up his initial victories and subduing Antigonos completely, Pyrrhos once again succumbs to the temptation to get involved in another conflict, this time in the Peloponnesos in support of Kleonymos, a claimant to the Spartan throne. Pyrrhos, says Pausanias, "was more ready [on this] and on other occasions to grasp what lay close to hand" (1.13.4).

Pyrrhos charges down into the Peloponnesos and invades Lakonia. Pausanias emphasizes the audacity of Pyrrhos' campaign by pausing at this point to ruminate on how rarely in recorded history a foreign army succeeded in penetrating the boundaries of the Spartan homeland (1.13.5). In Lakonia, however, Pyrrhos meets with a stiff resistance as he tries to capture the city of Sparta itself. Antigonos, meanwhile, had recovered the cities he lost in Macedonia and had begun marching into the Peloponnesos as well. Pyrrhos met Antigonos' army outside the city of Argos and defeated

[29] Cf. Plutarch *Pyrrhos* 25.   [30] Homer *Odyssey* 11.122.

it once again, but on pursuing the remnants of Antigonos' force into the narrow streets of the city, confusion ensued and Pyrrhos was killed. At least two (and possibly three) reports were known to Pausanias regarding his death. One source claims that Pyrrhos was crowned by a roof tile tossed from the roof of a nearby house by an unnamed woman. Yet "The Argives," according to Pausanias, dispute that account, saying that it was Demeter, in the likeness of a woman, who killed him (1.13.8). Why Demeter would have done so is left unclear.[31] Finally, Pausanias mentions that Hieronymos' account of Pyrrhos' death is different but that it was biased in favor of Antigonos. Whether Hieronymos' version is the one Pausanias just mentioned, whereby a mere mortal woman was responsible, or whether it was yet a third version that Pausanias doesn't specify, is impossible to say.[32]

As with the shorter digressions on Hellenistic kings, Pausanias' miniature biography of Pyrrhos is better literature than it is history. The Homeric references at the beginning of it and in the middle of it (when Pyrrhos is contemplating the attack on the Romans) are matched at the end when Pausanias reflects that – if the Argives are right about the cause of Pyrrhos' death – three members of Pyrrhos' family had come to an end "sent by a god" (ἐκ θεοῦ): Achilles was killed by Paris (with the help of Apollo, though Pausanias does not bother to mention that); Pyrrhos (son of Achilles) was killed by the Delphians in obedience to Apollo's oracle; finally, Pyrrhos (the latter-day Pyrrhos) was slain by Demeter (1.13.9). This same passage, with its multiple reasons being advanced for Pyrrhos' demise, also embodies another Herodotean parallel, this one more specific than those noted before. In the 490s BCE, King Kleomenes of Sparta, like Pyrrhos a volatile

---

[31] Pausanias says that the Argive version is corroborated by the poet Lykeas, whom Pausanias also designates as "the guide to local matters [in Argos, one assumes]" (ὁ τῶν ἐπιχωρίων ἐξηγητής). He also states that the Argives, in obedience to an oracle, founded a sanctuary of Demeter on the spot where Pyrrhos died, and buried Pyrrhos there. In describing the city of Argos, he claims that a monument in the center of the Argive agora commemorates the spot where Pyrrhos was cremated, but says that the bones of Pyrrhos lie in the sanctuary of Demeter, referring us back to the present passage (2.21.4). Plutarch, in contrast, places his death near the tomb of Likymnios (*Pyrrhos* 34), a monument which Pausanias sees in Argos, apparently at some distance from the Demeter shrine (2.22.8). Pausanias mentions no tie between this monument and Pyrrhos' death, while Plutarch mentions no role for supernatural forces, whether Demeter or otherwise. Cf. Justin *Epitome* 25.5 (an account which, with a little imagination, is generally compatible with that of Plutarch). Dionysios of Halikarnassos, *Roman Antiquities* 20.9.1–10.1, refers to a violation of a shrine of Persephone that Pyrrhos was induced to commit on his campaign in Italy (cf. Frazer 1898: 2.111; Hornblower 1981: 248). The wrath of the goddess is manifest for Dionysios in the defeats that Pyrrhos subsequently suffers on that campaign, but Pyrrhos makes conciliatory offerings to the goddess, and Dionysios mentions no role for her in Pyrrhos' subsequent career or his death.

[32] It is possible that Hieronymos' version of Pyrrhos' death is the one recorded by Plutarch (*Pyrrhos* 34), wherein Pyrrhos is dazed by being hit on the head with a tile and in his confusion allows himself to be apprehended and beheaded. Cf. Hornblower 1981: 248.

and adventuresome ruler, also won a military victory outside of the city of Argos. In the aftermath, he desecrated a sacred grove by burning it down, along with survivors from the Argive army who had taken refuge in it. When Herodotos recounts how Kleomenes later went mad and took his own life through gruesome self-mutilation, he reports that different people had a different explanation, all of them seeing Kleomenes' madness as god-sent retribution. As is the case with Pausanias' Pyrrhos, in Herodotos the Argives themselves are given a say in the interpretation of Kleomenes' fate: they allege the desecration of their own sacred spot as the reason for his madness. But the Athenians and the Delphians both propose other impieties that the king committed in their territories, while still others proposed a more mundane cause: the habit the king acquired from Scythian envoys of drinking undiluted wine.[33] Given Pausanias' penchant for Herodotean patterning, these parallels can scarcely be coincidental, and may help explain why Pausanias' version of Pyrrhos' end differs substantially from all other sources.[34]

With intimations of Herodotos, Homer, and perhaps even Thucydides (especially Thucydides' account of Athenian comeuppance in Sicily), Pausanias casts Pyrrhos as a myth-historic hero, a prodigiously talented and genetically well-endowed ruler with a tragic lack of moderation and patience. Unable to muster the perseverance to follow up on his successes, Pyrrhos meets an end that is either a manifestation of divine disapproval or a bathetically unheroic anticlimax (the sort of end, ironically, that heroes frequently meet in the Greek tradition: Theseus being pushed off a cliff, for instance, or Herakles being burnt alive by a love-potion). In this light, we might look back at some of the digressions that Pausanias devoted to other Hellenistic kings and see a similar mythico-moral discourse being enacted. Like Aristotle's tragic protagonists, none of the kings Pausanias tells us about is thoroughly evil, but their power and fortune make them susceptible to temptation and to envy. Hence the incest practiced by Ptolemy, which was "by no means customary for Macedonians" (1.7.1), and the untimely passion for a daughter-in-law that brought an end to Lysimachos' good fortune (1.10.3). Hence also the plots, betrayals, and internecine murders which form the focal point of most of Pausanias' Hellenistic histories. In a crescendo of expanding narratives, culminating in the treatment of Pyrrhos, Pausanias develops a consistent and subtle moral argument on the perils of power and the need for wisdom and moderation among rulers. The overall

---

[33] Hdt. 5.75, 84. Pausanias alludes to Kleomenes' attack on Argos at 2.20.8–10 and adds information supplementing Herodotos' account.

[34] Cf. Plutarch *Pyrrhos* 34; Justin 25.

effect is, once again, strongly Herodotean: Pyrrhos and Lysimachos serve as Pausanias' counterpart to Herodotean figures like the self-satisfied Croesus, the volatile Kleomenes, and the cruel and depraved Periander. Many of the faults of the Hellenistic kings replicate the charges made against tyrants in the pages of Herodotos: their disruptions of ancestral customs, their disrespect for women, their cruel and capricious behavior, and the catastrophic consequences of even their smallest personal foibles and failings.[35]

As is often the case in Pausanias, the climax of a series of descriptions or narratives is followed by something of a coda. After a short interval, Pausanias follows his Pyrrhos history with a far briefer digression on Seleukos I, whose statue he sees in front of the Stoa Poikile in the Agora (1.16.1–3). By this point, the reader has met Seleukos already a number of times: in the excursus on Ptolemies I and II (1.6.4, 1.6.7), where his flight from Babylon to Egypt under the pressure of Antigonos is mentioned, as is his role in helping to defeat Antigonos; in the brief paragraph on Attalos I (1.8.1), and in the digression on Lysimachos (1.10.2, 4–5). In the passage devoted to Seleukos himself, Pausanias first relates a miracle that presaged Seleukos' future greatness: in preparing to leave for Asia with Alexander, the wood with which he was preparing to light a fire to sacrifice to Zeus moved toward the statue of the god of its own accord and caught fire. Pausanias goes on to retell in somewhat greater detail the story of Seleukos' flight from Babylon, his later return, his defeat of Antigonos, and his defeat and capture of Antigonos' son Demetrios.[36] Palace intrigue plays a role in Seleukos' story, but here Seleukos is only the victim of a gruesome betrayal at the hands of someone who owed him his life: he is assassinated by Ptolemy Keraunos, who had come to him as a refugee with his sister from the disintegrating court of Lysimachos. Soon afterwards, Pausanias tells us, this Ptolemy is himself killed while fighting the Gauls, the same Gauls whose invasion was the subject of Pausanias' first Hellenistic digression.[37]

In conclusion to his excursus on Seleukos, Pausanias states: "I believe that out of all the kings Seleukos had an exceptional sense of what was right, especially in his piety toward the divine" (1.16.3). The evidence for this piety that Pausanias offers is that Seleukos restored to the citizens of Miletus a bronze statue of Apollo that had been taken from them by King Xerxes

---

[35] Cf. the "government debate" at Hdt. 3.80, where a Persian advocate for democracy characterizes the typical autocrat thus: "He disrupts traditional customs, violates women and kills men without trial."
[36] When Pausanias sees a statue of Seleukos at Olympia (6.16.2), he counts the capture of Demetrios as his most famous deed.
[37] Pausanias also mentions Ptolemy Keraunos' death in these circumstances in his longer narration of the Gallic invasion in Book 10 (10.19.7).

of Persia when he ruled that part of Anatolia, and he also respected the sanctuary of Bel in Babylon when he moved the city's inhabitants to his new city of Seleukeia.[38] Pausanias' hagiographic treatment of Seleukos contrasts with that of the previous Hellenistic kings, but focuses on some of the same issues, including the internecine strife and treachery and the destruction and despoliation of cities (which we also encountered particularly in the digression on Lysimachos). It thereby brings to a satisfying denouement this phase of Pausanias' excursions into the Greek past.

On the basis of this overview of Pausanias' Hellenistic histories, we can begin to address the role that they play in Book 1. As we have seen, Pausanias claims to be filling a gap in general knowledge when he begins his account of Ptolemy and Attalos. To the extent that this explanation meshes with Pausanias' tendency to operate *per differentiam*,[39] to tell things without telling what is already known, one could argue, as has Ameling,[40] that it applies equally to all of Pausanias' historical efforts. Some, however, have found the claim Pausanias makes in this specific instance to be a little suspicious. Many historians and other writers of the Roman era dealt with the same period. Plutarch, for instance, wrote biographies of many famous individuals of the era, including Pyrrhos,[41] and the histories of Diodoros and Appian both would have covered some of the same territory. Arrian wrote a separate work (no longer extant) entitled *History after Alexander*, although we cannot be sure it was published by the time Pausanias wrote Book 1.[42] Moreover, one of Pausanias' claims, that writers who were contemporary with the events described had fallen into oblivion long before, is demonstrably false since Hieronymos of Kardia, Douris of Samos, Myron of Priene, and a host of other third-century historians are frequently cited and alluded to in other historical literature of the Roman period. On the basis of this evidence, Ewen Bowie doubts Pausanias' sincerity at this point and proposes other motives that Pausanias prefers not to share with the reader:[43]

It seems to me that [Pausanias] has two different, though closely related, reasons for including [the Hellenistic material]. One is to do with his conception of his work: it is to blend narrative with monuments, and he badly needs some relevant

---

[38] The Seleucids seem to have practiced a policy of returning loot taken from Greek cities by Xerxes: Seleukos' son Antiochos is also said to have returned the statue of the tyrannicides taken by Xerxes to the Athenians (1.8.5). But they did not always return the items to the same city that they came from. Pausanias also mentions that Seleukos gave the wooden statue of Artemis taken from Brauron by Xerxes' troops not back to the Athenians but to the Laodiceans in Syria (3.16.8).

[39] Musti in Musti and Beschi 1982: xxxvii.   [40] Ameling 1996: 134.

[41] Also cf. Plutarch's *Phokion, Demetrios, Eumenes*.

[42] Bosworth 1980–1995: 4–5; Tonnet 1988: 1.68–69.   [43] Bowie 1996: 212.

but preferably not too familiar narrative to set alongside the monuments he is here discussing. The related reason is that his models, Herodotus and Thucydides, offered a preponderance of narrative over monuments, and he does not want to go further into Book I without some display of his Herodoto-Thucydidean mode.

Before discussing Bowie's suggestions, the point must be made that even if we accept his assessment of Pausanias' aims, we need not see Pausanias' expression of his motive as disingenuous. While we might expect that a person with Pausanias' education and intellectual ambitions would be familiar with other historical treatments of the period by contemporary writers, Pausanias may have been speaking to what he assumed to be his audience's level of knowledge rather than his own. On the other hand, while it is natural for us to expect that Pausanias read what are *our* best sources for the period in question (such as Plutarch and Appian), we have no firm evidence that he actually was aware of these other treatments. As A. R. Meadows has recently shown with relation to Pausanias' account of Spartan history in Book 3, when it comes to reading history, Pausanias seems to have the same antiquarian tastes that he has in the realms of architecture and statuary: he prefers older sources – sources closer to the time in question (like Hieronymos for the period of the Hellenistic kings) – and he betrays little knowledge of historical treatments that were written in his own time.[44] Though Plutarch wrote a *Life of Pyrrhos*, Pausanias' account and Plutarch's are as different as two accounts of the same historical figure can be. A telling passage later on in the first book (1.23.2) is Pausanias' anecdote about the courtesan named Leaina, an anecdote which, he says, "has never been put into a written account before." Actually, Plutarch had written up the same story in one of his philosophical essays just a few decades earlier.[45] In all, there is no reason not to take Pausanias' words as sincerely reflecting at least *one* of the reasons that he had for digressing on the Egyptian kings, especially since the reason that he gives is hardly incompatible with other reasons, including the ones Bowie suggests.

As for the alternative motives Bowie proposes, the former, "[Pausanias] badly needs some relevant but preferably not too familiar narrative to set alongside the monuments he is here discussing," is no doubt true in part, but errs in making it sound (perhaps unintentionally) as if Pausanias turned to the tales of the Hellenistic kings out of desperation and grabbed the first stories he could put his hands on in random fashion. As the analysis above

---

[44] Meadows 1995: 110–113; cf. also Bultrighini 2001, and the argument of Tuplin (1984) that Pausanias' supposed dependence on Plutarch's (lost) *Life of Epameinondas* for his own treatment of Epameinondas is questionable.

[45] *De garrulitate* 8.

showed, the histories of the Hellenistic kings were chosen with unmistakable deliberateness and woven together in a consistent narrative whole. Before he gets to the stories of the Ptolemies and Attalos, Pausanias has already demonstrated his ability to mix *logoi* and *theôrêmata*, both with the other Hellenistic narrative of the Gallic invasion and with other historical topics, such as his discourses on early Attic kings and heroes at 1.2.5–6 and 1.5.2–4. The foregoing analysis should also make it obvious that I would agree in part with Bowie's second proposed motive, except that I would argue that the "Herodoto-Thucydidean mode" (with emphasis on the Herodoto-) that Pausanias wants to display is not simply a "preponderance of narrative over monuments" but instead specifically Herodotean (and Thucydidean) themes and narrative strategies deployed on topics which neither Herodotos nor Thucydides covered.

The final, and, for our purposes, most important element of Pausanias' Herodotean *mimesis* in these digressions is their apparent lack of pertinence. As was mentioned in Chapter 6, one notable feature of Herodotos' style is the way he confidently jumps from one topic to another then back to the main topic again with apparent insouciance about the requirements of relevance. This is not the place to discuss the extent to which this style may stem from the quasi- or semi-oral compositional tradition in which Herodotos operated, the possible relation of it to the "Pindaric irrelevance" that is a feature of certain types of early classical poetry, or the possibility that deeper relevancies may be hidden beneath the surface impertinence of Herodotos' digressions. What is important is that this is one aspect of Herodotos' style that Pausanias emulates with particular eagerness, and nowhere more eagerly than in the first half of Book 1. While each of the royal stories Pausanias tells is relevant to a monument Pausanias sees in Athens (specifically, a statue of a king), almost everything in each of the accounts could have been applied just as well to a statue of the same king in some other city. Many of the kings in question were benefactors of Athens who left physical monuments of their generosity in the city's landscape, but aside from the statues themselves Pausanias is mostly silent on the physical evidence of those benefactions. The Attalos family endowed massive building projects in Athens, including the Stoa of Attalos in the old Agora and the Stoa of Eumenes on the south slope of the acropolis, but Pausanias famously omits mention of these and most other Attalid dedications both in the digressions devoted to that dynasty and in his topographical description of the city. One of Pausanias' longer digressions, moreover, is devoted to a figure, Lysimachos, who was, in Pausanias' own estimation *not* a benefactor of Athens (1.9.5), and Pausanias mentions no benefactions

Figure 8.2. The Stoa of Attalos in the Athenian Agora, one of the many Attalid donations to Athens that Pausanias does not mention. The stoa has been reconstructed to house the museum and the offices and workrooms of the Agora excavation.

or connections whatsoever between Athens and Pyrrhos, aside from the statue in the agora which serves as the jumping-off point for his lengthy digression on the Epeirote. How unimportant Athens is to Pausanias' purposes in these digressions is signaled at the end of his account of Ptolemy Philometor, when he says that "the Athenians, having been treated well by [Ptolemy] in ways that are numerous and not worth explaining (πολλά τε καὶ οὐκ ἄξια ἐξηγήσεως) set up a bronze statue of him and of Berenike, who was the only legitimate one of his children" (1.9.3).

Pausanias deserves credit for having a method to his Hellenistic fascination; his excursuses are not simply random historical topics bunged in as narrative fill. At the same time, however, they are hardly examples of most careful and punctilious history writing. While Pausanias apparently put some effort into researching and fact checking, his knowledge never seems to go far beneath the surface. The numerous inaccuracies and bouts of vagueness, together with the clear effort to produce literary effects, suggest that Pausanias' primary effort in these digressions was in enacting a *mimesis* of a historian rather than actually being a historian. This is not to deny that there is quite a bit of accurate and valuable material in them, but the image of Pausanias as the sedulous antiquarian who simply cannot restrain himself from sharing with us the vast amount of trivia he has carefully accumulated on Hellenistic monarchs is equally wide of the mark.

The degree to which Pausanias' Hellenistic histories appear to operate outside the sphere of the topographical context they occur in is somewhat dissonant with the image of Pausanias promulgated in the latest scholarship as an author who is supremely sensitive to issues of local identity in the places he visits and describes; but I would suggest that this concern for the local, and the impulse to focus not only his topographical efforts but also his historiographical efforts on capturing and explicating the local character of the Greek city-states is something that he *learns* to do as he advances in his topographical education. In Book 1, his primary concern, apart from the description of the antiquities he has seen in Athens, is the presentation of those antiquities in the multifaceted generic framework we suggested in the previous chapter, one that partakes of the spatial ordering and locally focused commentary of a geography or a *periplous* but which distends and enlivens the narrative limitations of those genres with the expansiveness, digressiveness, and thematic inclusiveness of Herodotean ethnography. For those purposes, a strict relevance of all the *logoi* of Book 1 to the city of Athens is not only unimportant; it is something to be avoided. In later books, however, that begins to change. Of course, Pausanias continues to display his capacity for Herodotean irrelevance in every book, but the major digressions – digressions of the scale of the Hellenistic histories in Book 1 – tend to be more intrinsically associated with the places Pausanias is describing. The extended passages on the careers of Aratos (2.8.2–9.5), Philopoimen (8.49.1–53.6), and Epameinondas (9.13.1–15.6) all occur not only in conjunction with monuments related to those figures but in conjunction with monuments in their native regions. The retelling of the Gallic invasion in Book 10 is more locally relevant there than the earlier digression in Book 1, not only because the Phocians played a crucial role in the fighting (as did the Athenians, according to Pausanias) but also because much of the action that Pausanias narrates occurs in and near the shrine of Delphi, which is the place that Pausanias is describing when he embarks on this digression.

At first glance, this might appear to be simply one of the many differences that scholars have long noted between Book 1 and other books. More evidence, that is, that Book 1 was written separately, or that at least a long gap of time intervened between the writing of Book 1 and the other books, time in which Pausanias could ponder his technique and crystallize his methods. What I am suggesting, though, is that Pausanias' evolving use of history is not just a change of technique but a change of attitude. I also would suggest that this change results not simply from the passage of time but, at least in part, from Pausanias' experience in visiting and researching the cities of Greece. What Pausanias learns is that the local identities of Greece are important and interesting subjects. And he also seems to come to a decision at some point in his career of traveling and writing that his ability to use history to communicate and support those local identities provides a more satisfying way to expend his energies as an author than a mimetic *tour de force* that has little intrinsic connection to the localities that his travels take him to. Most important for our present purposes, however, is the fact that these lessons are ones that Pausanias has not finished learning at the end of Book 1.

THE TOPOGRAPHY OF HISTORY

One of the peculiarities of Book 1 that has long been recognized is the lack of any local historical introduction for the city of Athens. Pausanias speaks of events in Athens' history, of course, but only in bits and pieces. Like the digressions on Hellenistic kings, all of Pausanias' comments on Athens' past come in connection with a particular monument. For instance, soon after tracing his initial route into the city, Pausanias describes a building (οἴκημα) with clay images portraying Amphiktyon, an ancient king of Athens, feasting Dionysos and other gods. Mention of this denizen of Athens' heroic age inspires a brief excursus on the (legendary) period when Athens was ruled by kings, beginning with Aktaios, the first king of Attica in Pausanias' reckoning, and stretching down to Erichthonios (1.2.5–6). An opportunity to deal with more of the legends of Athens' distant past comes at the monument of the Eponymous Heroes where, in addition to dilating upon the Hellenistic "heroes" that had been added to the monument, Pausanias also spends a section talking about the original ten (1.5.1–3). When Pausanias describes the graves of the *dêmosion sêma*, the hallowed cemetery where Athenian war-dead were buried at state expense (1.29.1–7),

each tomb provides an opportunity for Pausanias to mention a part of
Athens' past, and there are tombs from just about every historical period.
In this way, monument by monument, Pausanias manages to sketch a fair
picture of the most crucial events of Athens' history, but the various parts of
that picture are scattered throughout the text like pieces of a jigsaw puzzle.
This is not the way things are in other books. As we discussed in
Chapters 2 and 3, Pausanias' normal practice in later books is to present
for each territory and for each major site within the territories a historical
introduction that is not connected to any specific monument. The earliest
examples of this are actually in Book 1, when Pausanias is describing regions
outside of the city of Athens itself. For example, his description of the island
of Salamis begins as follows (1.35.1):

Salamis lies opposite Eleusis and stretches even as far as Megarian territory. The
first to give a name to the island was [Kychreus],[46] after his mother Salamis, the
daughter of Asopos; and later Aiginetans, led by Telamon, colonized it . . .

As this introduction continues, it emerges that one of the functions it
serves is to maintain the geographical coherence of Book 1: Salamis was
not always part of Attica, so its presence in Pausanias' account of Attica
needs some explaining: "They say that Philaios the son of Eurysakes, the
son of Ajax, gave the island to the Athenians after he had been enrolled
as an Athenian by them."[47] We see the same motive in Pausanias' briefer
remarks on the Attic deme of Oropos in the previous section (1.34.1):

The land of Oropos between Attica and Tanagran land was Boiotian to begin with,
but in our time the Athenians possess it, having waged war over it throughout
history but not acquiring secure control over it before Philip [II] gave it to them
after capturing Thebes.

And again, Pausanias' concern for asserting the congruence between the
geographical divisions he imposes on the Greek landscape and the traditional and historical identities of the communities within those divisions
surfaces in the longest (and last) historical introduction in Book 1, the one
for the city of Megara (1.39.4–6). As we discussed in Chapter 3, the problem
for Pausanias here is that the land of Megara, for much of recorded history,
was not part of Attica at all:

[46] The name Kychreus was suggested as a supplement by Hitzig on the basis of Diod. 4.72. But
Pausanias mentions this hero in 1.36.1 without referenece to the naming of the island.
[47] Interestingly, Pausanias says nothing in this passage about the historical war with Megara over the
possession of Salamis in the time of Solon (late seventh century BCE). He does mention it later in the
description of Megara, where he claims the Athenians were simply recapturing from the Megarians
what already belonged to them (1.40.5).

Adjacent to Eleusis is the land called Megaris. This also was part of the land of the Athenians in antiquity, since king Pylas left it to Pandion [king of Athens]. As evidence of what I say, the grave of Pandion is in the [Megarian] land . . .

The introductory history of Megara goes on at greater length than the one at Salamis, emphasizing the distinctness of Megara as a separate *polis* at the same time that it asserts Megara's connection to the territory dealt with in the rest of Book 1. But the same issues of geographical and ethnic affiliation predominate. In the course of his Megarian history Pausanias offers an explanation for why Megara stopped being part of Attica: an army of Peloponnesians, on an abortive invasion of Attica, had succeeded on their way home in seizing Megara and repopulating it with Peloponnesian colonists. "Thus," Pausanias says, "the Megarians changed their language and became Dorians" (1.39.5). The date of this invasion is set by Pausanias in the reign of the legendary Athenian king Kodros, and in this and other respects the introductory history for Megara never proceeds beyond what we would call the realms of myth and legend. Pausanias mentions later events in the city's history but, as in Athens, he only does so in connection with a specific site or monument. The reason that Pausanias confines himself to the distant past in Megarian history is not, as one might suppose, a simple bias that always makes him lean toward what is most ancient: in the course of his description of Athens, he shows no preference for the period of Athens' kings over later, better-attested periods. Instead, it makes better sense to look at this history, along with Pausanias' remarks on Salamis and Oropos, as responses to the specific problems he has in the case of these sites. The issues that Pausanias is concerned to address in these places, their geographic and demographic relation to Attica, are, in the case of Megara, resolved in that very ancient period. In the case of Oropos, apparently Pausanias felt its status was sufficiently vague that the reference to later history, the fourth-century donation of Philip, was necessary. In Salamis also, there is one historical event that affects the status of the population and its relation to the rest of Attica, so Pausanias includes that in his introductory history as well (1.35.3): "Many years later than this, the Athenians made the Salaminians exiles, accusing them of having acted traitorously in the war with Cassander and having given their city to the Macedonians mostly willingly." Pausanias is once again vague about the dates, but Cassander, the Macedonian king, occupied the island with a garrison in 318 BCE,[48] and the garrison apparently remained until the Achaean leader Aratos won the

---

[48] Cf. Polyainos 4.11.

island back for the Athenians in 229.[49] It was assumedly at this point that the Athenian punishment would have been enacted. Pausanias, our only source for that punishment, gives us to believe that the island was largely deserted ever since.

Origins, changes in population, changes in language, culture, and political affinities are the common themes of the local histories at the end of Book 1, and these themes continue into Book 2. In Book 2, as is well known, Pausanias makes the introductory local history a regular feature of his description of territories and cities, but in general the histories in Book 2 show the same characteristics as the ones we were looking at in Book 1. They confine themselves largely to the legendary period and focus mostly on foundations, migrations, name changes, and population changes. Typical (though briefer than most) is the introduction to Hermione (2.34.4):

> The Hermionians say that the founder of their ancient city was Hermion, the son of Europs. As for Europs – for his father was in fact Phoroneus – Herophanes of Troizen said that he was illegitimate; for never would the throne in Argos have devolved on Argos, Phoroneus' grandson through Niobe, if a legitimate son of Phoroneus were available . . . Later Dorians from Argos colonized Hermion also; but I don't think there was a war between them, for the Argives would have said so.

An interesting and somewhat less typical case is the history of Mycenae. Mycenae is the first major site in the Argolid proper that Pausanias deals with, and it, rather than the city of Argos, was the focus of much of the mythic tradition pertaining to that region. Consequently, the introductory history of Mycenae is longer than most in Book 2 (2.15.4–16.5), but in terms of content it is similar to the others. Pausanias begins by saying: "The Greeks know that Perseus was the founder of Mycenae; but I will write about the reason for its foundation . . ." Pausanias' explanation takes him back to the earliest inhabitants of the Argolid, Inachos (either a river or a human king) and his son Phoroneus, and to the royal line that descended from them, culminating in the great hero Perseus, who was the one that founded the city of Mycenae. Pausanias narrates in some detail the myth of Perseus, and offers three alternative explanations for the origin of the name of the city. But another crucial fact that Pausanias must explain is what happened to the people of Mycenae subsequently, since the town (as he describes it) is largely deserted in his own day. This takes him briefly into later history (2.16.5): "The Argives destroyed Mycenae out of spite, for while the Argives

---

[49] Pausanias mentions this at 2.8.6, as does Plutarch, *Aratos* 34. Neither mentions the subsequent fate of the Salaminians described in this passage.

held their peace during the Mede's invasion, the Mycenaeans sent eighty men to Thermopylai, who shared the exploit with the Spartans. This desire for glory on their part irritated the Argives and brought destruction down on them." The reference, of course, is to the Persian invasion of 480 BCE, in the face of which the Argives abstained from joining in the common Greek defense. Mycenae was destroyed by the Argives some time later, in 468 BCE,[50] so the reason for the destruction Pausanias attributes to the Argives is somewhat questionable and perhaps tendentious. Some have interpreted this reference as a slap at the Argives for not participating in the defense against the Persians.[51] A slap it may be, but the reference to Mycenae's destruction also functions in its context in a manner parallel to the mention of the depopulation of Salamis in the Hellenistic period: it completes Pausanias' explanation of who the people were (or weren't, as in the case of Mycenae) who inhabited the place he was describing.

Pausanias' introduction to Mycenae goes no further into the historical period, and the introductory history of the city of Argos itself which soon follows (2.18.4–19.2) is also largely confined to the realm of legendary kings and migrations. An important section deals with the return of the Herakleidai along with the Dorians (2.18.7–9). As we have already seen, and seen again most recently in the citation above of the introductory history of Hermione, the Dorification of cities in the northeastern Peloponnesos, which emanates from Argos, is an important motif for defining the interconnections of all the people in Book 2.[52] But the rest of the introductory history of Argos progresses only two generations beyond Temenos, the first of the Heraklid kings, with a quick reference to the later history of the Argive kingship, up to what Pausanias considers to be its end in the twelfth generation after Temenos (2.19.1–2). Pausanias makes no reference here to the lack of Argive participation in the Persian wars, nor to any subsequent event in Argos' history. All such references are conjoined with sites and monuments that Pausanias mentions in the course of his topography. The introductory history for the city of Troizen follows a pattern that is almost completely parallel (2.30.5–10): earliest inhabitants; early kings; foundation of the current city; arrival of the Herakleidai and Doricization; Troizen in Homer's Catalogue of Ships. At Aigina, Pausanias' introductory history does delve into later events (2.29.2–5): after describing the Doricizing of the island, Pausanias mentions the Aiginetans' participation in the battle of Salamis against the Persians – where they provided the most ships apart from Athens (2.29.5). But this reference serves most immediately as a foil

[50] Cf. Diod. 11.65.   [51] Alcock 1996: 254.   [52] See Piérart 2001.

to what is a more familiar theme in these histories: despite the power they possessed at the time of Salamis, "their good fortune was not permanent: they were driven out by the Athenians and given Thyrea in the Argolid to settle by the Spartans" (2.29.5). Later (after the Peloponnesian war), the Aiginetans recovered their island but never recovered their previous prosperity. A concern to track the demographic identity of the people in each *polis* also occasions the latest historical reference in any of the introductory histories of Book 2, the passage we have already examined in Chapter 5 wherein Pausanias recounts the destruction of Corinth and its refoundation as a Roman colony (2.1.2). So important an event is this in the history of Corinthian demography that Pausanias relegates a good portion of what he normally puts in introductory histories (especially stories of early kings and the Doricization of the city) to a later point in his description of the city and associates them with monuments (2.3.6–11; 2.4.1–4).

In Book 2, then, the use of local histories becomes regularized, but I would argue that in comparison to Book 1 this is more a difference of quantity than of essence. In the local histories of Book 2, you see the same limitations, in terms of chronology and subject-matter, that you see in the examples that come late in Book 1, and I would suggest that they can be ascribed to a similar impulse. In Attica, Pausanias faced the problem of cities and regions that had a challenged or complicated connection to Attica, and used history to forge a connection that justified the decisions he made in arranging his topography. In Book 2, as we saw in Chapter 3, Pausanias has to confront the same problem throughout the whole book: how does one make a unified whole out of Corinth, Argos, Sikyon, Aigina, and a number of other *poleis* that were, for most of their histories, adamantly independent of one another? Pausanias finds an answer in the traditions of the Greek heroic age; in the familial relations of the legendary royal houses; in the lists of cities subject to Agamemnon and Diomedes in the *Iliad*, and, most of all, in the legend of the Dorian invasion, and it is to place each of the cities of Book 2 into that unifying context that he begins to separate their histories from the monuments and put the history first. In the course of doing so, it is not unlikely that Pausanias gains greater appreciation for the individual histories of the cities and how the individualities of separate communities could combine to create an identity for the whole of Greece. At least by Book 2, and perhaps by the end of Book 1, he seems to have lost his taste for making history a vehicle for demonstrating his capacity for Herodotean irrelevance.

If we persist in reading the sequence of books as a temporal and developmental progression, we can see how subsequent books might provide further avenues for the development of Pausanias' historical sensibilities. In Lakonia (Book 3), a territory traditionally dominated by a single city with a rich and varied history, Pausanias provides only one introductory history of any length, that of Sparta itself, occupying over a third of the entire book (3.1.1–10.5). The example of Sparta's history indicates that Pausanias has begun to isolate the concept of his introductory histories from the exigencies that they served in Books 1 and 2, and, perhaps in consideration of Sparta's distinctive local custom of the dual kingship, he hits upon the novel (but somewhat confusing) plan of narrating the histories of the two royal houses consecutively. This takes him down into the third century with both lineages. One bit of evidence for the development of Pausanias' thinking might be worth noting here: in the course of his Pyrrhos digression in Book 1, Pausanias describes, with somewhat questionable pertinence, as we noted above, the lineage of Kleonymos, the claimant to the Spartan throne who invited Pyrrhos into Lakonia (1.12.4–5). In light of the fact that Pausanias is already referring to things in Book 1 that he will discuss in much later books, one wonders why Pausanias did not simply refer ahead to the slightly more detailed discussion of Kleonymos and his lineage in Book 3 (3.6.1–3). Perhaps Pausanias did not envisage writing such a detailed treatment of the Spartan kings until he sat down to the task of putting Book 3 into the form we now have. Having the experience of writing the Spartan history behind him, when he subsequently faces the problem of Messenia, a large territory with few of the sorts of monuments he thought worth describing, the large-scale introductory history is a concept he is already comfortable with. Hence, in part, the extended history of Messenia that fills twenty-nine out of the thirty-six chapters of Book 4.[53] In many ways, Pausanias' Messenian *logos* is an enormously magnified example of the same sort of introductory history we find in Book 2. It is a story of foundation, conquest, exile, and recovery explaining (in Pausanias' own words) "the many sufferings of the Messenians, and how the divinity scattered them to the ends of the earth and the furthest parts of the Peloponnesos, but at a later time brought them safely to their own land." As with the lesser examples in Book 2 (Aigina springs to mind), the story of banishment and return of the Messenians takes Pausanias well into the Hellenistic period; the Messenian history ends with the death of Philopoimen.

In Chapter 3 we saw that a feature of Pausanias' descriptions of many territories and cities are catalog-like lists of the participation of the people in question in panhellenic military efforts (8.6.1–3):

---

[53] On the balance of history and topography in Book 4, see Alcock 2001.

For the Arkadians in common the earliest noteworthy event was the war at Troy, and next was the fighting that they did in support of the Messenians against the Spartans. They also took part in the war against the Medes in the affair at Plataia. More by compulsion than out of good will for the Spartans, they joined in fighting the Athenians, crossed over to Asia with Agesilaos, and finally went along with the Spartans to Leuktra in Boiotia. But they showed their mistrust toward the Spartans often, and especially after the defeat of the Spartans at Leuktra, when right away they deserted them and went over to the Thebans. They were not among the Greeks who fought against Philip and the Macedonians at Chaironeia and later in Thessaly against Antipatros, but then they didn't fight against the Greeks either. When the Gauls threatened at Thermopylai, they say that they did not take part because of the Spartans, who, they feared, would ravage the land while their youth were away. As for the Achaean League, the Arkadians took part in it more eagerly than all the other Greeks.

Such roll-calls of panhellenic (or at least multi-*polis*) efforts appear on numerous occasions in the *Periegesis*, but what is rarely noted is that they all occur in the latter half of the work. Thus, they cannot really be said to be characteristic of Pausanias' treatment of history; if anything, they *become* characteristic, and the difference between being and becoming is in this case quite significant. The first example of this catalog-like list of participation or non-participation of a given people in great events comes in Book 5, when the subject is the Eleans (5.4.7–5.1). Up to that point – that is, up to 173 CE, when Pausanias tells us he was writing Book 5 – Pausanias employs and deploys history quite differently, as I have tried to demonstrate above. Pausanias mentions all these cardinal events to be sure – the Trojan war, the Persian war, the Peloponnesian war, the Lamian war – but shows little evidence of having abstracted a set of historical criteria by which the Greekness of a particular city or people could be measured on the basis of their involvement or non-involvement in these historical events.[54] This is something that Pausanias learns to do in the latter part of his work, and as such it represents an important development in the periegete's mental make-up. From the beginning, Pausanias has an antiquarian's attitude that values the monuments and memories of old Greece. He has the nostalgic attitude

---

[54] In this, I would disagree with Bearzot 1992: 17–18; Alcock 1996: 253–4 (cf. Swain 1996: 334 and Chamoux in Casevitz, Pouilloux, and Chamoux 1992: 214), who see the Persian wars in particular as serving as a defining point in Greek history and identity for Pausanias from the beginning of the work. Prior to Book 5 (and for much of the time afterwards, except in the introductory histories of cities), Pausanias tends to mention the Persian wars only where it is topographically relevant to do so. In Book 1, which includes the sites of Salamis and Marathon and the grave of Themistokles, opportunities to mention the Persian wars are rife. Still, the wars do not loom as large in Pausanias' account of the city as they do in the near-contemporary speech of Aelius Aristeides, *Panathenaikos* (on which, see Oliver 1968; Day 1980).

that allows him to see beyond the present reality of decline and decrepitude into the abiding reality in which Thebes, dilapidated and depopulated though it may be, is still the home of Dionysos and Epameinondas, and still the hub around which all Boiotia revolves. But over the course of his work, particularly in the structure of his historical *logoi*, you can sense that his devotion to this image of Greece is growing less academic and less abstract; you can sense a growing consciousness of the true import of Greece's unique heritage within the Roman world, and a growing emphasis on the points in history when the Greek cities were able to act as one while remaining autonomous and independent. The very image of Greece that Pausanias creates with his itineraries, a collection of independent entities that are nevertheless connected with one another intrinsically and integrated into a well-ordered whole, is one that Pausanias no longer views simply as a literary construct to be faced with a mixture of Herodotos and Hegesias and Polemon, but a reflection of the true nature of Greece, a nature that still has meaning for his own time.

A PILGRIM'S PROGRESS?

Other aspects of Pausanias' account and his self-presentation can benefit from this sort of diachronic analysis, and while I have no intention of expanding what is already a long chapter with a complete examination of any other topic, I will briefly canvass some areas in which the prospects for future study are promising. Religion is, of course, one of the crucial subjects to consider when dealing with Pausanias, and at first glance it might seem the obvious place to begin an appraisal of how Pausanias' stances evolve. This is one area, in fact, in which Pausanias himself acknowledges a change of attitude. In a well-known passage in the eighth book, Pausanias is discussing a Mantineian legend about the birth of Poseidon (8.8.2–3). In a doublet of the famous story of how Rhea prevented the infant Zeus from being devoured by his father Kronos by giving Kronos a rock wrapped in swaddling clothes, the Mantineians claim that Rhea similarly substituted a foal for the baby Poseidon. After reporting this tale, Pausanias informs the reader of his own opinion about such stories:

When I began my account I used to attribute more simple-mindedness (εὐηθία) to these stories of the Greeks, but having gotten as far as my account of the Arkadians I conceived the following idea (πρόνοια) about them: that those of the Greeks who were considered wise used to tell their stories through riddles (αἰνίγματα) in ancient times, and not directly; so I began to surmise that the things said about

Kronos were some sort of Greek wisdom. Regarding what pertains to divinity (τὸ θεῖον), I will make use of the things that are said.

This passage has attracted a lot of attention in the scholarship, particularly since Paul Veyne made it one of the keystones of his study of the nature of the Greeks' "belief" in their own myths.[55] What Pausanias is confessing here is apparently not skepticism toward the gods themselves but toward the stories told about them. And it is not necessarily all stories to which his statement applies but to "these stories," a phrase that could refer, in the context, to all stories about the gods, to tales of the early generation of gods, to accounts of the births of gods such as those found in Hesiod's *Theogony*, or, more specifically, to the various versions of the story of Kronos. What it is about these types of stories that used to trouble Pausanias is similarly unclear: was it the idea that a god could be born? that a god could procreate sexually? that a god would eat his own children? that the king of the universe could be fooled so easily by his wife?

In addition to these questions, it is also difficult to say exactly what Pausanias' new outlook on the matter consists of. At first glance, he would seem to be advocating an allegorical interpretation of "these stories": the ancients communicated deeper truths through such "riddles," hence that the story of Kronos is not really about Kronos at all but about something which Kronos, and the things he swallowed, symbolize. Pausanias offers no explanation as to *what* the Kronos story might symbolize, leaving open the possibility that this entire confession on his part is an elaborate and slightly sarcastic way of saying that he thought that the story about Kronos and Poseidon told by the Mantineians was bewilderingly silly. But it seems at least as likely that Pausanias is simply signaling a new way of looking at these stories without committing himself to a particular interpretation of them. The specific wording Pausanias uses to describe his new understanding may be significant in this regard. In the quote above, I have translated the word πρόνοια as "idea." This is similar to the choices that other English translators have made,[56] but in Greek the word has a much more specific meaning: πρόνοια is literally "forethought," and occurs in the literature with the connotations of "foresight," "precaution," and "(divine) providence." In all of Pausanias' other uses of the word, he varies between these standard connotations and never uses it as a simple synonym for "idea" or "opinion."[57] Though it is difficult to render a more accurate translation in

[55] Veyne 1988: 11–12, 95–102; earlier discussions include Frazer 1898: 1.lv–lx; Heer 1979: 250–254; Habicht 1998: 156–159; cf. Swain 1996: 342–3.
[56] Frazer: "opinion"; Jones: "more thoughtful view"; Levi: "point of view."
[57] "Foresight": 1.12.2; 4.7.6; "divine providence": 1.13.6; 2.31.1; "precaution": 4.8.1; 4.8.11; 10.34.8.

the context of the passage in question, I would suggest that what Pausanias means to say here is that he has come to have an attitude of "precaution" toward such tales. He has come to respect the ancients enough that he will refrain imputing foolishness to them too hastily, even if he is unable to divine the true meaning of the tales they told.

However we characterize the nature of Pausanias' new understanding, there remains the important question of what brought it about. Veyne suggests with some plausibility that it was the experiencing of Arkadia itself, a remote and relatively unspoiled territory whose inhabitants preserved traditions reaching back to the earliest days of creation, that engendered Pausanias' newfound respect for the wisdom of the ancients.[58] In the opening chapters of Book 8, Pausanias presents a thick series of declarations on mythico-religious matters that has no parallel elsewhere in the *Periegesis*. One example that casts an interesting light on the nature of Pausanias' "conversion" occurs only a few pages earlier in the text: in his account of legendary Arkadian kings, Pausanias must deal with King Lykaon, who, tradition maintains, was turned into a wolf upon offering the gods a human sacrifice. After recounting briefly the metamorphosis of Lykaon, Pausanias offers the following observation: "This story is persuasive to me; it has been told by the Arkadians since antiquity, and it has some plausibility" (8.2.4). Pausanias' ruminations on this topic (some of which we will return to later) go on at some length. The story is plausible because: "At that time humans were guests of the gods and shared the same table on account of their justice and piety"; the gods dealt out unequivocal honor to those who were good, and those who did wrong felt their wrath; at that time, "gods even arose from the ranks of humans (ἐξ ἀνθρώπου)," as did Aristaios, Britomartis, and Herakles, for example. This is why "someone might well believe that Lykaon became a wolf and that Niobe, the daughter of Tantalos, became a stone" (8.2.4–5). Pausanias goes on to explain why such things might seem incredible on the surface:

> In every period many things, things that occurred long ago and even things that are still happening, have been made unbelievable in the eyes of most people by those who construct falsehoods on top of what is true.

This statement, reminiscent of Thucydides' condemnation of "poets, who exaggerate the importance of their themes, and prose chroniclers who are less interested in telling the truth than in capturing the attention of their audience,"[59] seems to promise, like Thucydides, a critical method by

---

[58] Veyne 1988: 99–100; 151, n. 194. On the cults of Arkadia in Pausanias, see: Jost 1985; Jost 1998.
[59] Thucydides 1.21 (the translation is that of Warner 1954: 47).

which the truth can be winnowed from the chaff of fantasy and the tales of ancient gods and heroes can be made useful to the.serious student of antiquity. A subtle method it is, too, one that seems (to judge by Pausanias' comments on the Lykaon story) to privilege the age of the story and to weigh its plausibility (εἰκός). By engaging in this critical process, Pausanias can distinguish the truth of Lykaon's metamorphosis from a number of current falsehoods (8.3.6–7):

They say, for instance that after Lykaon someone always changes from a man (ἐξ ἀνθρώπου) to a wolf at the sacrifice to Zeus Lykaios . . . Similarly they say that on Mount Sipylos Niobe weeps in the summertime. I have even heard that griffins have spots like leopards and that tritons speak with a human voice; some even claim that they blow through a hollowed-out seashell.

Pausanias has already asserted that metamorphosis of humans is something that only happened in a bygone age: Lykaon may have become a wolf but no present-day person has done so. Niobe may have been transformed into a stone, and Pausanias elsewhere claims to have seen the Niobe stone on Mount Sipylos in the shape of "downcast and tearful woman" (1.21.3), but as a (presumed) native of the region of Mount Sipylos Pausanias can judge authoritatively that the stone does not actually "weep," as some claim. On the subject of griffins and tritons, it is important to note that, as in the case of the gods, what Pausanias questions is not the existence of these fabled beasts but the details that some people ascribe to their habits and appearance. Elsewhere, Pausanias claims to have seen the preserved bodies of tritons at both Tanagra and Rome (9.20.4–21.1), and reports without dispute things that he learned about griffins from sources that he evidently considers more reliable (1.24.6). In these comments, together with the "conversion" passage, Pausanias presents himself more explicitly than elsewhere as an arbiter between truth and falsehood, and he foregrounds his respect for the valuable religious information that lies beneath even the most implausible of legends. He chooses Arkadia as the locus for this new stance, and it may well be that the particularly rich and varied traditions he encountered in Arkadia have something to do with that choice, but his statements here may also reflect an attitude that develops over the entire stretch of time in which he was researching and writing the previous books. Pausanias' own words would seem to suggest this latter possibility: in 8.8.2, he tells us that he came to his new understanding about the wisdom of the ancients after "having gotten as far as my account of the Arkadians" (ἐς δὲ τὰ Ἀρκάδων προεληλυθώς). The contrast he draws between his thinking at this point and the time at which he began his account (ἀρχόμενος μὲν τῆς συγγραφῆς) suggests that the realization he is describing was a gradual development.

Does this mean that Pausanias' travels act as a sort of *rite de passage*, subjecting him to a number of transformative experiences and inspiring him to a deeper appreciation of matters religious, historical, and cultural? This is the suggestion of Elsner, who adduces this Arkadian "conversion" to support his argument for seeing Pausanias as not just a traveler but also a pilgrim.[60] The notion that Pausanias' change of heart in Book 8 reflects a pilgrim's insight is an attractive one, but can only be accepted with the addition of a number of provisos. First, since the composition of the *Periegesis* extended over a number of decades, and involved (probably) a number of separate journeys in addition to periods of sedentary study, any change we can perceive in Pausanias' attitudes cannot be assumed to have arisen solely from his on-site experiences. Many revelations may have come to Pausanias in the comfort of his own home, through reading and reflection and through the everyday experiences of living a normal life. If the *Periegesis* is the account of a pilgrimage, it is, as Elsner himself says, a "pilgrimage lasting many years,"[61] and one that is spiritual and intellectual as much as it is physical. Secondly, in this case and in all others, one must keep in mind the possibility that Pausanias' self-presentation is at least as much a literary stance as it is a sincere and spontaneous reflection of his inner self. As the parallel with Thucydides cited above suggests, one thing Pausanias accomplishes with his religious declarations at the beginning of Book 8 is the establishment of himself as a historian in the Thucydidean tradition in his handling of legendary and mythical matters. As Veyne points out, moreover, Pausanias' placement of his declaration of misgivings about the surface meaning of divine myth in the eighth of his ten books has a close parallel in the pages of Herodotos:[62] it is late in the seventh of his nine volumes that Herodotos makes the famous statement that "my business is to record what people say; but I am by no means bound to believe it – and that may be taken to apply to this book as a whole" (7.152.3), a statement that, as we have seen, Pausanias echoes more explicitly elsewhere.[63] Given Pausanias' deliberate pursuit of Herodotean *mimesis* throughout the work, this parallel can scarcely be coincidental. Of course, literary posturing and genuine sentiment are not completely exclusive of one another: we have no reason to believe that Pausanias is wholly fabricating the alteration

---

[60] Elsner 1992: 8; 1995: 144. Objections by Swain (1996: 342, n. 50) and Arafat (1996: 10) to Elsner's characterization of Pausanias as a pilgrim are valid only if one uses a rather narrow definition of what constitutes pilgrimage. On this issue, see Rutherford 2001, and cf. Hutton 2005b.

[61] Elsner 1995: 144.   [62] Veyne 1988: 11–12.   [63] 2.17.4; 6.3.8. See p. 194 above.

in his sentiments for literary effect, but undeniable attraction that the opportunity to align himself with Thucydides and Herodotos would have had for Pausanias needs to be taken into account when we estimate his motives for discussing the issue.

Thirdly, and most importantly, if there is some effect that Pausanias' "road to Damascus" experience[64] has on the way he handles particular stories about the gods, it is difficult to ascertain what that effect might be. One problem in judging this issue is that over the course of the *Periegesis* Pausanias does not actually deal very frequently with divine myth as such. Like Herodotos and Thucydides, he prefers to operate within the *spatium historicum*, the era of mortal history, which includes the deeds of demigod-heroes, legendary kings, and much else that we would call mythical, but generally does not include tales of gods playing any active role apart from averting evil from their mortal favorites and dispensing justice from a distance.[65] What we can say, however, is that when we compare Books 8 through 10 to the previous books, there is no measurable increase in the number of divine myths that Pausanias chooses to relate. Even in Book 8 itself, after his supposed discovery of the value of divine tales, Pausanias makes what Madeleine Jost has rightly identified as a particularly curious omission.[66] In spite of the fact that Pausanias reports the Arkadian claims that both Zeus (8.38.2) and Hera (8.22.2) were raised in their territory, when he is describing the territory around Mount Kyllene (8.17.1–5) he makes no explicit reference to the tradition that the god Hermes was born there.[67]

As an example of Pausanias' supposed old way of thinking, Habicht cites the Herodotean passage mentioned above.[68] In this passage from the second book (2.17.4), Pausanias encounters the statue of Hera in the Heraion of Argos. The locals have a story to tell about a cuckoo that is shown perched on the goddess' scepter: Zeus, they say, transformed himself into this bird while courting the still-virginal Hera. Pausanias reports this story but adds the now-familiar comment "this story (λόγος) and similar things said about the gods I write without accepting them, but I write them nonetheless." This rejection of a divine myth without reference to any possible deeper meaning to the tale might seem to be at variance with the attitude Pausanias

---

[64] The phrase is taken from Veyne 1988: 96.
[65] On this subject, see Veyne 1988: 5–15.   [66] Jost 1998: 235–236.
[67] Although he does record the presence of a temple of Hermes Kyllenios on the mountain (8.17.1), and the place nearby where Hermes found a tortoise and turned it into a lyre, an act which the *Homeric Hymn to Hermes* assigned to his first day of life (8.17.6). Not far away, in the direction of Pheneos, Pausanias notes a spring, in the waters of which the baby Hermes was alleged to have been bathed (8.16.1).
[68] Habicht 1998: 157.

professes in Book 8, but the problem is that he makes similar disavowals for other divine tales even after Book 8. For instance, in 9.2.3, Pausanias disputes the famous myth that the goddess Artemis punished Actaeon by turning him into a stag so that he would be torn apart by his own dogs. Pausanias ascribes to the view that Actaeon's dogs went mad and turned on their master without the involvement of Artemis. In considering both of these stories, it is important to note that while Pausanias does not mention the possibility of allegory in this case he does not explicitly reject it either. In neither instance can we assume that Pausanias would not have accepted the possible validity of such an interpretation, and in all there is no conclusive evidence over the course of the *Periegesis* that Pausanias either grows more accepting of tales about the gods or more prone to understanding myths allegorically. In fact, a closer look at the passage concerning the statue of Hera suggests that even in the second book Pausanias' attitude toward tales involving the divine is quite similar to the viewpoint he expresses in Book 8. Before discussing the story of the cuckoo, Pausanias describes the statue as follows:

The statue of Hera, large in size, sits upon a throne; it is made of gold and ivory, the work of Polykleitos. She wears a crown that has Graces and Seasons wrought upon it. As for her hands, in one she holds the fruit of the pomegranate and in the other a scepter. Now about the pomegranate – since the story (λόγος) is rather secret – I shall omit it, but they claim that the cuckoo . . .

There are thus two *logoi* told about the goddess' paraphernalia. One, the story about the cuckoo, is unworthy of the goddess, in Pausanias' view, while the other is one that he must deem plausible in some sense, since he observes the religious silence attached to it. Already in the second book we see that Pausanias neither accepts nor rejects divine myths on a wholesale basis. Some traditional tales have a measure of sacred validity about them while others are largely matters of worthless invention, and Pausanias exercises the authority to distinguish between the two.

If we compare the development of Pausanias' religious thought (at least those aspects of it we have examined so far) to the development of his historical thinking, a major difference is readily apparent. Despite the fact that Pausanias makes explicit statements about the evolution of his religious attitudes and does not do so for his historical attitudes, the changes in approach that we can trace in his text are far more pronounced in the historical realm than in the religious realm. It seems that while the role historical narrative plays in Pausanias' account is something that evolves in response to what he learns in the course of his travels and researches, the place assigned to religious narrative is established from the beginning and changes relatively little. In the discussion of Pausanias' use of history, we noted that Pausanias seems to develop a sense of the importance of place and of the power of local history. The diversities of local cult, however, and of local traditions regarding the divine, are of central concern for Pausanias from the beginning. In the first book, Pausanias congratulates the Athenians for being the only Greeks to have an altar to the god Mercy and for their exceptional piety to the gods in general (1.17.1), and observes without criticism that the demes in the Attic countryside have different traditions regarding the gods from those of the city-dwellers (1.14.7). As we have seen earlier, in Book 2 Pausanias laments the fact that the present-day Corinthians no longer observe the traditional Corinthian rites at the tomb of the children of Medea (2.3.7). Pausanias does not report what rites, if any, the current inhabitants of the city performed, but it could be that the settlers of the Roman colony instituted rites that were more in line with a version of Medea's story that was more well known, such as the one propagated by Euripides (which differs significantly from the traditional Corinthian version of the story that Pausanias reports). A comparable situation certainly prevails in the city of Argos: there, Pausanias sees a statue group of the famous "Seven against Thebes," seven Argive heroes who joined with Polyneikes, the son of Oedipus, in his attempt to wrest the throne of Thebes from his brother. Pausanias seems dismayed to find that the Argives – whose knowledge of their own traditional history Pausanias holds in particularly low regard[69] – have forgotten the original version of their heroes' story and have adopted the version made popular by an Athenian playwright: "These men Aeschylus reduced in number to only seven, though more leaders from Argos and from Messene and some even from the Arkadians joined the expedition . . . even the Argives have followed the poetry of Aeschylus" (2.20.5).[70] A fascination with local

---

[69] Cf. 2.19.8; 2.21.2; 2.21.4; 2.21.8; 2.21.10; 2.22.3; 2.23.3, and especially 2.23.5–6.

[70] Pausanias' relationship to the Athenian tragedians is an interesting topic. In general, he seems to regard them with little favor as a source of genuine mythical and religious traditions, and seems even to resent their creation of new versions of myths that crowd out more ancient local traditions. In Athens, Pausanias sees the shrine on the Areopagos for the goddesses of vengeance who pursued Orestes to Athens. He refers to these goddesses as the Semnai (Awesome Ones), and mentions Hesiod's name for them, Erinyes, but avoids the name for them found in Aeschylus' version of the story, the Eumenides (Kindly Ones). Pausanias claims that Aeschylus was the first to portray these goddesses with snakes in their hair, an iconographical detail that he does not see represented on the images of the goddesses at the shrine (1.28.6). In the very next section, he disputes Sophocles' version of the death of Oedipus because it conflicts with the poetry of Homer (1.28.7). Earlier in the first book, he delivers himself of the Thucydidean complaint: "Many untrue things are repeated among the multitudes, since they do not know history and they consider believable all the things they have heard from childhood in choruses and tragedies" (1.3.3).

religious and mythical traditions and, even more strikingly, a resistance to the homogenization of Greek traditions that time and Greece's integration into a wider, Hellenizing Mediterranean world made inevitable are present in Pausanias' work from the beginning.[71] It may be worth suggesting that this attitude toward the religious traditions of Greece inspired the direction in which Pausanias' use of historical narrative developed.

THE ORIGIN OF FORTUNE

Even if Pausanias' alleged conversion in Book 8 is not the watershed in his religious thinking that many have taken it for, there are some elements of his approach to religious matters that do undergo a perceptible evolution. Examples of this can be found in his treatment of divinities that stand outside the pantheon of traditional panhellenic gods. As Vincianne Pirenne-Delforge has recently pointed out, for Pausanias the traditional Greek pantheon of the twelve (plus or minus) Olympians serves as a sort of ground bass to the polyphony of local cult and local tradition that his pages articulate.[72] The gods traditionally worshiped by the Greeks serve as one means of bringing unity to the collection of Hellenic communities, in spite of their discordant mythical traditions and their varying cult practices, much as the litany of shared Greek historical efforts *becomes* for Pausanias a means of highlighting commonalities amongst the Greeks in the face of a tradition of vigorous disunity. For this reason, if for no other, it is somewhat important to Pausanias that the gods be universal rather than local. He records punctiliously the many and varied epithets applied to the major gods in cult, yet insists, mostly implicitly, on the fundamental identity of the deities who are given these various surnames and rites in the cities and sanctuaries of Greece: Artemis Kremaste in Arkadia and Artemis Ephesia in Ephesus are not separate goddesses to him; they are manifestations of one and the same goddess who adopts different names and appearances and who demands different signs of devotion from her worshipers from one place to the next.[73]

---

[71] This is not to say that there are not numerous anomalies and complications in Pausanias' approach to local traditions (cf. Frazer 1898: i.lviii). Sometimes local traditions will conflict with one another (e.g. 2.23.3); sometimes they will contradict a non-local source that Pausanias regards as unimpeachable (e.g. 1.30.4), and, as the example of Argos shows, Pausanias did not regard the present inhabitants of the Greek cities as being infallible. A detailed study of how Pausanias handles all these complications is beyond the scope of this chapter, but there are no evolutionary trends that I have been able to identify in the ways Pausanias chooses to handle these issues over the course of the *Periegesis*. For an interesting study of the tensions between competing local claims and "panhellenic" versions of myths in one book of the *Periegesis* (Book 8), see Jost, 1998.

[72] Pirenne-Delforge 1998. Cf. Calame 1998.   [73] Pirenne-Delforge 1998: 140–147.

Pirenne-Delforge points to a couple of phenomena that show that Pausanias' concept of the universality of the traditional pantheon is a normative one that guides his understanding of the manifold religious practices he encounters in his travels. With few exceptions, the word most commonly translated as "god," θεός, is applied only to the traditional gods worshiped widely throughout Greece, such as Zeus, Athena, Artemis, etc. If a figure is worshiped only in one place, and seems to Pausanias to be recognized as a god by the worshipers (either by calling him or her θεός, or by rituals which Pausanias recognizes to be appropriate to divinities rather than heroes), then he typically refers to the entity as a δαίμων ("spirit" or "divinity"), rather than a θεός,[74] or by asserting that despite the name the natives apply to it, the local god is in reality identical to one of the more familiar gods.[75] A θεός is almost never described as being ἐπιχώριος, "local," while heroes and δαίμονες are.[76]

By maintaining a unified and unifying concept of godhood in the face of local variation, Pausanias gives us a vivid portrait of the diverse unity of Hellenism. The gods who enjoy the status of universality in Pausanias' construction are the ones, by and large, that had been worshiped by the Greeks from time immemorial. As with the story of Lykaon's lycanthropy in 8.2.3–4, time, for Pausanias, is the surest guarantor of legitimacy. Left out of Pausanias' ideology of difference-within-sameness are the numerous new and foreign gods that had, since the late classical period, gained widespread popularity in the Greek world. Neither distinctively local nor venerably ancient, the cults of these had little chance to make a noticeable impact on Pausanias' view of what was important in Greek religious life. It is for this reason, perhaps, that Pausanias pays relatively little attention to newcomer gods like Isis and Serapis, and none at all to Christianity. Certain divinities, however, seem to hold more of an ambiguous position in Pausanias' mind: neither members of the Olympian pantheon nor noticeably foreign or adventitious. Concerning these gods, I would argue, Pausanias' attitude is not fixed at the start of the *Periegesis*, and occasionally we can catch glimpses

---

[74] Pirenne-Delforge 1998: 131.

[75] For instance, at 8.36.5, he argues that the god known as the *Agathos Theos* ("Good God") among the Megalopolitans is Zeus by another name (Pirenne-Delforge 1998: 136).

[76] Pirenne-Delforge 1998: 133–134. This is, of course, a generalization to which there are several exceptions. While it is true that there are no gods that Pausanias calls ἐπιχώριος, there are some θεοί who are strictly "local," even if Pausanias does not use the term ἐπιχώριος to describe them. One prominent example comes early on in the first book, in a place no more exotic than the "Roman agora" at Athens (1.17.1): "Among the things the Athenians have in their market-place that are not known to everyone is an altar of Mercy. Though this god, of all the gods (θεῶν), is most helpful in human life and in reversals of fortune, the Athenians are alone among the Greeks in worshiping him."

of his thought developing as he sees more and learns more over the course of the work's composition. An interesting case in point is his treatment of the goddess Tyche.[77]

Tyche, whose name is the word for "fortune" in Greek, was present as an anthropomorphic divinity in the earliest poetry known to Pausanias. The *Homeric Hymn to Demeter* (which Pausanias considers to be by Homer) mentions her as one of the Oceanids who were playing in a meadow with Persephone when she was abducted by Hades.[78] Hesiod also refers to her lineage in his grand genealogy of the gods, the *Theogony*.[79] As a force in the universe, either personified or not, Tyche (or *tyche*) had also gained importance in the realm of historiography in the post-classical period.[80] Having tasted the vicissitudes of F(/f)ortune in their defeat by the Macedonians, Greek intellectuals gained new appreciation for the power of this force in the affairs of men, an appreciation that is expressed famously by such writers as Polybios and Diodoros, but also by Pausanias on numerous occasions in his historical accounts. Ruminating, for instance, on the precipitous decline in Spartan fortune between their victory in the battle of Corinth (394 BCE) and their humiliation in the battle of Leuktra (371 BCE), Pausanias says: "In no minor way did the god make clear here [at Corinth] and again in Leuktra that those whom the Greeks call valorous are nothing without Tyche" (1.29.11). Later, in a passage that must be seen as one of the string of semi-religious manifestos that Pausanias delivers in Book 8, he discourses at length on the importance of *tyche* in the rise and fall of cities, a passage we have already examined as an example of Herodotean imitation (8.33.1–3).[81] In these passages, as elsewhere in Pausanias (and other authors), it is difficult to decide whether or not we should capitalize the word *tyche*. Ancient Greek manuscripts had no conventions such as capitalization to distinguish between proper names and impersonal concepts. Still, the importance of fortune to Pausanias as a force in history is clear, and as we shall see in later passages, there is little evident distinction in Pausanias' mind between the goddess and the concept.

In contrast to Tyche's early appearance in poetry and her importance in widespread views of the working of the universe, in actual cult she does not seem to become a popular figure until the late classical and Hellenistic

---

[77] For a different, but not incompatible study of Tyche in Pausanias, see Heer 1979: 307–312, and cf. Swain 1996: 340–341; Swain 1989b; Porter 2001: 74.

[78] *Homeric Hymn to Demeter* 420.   [79] Hesiod, *Theogony* 360.

[80] Which is not to deny, of course, that the importance of fortune was recognized even earlier (cf. Herodotos 1.5).

[81] Other passages in which *tyche* plays a role in historical events include: 4.13.4; 4.29.3; 7.17.2; 9.13.2.

periods.[82] It is perhaps because Pausanias suspected that the antiquity of the cults of Tyche in Greece was not comparable to that of the literary attestations of her power and significance that he puts what seems to be an unusual amount of effort into investigating the history of her worship. Pausanias mentions some sixteen shrines, temples, statues, altars, and other monuments sacred to the goddess[83] and in many of these cases, particularly the early ones, he takes pains to report to us what he has discovered regarding the cult's age and background. The most striking passage regarding the worship of Tyche comes in the description of the Messenian city of Pharai (4.30.3). Pausanias judges the cult image (ἄγαλμα) found in the Tyche temple there to be ancient (ἀρχαῖον), and the antiquity of it seems to inspire further thoughts. He takes this opportunity to report that Homer is the earliest writer to mention Tyche that he has been able to find. He quotes verbatim the lines from the *Homeric Hymn to Demeter* where Tyche is mentioned (lines 418–420), then seems to take Homer to task for not assigning Tyche a preeminent role in the affairs of humans, as he did for other important gods and goddesses:

But [Homer] did not explain further how this goddess is a very powerful one in human affairs and provides extraordinary power, as for instance in the *Iliad* he portrays Athena and Enyo as having dominance over those who are waging war . . . But this poet said nothing else about Tyche.

In pointed contrast to Homer's neglect, Pausanias goes on to credit the archaic artist Boupalos with the first representation of Tyche with what seem to have been the iconographical features that Pausanias most associated with her: a *polos* (cylindrical head-dress) and the "Horn of Amaltheia." Pausanias is not speaking here of the statue he saw in Pharai; instead, he is reporting a fact that he discovered about the Tyche cult that, implicitly, makes credible his claim for the age of the Messenian statue.

The display Pausanias makes here of his inquiries into the cultic and iconographical history of a minor goddess is unusual, as is his personal testimony to the goddess' prowess. One might wonder, with good reason, what motivated these statements at this particular point in his account. Pausanias had, up to this point in Book 4, dealt with several other temples, shrines, or statues of Tyche, and none of them produced this sort of response. In all of them, however, one can see, or easily imagine, a heightened concern on the part of Pausanias for the age of the cult in question. His first encounter

---

[82] For her representation, see: Edwards 1990; Matheson and Pollitt 1994.

[83] 2.2.8; 2.7.5; 2.11.8; 2.20.3; 2.35.3; 4.30.3; 4.31.10; 5.15.6; 5.17.3; 6.2.7; 6.25.4; 7.26.8; 8.30.7; 9.16.1; 9.26.8; 9.39.13.

with the cult of Tyche comes (in a passage we have examined already) in his description of Corinth, where he sees a temple of Tyche with an upright marble statue of the goddess (2.2.8). While Pausanias expresses no misgivings about this particular establishment, the doubts he had about the relationship of the present-day Corinthians to traditional cults may well have bled over into a concern about the traditional nature of this Tyche. Perhaps in response to this, Pausanias points out in the cases of the next two Tyche cults he encounters, at Sikyon (2.7.5) and Titane (2.11.8), that their cult statues were of the archaic *xoanon*-type. The next opportunity Pausanias has to discuss Tyche comes in Argos. Here, he makes his concern with the age of the cult explicit for the first time, but the way he does so is problematic (2.20.3):

πέραν δὲ τοῦ Νεμείου Διὸς Τύχης ἔστιν ἐκ παλαιοτάτου ναός, εἰ δὴ Παλαμήδης κύβους εὑρὼν ἀνέθηκεν ἐς τοῦτον τὸν ναόν.

Beyond the Nemean Zeus there is a temple of Tyche of very old age, if indeed Palamedes, after discovering dice, dedicated them in this temple.

It is not out of the question that Pausanias was actually willing to believe that the temple he saw here in Argos was old enough to house a dedication by the Trojan-war-era hero Palamedes,[84] but given Pausanias' jaundiced attitude toward what the Argives tell him about their antiquities, it is perhaps better to view this statement as subtly sarcastic. Even so, whether the lesson Pausanias derives from his encounter with the monument is that the cult of Tyche is very old, or that the Argives can't be trusted when they call something old, this passage attests to his interest in the age of the Tyche cult. This interest appears again when Pausanias comes to the city of Hermione in the eastern Argolid. Here, he reports that the shrine of Tyche, with its colossal marble statue, is said by the inhabitants to be the newest of their shrines (2.25.3). In all, Pausanias makes five references to the Tyche cult in Book 2, more references than he makes in any other book, and here is an approximation of what he might have ended up asking himself after getting through with them: Is the Tyche cult a new cult in Greece? Is it, perhaps, one even brought in by the Roman settlers of Corinth? The Argives say their cult is extremely old, but who can believe what they say? And the Hermionians say that their shrine is the newest. Then again, the people of Sikyon and Titane have old-style *xoana* of the goddess. With his attitudes toward the goddess having reached (hypothetically) this ambiguous juncture, Pausanias

---

[84] Pausanias discusses with no *obvious* irony other artifacts of the era (9.40.11, for instance, on Agamemnon's scepter; cf. Veyne 1988: 100–101).

remains silent about her throughout the third Book before reemerging in the fourth book with the extended disquisition cited above.

Of course, my reconstruction of Pausanias' thought processes above is completely speculative, but something of the sort would explain what we see in Book 4: having been made curious by what he learned about the cult of Tyche in composing his account of the first three books (particularly Book 2), he does more research, and by the time he comes to write Book 4 he can report the results of that research, results that unsurprisingly confirm the goddess' antiquity and, consequently, Pausanias' own sense of her importance in literary and historic terms. In subsequent references to the Tyche cult, the age of the cult is less of an issue, although Pausanias does mention on one occasion (in Elis) that the cult statue of the goddess is a *xoanon* (gilt and acrolithic),[85] and on another occasion (at Aigeira in Achaea) he points out that the local shrine of Tyche houses a statue with the Horn of Amaltheia, one of the hallmarks of the archaic iconography he ascribes to Boupalos.[86]

Through the combination of sightseeing and research, Pausanias is able to bridge the discrepancy between Tyche's literary and historical importance and her representation in the physical plane of Greek cult, and he can thereby allow this goddess to take her rightful place among the major gods of Greece. When he sees her statue at Aigeira (7.26.8), he makes note of the fact that she is portrayed in the company of Eros and takes the opportunity to comment on the appropriateness of having Tyche and Eros paired. In this connection, he cites some lines of Pindar, whose statements regarding the goddess were mentioned by Pausanias in his essay on Tyche in Book 4 (4.30.3), but not actually quoted or paraphrased. At Aigeira, we learn that what Pindar says actually conflicts with the passage Pausanias previously cited from the Homeric Hymn: instead of one of the feckless virginal daughters of Okeanos, Pindar calls Tyche one of the Fates, and in fact the strongest of the three sisters. Pausanias makes no comment on the contradiction, and instead praises Pindar for the aptness of his mythologizing. We see here an appearance, before his "conversion" in Book 8, of Pausanias the allegorist, a searcher for truth in divine representations in spite of contradictory and confusing surface messages of their myths, and it is an allegorical interpretation he places on the combination of Tyche and Eros: the fact that luck is more important than beauty in the matters of the

---

[85] 6.25.4.

[86] 7.26.8. In 5.17.3, in the description of Olympia, Pausanias also inquires into the age of a statue of Tyche, along with several other statues in the temple of Hera, and determines that they are all ancient (ἀρχαῖον; 5.17.3).

heart. In the end, he might say, it doesn't really matter whether you call Tyche one of the Fates or one of Persephone's playmates; both can be ways of revealing important truths about the nature of fortune. At the same time, the uncorrected doubling of the tale of Tyche's origins also echoes some of the unhomogenized polyphony of early myth, and this may reflect the fact that by the time he was writing the description of Aigeira, Pausanias had reached a level of comfort in thinking of Tyche as one of the old-time gods like Aphrodite, who likewise had double origins,[87] or like Hesiod's two kinds of Strife,[88] or like the Fates themselves, whom Hesiod alternately identifies as the daughters of Night or the daughters of Zeus and Themis.

Thus, we can see Pausanias confronting a dilemma in the case of Tyche; a goddess who should be among the foremost of the Greek goddesses, but one whose actual cult seems to be sporadic and bereft of antiquity. By the time he has come to write the latter portion of the *Periegesis*, however, he seems to have learned enough about the goddess and her representations that he can classify the cult as an ancient and valid part of the Greek cultic landscape. The value of Tyche is one aspect of Pausanias' religious life where he seems to learn something as he goes on, and it may be worth suggesting that it is no coincidence that his discoveries about Tyche are presented in Book 4, where we also see the apex of Pausanias' developing appreciation of local history in his extended narrative of the history of the Messenians, a history in which the power of Tyche, or just plain fortune, is illustrated as well as it is illustrated anywhere in the *Periegesis*.

GODS FROM MEN?

Using Pausanias' self-education on the subject of Tyche as precedent, I will close this chapter with a more tentative suggestion: that a similar progress can be traced in Pausanias' relation to another late arrival on the religious terrain of Greece, the cult of the Roman emperors. As was mentioned in Chapter 2, the imperial cult was an everyday part of life in most communities of the Greek east, and included some of the leading Greek intellectuals and statesmen in its priesthood. As with all of the provinces of the empire, there were many temples, shrines, altars, and statues devoted to the imperial cult in Roman Greece. Pausanias mentions few of them, which in itself is nothing remarkable. As was noted above, Pausanias is generally indifferent to newcomer deities of all sorts, and there is no possibility that, like Tyche,

---

[87] In Hesiod, she is born from the foam cast up on the sea by the castrated genitals of Ouranos. In Homer, she is the daughter of Zeus and Dione.

[88] Hesiod, *Works and Days* 11–20.

the imperial cult could be found to have a genuine ancient pedigree. There is one passage, however, where Pausanias reveals considerably stronger sentiments than mere indifference, and it is actually a passage that we have partially examined already. When Pausanias is discussing the issue of the metamorphosis of Lykaon at the beginning of Book 8, he asserts, as we have seen, that in ancient times men and gods associated with one another, and that men could even become gods. At that point, his comments continue as follows (8.2.5):

ἐπ' ἐμοῦ δέ – κακία γὰρ δὴ ἐπὶ πλεῖστον ηὔξετο καὶ γῆν τε ἐπενέμετο πᾶσαν καὶ πόλεις πάσας – οὔτε θεὸς ἐγένετο οὐδεὶς ἔτι ἐξ ἀνθρώπου, πλὴν ὅσον λόγῳ καὶ κολακείᾳ πρὸς τὸ ὑπερέχον . . .

In my day, however, since evil has grown to such an extent and has spread over the entire land and into every city, no one from the ranks of humans (ἐξ ἀνθρώπου) ever becomes a god any more, except in name only, and in flattery addressed to the powerful.

As I have pointed out elsewhere, this passage is the strongest and most unequivocal condemnation of the practice of ruler worship by any non-Christian author of the Roman period.[89] While Pausanias does not mention Romans or emperors explicitly here, his assertion that he is talking about what happens in his own day (ἐπ' ἐμοῦ) leaves little doubt that he has in mind the emperors and their familiars, and not Hellenistic kings or other recipients of deification ensconced safely in the distant past.[90] I would also argue that this statement must be read as part of the moral and religious discourse that Pausanias works so hard to develop in the opening chapters of Book 8. This discourse, I submit, includes the following statement, which Pausanias makes about a shrine that he encountered in the city of Mantineia (8.9.7):

Even Antinoos is considered to be a god (θεός) by [the Mantineians], and of the temples in Mantineia the temple of Antinoos is the youngest. The passion that the emperor Hadrian felt for him was certainly extraordinary. I never saw him while he was still among humans (μετ' ἀνθρώπων), but I have seen him in statues and paintings.

---

[89] Hutton 2005b pp. 307–309. Other scholars have seen this passage as criticism of imperial deification (e.g. Habicht 1998: 152; Torelli 2001: 179–185), but surprisingly the sentiment is not unanimous. Other writers, such as Plutarch, for instance (*Romulus* 28), criticize the notion of granting divinity by senatorial decree, but do not rule out the possibility of mortals earning godhood by their virtue. On the response to the imperial cult by Greek intellectuals (not including Pausanias), see Bowersock 1973.

[90] As suggested by Swain 1996: 346. Although Swain recognizes that the remark refers to the present, he finds its contemporary relevance blunted by the fact that "the context is not connected to Rome." Hellenistic kings, however, are even further removed from the context.

The interest scholars have taken in this passage previously has been mainly for the evidence it gives for Pausanias' date of birth: he would not say that he hadn't seen Antinoos "among humans" unless it were a possibility for him to have done so. Since Antinoos, Hadrian's beautiful favorite, died at a tragically young age in 130 CE, Pausanias must have reached an age of discretion by at least that date.[91] What no one to my knowledge has noticed, however, is that this passage is also one of the clearest examples of sarcasm that we have in all the pages of Pausanias. Crucial is the phrase "among humans" (μετ᾽ ἀνθρώπων), which is not a euphemism along the lines of "among the living." Instead, every other time Pausanias uses this expression he is referring to a divinized hero's state prior to becoming an immortal.[92] In one informative instance, the talk is of Herakles (one of the legitimate beneficiaries of apotheosis that Pausanias mentions in 8.2.4), and in light of Pausanias' earlier references to deification this passage can also be seen as an indirect criticism of emperor cult. The topic in this passage is the claim of the people of Thespiai in Boiotia that Herakles established a temple to himself in the city and forced the daughter of the king, who had refused his sexual advances, to live a life of chastity as his priestess (9.27.7):

There is no way I can consider it credible that Herakles would be driven to such rage against the daughter of a man who was his friend. In addition, when he was still among humans (μετ᾽ ἀνθρώπων) . . . he would not himself have established a temple and a priesthood for himself as though he were a god (θεός).

What Pausanias is saying about Antinoos, then, is not simply that he had never seen him while he was still alive but that he had never seen him before his metamorphosis into a god. In combination with the statement he made only a few pages earlier that in these days of wickedness *no one* becomes a god any more "from the ranks of humans" (ἐξ ἀνθρώπου), the sarcasm could scarcely be more conspicuous. Swain suggests that on this occasion Pausanias was induced by his profound admiration for Hadrian to forget his previous objection to deification and to accept Antinoos' godhood without complaint.[93] But surely it is preferable to assume that Pausanias knew exactly what he was doing in the near-juxtaposition of

[91] See Habicht 1998: 12; Bowie 2001: 23, both with references to previous scholars drawing the same conclusion.
[92] 3.16.2 (Dioskouroi); 7.17.8 (Herakles). 4.32.4 is a bit different: there, it is applied not to a divinized individual but to a heroized one (Aristomenes the Messenian), who is said to have aided the Thebans at the battle of Leuktra even though he was no longer "among humans" (he lived some three hundred years before the battle).
[93] Swain 1996: 349; cf. Arafat 1996: 187.

Figure 8.3. Antinoos: beloved of Hadrian and a god in Mantineia.

these two extraordinary passages. I would venture so far as to suggest that his encounter at Mantineia with the cult of Antinoos – a particularly extreme example of imperial deification, in which it is not even the emperor himself but his male consort who receives the honor of immortality – is what motivated his strong condemnation of deification earlier in the book.

To criticize the imperial cult, at a time when the elites of the Greek communities regularly sought connections to the cult as a route to local prominence and imperial advancement, is to stake out an interesting position for one's self. The same can be said for the ridicule of Antinoos, whose image was ubiquitous in Greece, and who was honored with games, coinage, sacrifices, and statuary long after his death.[94] When I first began to write this book, I believed that these passages signaled a basic disdain for the imperial cult on Pausanias' part. Having arrived at this point in my account, however, I have begun to wonder if this disdain is something that Pausanias did not start out with but rather acquired as he worked on the *Periegesis*. While it is true that Pausanias passes up the vast majority of opportunities to discuss monuments related to the imperial cult in Greece,[95] that choice, as was mentioned above, can be ascribed to the antiquarian nature of Pausanias' project and implies in itself no active distaste. We have seen how Pausanias' lack of interest in the imperial cult may have led him to misidentify one of the more impressive religious structures in Corinth, Temple E,[96] but again, neglect is not the same as antipathy. Where Pausanias does mention the cult, his statements are brief and void of commentary, either positive or negative. For instance, in the third book he describes what there is to see in the Lakonian town of Akriai in the following way: "In it there is a temple for the Roman emperors and upland from the city, at a distance of about twelve stadia, is a shrine of Asklepios" (3.22.9). In Sparta, he is more verbose but similarly matter-of-fact (3.11.4):[97]

There are temples on the agora: one for Caesar, who was the first to pursue a monarchy at Rome and who first obtained the established power, and one made for Augustus, his son, who put the principate on a sounder footing and advanced further than his father in reputation and power. His name was Augustus, which means "revered" in the Greek tongue.

If one is determined to find criticism of the emperor cult here, one might suggest that the way Pausanias regales the reader with very elementary information about these world-famous additions to the pantheon amounts to a subtle form of ridicule, but I suspect that such an interpretation would depend on reading the attitude he displays in Book 8 back into this earlier part of the work. There is certainly nothing on the surface of this passage that amounts to criticism.

Perhaps the strongest case for a negative reflection on the imperial cult prior to Book 8 comes in Pausanias' description of Sikyon, where he informs the reader that the precinct (τέμενος) currently dedicated to the Roman emperors was formerly the house of one of the tyrants who ruled Sikyon

---

[94] On the spread of Antinoos-related monuments and artifacts throughout Greece, consult Meyer 1991: 194–211. On the Antinoos cult in Mantineia in particular, see: Meyer 1991: 251–262; Jost 1985: 128–9, 541–2. On elite participation in the cult, see also Spawforth 1978: 249–260.
[95] For two major monuments that Pausanias neglects in Athens alone, see Hoff 1996.
[96] See above, pp. 168–169.   [97] On this passage, see Arafat 1996: 131–2.

in earlier times (2.8.1). Elsner has suggested that Pausanias is making anti-
imperial insinuations when he chooses to tell the reader that the house of the
old tyrant is now inhabited (so to speak) by the modern-day rulers: it is as
if he were implying that the character of the occupants had not changed.[98]
Such subtlety would hardly be beyond our author, but as Matthaias Steinhart has recently argued, Pausanias frequently mentions cases where what
was formerly a private house has been converted to a new use, and in none
of those cases is it possible to detect any implicit criticism of the new occu-
pant(s).[99] Whether one agrees with Elsner or Steinhart on this issue, however, the criticism here, if any, is far less scathing than what we find in Book 8.

The question, then, is: what happens between the early books and Book 8
that hardens Pausanias' attitude against the imperial cult? I would suggest
that a possible answer lies in the evolution of Pausanias' thinking in the other
areas that we have been examining in this chapter. Perhaps as Pausanias'
understanding of the importance of Greece's independent history develops,
and as he gains a clearer sense of what constitutes valid additions to both
the local and panhellenic aspects of Greek religion, the imperial cult begins
to look more and more to him like an illegitimate accretion. Before leaving
this topic, we might ask whether a different attitude toward the imperial
cult implies a different attitude toward the empire in general. The answer
I would give is yes. In his ridicule of Antinoos, Pausanias is also, indirectly,
ridiculing Hadrian, the same emperor whose benefactions for Greece he
praised unreservedly in the first and second books. The reader will, I hope,
be relieved rather than disappointed if I decline to begin unraveling the
hoorah's nest of Pausanias' relation to Rome at this stage of the present work,
but in brief I would reiterate a point I made in Chapter 2: that one should
not speak of Pausanias' attitude toward Rome but rather his attitudes, and
that one characteristic of the multiplicity of attitudes that Pausanias displays
is that they are not completely the same from the beginning of the work to
the end.

CONCLUSION

The author of the *Periegesis* begins with a well-formed image of Greece, and
a well-thought-out plan for transmitting what was meaningful to him about

[98] Elsner 1992: 19; 1995: 143.
[99] Steinhart 2002a. Examples he cites include: 1.2.5; 1.29.2; 8.51.2; 9.12.3; 9.16.5. One might respond to
Steinhart that the context of these passages is important: none of the other cases involve the ruler
of the current regime, and hence innuendo or sarcasm is scarcely even a possibility. It is because the
Roman emperors are people whom Pausanias *might* want to criticize that the suggestion that he *is*
criticizing them is plausible. Moreover, Pausanias' reference to the emperor cult at Sikyon is followed
almost immediately by his lengthy account of the career of Aratos, one of the last great leaders of
independent Greece (2.8.2–9.5): another pregnant juxtaposition?

Greece using the medium of language and literature. Even those aspects of his project that were in place from the beginning show that Pausanias – far from being a dependable dullard – was a creative and innovative, one might even say audacious, literary craftsman. Presented at every phase of the composition of his work with the opportunity to follow established and accepted patterns, he consistently refuses to do so. He could have fixed the scope of his work within the limits of the Roman province of Achaia, or within the boundaries set by a previous geographer, but instead he chose to define the physical extent of *Hellas* by his own cultural and personal criteria. In selecting and arranging the content of his work, he could have followed the rules of the established genres of geography, history, or antiquarian *periegesis*, but chose instead to forge an unprecedented combination of the three. In his language, he could have chosen to echo canonical masters that everyone admired, but instead elected to strive for something completely new in the arena of *mimesis:* a highly idiosyncratic style that recalled most strongly predecessors whose status was either ambiguous (in the case of Herodotos) or utterly discredited (Hegesias) in the eyes of the intelligentsia.

All of these choices cooperate to characterize the author as someone who is highly individualistic and who cultivates a studied indifference both to the way that writers were supposed to write and to the way that intellectuals were supposed to relate to the cosmopolitan society of the empire. Pausanias was hardly alone in the field of literary innovation in this period, but his creativeness and willfulness in literary matters and in matters of self-presentation are a strong contrast from the common prejudice against him as a dull and unimaginative keeper of antiquarian laundry-lists. Among Pausanias' most innovative decisions was to deal with Greece as an eyewitness. At a time when everyone talked about Greece but few of those who even went to Greece ventured far beyond the major tourist draws, Pausanias offers himself as a guide to the Greece that was not taught in the history books. His firsthand testimony, vivified though it is by the passionate idealization of bygone *Hellas*, is also a corrective, an unparalleled corrective, to that idealization.

However singular Pausanias' stance is at the beginning of his work, this final chapter has attempted to show Pausanias developing still more avenues of singularity as he progresses through his work on the *Periegesis*. While his overall attitude toward religion was already close to its final form at the start, in many respects what he thinks about religion is not what distinguishes him most strongly. As Jane Lightfoot has noted,[100] "religion was a major, if not *the* main area in which patriotic localism could coexist with allegiance

---

[100] Lightfoot 2003: 207.

to the center" in the period in which Pausanias wrote. Religion, in other words, was one area where resistence to imperial homogeneity was relatively safe (up to a point, as certain sects learned) and even, in some periods and circumstances, encouraged. As he composes the latter books of the *Periegesis*, we see Pausanias developing his own personal vision of Hellenism in new directions, to places where even Hadrian himself is not immune from criticism if his interventions conflict with the character of *Hellas* as a whole and of all its eternally varying constituent parts. How far Pausanias goes in these new directions is an important question worth further study. With any luck I, or the next generation of Pausanias' admirers, will be able to say more about that in the future. What we can say for the present is that Pausanias serves as a good example, perhaps our best example, of how a classical Greek mind perceives and communicates both physical landscapes and the cultural associations that adhere to the objects and people in those landscapes. But while Pausanias' cognitive, cultural, and intellectual proclivities give shape and structure to the landscape, the process is not a one-way street. The places Pausanias visits, the monuments he sees, and the peoples he encounters contribute to the evolution of his way of seeing and describing Greece.

Bibliography

Ackerman, R. 1974. "Sir James G. Frazer and A. E. Housman: a Relationship in Letters." *GRBS* 15: 339–364.

Adam, Jean-Michel, ed. 1990. *Le discours anthropologique: description, narration, savoir*. Paris.

Adams, A. 1989. "The Arch of Hadrian at Athens." In Walker and Cameron, eds.: 10–15.

Ahl, F. 1989. "The Art of Safe Criticism in Greece and Rome." *AJP* 105: 174–208.

Alcock, Susan E. 1993. *Graecia Capta: The Landscapes of Roman Greece*. Cambridge.

———. 1994. "Minding the Gap in Hellenistic and Roman Greece." In Alcock and Osborne, eds.: 247–261.

———. 1995. "Pausanias and the *Polis*: Use and Abuse." In Hansen, ed.: 326–344.

———. 1996. "Landscapes of Memory and the Authority of Pausanias." In Bingen, ed.: 241–267.

———. 1997. "Greece: a Landscape of Resistance?" In Mattingly, ed.: 103–115.

———. 1997, ed. *The Early Roman Empire in the East*. Oxford.

———. 2001. "The Peculiar Book IV and the Problem of the Messenian Past." In Alcock, Cherry, and Elsner, eds.: 142–166.

Alcock, Susan E., John F. Cherry, and J. Elsner, eds. 2001. *Pausanias: Travel and Memory in Roman Greece*. Oxford.

Alcock, Susan E., and Robin Osborne, eds. 1994. *Placing the Gods: Sanctuaries and Sacred Space in Ancient Greece*. Oxford.

Alföldy, Geza. 1996. "Subject and Ruler, Subjects and Methods: an Attempt at a Conclusion." In Small, ed.: 254–261.

Allinson, F. G. 1886. "Pseudo-Ionism in the Second Century A.D." *AJP* 7: 203–217.

Amandry, Michel. 1988. *Le monnayage des duovirs corinthiens*. *BCH* Suppl. 15. Paris.

Ameling, Walter. 1983. *Herodes Atticus*. 2 vols. Hildesheim.

———. 1996. "Pausanias und die hellenistische Geschichte." In Bingen, ed.: 117–160.

Anderson, Graham. 1976. *Studies in Lucian's Comic Fiction*. Leiden.

———. 1993. *The Second Sophistic: a Cultural Phenomenon in the Roman Empire*. London.

———. 1994. *Sage, Saint and Sophist: Holy Men and their Associates in the Early Roman Empire*. London.

André, J.-M., and M.-F. Baslez. 1993. *Voyager dans l'antiquité*. Paris.

Arafat, K. W. 1992. "Pausanias' Attitude to Antiquities." *BSA* 87: 387–409.

———. 1995. "Pausanias and the Temple of Hera at Olympia." *BSA* 90: 461–473.

Bibliography

1996. *Pausanias' Greece: Ancient Artists and Roman Rulers.* Cambridge.

2000. "The Recalcitrant Mass: Athenaeus and Pausanias." In Braund and Wilkins, eds.: 191–202.

Arnaud, Pascal, and Patrick Counillon, eds. 1998. *Geographica Historica.* Bordeaux.

Atherton, Catherine. 1998. "Children, Animals, Slaves and Grammar." In Too and Livingstone, eds.: 214–244.

Auberger, Jannick. 1992. "Pausanias et les Messéniens: une histoire d'amour!" *REA* 94: 187–197.

1994. "Les mots du courage chez Pausanias." *RPh* 68: 7–18.

2000. "Pausanias et le livre 4: une leçon pour l'empire." *Phoenix* 54: 255–281.

2001. "D'un héros à l'autre: Pausanias au pied de l'Ithôme." In Knoepfler and Piérart, eds.: 261–273.

Aupert, Pierre. 1985. "Un Serapieion argien?" *CRAI*: 151–175.

1987. "Pausanias et l'Asclepieion d'Argos." *BCH* III: 511–517.

Avenarius, Gert. 1956. *Lukians Schrift zur Geschichtsschreibung.* Meisenheim am Glan.

Badian, E. 1996. "Alexander the Great Between Two Thrones and Heaven: Variations on an Old Theme." In Small, ed.: 11–26.

Baladié, Raoul. 1980. *Le Péloponnèse de Strabon.* Paris.

2001. "Structure et particularités du livre IV de Pausanias." In Knoepfler and Piérart, eds.: 275–282.

Baldwin, Barry. 1973. *Studies in Lucian.* Toronto.

Barnes, Jonathan, and Griffin, Miriam, eds. 1997. *Philosophia Togata II.* Oxford.

Bartsch, Shadi. 1989. *Decoding the Ancient Novel.* Princeton.

Baslez, M.-F. 1994. "L'auteur du *De Dea Syria* et les réalités religieuses de Hiérapolis." In Billault, ed.: 171–176.

Beagon, Mary. 1996. "Nature and Views of her Landscapes in Pliny the Elder." In Shipley and Salmon, eds.: 284–309.

Beard, Mary. 2001. "'Pausanias in Petticoats,' or *The Blue Jane*." In Alcock, Cherry, and Elsner, eds.: 224–239.

Bearzot, Cinzia. 1988. "La Grecia di Pausania, geografia e cultura nella definizione del concetto di Ἑλλάς." In Sordi: 90–112.

1992. *Storia e storiografia ellenistica in Pausania il Periegeta.* Venice.

2001. "La nozione di κοινόν in Pausania." In Knoepfler and Piérart, eds.: 93–108.

Becker, A. S. 1992. "Reading Poetry Through a Distant Lens: Ecphrasis, Ancient Greek Rhetoricians, and the Pseudo-Hesiodic 'Shield of Herakles.'" *AJP* 113: 5–24.

Behr, C. A. 1968. *Aelius Aristides and the Sacred Tales.* Amsterdam.

1994. "Studies on the Biography of Aelius Aristides." *ANWR* 34.2: 1140–1233.

Bender, Barbara. 1999. "Subverting the Western Gaze: Mapping Alternative Worlds." In Ucko and Layton: 31–45.

Bengtson, Hermann. 1975. *Herrschergestalten des Hellenismus.* Munich.

Berggren, J. Lennart, and Alexander Jones. 2000. *Ptolemy's Geography: an Annotated Translation of the Theoretical Chapters.* Princeton.

Biers, J. C. 1985. *Corinth XVII: the Great Bath on the Lechaion Road.* Princeton.

2003. "*Lavari est vivere*: Baths in Roman Corinth." In Williams and Bookidis, eds.: 303–319.

Biers, W. 1978. "Water from Stymphalos." *Hesperia* 47: 171–184.

Billault, A., ed. 1994. *Lucien de Samosate*. Paris.

Bingen, Jean, ed. 1996. *Pausanias Historien*. (Fondation Hardt Entretiens sur l'antiquité classique XLI) Geneva.

Birge, Darice. 1994. "Trees in the Landscape of Pausanias' *Periegesis*." In Alcock and Osborne, eds.: 231–245.

Bischoff, E. 1938. "Perieget." In *Realencyclopädie der klassischen Altertumswissenschaft*. Vol. 19: 725–742. Stuttgart.

Blass, Friedrich. 1865. *Die griechische Beredsamkeit in dem Zeitraum von Alexander bis auf Augustus*. Berlin.

Boatwright, Mary. 2000. *Hadrian and the Cities of the Roman Empire*. Princeton.

Boeckh, August. 1874. *Gesammelte kleine Schriften*. Leipzig.

Boer, Willem den. 1973. *Le culte des souverains dans l'empire romain*. (Fondation Hardt Entretiens sur l'antiquité classique XIX) Geneva.

Bommelaer, Jean-François. 1999. *Traces de l'épigraphie delphique dans le texte de Pausanias*. In Khoury, ed.: 83–93.

   2001. "Les procédés de la localisation dans le livre X." In Knoepfler and Piérart, eds.: 375–386.

Bommelaer, J. F., and Y. Grandjean. 1972. "Recherches dans le quartier sud d'Argos." *BCH* 96: 155–228.

Bommeljé, S., K. Doorn, M. Deylius, et al. 1987. *Aetolia and the Aetolians*. Studia Aetolica I. Utrecht.

Bompaire, J. 1958. *Lucien écrivain: imitation et création*. Paris.

   1994. "L'atticisme de Lucien." In Billault, ed.: 65–75.

Bookidis, Nancy. 2003. "The Sanctuaries of Corinth." In Williams and Bookidis, eds.: 247–259.

Bookidis, Nancy, and Ronald S. Stroud. 1997. *The Sanctuary of Demeter and Kore: Topgraphy and Architecture* (*Corinth XVIII.iii.*). Princeton.

Bosworth, A. B. 1980–1995. *A Historical Commentary on Arrian's History of Alexander*. 2 vols. Oxford.

   1993. "Arrian and Rome: the Minor Works." *ANRW* 34.1: 226–275.

Boulanger, André. 1923. *Aelius Aristide et la Sophistique dans la province d'Asie au IIe siècle de notre ère*. Paris.

Bowersock, G. W. 1969. *Greek Sophists in the Roman Empire*. Oxford.

   1973. "Greek Intellectuals and the Imperial Cult in the Second Century, A.D." In den Boer, ed.: 179–206.

   1974, ed. *Approaches to the Second Sophistic*. University Park, PA.

   1990. *Hellenism in Late Antiquity*. Ann Arbor.

Bowersock, G. W., and C. P. Jones. 1974. "A Guide to the Sophists in Philostratus' *Vitae Sophistarum*." In Bowersock, ed.: 35–40.

Bowie, Ewen. 1970. "Greeks and their Past in the Second Sophistic." *Past & Present* 46: 3–41.

   1982. "The Importance of Sophists." *YClS* 27: 29–59.

Bibliography

1991. "Hellenes and Hellenism in Writers of the Early Second Sophistic." In Saïd, ed.: 183–204.

1996. "Past and Present in Pausanias." In Bingen, ed.: 207–230.

2001. "Inspiration and Aspiration: Date, Genre, and Readership." In Alcock, Cherry, and Elsner, eds.: 21–32.

Branham, R. B. 1989. *Unruly Eloquence: Lucian and the Comedy of Traditions.* Cambridge, MA.

Braund, David. 1994. *Georgia in Antiquity: a History of Colchis and Transcaucasian Iberia 550 BC–AD 562.* Oxford.

Braund, David, and John Wilkins, eds. 2000. *Athenaeus and his World: Reading Greek Culture in the Roman Empire.* Exeter.

Brixhe, C. 1987. *Essai sur le grec anatolien au début de notre ère.* Nancy.

Broneer, O. 1954. *Corinth I.iv: the South Stoa and its Roman Successors.* Princeton.

1971. *Isthmia I: Temple of Poseidon.* Princeton.

1973. *Isthmia II: Topography and Architecture.* Princeton.

Browning, R. 1983. *Medieval and Modern Greek* (2nd edition). Cambridge.

Brunt, P. A. 1976–1983. *Arrian.* 2 vols. Cambridge, MA.

1994. "The Bubble of the Second Sophistic." *PCPhS* 40: 25–52.

Bryson, Norman. 1994. "Philostratus and the Imaginary Museum." In Goldhill and Osborne, eds.: 255–283.

Bucher, W. 1919. *De Pausaniae studiis Homericis.* Halle.

Bultrighini, Umberto. 1990a. *Pausania e le tradizioni democratiche: Argo ed Elide.* Padua.

1990b. "La Grecia descritta da Pausania. Trattazione diretta e trattazione indiretta." *RFIC* 118: 282–305.

2001. "'Errori' in Pausania: III 8, 10." In Knoepfler and Piérart, eds.: 239–260.

Bursian, C. 1872. *Geographie von Griechenland.* Leipzig.

Calame, Claude. 1990. "Pausanias le périégète en ethnographe, ou comment décrire un culte grec." In Adam, ed.: 227–250.

1998. "Logiques du temps légendaire et de l'espace culturel selon Pausanias: une représentation discursive du 'panthéon' de Trézène." In Pirenne-Delforge, ed.: 149–163.

Camerotto, Alberto. 1998. *La metamorfosi della parola: studi sulla parodia in Luciano di Samosata.* Pisa.

Camp, J. 1986. *The Athenian Agora: Excavations in the Heart of Classical Athens.* New York.

Campbell, M. B. 1988. *The Witness and the Other World.* Ithaca.

1991. "'The Object of One's Gaze': Landscape, Writing, and Early Medieval Pilgrimage." In Westrem, ed.: 3–15.

Carpenter, R., and A. Bon. 1931. *Corinth III.ii: The Defenses of Acrocorinth and the Lower Town.* Cambridge, MA.

Cartledge, P. 1979. *Sparta and Lakonia: a Regional History 1300–362 BC.* London.

Cartledge, P., and A. Spawforth. 1989. *Hellenistic and Roman Sparta: a Tale of Two Cities.* London.

Casevitz, Michel. 2001. "Sur les scholies à Pausanias et les fragments de Pausanias." In Knoepfler and Piérart, eds.: 33–42.

Casevitz, Michel, Madeleine Jost, and Jean Marcadé. 1992. *Pausanias, Description de la Grèce Livre VIII, L'Arcadie.* Paris.

Casevitz, Michel, Jean Pouilloux, and F. Chamoux. 1992. *Description de la Grèce. Tome I: Livre I, Introduction générale, l'Attique.* Paris.

Casevitz, Michel, Jean Pouilloux, and Anne Jacquemin. 1999. *Pausanias, Description de la Grèce Tome V: Livre V, L'Élide (I).* Paris.

Casson, L. 1974. *Travel in the Ancient World.* London.

   1989. *The* Periplus Maris Erythraei. Princeton.

Cavanagh, W., J. Crouwel, R. W. V. Catling, and G. Shipley, eds. 1996. *Continuity and Change in a Greek Rural Landscape: the Laconia Survey.* Vol. 2. London.

Chamoux, F. 1974. "Pausanias géographe." In *Littérature gréco-romaine et géographie historique.* R. Chevallier, ed.: 83–90. Paris.

   1996. "La méthode historique de Pausanias." In Bingen, ed.: 45–69.

   2001. "Les épigrammes dans Pausanias." In Knoepfler and Piérart, eds.: 79–91.

Chevallier, Raymond. 1998. "Géographie, topographie, archéologie et histoire de la Gaule." In Arnaud and Counillon, eds.: 25–39.

Christ, Wilhelm. 1898. *Geschichte der griechischen Litteratur bis auf die Zeit Justinians* (3rd edition; *Handbuch der Altertumswissenschaft* VII). Munich.

Christ, W., W. Schmid, and O. Stählin. 1920–1924. *Geschichte der griechischen Litteratur* (2 vols., 6th edition; *Handbuch der Altertumswissenschaft* VII.2.). Munich.

Clark, Gillian. 1996. "Cosmic Sympathies: Nature as the Expression of Divine Purpose." In Shipley and Salmon, eds.: 310–329.

Clarke, Katherine. 1997. "In Search of the Author of Strabo's *Geography.*" *JRS* 87: 92–110.

   1999. *Between Geography and History: Hellenistic Constructions of the Roman World.* Oxford.

Clinton, K. 1989a. "Hadrian's Contribution to the Renaissance of Eleusis." In Walker and Cameron, eds.: 56–68.

   1989b. "The Eleusinian Mysteries: Roman Initiates and Benefactors: Second Century B.C.–267 A.D." *ANRW* II 18.2: 1499–1537.

Cohen, Ada. 2001. "Art, Myth and Travel in the Hellenistic World." In Alcock, Cherry, and Elsner, eds.: 93–126.

Cohen, Erik, 1992. "Pilgrimage and Tourism: Convergence and Divergence." In Morinis, ed.: 47–61.

Comfort, H. 1931. "The Date of Pausanias, Book II." *AJA* 35: 310–314.

Connolly, Joy. 2001. "Problems of the Past in Imperial Greek Education." In Too, ed.: 289–316.

Cooper, Guy L. III. 1998. *Attic Greek Prose Syntax.* 2 vols. Ann Arbor.

Cosgrove, Denis. 1984. "Prospect, Perspective and the Evolution of the Landscape Idea." *Transactions of the Institute of British Geographers* 10: 45–62.

Cosgrove, Denis, and Stephen Daniels, eds. 1988. *The Iconography of Landscape: Essays on the Symbolic Representation, Design and Use of Past Environments.* Cambridge.

Cribiore, Raffaella. 2001a. *Gymnastics of the Mind: Greek Education in Hellenistic and Roman Egypt*. Princeton.

2001b. "Euripides' *Phoenissae* in Hellenistic and Roman Education." In Too, ed.: 241–259.

Croissant, F. 1972. "Note de topographie argienne." *BCH* 96: 137–154.

Culler, Jonathan. 1981. "The Semiotics of Tourism." *American Journal of Semiotics* 1: 127–140.

Curtius, Ernst. 1852. *Peloponnesos: eine historisch-geographische Beschreibung der Halbinsel*. Gotha.

Dalimier, C. 1991. "Sextus Empiricus contre les grammairiens: ce que parler grec veut dire." In Saïd: 17–32.

Daux, Georges. 1936. *Pausanias à Delphes*. Paris.

Day, Joseph W. 1980. *The Glory of Athens: the Popular Tradition as Reflected in the Panathenaicus of Aelius Aristides*. Chicago.

Deferrari, Roy J. 1916 (1969). *Lucian's Atticism: the Morphology of the Verb*. Princeton (Amsterdam).

De Groot, A. W. 1921 (1967). *Der antike Prosarhythmus*. Groningen.

Deicke, Ludwig. 1935. *Quaestiones Pausanianae*. Göttingen.

Denniston J. D. 1950. *Greek Word Order*. London.

1954. *The Greek Particles* (2nd edition). Oxford.

des Courtils, J. 1981. "Note de topographie argienne." *BCH* 105: 607–610.

Deutsche, R. 1991. "Boys Town." *Environment and Planning D: Society and Space* 9: 5–30.

Devine, A. M. and L. D. Stephens. 2000. *Discontinuous Syntax: Hyperbaton in Greek*. Oxford.

Dewald, Carolyn. 1987. "Narrative Surface and Authorial Voice in Herodotus' *Histories*." *Arethusa* 20: 147–170.

1997. "Wanton Kings, Pickled Heroes, and Gnomic Founding Fathers: Strategies of Meaning at the End of Herodotus's *Histories*." In Roberts, Dunn, and Fowler, eds.: 62–82.

Dihle, Albrecht. 1977. "Der Beginn des Attizismus." *Antike und Abenland* 23: 162–177.

1994. *Greek and Latin Literature of the Roman Empire: From Augustus to Justinian*. Manfred Malzahn, tr. London (= *Griechische Literaturgeschichte*. Munich, 1989).

Dik, Helma. 1995. *Word Order in Ancient Greek: a Pragmatic Account of Word Order Variation in Herodotus*. Amsterdam.

Dilke, O. A. W. 1985. *Greek and Roman Maps*. Ithaca.

Diller, A. 1955. "The Authors Named Pausanias." *TAPA* 86: 268–279.

1956. "Pausanias in the Middle Ages." *TAPA* 87: 84–97.

1957. "The Manuscripts of Pausanias." *TAPA* 88: 169–188.

Dillon, Matthew. 1997. *Pilgrims and Pilgrimage in Ancient Greece*. London.

Dinsmoor, W. B. 1949. "The Largest Temple in the Peloponnese." *Hesperia* Supplement 8: 104–115. Princeton.

Dinsmoor, W. B., Jr. 1974. "The Temple of Poseidon: a Missing Sima and Other Matters." *AJA* 78: 211–238.

Dorati, Marco. 2000. *Le* Storie *di Erodoto: Etnografia e racconto.* Pisa.

Dover, K. J. 1960. *Greek Word Order.* Cambridge.

1973. *Thucydides* (Greece & Rome New Surveys in the Classics 7). Oxford.

1997. *The Evolution of Greek Prose Style.* Oxford.

Dueck, Daniela. 2000. *Strabo of Amasia: a Greek Man of Letters in Augustan Rome.* London.

Duff, Tim. 1999. *Plutarch's* Lives: *Exploring Virtue and Vice.* Oxford.

Eade, John, and Michael J. Sallnow. 1991. "Introduction." In Eade and Sallnow, eds.: 1–29.

Eade, John, and Michael J. Sallnow, eds. 1991. *Contesting the Sacred: the Anthropology of Christian Pilgrimage.* London.

Ebner, M., H. Gzella, H.-G. Nesselrath, and E. Ribbat, eds. 2001. *Lukian:* Lügenfreunde oder: der ungläubige. Darmstadt.

Edlow, R. B. 1977. *Galen on Language and Ambiguity.* Leiden.

Edwards, C. M. 1990. "Tyche at Corinth." *Hesperia* 59: 529–542.

Eide, Tormod. 1992. "Pausanias and Thucydides." *SO* 67: 124–137.

Eisner, R. 1991. *Travelers to an Antique Land.* Ann Arbor.

Ekroth, Gunnel. 1999. "Pausanias and the Sacrificial Rituals of Greek Hero-Cults." In Hägg, ed.: 146–158.

Elsner, J. 1992. "Pausanias: a Greek Pilgrim in the Roman World." *Past and Present* 135: 3–29.

1994. "From the Pyramids to Pausanias and Piglet: Monuments, Travel and Writing." In Goldhill and Osborne, eds.: 224–254.

1995. *Art and the Roman Viewer: the Transformation of Art from the Pagan World to Christianity.* Cambridge.

1997a. "Pilgrimage, Religion and Visual Culture in the Roman East." In Alcock, ed.: 178–199.

1997b. "Hagiographic Geography: Travel and Allegory in the *Life of Apollonius of Tyana.*" *JHS* 117: 22–37.

2001a. "Describing Self in the Language of Other: Pseudo (?) Lucian at the Temple of Hierapolis." In Goldhill, ed.: 123–153.

2001b. "Structuring 'Greece': Pausanias's *Periegesis* as a Literary Construct." In Alcock, Cherry, and Elsner, eds.: 3–20.

Elsner, J., and I. Rutherford, eds. 2005. *Pilgrimage in Greco-Roman and Christian Antiquity.* Oxford (forthcoming).

Engeli, Adolf. 1907. *Die Oratio variata bei Pausanias.* Berlin.

Engels, D. 1990. *Roman Corinth.* Chicago.

Faraklas, N. 1971. Σικυωνία. *Ancient Greek Cities* 8. Athens.

1972a. Ἐπιδαυρία. *Ancient Greek Cities* 12. Athens.

1972b. Φλειασία. *Ancient Greek Cities* 11. Athens.

1972c. Τροιζηνία, Καλαύρεια, Μέθανα. *Ancient Greek Cities* 10. Athens.

1973. Ἑρμιονίς- Ἁλιάς. *Ancient Greek Cities* 19. Athens.

Fehling, D. 1988. "A Guide to Pausanias. Christian Habicht: *Pausanias' Guide to Ancient Greece.*" *CR* 38: 18–19.

Fein, Sylvia. 1994. *Die Beziehungen der Kaiser Trajan und Hadrian zu den* litterati. Stuttgart.

Fischbach, O. 1893. "Die Benutzung des thukydideischen Geschichtswerkes durch den Periegeten Pausanias." *WS* 15: 161–191.

Flashar, Hellmut, ed. 1979. *Le classicisme à Rome aux 1ers siècles avant et après J.-C.* (Fondation Hardt Entretiens sur l'antiquité classique XXV). Geneva.

Flinterman, Jaap-Jaan. 1995. *Power, Paideia, and Pythagoreanism: Greek Identity, Conceptions of the Relationship between Philosophers and Monarchs and Political Ideas in Philostratus'* Life of Apollonius. Amsterdam.

Flory, Stewart. 1990. "The Meaning of τὸ μὴ μυθῶδες (1.22.4) and the Usefulness of Thucydides' History." *CJ* 85: 193–208.

Folch-Serra, M. 1990. "Place, Voice, Space: Mikhail Bakhtin's Dialogical Landscape." *Environment and Planning D: Society and Space* 8: 255–274.

Foley, A. 1988. *The Argolid 800–600 B.C.: an Archaeological Survey.* Göteborg.

Foresti, Luciana Aigner, ed. 1998. *L'ecumenismo politico nella coscienza dell'occidente.* Rome.

Forte, B. 1972. *Rome and the Romans as the Greeks Saw Them.* Rome.

Fossey, J. 1988. *Topography and Population of Ancient Boiotia.* Chicago.

Fowler, D. P. 1991. "Narrate and Describe: the Problem of Ekphrasis." *JRS* 81: 25–35.

Fowler, H. N., R. Stillwell, C. W. Blegen, B. Powell, and C. A. Robinson. 1932. *Introduction: Topography, Architecture* (*Corinth I.i*). Cambridge, MA.

Frank, Georgia. 2000. *The Memory of the Eyes: Pilgrims to Living Saints in Christian Late Antiquity.* Berkeley.

Frazer, J. G. 1898. *Pausanias' Description of Greece.* 6 vols. London.

Freeman, P. W. M. 1993. "Romanisation and Roman Material Culture." *JRA* 6: 438–445.

Frézouls, E. 1991. "L'hellénisme dans l'épigraphie de l'Asie Mineure romaine." In Saïd, ed.: 125–147.

Friedländer, P. 1921–1923. *Darstellungen aus der Sittengeschichte Röms.* 3 vols. Leipzig.

Frösén, Jaakko. 1974. *Prolegomena to the Study of the Greek Language in the First Centuries A.D.: the Problem of Koiné and Atticism.*

Frost, Frank. 1980. *Plutarch's* Themistocles: *a Historical Commentary.* Princeton.

Gabbert, Janice J. 1997. *Antigonus II Gonatas: a Political Biography.* London.

Galli, M. 2002. *Die Lebenswelt eines Sophisten: Untersuchungen zu den Bauten und Stiftungen des Herodes Atticus.* Mainz am Rhein.

Galsterer, Hartmut. 1998. "Einheit und Vielfalt im römischen Reich." In Foresti, ed.: 319–332.

Gardner, E. A., W. Loring, G. C. Richards, and W. J. Woodhouse. 1892. *Excavations at Megalopolis 1890–1891.* London.

Garoufalias, Petros. 1979. *Pyrrhus, King of Epirus.* 2nd edition. London.

Gebhard, E. 1973. *The Theater at Isthmia.* Chicago.

Gebhard, E., and M. Dickie. 2003. "The View from the Isthmus, ca. 200 to 44 B.C." In Williams and Bookidis, eds.: 261–278.

Gelzer, Thomas. 1979. "Klassizismus, Attizismus und Asianismus." In Flashar, ed.: 1–41.

Georgiadou, A., and D. H. J. Larmour. 1994. "Lucian and Historiography: 'De Historia Conscribenda' and 'Verae Historiae.'" *ANRW* II.34.2: 1448–1509.

Gignac, F. T. 1981. *A Grammar of the Greek Papyri of the Roman and Byzantine Periods*. 2 vols. Milan.

Gingras, G. E. 1970. *Egeria: Diary of a Pilgrimage* (Ancient Christian Writers 38). New York.

Gleason, Maud W. 1995. *Making Men: Sophists and Self-Presentation in Ancient Rome*. Princeton.

Gogos, Savas. 1988. "Das Antike Theater in der Periegese des Pausanias." *Klio* 70: 329–339.

Goldhill, Simon. 2001 "The Erotic Eye: Visual Stimulation and Cultural Conflict." In Goldhill, ed.: 154–194.

    2001, ed. *Being Greek Under Rome: Cultural Identity, the Second Sophistic and the Development of Empire*. Cambridge.

    2002. *The Invention of Prose* (Greece & Rome New Surveys in the Classics 32). Oxford.

Goldhill, Simon, and Robin Osborne, eds. 1994. *Art and Text in Ancient Greek Culture*. Cambridge.

Golledge, Reginald G., and Robert J. Stimson. 1997. *Spatial Behavior: a Geographic Perspective*. New York.

Gomme, A. W. 1956. *A Historical Commentary on Thucydides*. Vol. III. Oxford.

Gregory, T., ed. 1993. *The Corinthia in the Roman Period*. Ann Arbor.

Griffin, Miriam, and J. Barnes, eds. 1989. *Philosophia Togata*. Oxford.

Groag, Edmund. 1939. *Die Römischen Reichsbeamten von Achaia bis auf Diokletian*. Vienna.

Grundmann, H. R. 1885. "Quid in elocutione Arriani Herodoto debeatur." *Berliner Studien* 2: 12–268.

Gurlitt, W. 1890. *Über Pausanias*. Graz.

Habicht, C. 1956. *Gottmenschentum und griechische Städte*. Munich.

    1984. "Pausanias and the Evidence of Inscriptions." *CA* 3: 40–56.

    1997. *Athens from Alexander to Anthony*. Tr. D. L. Schneider. Cambridge, MA (= *Athen. Die Geschichte der Stadt in hellenistischen Zeit*. Munich 1995).

    1998. *Pausanias' Guide to Ancient Greece* (2nd edition). Berkeley.

Habinek, Thomas N. 1990. "Toward a History of Friendly Advice: the Politics of Candor in Cicero's *de Amicitia*." In Nussbaum, ed.: 165–186.

Hägg, Robin, ed. 1999. *Ancient Greek Hero Cult* (Proceedings of the Fifth International Seminar on Ancient Greek Cult. Göteborg University, 1995). Stockholm.

Halfmann, Helmut. 1986. *Itinera principum: Geschichte und Typologie der Kaiserreisen im Römischen Reich*. Stuttgart.

Hall, E. 1989. *Inventing the Barbarian: Greek Self-Definition Through Tragedy*. Oxford.

Hall, J. 1981. *Lucian's Satire*. New York.

Hammond, N. G. L. 1967. *Epirus*. Oxford.

Hankinson, R. J. 1991. *Galen on the Therapeutic Method, Books I and II*. Oxford. 1998. *Galen on Antecedent Causes*. Cambridge.

Hansen, Mogens Herman, ed. 1994. *Sources for the Ancient Greek City-State* (Acts of the Copenhagen Polis Centre vol. 2). Copenhagen.

1997, ed. *The Polis as an Urban Centre and as a Political Community* (Acts of the Copenhagen Polis Centre vol. 4). Copenhagen.

Harrison, G. W. M. 2000. "Problems with the Genre of *Problems*: Plutarch's Literary Innovations." *CP* 95: 193–199.

Hartog, François. 1988. *The Mirror of Herodotus: the Representation of the Other in the Writing of History*. Janet Lloyd, tr. Berkeley (= *Le miroir d'Hérodote: Essai sur la représentation de l'autre*. Paris, 1980).

1991. "Rome et la Grèce: les choix de Denys d'Halicarnasse." In Saïd, ed.: 149–157.

2001. *Memories of Odysseus: Frontier Tales from Ancient Greece*. Janet Lloyd, tr. Chicago (= *Mémoire d'Ulysse: Récits sur la frontière en Grèce ancienne*. Paris, 1996).

Heath, Malcolm. 1999. "Longinus, *On Sublimity*." *PCPhS* 45: 43–74.

Heberdey, R. 1894. *Die Reisen des Pausanias in Griechenland*. Vienna.

Heer, Joyce. 1979. *La personnalité de Pausanias*. Paris.

Henderson, John. 2001. "Farnell's *Cults*: the Making and Breaking of Pausanias in Victorian Archaeology and Anthropology." In Alcock, Cherry, and Elsner, eds.: 207–223.

Hershbell. 1993. "Plutarch and Herodotus: the Beetle and the Rose." *RhM* 136: 143–163.

Herz, Peter. 1996. "Hellenistische Könige. Zwischen griechischen Vorstellungen vom Königtum und Vorstellungen ihrer einheimischen Untertanen." In Small, ed.: 27–40.

Hidber, Thomas. 1996. *Das klassizistische Manifest des Dionys von Halikarnass*. Stuttgart.

Hill, B. H. 1964. *Corinth I.vi: the Springs: Peirene, Sacred Spring, Glauke*. Princeton.

Hitzig, Hermann, and Hugo Blümner. 1896–1910. *Pausaniae Graeciae Descriptio* [edition and commentary]. 3 vols. Berlin.

Hodkinson, Stephen, and Anton Powell, eds. 1999. *Sparta: New Perspectives*. London.

Hoff, Michael. 1989. "The Early History of the Roman Agora at Athens." In Walker and Cameron, eds.: 1–8.

1996. "The Politics and Architecture of the Athenian Imperial Cult." In Small, ed.: 185–200.

Hoff, Michael C., and Susan I. Rotroff, eds. 1997. *The Romanization of Athens*. Oxford.

Hohmeyer, H. 1965. *Lukian: Wie man Geschichte schreiben soll* (text, translation and commentary). Munich.

1967. "Zu Plutarchs *De malignitate Herodoti*." *Klio* 49: 181–7.

Hölbl, Günther. 2001. *A History of the Ptolemaic Empire.* T. Saavedra, tr. London (= *Geschichte des Ptolemäerreiches.* Darmstadt, 1994).

Holford-Strevens, Leofranc. 1997. "Favorinus: the Man of Paradoxes." In Barnes and Griffin, eds.: 188–217.

Holum, K. 1990. "Hadrian and St. Helena: Imperial Travel and the Origins of Christian Holy Land Pilgrimage." In R. Ousterhout, ed.: 61–81.

Hornblower, Jane. 1981. *Hieronymus of Cardia.* Oxford.

Hornblower, Simon. 1996. *A Commentary on Thucydides.* Vol. II. Oxford.

Hunt, E. D. 1982. *Holy Land Pilgrimage in the Later Roman Empire, AD 312–460.* Oxford.

    1984. "Travel, Tourism and Piety in the Roman Empire." *EMC* 28 (n.s. 3): 391–417.

Hutton, W. E. 1995. *The Topographical Methods of Pausanias.* Diss. University of Texas – Austin.

    2005a. "Asine: a Lost City in Lakonia?" *AHB* 18: 22–44.

    2005b. "The Construction of Religious Space in Pausanias." In Elsner and Rutherford, eds. (pp. 291–317).

Ihnken, Thomas. 1978. *Die Inschriften von Magnesia am Sipylos* (*Inschriften griechischer Städte aus Kleinasien* Bd. 8).

Imhoof-Blumer, F., and P. Gardner. 1887, first edition. *A Numismatic Commentary on Pausanias.* London (new edition by A. Oikonomides published as *Ancient Coins Illustrating Lost Masterpieces of Greek Art: a Numismatic Commentary on Pausanias.* Chicago. 1964).

Irigoin, Jean. 2001. "Les manuscrits de Pausanias, quarante ans après. Hommage à la mémoire d'Aubrey Diller." In Knoepfler and Piérart, eds.: 9–24.

Jackson, J. 1984. *Discovering the Vernacular Landscape.* New Haven.

Jacob, Christian. 1991. *Géographie et ethnographie en Grèce ancienne.* Paris.

Jacoby, F. 1944. "*Patrios Nomos*: State Burial in Athens and the Public Cemetery in the Kerameikos." *JHS* 64: 37–66.

Jacquemin, Anne. 1991a. "Delphes au IIe siècle après J.-C.: un lieu de la mémoire grecque." In Saïd: 217–231.

    1991b. "Les curiosités naturelles chez Pausanias." *Ktema* 16: 123–130.

    1996. "Pausanias et les empereurs romains." *Ktema* 21: 29–42.

    2000. "Pausanias à Delos, ou – un chapître recomposé du livre imaginé des 'Kykladika.'" *Ktema* 25: 19–36.

Jameson, M. H., C. N. Runnels, and T. H. van Andel. 1994. *A Greek Countryside: the Southern Argolid from Prehistory to the Present Day.* Stanford.

Janni, Pietro. 1984. *La mappa e il periplo: Cartografia antica e spazio odologico.* Rome.

    1998. "Cartographie et art nautique dans le monde ancien." In Arnaud and Counillon, eds.: 41–53.

Jones, C. P. 1972. *Plutarch and Rome.* Oxford.

    1978a. "Three Foreigners in Attica." *Phoenix* 32: 222–234.

    1978b. *The Roman World of Dio Chrysostom.* Cambridge, MA.

1986. *Culture and Society in Lucian.* Cambridge, MA.

1996. "The Panhellenion." *Chiron* 26: 29–56.

2001. "Pausanias and his Guides." In Alcock, Cherry, and Elsner, eds.: 33–39.

Jones, W. H. S., H. A. Ormerod, and R. E. Wycherley. 1971–1978. *Pausanias, Description of Greece.* 5 vols. Cambridge, MA.

Jost, Madeleine. 1973. "Pausanias en Mégalopolitide." *REA* 75: 241–267.

1985. *Sanctuaires et cultes d'Arcadie.* Paris.

1992. "Sanctuaires ruraux et sanctuaires urbains en Arcadie." In Schachter, ed.: 205–245.

1994. "The Distribution of Sanctuaries in Civic Space in Arcadia." In Alcock and Osborne, eds.: 217–230.

1998. "Versions locales et versions 'panhelléniques' des myths arcadiens chez Pausanias." In Pirenne-Delforge, ed.: 209–226.

Jourdain-Annequin, C. 1998. "Représenter les dieux: Pausanias et le panthéon des cités." In Pirenne-Delforge, ed.: 241–261.

Kahrstedt, U. 1954. *Das wirtschaftliche Gesicht Griechenlands in der Kaiserzeit.* Bern.

Kalkmann, A. 1886. *Pausanias der Perieget: Untersuchungen über seine Schriftstellerei und seine Quellen.* Berlin.

Karadimas, D. 1996. *Sextus Empiricus against Aelius Aristides.* Diss.: Lund University.

Kaster, Robert. 1988. *Guardians of Language: the Grammarian and Society in Late Antiquity.* Berkeley.

2001. "Controlling Reason: Declamation in Rhetorical Education at Rome." In Too, ed.: 317–337.

Kelly, T. 1976. *A History of Argos to 500 B.C.* Minneapolis.

Kennedy, G. 1963. *The Art of Persuasion in Greece.* Princeton.

1972. *The Art of Rhetoric in the Roman World.* Princeton.

1999. *Classical Rhetoric and its Christian and Secular Tradition from Ancient to Modern Times.* Chapel Hill.

Kennell, Nigel. 1999. "From *Perioikoi* to *Poleis*: the Laconian Cities in the Late Hellenistic Period." In Hodkinson and Powell, eds.: 189–210.

Kent, J. H. 1966. *Corinth VIII.iii: the Inscriptions 1926–1950.* Princeton.

Khoury, Raif Georges, ed. 1999. *Urkunden und Urkundenformulare im klassischen Altertum und in den orientalischen Kulturen.* Heidelberg.

Kiefner, G. 1964. *Die Versparung.* Wiesbaden.

Kleiner, D. E. E. 1983. *The Monument of Philopappos in Athens.* Rome.

Knoepfler, Denis. 1996. "Sur une interprétation historique de Pausanias dans sa description du *Dêmosion Sêma* athénien." In Bingen, ed.: 277–311.

2001. "La fête des *Daidala* de Platées chez Pausanias: une clef pour l'histoire de la Béotie hellénistique." In Knoepfler and Piérart, eds.: 343–374.

Knoepfler, Denis, and Marcel Piérart, eds. 2001. *Éditer, traduire, commenter Pausanias en l'an 2000.* Actes du colloque de Neuchâtel et de Fribourg (18–22 septembre 1998). Geneva.

Konstan, David. 2001a. "The Joys of Pausanias." In Alcock, Cherry, and Elsner, eds.: 57–60.

2001b. "*To Hellenikon ethnos:* Ethnicity and the Construction of Ancient Greek Identity." In Malkin, ed.: 29–50.

Kourinou, E. 2000. Σπάρτη· Συμβολή στὴ μνημιακὴ τοπογραφία της. Athens.

Kreilinger, Ulla. 1997. "Τὰ ἀξιολογώτατα τοῦ Παυσανίου: die Kunstauswahlkriterien des Pausanias." *Hermes* 125: 470–491.

Kühner, R., and B. Gerth. 1890–1904. *Ausführliche Grammatik der griechischen Sprache.* 4 vols. Hanover.

Lacroix, Léon. 1992. "À propos des offrandes à l'Apollon de Delphes et du témoignage de Pausanias: du réel à l'imaginaire." *BCH* 116: 157–176.

Lafond, Yves. 1994. "Pausanias et les paysages d'Achaïe." *REA* 96: 485–497.

1996. "Pausanias et l'histoire du Péloponnèse depuis la conquête romaine." In Bingen, ed.: 167–198.

1998. "Pausanias et le panthéon de Patras: l'identité religieuse d'une cité grecque devenue colonie romaine." In Pirenne-Delforge, ed.: 195–208.

2001. "Lire Pausanias à l'époque des Antonins. Réflexions sur la place de la *Périégèse* dans l'histoire culturelle, religieuse et sociale de la Grèce romaine." In Knoepfler and Piérart, eds.: 387–406.

Lambrinoudakis, V. K. 1969–70. "Προβλήματα περὶ τὴν ἀρχαίαν τοπογραφίαν τοῦ Ἄργους." *Athena* 71: 47–72.

Larner, J. 1999. *Marco Polo and the Discovery of the World.* New Haven.

Laurence, Ray, and Joanne Berry, eds. 1998. *Cultural Identity in the Roman Empire.* London.

Lausberg, H. 1973. *Handbuch der literarischen Rhetorik: eine Grundlegung der Literaturwissenschaft.* Munich.

Layton, Robert, and Peter J. Ucko, eds. 1999. *The Archaeology and Anthropology of Landscape: Shaping your Landscape.* London.

Leach, E. W. 1988. *The Rhetoric of Space: Literary and Artistic Representations of Landscape in Republican and Augustan Rome.* Princeton.

Leake, W. M. 1830. *Travels in the Morea.* 3 vols. London.

1831. *The Topography of Athens with Some Remarks on its Antiquities.* London.

1835. *Travels in Northern Greece.* 4 vols. London.

1846. *Peloponnesiaca: a Supplement to* Travels in the Morea. London.

Leontis, Artemis. 1995. *Topographies of Hellenism: Mapping the Homeland.* Ithaca, NY.

Le Roy, Christian. 1961. "Lakonika." *BCH* 85: 206–235.

1965. "Lakonika II." *BCH* 89: 358–382.

2001. "Pausanias et la Laconie, ou la recherche d'un équilibre." In Knoepfler and Piérart., eds.: 223–237.

Levi, Peter, tr. 1971. *Pausanias: Guide to Greece.* 2 vols. Harmondsworth.

Lévy, E. 1991. "Apparition des notions de Grèce et de grecs." In Saïd, ed.: 49–69.

Leyerle, Blake. 1996. "Landscape as Cartography in Early Christian Pilgrimage Narratives." *Jounal of the American Academy of Religion* 64: 119–143.

Lightfoot, J. L. 2003. *Lucian: On the Syrian Goddess.* Oxford.

Lolos, Y. A. 1997. "The Hadrianic aqueduct of Corinth." *Hesperia* 66: 271–314.

1998. *Studies in the Topography of Sikyonia.* Diss.: Berkeley.

Lolling, H. G. 1879. "Der hermioneische Archipel." *MDAI(A)* 4: 107–113.

Lord, L. E. 1939. "Watchtowers and Fortresses of the Argolid." *AJA* 43: 78–84.

1941. "Blockhouses in the Argolid," *Hesperia* 10: 93–112.

MacCormack, Sabine. 1990. "*Loca sancta*: the Organization of Sacred Topography in Late Antiquity." In R. Ousterhout, ed.: 9–20.

Macready, Sarah, and F. H. Thompson, eds. 1987. *Roman Architecture in the Greek World.* London.

Maddoli, Gianfranco, and Vincenzo Saladino. 1995. *Pausania: Libro V L'Elide e Olimpia.* Milan.

Malkin, Irad, ed. 2001. *Ancient Perceptions of Greek Ethnicity.* Cambridge, MA.

Marasco, Gabriele. 1978. *I viaggi nella Grecia antica.* Rome.

Marchetti, P. 1993. "Recherches sur les mythes et la topographie d' Argos I: Hermès et Aphrodite." *BCH* 117: 211–223.

Marchetti, Patrick, and Kostas Kolokotsas. 1995. *Le nymphée de l'agora d'Argos: Fouille, étude architecturale et historique.* (École française d'Athènes, Études Péloponnésiennes XI). Paris.

Marchetti, P., and Y. Rizakis. 1995. "Recherches sur les mythes et la topographie d' Argos IV: l'agora revisitée." *BCH* 119: 437–472.

Marincola, John. 1987. "Herodotean Narrative and the Narrator's Presence." *Arethusa* 20: 121–137.

1994: "Plutarch's Refutation of Herodotus." *AncW* 25: 191–203.

1997. *Authority and Tradition in Ancient Historiography.* Cambridge.

Martin, Hubert J. 1997. "Plutarch." In Porter, ed.: 715–736.

Martin, Paul M. 1998. "L'œcuménisme dans la vision de Rome par l'historien Denys d'Halicarnasse." In Foresti, ed.: 295–306.

Matheson S. B., and J. J. Pollitt. 1994. *An Obsession with Fortune. Tyche in Greek and Roman Art.* New Haven.

Mattingly, D. J., ed. 1997. *Dialogues in Roman Imperialism: Power, Discourse, and Discrepant Experience in the Roman Empire* (Journal of Roman Archaeology Supplementary Series, no. 23). Portsmouth, RI.

May, James M., ed. 2002. *Brill's Companion to Cicero: Oratory and Rhetoric.* Leiden.

McInerney, J. 1999. *The Folds of Parnassos: Land and Ethnicity in Ancient Phokis.* Austin.

Meadows, A. R. 1995. "Pausanias and the Historiography of Classical Sparta." *CQ* 89: 92–113.

Mette, L. 1978. "Die 'kleine griechischen Historiker' heute." *Lustrum* 21: 3–34.

Meyer, E. 1939. *Peloponnesische Wanderungen.* Zürich.

1954. *Pausanias: Beschreibung Griechenlands* (translation and commentary). Zürich.

Meyer, Hugo. 1991. *Antinoos: Die archäologischen Denkmäler unter Einbeziehung des numismatischen und epigraphischen Materials sowie der literarischen Nachrichten.* Munich.

Millar, Fergus. 1977. *The Emperor in the Roman World (31 BC–AD 337).* Ithaca, NY.

Miller, K. 1916. *Itineraria Romana. Römische Reisewege an der Hand der Tabula Peutingeriana.* Rome.

Millis, B. 2004. "Work on Corinth Guide Progresses." *Akoue* (Newsletter of the American School of Classical Studies at Athens) 51: 4, 16.

Mitchell, Stephen. 1993. *Anatolia: Land, Men, and Gods in Asia Minor.* Vol. I. Oxford.

Moggi, M. 1993. "Scrittura e riscrittura della storia in Pausania." *RFIC* 121: 396–418.

1996. "L'*excursus* di Pausania sulla Ionia." In Bingen, ed.: 79–105.

2001. "Pausania e la Mainalia." In Knoepfler and Piérart, eds.: 323–341.

Moles, J. L. 1990. "The *Kingship Orations* of Dio Chrysostom." *Proceedings of the Leeds Latin Seminar* 6: 297–375.

Momigliano, A. 1958. "The Place of Herodotus in the History of Historiography." *History* 43: 1–13 (cited with the page numbering of its reprinting in Momigliano 1966: 127–142).

1966. *Studies in Historiography.* London.

Morgan, J. R. 1985. "Lucian's *True Histories* and the *Wonders Beyond Thule* of Antonius Diogenes." *CQ* 25: 475–90.

Morgan, Teresa. 1998. *Literate Education in the Hellenistic and Roman Worlds.* Cambridge.

Morinis, Alan, 1992. "Introduction." In Morinis, ed.: 1–28.

1992, ed. *Sacred Journeys: the Anthropology of Pilgrimage.* Westport, CT.

Moschou, L. 1975. "Τοπογραφικὰ Μάνης." *AAA* 8: 160–177.

Moskou, Lida [= L. Moschou] 1976–78. "Topographie du Magne." In Πρακτικά του α' διεθνούς σθνεδρίου Πελοποννησιακῶν Σπουδῶν, vol. 2: 45–54.

Mossman, J. 1988. "Tragedy and Epic in Plutarch's *Alexander.*" *JHS* 108: 83–93.

Muller, Arthur. 1980. "Megarika" *BCH* 104: 83–92.

1981. "Megarika." *BCH* 105: 203–225.

1982. "Megarika." *BCH* 106: 379–407.

1983. "Megarika." *BCH* 107: 157–179.

1984. "Megarika." *BCH* 108: 249–266.

Müller, K. 1861. *Geographi Graeci minores.* 3 vols. (Reprint: Hildesheim, 1965).

1868–1883. *Fragmenta historicorum Graecorum.* 5 vols. Paris.

Musti, D. 1984. "L'itinerario di Pausania: dal viaggio alla storia." *QUCC* 46: 7–18.

1988. "La struttura del libro di Pausania sulla Beozia," Επετηρίς της εταιρείας βοιωτικῶν μελετῶν ι.ι (Α' διεθνές συνέδριο βοιωτικῶν μελετῶν): 333–344.

1996. "La struttura del discorso storico in Pausania." In Bingen, ed.: 9–34.

2001. "L''ora' di Pausania. Sequenze cronologiche nella *Guida della Grecia* (sull'Anfizionia di Delfi e altri argomenti)." In Knoepfler and Piérart, eds.: 43–78.

Musti, Domenico, and Luighi Beschi. 1982. *Pausania, Guida della grecia Libro I: L'Attica.* Milan.

Musti, D., and M. Torelli, 1986. *Pausania. Guida della Grecia, Libro II: La Corinzia e l'Argolida.* Milan.

1991a. *Pausania, Guida della grecia Libro III: La Laconia.* Milan.

1991b. *Pausania, Guida della grecia Libro IV: La Messenia.* Milan.

Nachtergael, Georges. 1975. *Les Galates en Grèce et les Sôtéria de Delphes*. Brussels.
Narducci, Emanuele. 2002. "*Brutus:* the History of Roman Eloquence." In May, ed.: 401–425.
Nesselrath, H.-G. 2001. "Lukian und die Magie." In Ebner et al., eds.: 153–166.
Nicolet, Claude. 1991. *Space, Geography and Politics in the Early Roman Empire*. Ann Arbor.
Norden, E. 1915. *Die antike Kunstprosa*. 3 vols. Leipzig.
Nörenberg, Heinz-Werner. 1973. "Untersuchungen zum Schluß der Περιήγησις τῆς Ἑλλάδος des Pausanias." *Hermes* 101: 235–252.
Nussbaum, Martha C., ed. 1990. *The Poetics of Therapy: Hellenistic Ethics in its Rhetorical and Literary Context (Apeiron 23.4)*. Edmonton.
Obrecht, Joseph. 1919. *Der echte und soziative Dativ bei Pausanias*. Zürich.
Oliver, J. H. 1953. *The Ruling Power: a Study of the Roman Empire in the Second Century after Christ through the Roman Oration of Aelius Aristides (Transactions of the American Philosophical Society n.s. 43.4)*. Philadelphia.
  1968. *The Civilizing Power: a Study of the Panathenaic Discourse of Aelius Aristides against the Background of Literature and Cultural Conflict (Transactions of the American Philosophical Society n.s. 58.1)*. Philadelphia.
  1972. "The Conversion of the Periegete Pausanias." In *Homenaje a Antonio Tovar*. Madrid.
O'Neill, J. G. 1930. *Ancient Corinth with a Topographical Sketch of the Corinthia, I. From the Earliest Times to 404 B.C.* Baltimore.
Osanna, M. 1998. "Descrizione autoptica e rielaborazione 'a tavolino' in Pausania: il caso di Aigeira." In Pirenne-Delforge, ed.: 209–226.
  2001. "Tra Monumenti, *Agalmata* e *Mirabilia:* Organizzazione del percorso urbano di Corinto nella *Periegesi* di Pausania." In Knoepfler and Piérart, eds.: 185–202.
Ousterhout, Robert G., ed. 1990. *The Blessings of Pilgrimage*. Urbana, IL.
Palm. J. 1959. *Rom, Römertum und Imperium in der griechischen Literatur der Kaiserzeit*. Lund.
Palmer L. R. 1980. *The Greek Language*. London.
Papachatzes, N. 1974–1981. Παυσανίου Ἑλλάδος περιήγησις. 5 vols. Athens.
Pariente, A. 1987. "Terrain Karmoyannis." *BCH* 111: 591–597.
  1992. "Le monument argien des 'Sept contre Thèbes.'" In Piérart, ed.: 195–225.
Parks, G. B. 1971. "Pausanias." In *Catalogus translationum et commentariorum: Medieval and Renaissance Latin Translations and Commentaries*. P. O. Kristeller, ed. Vol. II: 215–220. Washington, DC.
Pasquali, G. 1913. "Die schrifstellerische Form des Pausanias." *Hermes* 48: 161–223.
Pelling, Christopher. 1989. "Plutarch: Roman Heroes and Greek Culture." In Griffin and Barnes, eds.: 199–232.
  2002. *Plutarch and History*. London.
Petrakos, V. 1968. Ὁ Ὠρωπὸς καὶ τὸ ἱερὸν τοῦ Ἀμφιαράου. Athens.
Pfaff, C. 2003. "Archaic Corinthian Architecture, ca. 600 to 480 B.C." In Williams and Bookidis, eds.: 95–140.
Pfister, F. 1951. *Die Reisebilder des Herakleides*. Vienna.

Pfundtner, Joannes Otto. 1866. *Pausanias periegeta imitator Herodoti*. Königsberg.

Phaklares, P. 1990. Ἀρχαία Κυνουρία. Thessaloniki.

Piérart, M. 1982. "Deux notes sur l'itinéraire argien de Pausanias." *BCH* 106: 139–152.

1992, ed. *Polydipsion Argos. BCH* Supplement 22. Paris.

1998a. "Omissions et malentendus dans la 'Périégèse': Danaos et ses filles à Argos." In Pirenne-Delforge, ed.: 165–193.

1998b. "ΡΩΜΑΙΟΣ ΩΝ ΑΦΕΛΛΗΝΙΣΘΗ: la place de Rome dans la vision culturelle de Pausanias d'après le livre II." In Foresti, ed.: 149–162.

2001. "Observations sur la structure du livre II de la *Périégèse*: Argos, l'Argolide et la Thyréatide." In Knoepfler and Piérart, eds.: 203–221.

Piérart, M., and J. P. Thalmann. 1978. "Problemes de topographie argienne." *BCH* 102: 777–790.

Pikoulas, G. A. 1989. "Τὸ ὁδικὸ δίκτυο τῆς ἀρχαίας Οἰνόης (Μερκούρι)." Πρακτικὰ τοῦ Β' τοπικοῦ συνεδρίου Ἀργολικῶν σπουδῶν: 296–299. Athens.

1992–3. "Τὸ ὁδικὸ δίκτυο τῆς Κεντρικῆς Ἀρκαδίας." In Πρακτικά δ' διεθνούς συνεδρίου Πελοποννησιακῶν Σπουδῶν, vol. II: 201–206.

1995. Οδικό δίκτυο και άμυνα, απο την Κόρινθο στο Ἀργος και την Αρκαδία. Athens.

Pikoulas, Yanis A. (= G. A.) 1998. "The Road-Network of Arkadia." In Thomas Heine Nielsen and James Roy, eds., *Defining Ancient Arkadia* (Acts of the Copenhagen Polis Center, vol. 6). Copenhagen.

Pirenne-Delforge, Vinciane. 1998. "La notion de 'panthéon' dans la *Périégèse* de Pausanias." In Pirenne-Delforge, ed. 129–148.

1998, ed. *Les Panthéons des cités: des origines à la* Périégèse *de Pausanias* (*Kernos*, Suppl. 8). Liège.

Pirenne-Delforge, Vinciane, and Gérald Purnelle, eds. 1997. *Pausanias, Periegesis.* 2 vols. Liège.

Polánski, T. 1998. *Oriental Art in Greek Imperial Literature*. Trier.

Porter, James I. 2001. "Ideals and Ruins: Pausanias, Longinus, and the Second Sophistic." In Alcock, Cherry and Elsner, eds.: 63–92.

Porter, Stanley E., ed. 1997. *Handbook of Classical Rhetoric in the Hellenistic Period 330 B.C.–A.D. 400*. Leiden.

Portugali, Juval, ed. 1996. *The Construction of Cognitive Maps*. Dordrecht.

Pothecary, Sarah. 1997. "The Expression 'Our Times' in Strabo's Geography." *CP* 92: 235–246.

Pratt, Mary Louise. 1992. *Imperial Eyes: Travel Writing and Transculturation*. London.

Pred, Allan. 1990. *Making Histories and Constructing Human Geographies: the Local Transformations of Practice, Power Relations and Consciousness*. Boulder, CO.

Preller, L. 1838. *Polemonis periegetae fragmenta*. Leipzig.

Price, Simon. 1984a. *Rituals and Power: the Roman Imperial Cult in the Greek East*. Cambridge.

1984b. "Gods and Emperors: the Greek Language of the Roman Imperial Cult." *JHS* 104: 79–95.

Pritchett, W. Kendrick. 1965. *Studies in Ancient Greek Topography, Part I.* Berkeley.
    1980. *Studies in Ancient Greek Topography, Part III (Roads).* Berkeley.
    1982. *Studies in Ancient Greek Topography, Part IV (Passes).* Berkeley.
    1991. *Studies in Ancient Greek Topography, Part VII.* Amsterdam.
    1993. *The Liar School of Herodotos.* Amsterdam.
    1998. *Pausanias Periegetes I.* Amsterdam.
    1999. *Pausanias Periegetes II.* Amsterdam.
Puech, B. 1983. "Grandes prêtes et helladarques d'Achaïe." *REA* 85: 5–43.
    1991. "Prosopographie des amis de Plutarque." *ANRW* ii 33.6: 4831–4893.
Puillon de Boblaye, Emile. 1835. *Récherches géographiques sur les ruines de la Morée* (Expédition Scientifique de Morée). Paris.
Quass, F. 1982. "Zur politischen Tätigkeit der munizipalen Aristokratie des griechischen Ostens in der Kaiserzeit." *Historia* 31: 188–213.
    1993. *Die Honoratioren Schicht in der städten des griechischen Ostens: Untersuchungen zur politischen und sozialen Entwicklung in hellenistischer und römischer Zeit.* Stuttgart.
Ramón Palerm, V. 2000. "El *De Herodoti malignitate* de Plutarco como *epideixis* retórica." In Van der Stockt, ed.: 387–398.
Raubitschek. 1946. "Octavia's Deification at Athens." *TAPA* 77: 146–150.
Rawson, Elizabeth. 1989. "Roman Rulers and the Philosophic Adviser." In Griffin and Barnes, eds.: 233–252.
Reardon, B. P. 1971. *Courants littéraires grecs des IIe et IIIe siècles après J.-C.* Paris.
Regenbogen, O. 1956. "Pausanias." In *Realencyclopädie der klassischen Altertumswissenschaft.* Supp. VIII: 1008–1097. Stuttgart.
Reitz, Eduard. 1891. *De praepositionis* ΥΠΕΡ apud Pausaniam periegetem usu locali. Freiburg.
Reynolds, L. D., and N. G. Wilson 1991. *Scribes and Scholars: a Guide to the Transmission of Greek and Latin Literature.* 2nd edition. Oxford.
Rizakis, A. D. 1996, ed. *Roman Onomastics in the Greek East* (Proceedings of the International Colloquium on Roman Onomastics, Athens 7–9 September 1993). Athens.
    1997. "Roman Colonies in the Province of Achaia: Territories, Land and Population. In Alcock, ed.: 15–36.
Robert, C. 1909. *Pausanias als Schriftsteller.* Berlin.
Roberts, D. H., F. M. Dunn and D. Fowler, eds. 1997. *Classical Closure: Reading the End in Greek and Latin Literature.* Princeton.
Robinson, H. S. 1976. "Excavations at Corinth: Temple Hill: 1968–1972." *Hesperia* 45: 203–239.
Rocha-Pereira, Maria Helena. 1989–90. *Pausaniae Graeciae descriptio.* Biblotheca Teubneriana. Leipzig.
Rodaway, Paul. 1994. *Sensuous Geography: Body, Sense and Place.* London.
Roebuck, C. 1951. *Corinth XIV: the Asklepieion and Lerna.* Princeton.
Romano, David G. 1993. "Post 146 B.C. Land Use in Corinth, and Planning of the Roman Colony of 44 B.C." In Gregory, ed.: 9–30.

2003. "City Planning, Centuriation, and Land Division in Roman Corinth: *Colonia Laus Iulia Corinthiensis* and *Colonia Flavia Augusta Corinthiensis.*" In Williams and Bookidis: 279–301.

Romeri, Luciana. 2000. "The λογόδειπνον: Athenaeus between Banquet and Anti-Banquet." In Braund and Wilkins, eds.: 256–271.

Romm, James S. 1992. *The Edges of the Earth in Ancient Thought: Geography, Exploration, and Fiction.* Princeton.

Roos, A. G. 1927. "De Arriani Indicae dialecto Ionica." *Mnemosyne* 55: 23–43.

Ros, J. 1938 (1968). *Die* μεταβολή (Variatio) *als Stilprinzip des Thukydides.* Nijmegen (Amsterdam).

Rose, Gillian. 1993. *Feminism and Geography: the Limits of Geographical Knowledge.* Minneapolis.

Roux, G. 1958. *Pausanias en Corinthie.* Paris.

Roy, J., J. A. Lloyd, and E. J. Owens. 1989. "Megalopolis under the Roman Empire." In S. Walker and A. Cameron, eds.: 146–150.

Russell, D. A. 1972. *Plutarch.* London.

1983. *Greek Declamation.* Cambridge.

1990, ed. *Antonine Literature.* Oxford.

Rutherford, Ian. 1998. *Canons of Style in the Antonine Age: Idea-Theory in its Literary Context.* Oxford.

2001. "Tourism and the Sacred: Pausanias and the Traditions of Greek Pilgrimage." In Alcock, Cherry, and Elsner, eds.: 40–52.

Sacks, Kenneth. 1990. *Diodorus Siculus and the First Century.* Princeton.

Saïd, Suzanne, ed. 1991. *ΕΛΛΗΝΙΣΜΟΣ: Quelques jalons pour une histoire de l'identité grecque.* Leiden.

1994. "Lucien ethnographe." In Billault, ed.: 149–170.

2001. "The Discourse of Identity in Greek Rhetoric from Isocrates to Aristides." In Malkin, ed.: 275–299.

Sakellariou, M., and N. Faraklas. 1971. *Corinthia – Cleonaea.* Ancient Greek Cities 3. Athens.

Sanders, Jan Motyka, ed. 1992. *Philolakon: Lakonian Studies in Honour of Hector Catling.* London.

Schachter, Albert, ed. 1992. *Le sanctuaire grec* (Fondation Hardt Entretiens sur l'antiquité classique XXXVII). Geneva.

Schepens, Guido. 1998. "Between Utopianism and Hegemony. Some Reflections on the Limits of Political Ecumenism in the Graeco-Roman World." In Foresti, ed.: 117–147.

Schmid, Wilhelm. 1887–1897. *Der Atticismus in seinen Hauptvertretern von Dionysius von Halikarnass bis auf den zweiten Philostratus.* 5 vols. Stuttgart.

Schmid, W., and O. Stählin. 1929–1948. *Geschichte der griechischen Litteratur* (5 vols.; *Handbuch der Altertumswissenschaft* VII.1). Munich.

Schmitz, Thomas. 1997. *Bildung und Macht: zur sozialen und politischen Funktion der zweiten Sophistik in der griechischen Welt der Kaiserzeit.* Munich.

Schneider, Werner. 1997. "Ein kryptisches Denkmal im Zentrum der Pausanias-Perihegese." *Hermes* 125: 492–505.

1999. "Eine Polemik Polemons in der Propyläen. Ein Votivgemälde des Alkibiades – Kontext und Rezeption." *Klio* 81: 18–44.

Schouler, Bernard. 1984. *La tradition hellénique chez Libanius.* 2 vols. Paris.

Scott, Kenneth. 1929. "Plutarch and the Ruler Cult." *TAPA* 60: 117–135.

Scranton, R. L. 1951. *Corinth I.iii: Monuments in the Lower Agora and North of the Archaic Temple.* Princeton.

Seavey, W. 1991. "Forensic Epistolography and Plutarch's *De Herodoti malignitate.*" *Hellas* 2: 33–45.

Seeman, E. 1880. *Quaestiones grammaticae et criticae ad Pausaniam spectantes.* Jena.

Segre, M. 1927. "Pausania come fonte storica." *Historia* 1: 202–234.

Settis, S. 1963. *Il ninfeo di Erode Attico a Olimpia e il problema della composizione della Periegesi di Pausania.* Pisa.

Sheedy, Kenneth, ed. 1994. *Archaeology in the Peloponnese: New Excavations and Research.* Oxford.

Shipley, Graham. 1992. "*Perioikos*: the Discovery of Classical Lakonia." In Sanders, ed.: 211–238.

1996a. "Archaeological Sites in Laconia and the Thyreatis." In Cavanagh et al., eds.: 263–313.

1996b. "Ancient History and Landscape Histories." In Shipley and Salmon, eds.: 1–15.

1997. "'The Other Lakedaimonians'; the Dependent Perioikic *Poleis* of Lakonia and Messenia." In Hansen, ed. 1997: 189–281.

Shipley, Graham, and John Salmon, eds. 1996. *Human Landscapes in Classical Antiquity: Environment and Culture.* London.

Silberman, Alain. 1993. "Arrien, 'Périple du Pont-Euxin': essai d'interprétation et d'évaluation des données historiques et géographiques." *ANRW* 34.1: 276–311.

1995. *Arrien: Périple du Pont-Euxin.* Paris.

Sisti, Francesco. 2001. *Arriano: Anabasi di Alessandro* (text, translation, and commentary). Vol. I. Milan.

Sivan, Hagith. 1988a. "Who Was Egeria? Piety and Pilgrimage in the Age of Gratian." *HThR* 81: 59–72.

1988b. "Holy Land Pilgrimages and Western Audiences: Some Reflections on Egeria and her Circle." *CQ* 38: 528–535.

Small, Alastair, ed. 1996. *Subject and Ruler: the Cult of the Ruling Power in Classical Antiquity. Journal of Roman Archaeology Supplementary Series* 17. Ann Arbor.

Snodgrass, A. 1987. *An Archaeology of Greece.* Berkeley.

2001. "Pausanias and the Chest of Kypselos." In Alcock, Cherry, and Elsner, eds.: 127–153.

Sordi, M. 1988. *Geografia e storiografia nel mondo classico.* Milan.

Spawforth, A. J. S. 1978. "Balbilla, the Euryclids and Memorials for a Greek Magnate." *BSA* 73: 249–260.

1994. "Corinth, Argos, and the Imperial Cult: Pseudo-Julian, *Letters* 198." *Hesperia* 63: 211–232.

1996. "Roman Corinth: the Formation of a Colonial Elite." In Rizakis, ed.: 167–182.

2001. "Shades of Greekness: a Lydian Case Study." In Malkin, ed.: 375–400.

Spawforth A. J. S., and Walker, S. 1985. "The World of the Panhellenion I. Athens and Eleusis." *JRS* 75: 78–104.

1986. "The World of the Panhellenion II. Three Dorian Cities." *JRS* 76: 88–105.

Stadter, Philip A. 1980. *Arrian of Nicomedia.* Chapel Hill, NC.

Steinhart, Matthias. 2002a. "Tyrannenhaus und Kaiserkult: zu einer angeblich römerfeindlichen Bemerkung bei Pausanias." *Thetis* 9: 95–96.

2002b. "Das Unglück der römischen Herrschaft? zum Verständnis von Pausanias 8,27,1." *Würzburger Jahrbücher für die Altertumswissenschaft* 26: 145–150.

2003. "Pausanias und das Philopappos-Monument – ein Fall von *Damnatio Memoriae?*" *Klio* 85: 171–188.

Stertz, Steven A. 1994. "Aelius Aristides' Political Ideas." *ANRW* 34.2: 1248–1270.

Stibbe, Conrad M. 1989. "Beobachtungen zur Topographie des antiken Sparta." *Babesch (Bulletin Antieke Beschaving)* 64: 61–99.

Stillwell, R., R. L. Scranton, and S. E. Freeman. 1941. *Corinth I.ii: Architecture.* Cambridge, MA.

Storch, O. 1869. *Syntaxeos pausanianae particula prima: de anacoluthis.* Breslau.

Strid, Ove. 1976. *Über Sprache und Stil des Periegeten Pausanias.* Uppsala.

Strobel, K. 1994. "Historiker des Partherkrieges des Lucius Verus." *ANRW* II.34.2: 1315–1360.

Stroud, R. 1965. "The Sanctuary of Demeter and Kore on Acrocorinth, Preliminary Report I: 1961–1962." *Hesperia* 34: 1–24.

Sutton, Susan Buck. 2001. "A Temple Worth Seeing: Pausanias, Travelers, and the Narrative Landscape at Nemea." In Alcock, Cherry, and Elsner, eds.: 175–189.

Swain, Simon. 1989a. "Plutarch's *De fortuna Romanorum.*" *CQ* 39: 504–516.

1989b. "Plutarch, Chance, Providence and History." *AJP* 110: 272–302.

1996. *Hellenism and Empire: Language, Classicism, and Power in the Greek World, AD 50–250.* Oxford.

1997. "Plutarch, Plato, Athens, and Rome." In Barnes and Griffin, eds.: 165–187.

Symeonoglou, S. 1985. *The Topography of Thebes from the Bronze Age to Modern Times.* Princeton.

Szelest, Hanna. 1953. *De Pausaniae clausulis* (Auctarium Maeandreum, Vol. III). Warsaw.

Thompson, H. A., and R. E. Wycherley. 1972. *The Athenian Agora XIV: the Agora of Athens: the History, Shape and Uses of an Ancient City Center.* Princeton.

Tilley, Christopher. 1994. *A Phenomenology of Landscape: Places, Paths and Monuments.* Oxford.

Tobin, Jennifer. 1997. *Herodes Attikos and the City of Athens: Patronage and Conflict under the Antonines.* Amsterdam.

Tod, Marcus, and A. J. B. Wace. 1906. *Catalogue of the Sparta Museum.* Oxford.

Tolman, Edward C. 1948. "Cognitive Maps in Rats and Men." *Psychological Review* 55: 189–208.

Tomasch, Sylvia, and Sealy Gilles, eds. 1998. *Text and Territory: Geographical Imagination in the European Middle Ages*. Philadelphia.

Tomlinson, R. A. 1972. *Argos and the Argolid from the End of the Bronze Age to the Roman Occupation*. London.

1983. *Epidauros*. London.

Tonnet, Henry. 1988. *Recherches sur Arrien: Sa personnalité et ses écrits atticistes*. Amsterdam.

Too, Yun Lee, ed. 2001. *Education in Greek and Roman Antiquity*. Leiden.

Too, Yun Lee, and Niall Livingstone, eds. 1998. *Pedagogy and Power: Rhetorics of Classical Learning*. Cambridge.

Torelli, Mario. 2001. "Pausania a Corinto. Un intellettuale greco del secondo secolo e la propaganda imperiale romana." In Knoepfler and Piérart, eds.: 135–184.

Trendelenburg, Adolf. 1911. *Pausanias* Hellenika. Berlin.

1914. *Pausanias in Olympia*. Berlin.

Tuplin, C. J. 1984. "Pausanias and Plutarch's *Epaminondas*." *CQ* 34: 346–58.

Turner, Victor, and Edith L. B. Turner. 1978. *Image and Pilgrimage in Christian Culture*. New York.

Tzifopoulos, Yannis Z. 1991. *Pausanias as a "Steloskopas": an Epigraphical Commentary of Pausanias' Eliakon A' and B'*. Diss. The Ohio State University.

1993. "Mummius' Dedications at Olympia and Pausanias' Attitude to the Romans." *GRBS* 34: 93–100.

Ucko, P., and R. Layton. 1999. *The Archaeology and Anthropology of Landscape*. London.

Van der Stockt, L., ed. 2000. *Rhetorical Theory and Praxis in Plutarch*. Louvain.

Vanderpool, E. 1949. "The Route of Pausanias in the Athenian Agora." *Hesperia* 18: 128–137.

1974. "The 'Agora' of Pausanias I.17.1–2." *Hesperia* 43: 308–310.

Vasaly, A. 2002. "Cicero's Early Speeches." In May, ed.: 71–112.

Veyne, Paul. 1988. *Did the Greeks Believe in their Myths?* Trans. Paula Wissing. Chicago.

Vollgraff, W. 1907. "Fouilles d'Argos." *BCH* 31: 139–184.

Wagstaff, J. M. 2001. "Pausanias and the Topographers: the Case of Colonel Leake." In Alcock, Cherry, and Elsner, eds.: 190–206.

Walbank, Mary E. H. 1989. "Pausanias, Octavia and Temple E at Corinth." *BSA* 84: 361–394.

1996. "Evidence for the Imperial Cult in Julio-Claudian Corinth." In Small, ed.: 201–212.

1997. "The Foundation and Planning of Early Roman Corinth." *JRA* 10: 95–130.

2003. "Aspects of Corinthian Coinage in the Late 1st and Early 2nd Centuries A.C." In Williams and Bookidis: 337–349.

Walker, Andrew D. 1993. "*Enargeia* and the Spectator in Greek Historiography." *TAPA* 123: 353–377.

Walker, Jeffrey. 2000. *Rhetoric and Poetics in Antiquity*. Oxford.

Walker, Susan, and Averil Cameron, eds. 1989. *The Greek Renaissance in the Roman Empire.* London.

Wallace, P. W. 1979. *Strabo's Description of Boiotia: a Commentary.* Heidelberg.

Wardman, Alan. 1974. *Plutarch's Lives.* London.

Warner, R., tr. 1954. *Thucydides: History of the Peloponnesian War.* Harmondsworth.

Webb, Ruth. 2001. "The *Progymnasmata* as Practice." In Too, ed.: 289–316.

Webster, Jane, and Nicholas J. Cooper, eds. 1996. *Roman Imperialism: Post-Colonial Perspectives.* Leicester.

Weissenberger, M. 1996. *Literaturtheorie bei Lukian: Untersuchungen zum Dialog Lexiphanes.* Stuttgart.

Wernicke, Conrad. 1884. *De Pausaniae periegetae studiis Herodoteis.* Berlin.

West, A. B. 1931. *Corinth VIII.ii: Latin Inscriptions 1896–1926.* Cambridge, MA.

West, Martin. 1973. *Textual Criticism and Editorial Technique.* Stuttgart.

Westra, H. J. 1995. "The Pilgrim Egeria's Concept of Place." *Mittellateinisches Jahrbuch* 30: 93–100.

Westrem, Scott D., ed. 1991. *Discovering New Worlds: Essays on Medieval Exploration and Imagination.* New York.

Whitmarsh, Tim. 1998. "Reading Power in Roman Greece: the *Paideia* of Dio Chrysostom." In Too and Livingstone, eds.: 192–213.

———. 1999. "Greek and Roman in Dialogue: the Pseudo-Lucianic *Nero*." *JHS* 119: 142–160.

———. 2001. *Greek Literature and the Roman Empire.* Oxford.

Wide, S. 1893. *Lakonische kulte.* Leipzig.

Wilamowitz-Möllendorff, U. von. 1877. "Die Thukydideslegende." *Hermes* 12: 326–367.

———. 1900. "Asianismus und Atticismus." *Hermes* 35: 1–52.

Wilcken, Ulrich. 1910. "Die attische Periegese von Hawara." In *Genethliakon* (Festschrift Carl Robert, Berlin): 191–225.

Wilkinson, John. 1999. *Egeria's Travels* (3rd edition). Warminster.

Willers, D. 1990. *Hadrians panhellenisches Programm. Archäologische Beiträge zur Neugestaltung Athens durch Hadrian.* Basel.

Williams, C. K., II. 1969. "Excavations at Corinth, 1968." *Hesperia* 38: 36–63.

———. 1987. "The Refounding of Corinth: Some Roman Religious Attitudes." In Macready and Thompson, eds.: 26–37.

———. 1989. "A Re-evaluation of Temple E and the West End of the Forum of Corinth." In Walker and Cameron, eds.: 156–162.

Williams, C. K., II, and Nancy Bookidis, eds.: 2003. *Corinth, the Centenary: 1896–1996 (Corinth XX).* Athens.

Williams, C. K., II, and J. E. Fisher. 1975. "Corinth, 1974: Forum Southwest." *Hesperia* 44: 1–50.

Williams, C. K., II, Jean MacIntosh, and Joan E. Fisher. 1974. "Excavations at Corinth, 1973." *Hesperia* 43: 1–76.

Williams, C. K., II, and O. Zervos. 1984. "Corinth, 1983: the Route to Sikyon." *Hesperia* 53: 83–122.

1990. "Excavations at Corinth, 1989: the Temenos of Temple E." *Hesperia* 59: 325–369.

Wiseman, J. 1967. "Excavations at Corinth, the Gymnasium Area, 1965." *Hesperia* 36: 13–41.

1969. "Excavations in Corinth, the Gymnasium Area, 1967–1968." *Hesperia* 38: 64–106.

1972. "The Gymnasium Area at Corinth 1969–1970." *Hesperia* 41: 1–42.

1978. *The Land of the Ancient Corinthians.* Göteborg.

1979. "Corinth and Rome I: 228 BC–AD 267." *ANRW* 11.7.1: 438–548.

Woodman, A. J. 1988. *Rhetoric in Classical Historiography.* London.

Woodward, Christopher. 2001. *In Ruins.* London.

Woolf, G. 1994. "Becoming Roman, Staying Greek: Culture, Identity and the Civilizing Process in the Roman East." *PCPhS* 40: 116–143.

1997. "The Roman Urbanization of the East." In Alcock, ed.: 1–14.

Worthington, Ian, ed. 1994. *Persuasion: Greek Rhetoric in Action.* London.

Wycherley, R. E. 1957. *The Athenian Agora III: Literary and Epigraphical Testimonia.* Princeton.

1959. "Pausanias in the Agora of Athens." *GRBS* 2: 21–24.

1963. "Pausanias at Athens, II." *GRBS* 4: 157–175.

Xylander, W., and F. Sylburg. 1583. *Pausaniae accurata Graeciae descriptio.* Frankfurt.

Yegül, F. K. 1991. "Roman Architecture in the Greek World" (Review of MacReady and Thompson [1987]). *JRA* 4: 345–355.

Zanker, G. 1981. "Enargeia in the Ancient Criticism of Poetry." *RM* 124: 291–311.

Ziegler, K. 1951. "Plutarchos." In *Realencyclopädie der klassischen Altertumswissenschaft.* 21.1: 636–962.

Index of passages

349

General index

Atticism 52, 178, 181–190, 210, 213, 222, 224,
    227, 228, 229, 235–237, 240, 262
Augustus 43, 44, 74, 76, 77, 86, 132, 153, 168, 321
Aulis 96
Ausculum, battle 285
autopsia: *see* autopsy
autopsy 6, 7, 25, 67, 80, 81, 111, 112, 114, 137, 198,
    202, 209, 211, 234, 250, 263, 264, 268,
    269, *see also* Pausanias as eyewitness

Babylon 289, 290
Baedeker Guide 24, 242
Baslez, M.-F. 196
Bassai 94
baths 32, 39, 155–156, 157, 169
Battle of the Champions 116
Beard, M. 29
Bellerophon 156, 158, 172–173, 286
Berenike 280
Bia (goddess) 163
Bischoff, E. 249, 250, 255, 256
Bithynia 32
Black Sea 31, 266, 270
Blue Guides 24, 242, 244
Boeckh, A. 128, 222, 227–228
Boiotia 68, 70, 71, 73, 77, 79, 81–82, 85, 88–89,
    112, 117–118, 124, 127, 137, 206, 259, 303
Boleoi 114
borders 73–77
Boulis 88
Boupalos 314
Bowie, E. 34, 220, 290–292
Brasiai: *see* Prasiai
Britain 31
Britomartis 305
Brunt, P. A. 33
Byblos 203

Caecilius of Kale Akte 181
Caesar, Gaius Julius: *see* Julius Caesar
Calaurean League 74
Capitoline triad 168
Cappadocia 240, 266
Caria 236
Casevitz, M. 183
Cassander 12, 297
Cebes *see Tabula of Cebes*
Chaironeia 32, 79, 86, 88, 130, 205
    Battle of Chaironeia 63, 64, 73, 302
Chalkis 259, 260
Chaon (Mt.) 108
Charadra (Phokis) 87
Chariton 229
Cheimarros (river) 115
Chorseiai 124

Chremonidean war 278, 283
Christianity 48, 51, 312
Cicero 45, 231
Clarke, K. 263
clausulae 224, *see also* Pausanias: style; prose
    rhythm
Cleisthenes 195
Clytemnestra 3
cognitive topography 8–9, 54, 84, 95, 117–118,
    139, 145, 147, 166, 173
coinage 148
colonialism 42
Commagene 1
Commodus 184
Corcyra 283
Cordatus 196
Corfu: *see* Corcyra
Corinth 3, 15–16, 17, 39, 46, 69, 70, 71, 72, 73,
    91, 100, 101, 102–103, 104, 107, 116, 117,
    118, 127, 135, 136–137, 201, 206, 245, 300,
    310
  Acrocorinth 101, 137, 165, 166
  Acrocorinth road 163–165, 171
  agora: *see* 'forum'
  Archaic Temple: *see* Temple of Apollo
  Asklepieion 159, 160, 162
  Athena Chalinitis shrine 158, 161, 172, 173
  Babbius Monument 151, 167
  Baths of Eurykles 155–156, 157
  Demeter and Kore sanctuary 163
  forum 149, 150–154, 155, 157, 160, 163, 164,
    166, 167, 168, 215
  Glauke 158, 160, 161
  gymnasium 162
  Isthmus of Corinth: *see* Isthmus
  Kraneion 101, 136, 149, 254
  "largest temple in the Peloponnesos" 162–163,
    165
  Lechaion road 155–157, 169, 170, 171
  Lerna 158, 162
  odeion 158, 159, 161, 162
  Peirene 155, 156
  Sikyon road 158–163, 171, 172–173
  Temple C 161, 163
  Temple D 151, 167, 315
  Temple E 153–154, 168, 169, 173, 174, 321
  Temple F 151–153, 161, 167, 168
  Temple G 151, 167
  Temple K 151, 167
  Temple of Apollo 3, 146, 160, 163, 173
  Temple of Tyche: *see* Temple D
  theater 158, 159, 162, 166
  western terrace of forum 151–153, 160, 161,
    167, 170
  Zeus Kapitolios shrine 162, 169

Greek index